Media Organisations in Society

Media Organisations in Society

Edited by

JAMES CURRAN

Professor of Communications,
Goldsmiths College,
University of London

A member of the Hodder Headline Group
LONDON
Co-published in the United States of America by
Oxford University Press Inc., New York

First published in Great Britain in 2000 by
Arnold, a member of the Hodder Headline Group,
338 Euston Road, London NW1 3BH

http://www.arnoldpublishers.com

Co-published in the United States of America by
Oxford University Press Inc.,
198 Madison Avenue, New York 10016

Chapter 2 © Jonathan Burston
Chapter 3 © Korinna Patelis
Chapter 4 © David Hesmondhalgh
Chapter 5 © Dilruba Çatalbaş
Chapter 6 © Sonia Serra
Chapter 7 © Aeron Davis
Chapter 8 © Herbert F. Pimlott
Chapter 9 © James Curran
Chapter 10 © Keith Negus
Chapter 11 © Eric Kit-Wai Ma
Chapter 12 © Nick Couldry

The advice and information in this book are believed to be true and
accurate at the date of going to press, but neither the authors nor the
publisher can accept any legal responsibility or liability for any errors or omissions.

British Library Cataloguing in Publication Data
A catalogue entry for this book is available from the British Library

Library of Congress Cataloging-in-Publication Data
A catalog record for this book is available from the Library of Congress

ISBN 0 340 72014 X (hb)
ISBN 0 340 72015 8 (pb)

1 2 3 4 5 6 7 8 9 10

Production Editor: Rada Radojicic
Production Controller: Priya Gohil
Cover Design: Terry Griffiths

Typeset in 10/12pt Sabon by Phoenix Photosetting, Chatham, Kent
Printed and bound in Great Britain by
MPG Books, Bodmin, Cornwall

What do you think about this book? Or any other Arnold title?
Please send your comments to feedback.arnold@hodder.co.uk

Contents

Contributors

Jonathan Burston	Visiting Scholar, Department of Culture and Communication, New York University, USA
Dilruba Çatalbaş	Lecturer in Communications, Galatasaray University, Istanbul, Turkey
Nick Couldry	Lecturer in Communications, Goldsmiths College, University of London, UK
James Curran	Professor of Communications, Goldsmiths College, University of London, UK
Aeron Davis	Research Student, Goldsmiths College, University of London, UK
David Hesmondhalgh	Research Fellow in Sociology, Open University, UK
Eric Kit-Wai Ma	Lecturer in Journalism and Communication, Chinese University of Hong Kong, China
Keith Negus	Lecturer in Communications, Goldsmiths College, University of London, UK
Korinna Patelis	Research Student, Goldsmiths College, University of London, UK
Herbert F. Pimlott	Lecturer in Writing and Publishing Studies, Middlesex University, UK
Sonia Serra	Research Student, Goldsmiths College, University of London, UK

Introduction

JAMES CURRAN

This book is part of a general reappraisal that is taking place in the field. The study of media institutions seemed uninteresting when audiences were judged to be overwhelmingly dominant. Why study media production when audiences are the main producers of meaning? However, there is now a growing recognition that audience activity should not be equated with audience control, a point that is made emphatically by key pioneers of the new audience research (Morley 1992, Ang 1995). This more realistic assessment of the limits of audience power points by implication to the significance of media organisations, and the need to study them more fully. How they function, and how they relate to the power structure of society, matter.

There has also been a reaction against textual populism. The initial insight that communications are not best understood as 'messages', whose meanings are fixed, transparent and self-contained, was once a liberation. It gave rise to a rich vein of analysis that drew attention to tensions, ambivalences, unstable meanings and discursive spaces in media content. Everything suddenly seemed fissured, fluid, intertextual, susceptible to multiple interpretation. Containers of meaning, once shunted so to speak on rail tracks to the mass audience, were cracked open and their contents distributed according to the whim of the guerrilla 'reader'. But there is now increased awareness that audience understandings are cued (though not necessarily determined) by the ways in which communications are encoded (Hoijer 1992, Corner 1996). How the media structure meaning, and what influences media processes, have assumed by implication a greater importance.

Widescreen approach

If 'media-making' should be the subject of more systematic attention, however, how should this be done? There are two broad approaches, each of which tends to be critical of the other. Within each of these two approaches, there are also warring factions.

The traditional way is to look at media production. There is a long and distinguished record of research, rooted in organisational sociology, which foregrounds internal processes within media organisations (Tunstall 1996). There is another related tradition which looks at media occupations in terms of the recruitment, career paths, culture and norms of groups of media workers (Weaver and Wilhoit 1991). There is a third tradition, now enjoying a vogue, which focuses on the influence of the suppliers of news (Schlesinger and Tumber 1994). A fourth tradition, radical political economy, has an expansive theoretical reach but tends in practice to focus on media ownership and control, and its links to power in society, as well as to related issues such as the functioning of markets (Murdock 1990). There is also a fifth tradition, concerned with public policy and the social administration of the media, often viewed in a comparative perspective (Humphreys 1996). There are two other cognate traditions – one which reviews the performance of the media in terms of normative theory (McQuail 1992) and the other which interprets the media from a historical political economy (Curran and Seaton 1997) – which belong to the same family. All these different approaches are, to a lesser or greater degree, media-centred. Their main sources of evidence are interviews with journalists and news sources, participant observation of media organisations, company records and industrial data, or reports of public enquiries into the media. They tend to 'explain' the media mainly, but not exclusively, as organisations.

By contrast the main tradition in cultural studies, and also in much theoretically oriented media studies, sees the media primarily as cultural products. Their principal (and indeed often only) source of evidence is the content of the media. Thus, the media are viewed as an index of shared values in the 'cultural-indicator' approach (Nowak 1984); as a conduit of dominant ideologies, in a traditional Marxist perspective (Parenti 1993); and as an extension of the power structure, in the radical-structuralist tradition (Hallin 1994). In Gramscian analysis, the media are contested 'spaces' reflecting the struggle for ascendancy (Hall 1982); in liberal pluralism, they are cultural fora reproducing the collective debate of society (Newcomb and Hirsch 1984); and in a functionalist Durkheimian tradition they reflect both normative competition and achieved agreement (Alexander and Jacobs 1998). There are also: an anthropological tradition which sees the media as expressing the mythic forms, archetypes and symbolic system of society (Bird and Dardenne 1988); a postmodern tradition in which the media connect to the multiple, mobile and fractured identities of the public (McRobbie 1994); and a psychoanalytic perspective in which the media are said to voice the transgressive desires, collective fantasies and structures of feeling of their audiences (Modleski 1984). Common to all these perspectives – and this is only a condensed and selective shortlist – is a tacit assumption that control of the media lies outside the media, in forces and agencies external to it. Indeed, some of these studies give the impression that the media are little more than panes of glass through which it is possible to discern the structure of society, its values and innermost tensions, in ways that are wholly unaffected by institutional mediation.

Both approaches, one seeing the media primarily as organisations and the other as cultural products, are potentially complementary. An influential essay by Schlesinger (1990) argued persuasively that the sociology of journalism is unduly media-centred, and should pay more attention to 'externalist' influences (that is, to those outside media organisations). The reverse argument could be mounted equally effectively in relation to cultural studies. It tends to be socio-centric, and should pay more attention to the organisational/industrial dimension of the media.

This book deliberately makes space for both media-centric and socio-centric perspectives in order to promote a widescreen approach to the study of the media. It begins with a view of the media as an industry, broadens out to consider the media in relation to conflict, and concludes with essays that seek to form a bridge between production and cultural studies.

Panglossian moment

However, in one sense, this books rows against the tide of opinion. It is argued in an incisive and elegant essay that the media's concern for public legitimacy helps to shield it from big-business manipulation (Schudson 1996). The division of labour within media organisations has given rise, it is assumed, to a significant degree of journalistic autonomy (Kaniss 1997). The emergence of new market forms – niche markets, specialised companies and flexible working – has made the media more responsive and dynamic (Waters 1995). The trend towards media globalisation is promoting a more efficient way of recruiting and mobilising talent (Frith 1996), and is bypassing established national and elite structures of control in ways that can be progressive (Ang 1995). The drive towards media deregulation has reduced state and elite control, and is empowering the public (Murdoch 1989). The wider environment of flux and change is creating new opportunities for postmodern media to break rules and subvert conventions (McRobbie 1996), while the feminisation of the media workforce and the introduction of new participant television formats amounts to a form of democratisation (Shattuc 1997). Above all, new technologies of information are extending the freedom and diversity of the media (Negroponte 1996). Some of these arguments are substantial, some half right and some flawed. Taken as a whole, they amount to a Panglossian moment in media studies, a gathering movement of affirmation.

This book questions the broad thrust of this affirmative tradition. It begins with a stock-taking chapter which candidly acknowledges some of the weaknesses of the radical political economy approach. This review then turns its critical attention to revisionist argument, some of which is also problematic. It concludes by arguing that democratic theory provides a valuable alternative way of judging the media which is different from ubiquitous market theory. In brief, the first chapter provides an initial spring clean of existing intellectual furniture.

Central themes

The following four chapters illustrate the value of looking at the political and economic organisation of the media. Nothing exemplifies better the infectious optimism generated by new communications technology than the hopes that are being invested currently in the Internet. Yet, Korinna Patelis questions whether the Internet is really the neutral zone of free expression that it is widely thought to be. On the contrary, she argues, it is heavily distorted by inequalities between nations, citizens and commercial and non-commercial organisations. Its information is also structured by a signposting system that prioritises.

At a time when post-Fordism (the supposed move away from industrial production for mass consumption) is widely understood to be the driving force behind changes in the cultural industries, Jonathan Burston offers a dissenting view. In fact, he argues, mass-production methods are being *introduced* in live performances of megamusicals on a global basis. This is leading to increased standardisation, and the loss of autonomy and creativity among performers.

Globalisation is also part of Dilruba Çatalbaş's narrative of deregulation in Turkey, a country where public broadcasting has traditionally been associated with government control. She concludes that deregulation has indeed encouraged some degree of political liberalisation. However, she also argues that it has led to homogenisation around entertainment and infotainment. 'Uniformity within diversity' is her paradoxical verdict on the outcome of a liberal political experiment.

By contrast, radical experiment is the focus of Chapter 4, in which David Hesmondhalgh extracts from analysis of alternative media and Marxist aesthetics an ideal-typical model of how the media might be organised. It is intended as a benchmark of idealistic thinking in the context of 'defeatism and miserable pragmatism'.

The next section (Part III) looks at the media and conflict. All three chapters focus on radical groups in society. They feature Amnesty and the radical wing of the Catholic Church, trade unions and the former British Communist Party, which are all shown to have significantly influenced mainstream media.

Thus, Sonia Serra describes the way in which an international media outcry against the killing of Brazilian street children in the early 1990s strengthened the hand of domestic reformers. External media pressure influenced

Brazilian journalists, public and government, and contributed to a change in the law. This shows, she argues, that the international public sphere can be mobilised in defence of those outside the structure of power.

Public relations is sometimes viewed as a means by which elite groups exercise control over the media and public. But in fact public relations is a relatively low-cost activity, and is not restricted to the powerful. As Aeron Davis points out, British trade unions sought to recover from their defeat and marginalisation in the Thatcher era by modernising their communications apparatus. This retooling met with some success, as his case study of the defeat of the government's plans in 1994 to privatise the post office demonstrates.

The last chapter in this section documents the rise of an obscure journal, published by a fringe political organisation, into a position of prominence and influence. Winning editorial autonomy, shifting to a magazine format, gaining national distribution, and publishing original ideas were, according to Herbert Pimlott, key elements in the rise of *Marxism Today*. But its critical success also had something to do, he argues, with the political agenda that was being pursued by part of the press.

The central theme of these chapters is similar to that of other work in the university department in which they originate. This other work could not be presented here either because material is still being gathered or because deadlines for this book clashed with the more important deadline of delivering a completed thesis. Wilma de Jong's research is revealing how Greenpeace defeated Europe's largest conglomerate, Shell, in media battles conducted in Germany, The Netherlands and, to a lesser extent, Britain, forcing the company to abandon its plan to dump the Brent Spar oil rig in the sea. Aristotelis Nikolaidis (1999) shows how a section of the Greek press assumed almost the role of opposition during a period in the 1990s when there was a crisis of legitimated political authority. Christian Cornel argues that East German television gave expression to radical civic voices in the dying days of the communist regime, only for these to be muzzled by the West German take-over of broadcasting in a way that impaired German unification. What all these projects have in common with the three studies published here is that they see the media as a site of contest, and reject a reductionist view of the media as an unchanging agency of control.

The last section in the book (Part IV) looks at the way in which the media are socially produced. James Curran asks why many of the books that are reviewed in the British national press are neither popular nor necessarily very important. The answer, he suggests, lies partly in the literary-humanities backgrounds and values of books editors. However, these are reinforced by social networks, pre-selection by publishers and cultural tradition rooted in Britain's social history. In other words, what is reviewed does not simply reflect what literary editors find interesting but is the outcome of a range of influences, both internal and external, current and embedded in the past.

Similarly, Keith Negus argues that much of the literature on media organisations, and in particular the music industry, is too narrowly framed. It fails to take adequate account of the many ways in which 'culture produces industry'. Thus, corporate judgements about musical quality and commercial potential were influenced by the personal preferences of the elite educated male executives who dominated the music industry in the late 1980s. This led to the privileging of certain kinds of music ('authentic', live, male rock) for acquisition and development at the expense of other kinds.

Eric Kit-Wai Ma also focuses on the complex interaction between media and society. He argues that Hong Kong soap opera responded to the dominant group in the 1970s by stigmatising recent Chinese mainland immigrants as lazy and deviant. However, the balance of power shifted in the 1990s in anticipation of Hong Kong being handed back to China. The backwash of populist anti-mainlander sentiment clashed with political prudence, producing contradictory images in Hong Kong soap opera. In effect, there developed a tension between audience and political power which was handled differently within commercial and public-service television.

Nick Couldry frames the interaction between media and society in a new way by looking at the encounters of non-media people with media organisations, whether this be queuing up to go into a TV studio or being the subject of a news report. From these can be gleaned, he argues, the underlying assumptions about the media that help to explain the nature of the influence they exert. The chapter also illustrates the need to bridge the gap between studies of media production and consumption.

In short, this book is constructed around three core arguments. The media are influenced by their political and economic organisation. They are also influenced by the ways in which conflicts and rivalries are played out in society. Third, the media are conditioned by the culture of society, through complex processes of institutional mediation. This summary perhaps makes this book appear tidier than it really is. There are tensions and differences within it (contrast for example the opposing positions tacitly taken by Burston and Negus). But it also has a certain degree of internal coherence as a consequence of the discussions that have taken place between individual contributors.

Every contributor to this book (apart from the editor) is or has been a student in the Department of Media and Communications, Goldsmiths College, University of London. This is the first time that such a venture has been attempted in this field since the brilliant, innovative publications of the staff and students at Birmingham University in the 1970s and early 1980s. While this book does not claim to emulate their achievements, or even to mix in the same distinguished company, we hope it is of some use. It draws attention to an area that needs to be fully researched, indicates ways in which this might be done and offers insights based on new empirical work.

The book originates from regular meetings of the media political economy group convened by James Curran (and, in its first year, Georgina

Born). This was, and is, a minority grouping within a department dominated by cultural studies and creative media practice. But it is a harmonious department in which an interest in media political economy has been actively supported, not least by colleagues who have supervised some of the contributors to this book. Out of this atmosphere of good will has grown a desire to look for ways of drawing together the traditions of political economy and cultural studies. This is the underlying agenda of this book.

My grateful thanks go to Herbert Pimlott, who subbed two chapters, to Sam Lay, who checked the bibliography of Part I of this book, and to Korinna Patelis, who displayed the co-ordinating abilities she has always denied having. All the contributors to the book are thanked for leaning on the oar in writing Chapter 1. Although this chapter is a collective effort, David Hesmondhalgh, Aeron Davis and Nick Couldry ended up writing much of it.

References

Alexander, J. and Jacobs, R. (1998) 'Mass Communication, Ritual and Civil Society', in T. Liebes and J. Curran (eds), *Media, Ritual and Identity*, London: Routledge.

Ang, I. (1995) *Living Room Wars*, London: Routledge.

Bird, S. and Dardenne, R. (1988) 'Myth, Chronicle and Story: Exploring the Narrative Quality of News', in J. Carey (ed.), *Media, Myths and Narratives*, Newbury Park, CA: Sage.

Corner, J. (1996) 'Reappraising Reception: Aims, Concepts and Methods', in J. Curran and M. Gurevitch (eds), *Mass Media and Society*, 2nd edn, London: Arnold.

Curran, J. and Seaton, J. (1997) *Power Without Responsibility*, 5th edn, London: Routledge.

Frith, S. (1996) 'Entertainment', in J. Curran and M. Gurevitch (eds), *Mass Media and Society*, 2nd edn, London: Arnold.

Hall, S. (1982) 'The Rediscovery of "Ideology": Return of the Repressed in Media Studies', in M. Gurevitch, T. Bennett, J. Curran and J. Wollacott (eds), *Culture, Society and the Media*, London: Methuen.

Hallin, D. (1994) *We Keep America on Top of the World*, London: Routledge.

Hoijer, B. (1992) 'Socio-cognitive Structures and Television Reception', *Media, Culture and Society*, 14.

Humphreys, P. (1996) *Mass Media and Media Policy in Western Europe*, Manchester: Manchester University Press.

Kaniss, P. (1997) *Making Local News*, Chicago: University of Chicago Press.

McQuail, D. (1992) *Media Performance*, London: Sage.

McRobbie, A. (1994) *Postmodernism and Popular Culture*, London: Routledge.

McRobbie, A. (1996) '*More!*: New Sexualities in Girls' and Women's Magazines', in J. Curran, D. Morley and V. Walkerdine (eds), *Cultural Studies and Communications*, London: Arnold.

Modleski, T. (1984) *Loving with a Vengeance*, New York: Methuen.

Morley, D. (1992) *Television, Audiences and Cultural Studies*, London: Routledge.

Murdoch, R. (1989) *Freedom in Broadcasting*, London: News International.

Murdock, G. (1990) 'Redrawing the Map of Communication Industries: Concentration and Ownership in the Era of Privatization', in M. Ferguson (ed.), *Public Communication*, London: Sage.

Negroponte, N. (1996) *Being Digital*, London: Coronet.

Nikolaidis, A. (1999) 'The Media Under Restrictive Legislation: The Case of the Greek Press in the 1990s', unpub. PhD thesis, Goldsmiths College, University of London.

Newcomb, H. and Hirsch, P. (1984) 'Television as a Cultural Forum: Implications for Research', in W. Rowland and B. Watkins (eds), *Interpreting Television*, London: Sage.

Nowak, K. (1984) 'Cultural Indicators in Swedish Advertising 1950–75', in G. Melischek, K. Rosengren and J. Stappers (eds), *Cultural Indicators: An International Symposium*, Vienna: Verlag der Osterriechisen Akademie der Wissenschaften.

Parenti, M. (1993) *Inventing Reality*, 2nd edn, New York: St. Martin's Press.

Schlesinger, P. (1990) 'Rethinking the Sociology of Journalism: Source Strategies and the Limits of Media-Centrism', in M. Ferguson (ed.), *Public Communication*, London: Sage.

Schlesinger, P. and Tumber, H. (1994) *Reporting Crime*, Oxford: Clarendon Press.

Schudson, M. (1996) 'The Sociology of News Production Revisited', in J. Curran and M. Gurevitch (eds), *Mass Media and Society*, 2nd edn, London: Arnold.

Shattuc, J. (1997) *The Talking Cure*, New York: Routledge.

Tunstall, J. (1996) *Newspaper Power*, Oxford: Oxford University Press.

Waters, M. (1995) *Globalization*, London: Routledge.

Weaver, D. and Wilhoit, G. (1991) *The American Journalist*, 2nd edn, Bloomington: Indiana University Press.

PART

I

OVERVIEW

|1|

Media organisations in society

Central issues

GOLDSMITHS MEDIA GROUP[1]

The twentieth century has seen a transformation in the nature of communication. Much of it is now mediated through print or electronic technology; bought and sold in a market system; and produced in institutions marked by a complex division of labour. The conservative response has been divided between those who mourn the rise of mass culture, and those who see the hidden hand of the market as benignly ensuring that people get what they want in terms of information and entertainment. For both camps, media organisations are of little interest. They are either, in the first case, the transmitters of a trivial, fragmented culture; or, in the second, neutral respondents to public opinion, who need merely to be protected from state intervention in order to work effectively.

Media and communication studies, generally undertaken by those of the centre and of the left, have by contrast seen media organisations as crucial to an understanding of the consequences of the rise of mass communication. But a schism has marked the field for half a century, between liberals who find in modern mass media a multiplication of representative voices, forming a collective conversation, and radicals who see a worrying concentration of power. In this first section, we want to outline the basis of the radical approach to the political economy of communications, which informs many of the essays in this book; and in the second and third sections we proceed to outline some of the ways in which the radical approach has evolved in the light of new developments and debates.

The cultural industries

The cornerstone of the radical case is to see the mass media as capitalist enterprises. The most developed version of this argument is what has been called the 'cultural industries' approach, which has its root in the Frankfurt School's critique of the 'Culture Industry' (Adorno and Horkheimer 1978

[1941]), but has been developed in recent years by critical media economists such as Bernard Miège (1989) and Nicholas Garnham (1990). This school of writing takes its name from the adherence of its writers to the view that, in the modern world, the production of culture has been largely industrialised; but that the particular features of this industrialisation are distinct from those of other sectors.

At the heart of capitalism is the requirement to generate profit. Yet, according to Nicholas Garnham, there is a contradiction in entertainment capitalism which complicates considerably the way that capitalists seek to make a profit in the field of culture. A tension exists between a general drive towards audience maximisation on the part of cultural firms and a countervailing drive by the same firms to limit access in order to achieve scarcity (thereby keeping unit prices high). Both of these contradictory features derive from the way that consumers use the cultural commodity.

One of these use-values of the cultural commodity is novelty. Consumers require cultural products to be distinguishable from each other. Garnham notes that this makes every film, record or book more like a prototype than a copy. The drive for novelty, achieved through intensive development activity, means that, in the cultural industries, production costs are high relative to the costs of reproduction. The music on a compact disc costs far more to produce in a studio and to publicise in advance of its release than does its subsequent mechanical reproduction in a factory. Marginal returns grow significantly with each unit sold, and this puts an emphasis on audience maximisation as a source of profit. In order to meet this challenge of audience maximisation, media transnationals have become particularly expert in deploying strategies of concentration, internationalisation and cross-sector ownership (though these are of course features of other industries too).

Another feature of the cultural commodity, however, is that it is not destroyed in use. A video tape of a film can be lent to dozens, if not hundreds, of people; a chocolate bar can only be consumed once. In order to achieve scarcity, then, cultural firms must, besides working with the state to control piracy, aim to limit access to cultural goods and services by artificial means. Garnham identifies a number of ways in which scarcity is achieved. Primary among them is vertical integration. The ownership of distribution and retail channels allows companies to control release and re-release schedules of videos (think of Disney 'classics' such as *Snow White*), films, records, new magazines, etc., thereby ensuring the adequate availability (or strategic unavailability) of goods.

A third feature of cultural commodities is that audiences tend to use them in their efforts to achieve difference and distinction from other users (see Bourdieu 1984). Because the criteria for judging difference and distinction fluctuate with fashion, the demand for any given cultural commodity is unpredictable. As a consequence, risk needs to be spread across as diverse a repertoire of cultural products as possible. This creates an especially strong drive towards concentration and oligopoly, as those companies which cannot afford to spread their risks via a wide range of products tend either to be absorbed into larger corporations, or to disappear altogether.

Garnham's model, then, helps to explain some striking features about contemporary media organisations. Internationalisation has been a feature of the cultural industries for many decades (think of Hollywood's domination of the international film market from the 1920s on) but has intensified in recent years. The importance of cross-media ownership can be seen in the daily manoeuvres of various British press concerns as they continue to diversify into electronic media, thus circumventing ownership restrictions originally constructed to ensure a plurality of voices in society (Williams 1996). Evidence of the viability of vertical integration is provided by the fact that 'the five largest media firms in the world in terms of sales – Time Warner, Disney, Bertelsmann, Viacom and News Corporation – are also the most fully integrated global giants' (Herman and McChesney 1997: 70). And though neither concentration nor oligopoly is new to the realm of international entertainment capitalism, recent giant purchases – of ABC/Capital Cities by Disney, of Ted Turner's CNN by Time Warner, of CBS by Westinghouse – are only the most prominent of the myriad alliances, partnerships, mergers, acquisitions and anti-competitive manoeuvres that the climate of 'deregulation' in the 1980s and 1990s has especially encouraged (Herman and McChesney 1997: 41–69).

So features of the cultural industries, rooted in the way that audiences use cultural commodities, make profit-making complex and difficult; but the extraordinary successes of transnational media and entertainment corporations attest to the possibility of doing so. These strategies are worrying to radical critics because they mean that the means of communication will tend to be owned by the powerful and wealthy, for the simple reason that all the strategies referred to require huge resources. The implication of this political economy approach is that there is an inbuilt tendency in capitalism for those who already have power to be reinforced.

The features of the cultural commodity analysed by Garnham should not, however, be seen as iron laws which determine all that takes place in the cultural market. This is merely a starting-point for understanding the dynamics underlying industrial strategies in the sector. Media sociology can serve as the sister-discipline to such a political economy, by examining how regulation policy, political action, aesthetic ideologies, professional codes and histories of class, gender and ethnic relationships can all affect the production processes and outcomes within media organisations. In some cases, sociologists have found that what happens in media entertainment organisations is largely determined by the patterns of ownership described above: media workers ultimately, whatever their intentions, engage in actions, and produce content, which reinforces existing patterns of class, gender and ethnic-group power (Gitlin 1994). In other cases, however, analysts have emphasised the production of unusual and innovative work, which cannot be understood as the product of a coherent 'dominant ideology' (e.g. Frith 1983).

The news media

While radical critiques of the cultural industries have been largely concerned with the production and consumption of cultural commodities, authors investigating the news media have tended to prioritise another set of concerns. The news media play an important part in any political system and are expected to fulfil a number of 'ideal' functions in liberal democratic states (see Keane 1991, McNair 1995 and Negrine 1996, for discussions). These include providing: access for a wide range of citizens to put forward their views; an arena for rational debate on the issues affecting society and the state; a source of objective information, widely available to all citizens; and a check ('watchdog role') on the activities of powerful institutions and individuals. Thus, although news is itself a cultural commodity, produced both privately and publicly, it is also observed and critiqued in terms of its ability to fulfil these 'ideal' functions in democratic societies.

In contrast to liberal and neo-liberal accounts, radicals have sought to demonstrate that news media in capitalist democracies fail to be objective, present rational debate or offer equal access. Radical explanations for this are varied, employing different methods, emphases and perspectives. They have, however, tended to agree on a number of key tenets in their critique. The news media, although a site of social conflict, relay the 'dominant ideology' of the ruling class. Economic concerns ('economic determinism'), to a greater or lesser extent, guide the production of news. Journalists and consumers, while believing that they act autonomously, are in fact socialised and guided by economic conditions and the dominant ideology of the ruling class.

One consistent approach taken by radicals is to look at the ownership and control of organisations that produce news. In Europe broadcasting has, for most of the century, been state owned and/or regulated. This has involved the state appointing directors and determining funding. Where the government of the day has not directly controlled the news media, it still has been responsible for regulating it through legislation on censorship, libel and media ownership. As many radical (Schlesinger et al. 1983, Glasgow University Media Group 1985, Hollingsworth 1986, Schiller 1992) and neo-liberal accounts have demonstrated, states have frequently been prone to abuse their privileged positions in all these matters. State control and ownership, however, have slowly given way to control by large corporations and 'media moguls'. Broadcasting and news media, like the press traditionally, have become predominately private concerns. Once again, many accounts (Evans 1983, Schiller 1989, Tunstall and Palmer 1991, Curran and Seaton 1997) have documented abuse by owners who seek to influence the work of their employees and the political process to their own corporate ends. Thus, news is powerfully distorted by governments and corporations. Objective reporting and rational debate are understandably threatened when it comes to reporting on issues that involve the interests of these sectors.

Independent journalism is also affected by the fact that news is a business and is widely influenced by economic considerations. First, corporate elites are key shareholders and/or directors of boards for media organisations and businesses are the prime funders of news through the purchase of advertising. They can therefore apply financial pressures when necessary – to censor texts, to gain favourable coverage or simply to appeal to particular audiences (Murdock 1982, Curran 1986, Bagdikian 1992, Gitlin 1994). Second, news production and distribution is expensive and more economically viable when conducted by large corporations that can make maximum use of facilities and networks. The demands of advertisers, coupled with the increased costs of market entry, mean that corporations increasingly influence news production and that alternative and critical news producers decline and gain less access to the process. Thus, the news industry, like other cultural industries, has been subject to a steady process of concentration and conglomeration – one that involves news being produced by fewer interests (Murdock 1982, Chomsky and Herman 1988, Garnham 1990, Curran and Seaton 1997). Third, news is a cultural commodity, but one that is less subject to fashion and ill-equipped to maximise the returns on successful products by simply producing more of them. Instead news producers can only increase profits by making production cuts, recycling news texts (as in 24-hour news) and maximising audiences (or elite audiences) and therefore increasing advertising revenues. As other radical and some liberal commentators have observed, as news has become more privatised and commodified, so its editorial quality has declined and its need to entertain has risen (McNair 1994, Barnett and Curry 1994, Williams 1996). Expensive investigative journalism and foreign news is reduced and business and celebrity news rise (Sigal 1973, Fishman 1980, Tunstall 1996). Thus, economic considerations diminish access, objectivity and rational debate further.

A third general radical approach looks at the cultural and organisational factors which affect journalists involved in the news media. Several studies have attempted to demonstrate that journalists are guided in their news gathering and reporting by the ideas and arguments of corporate and government elites. Content analysis (Glasgow University Media Group 1976, 1980, 1982) of news texts has been used to argue that such elites frequently set news agendas and are reported more favourably than oppositions and non-elites. Sociological studies of news reporting and journalists in action (Hall et al. 1978, Fishman 1980, Ericson et al. 1989, Hallin 1994) have supported this contention. They have demonstrated that government and institutional news sources consistently outnumber others and that ordinary workers and consumers are rarely reported. Journalist routines and their attempts to appear impartial and objective have resulted in a reporting process that enforces the authority ('primary definer' status) of those in power and marginalises others. Once again, access and objectivity have become narrowly constrained in the news media.

Recent developments

Radical critiques of the media were clearly in the ascendancy in the early 1980s. Since then, research emanating from cultural studies and sociology, coupled with postmodern theory, have argued that many of the foundations of the radical critique are highly dubious. Broadcast journalists and liberal sociologists (Annan 1977, Tiffen 1989, Schudson 1991) have countered claims of journalistic bias and argued that pressures imposed from above cannot affect the day-to-day autonomy of working journalists. Audience-reception theorists have argued that audiences interpret texts with a substantial degree of autonomy (Morley 1980, 1992, Ang 1985, Fiske 1987 and Corner 1991). They have forcefully countered the notions that audiences are passive consumers and texts rigidly determined. Coherent elite ideology and economically defined classes were also perceived to be flawed concepts. Several studies (Abercrombie et al. 1984, Hallin 1994, Miller 1994) showed that elites were too fractured and too much in conflict to provide a coherent ideological consensus. Studies of ethnic subcultures (Hebdige 1979, Chambers 1985) and female experiences (Radway 1987, McRobbie 1994), as well as suggesting that there were groups in society that did not submit to any perceived dominant cultural norms, also undermined the credibility of the notion of culture determined by economic conditions alone. Thus, in the academic sphere, dynamic interaction, individual autonomy and/or action, fracture and change have countered the rigid structures and totalising theories that were associated with radical critiques.

During this same period of academic change, the political landscape and the shape of the media industries have simultaneously been transformed. Free-market arguments have become dominant with the collapse of Eastern European communism and the succession of neo-liberal governments worldwide. Globalisation, privatisation and deregulation of the media (including news media) industries has proceeded rapidly. Conservative politicians and media owners (Veljanovski 1989, 1990, Sola Pool 1990), arguing for consumer choice and free private industry rather than elite preference and state inefficiency and corruption, appear to have won through and continue to guide current legislative policy (see Williams 1996, Franklin 1997, Curran and Seaton 1997). Thus, in theory, radical perspectives appear to have lost tremendous ground. In practice, their concerns have been ignored by prevailing political opinion.

However, although radical critiques have proved to be conceptually vulnerable, continuing trends in media production indicate that their concerns are more justified than ever. Deregulation, concentration and conglomeration proceed, despite the arrival of left-leaning governments. Abuses by governments, powerful media owners, advertisers and corporate bodies have not diminished. Cuts in editorial budgets and the casualisation of the journalist workforce is further reducing reporter autonomy. 'Serious' news is being further commodified and coming to resemble 'infotainment' or 'newszak'. Institutional sources still dominate news texts and many sections of the public are being further excluded from news agendas. All these trends continue to be documented in the UK (Murdock 1990, Tunstall 1996, Williams 1996, Curran and Seaton 1997, Franklin 1997) and the US (Schiller 1989, Bagdikian 1992, Mancini and Swanson 1996, Herman and McChesney 1997, McChesney 1997). Even liberal theorists and journalists (Blumler and Gurevitch 1995, Fallows 1996) are showing extreme concern about the profession of journalism and the 'crisis of public communication'. Thus the radical critique of news media lacking objectivity, information, rational debate and wide access is no less valid than it was two decades ago. Much of traditional radical theory, in contrast, is in need of a major overhaul.

DISPERSAL OF MEDIA POWER: AUTONOMY AND RESISTANCE WITHIN PRODUCTION

The opening section of this chapter outlined the more established radical approaches to the study of entertainment and news-media production. It argued that, despite the range of significant critiques of radical political economy that emerged during the 1980s and 1990s, the relevance of the approach was as important as ever. In spite of its shortcomings, radical political economy needed to be refined and reformulated rather than rejected. One way in which this tradition sought to renew itself was through a Gramscian reappraisal that emphasised conflict (Curran 1996d). This led to the media being conceived of as a battlefield between contending groups rather than as a top-down instrument of control. However, Gramscianism was a rather unstable basis of reformulation since it tended to mean different things to different analysts. This rethinking also raised a number of questions. In what way is a radical approach emphasising social conflict different from a liberal pluralist one stressing rivalry and disagreement? More generally, how is a 'loosened-up' version of radical political economy different from liberal argument?

This is explored further here in relation to three areas: changing patterns of ownership and organisation; news sources and media–source relations; and the impact of new technologies. In each of these research areas, radical

and liberal perspectives have been applied but with different emphases and different terminology. In each case a strong liberal-pluralist line has emerged to challenge many of the central tenets of radical political economy. 'Individual autonomy' and 'dynamic processes of contestation' have replaced 'dominant ideology' and 'structures'; cultural and technological factors have been highlighted over 'economic determinism' and 'class'; and 'the micro-physics of power' and bottom-up influences have challenged 'macro explanations' of 'top-down power'. Throughout, a strong liberal line has emerged – one that emphasises the autonomy of the individual and the dispersal of power within media production. Whether it be independent production companies, or environmentalists using the Internet, or opposition sources setting news agendas, there is a sense that traditional top-down power structures have been weakened or broken. Just as audiences can actively consume media products, so individual media workers and opposition organisations can affect the media production process – regardless of the increasing trends towards concentrated ownership and globalisation of media corporations.

The aims of this section are therefore to present and critically explore some of these alternative areas of debate. It concludes that many of these studies and perspectives offer some useful challenges and provide further grounds for research for those interested in production issues. However, it also finds problems in a number of liberal positions that have over-emphasised small gains and ignored great losses of individual autonomy and the continued exclusion of opposition groups. The exercise of political power may be more mediated and complex than many radical political economists have acknowledged; but its effects are just as keenly felt, no matter the level of production or individual opposition.

One strong area of liberal challenge to radical political economy is in relation to questions of control and individual autonomy within media organisations. The radical approach to the political economy of the media traditionally assumes that the media industries reinforce social power because the wealthy and powerful own them. Ownership entails a large degree of control over operations, the recruitment and reward of cultural labour and, ultimately, media content. Consequently, larger media conglomerates and more powerful media owners result in greater control of the media. However, if the power of ownership is more limited, and the levels of individual autonomy greater than radicals have assumed, then the arguments about ownership become rather less relevant. The findings of much recent work on media production have indeed emphasised such devolved patterns of control.

Work on the 'managerial revolution' (Burnham 1962, Berle and Means 1968) has provided one key component for a thesis emphasising independence and autonomy for those working within many types of industry. This stressed that, as the twentieth century has progressed, control of companies has passed from single owners to complex networks of shareholders and 'managerial elites'. As companies become larger, shareholders become more dispersed and anonymous. Companies consequently become more controlled by highly skilled professional elites with outlooks and rewards that are different from those of traditional capitalist owners. A second wave of research on post-Fordism and 'flexible specialisation' (e.g. Aglietta 1979, Piore and Sabel 1984) has more recently emerged to complement this thesis. These studies have identified a transition in industry away from Fordist structures of production that involved large-scale centralised production, rigid bureaucratic managerial hierarchies and the use of mass, unskilled, cheap labour. Instead, post-Fordist production methods have, among other things, introduced decentralised networks of companies and highly skilled, flexible and professional workforces. Expanding multinational companies may be bigger and richer but are not necessarily controlled more rigidly from the centre. Instead, new consensual networks are made up of large corporations and small, specialist companies that service them, often in regional agglomerations which serve to bolster local economies. Indeed, for writers such as Castells (1996), the logic of the network is more significant than power in any particular part of that network.

These positions have clearly provided the focus for a number of recent studies on 'independent producers' operating within the media industries. Independent producers (that is, small companies with no direct ties to major corporations) have frequently been a feature of media production. They have been credited with a number of innovations in popular music (Gillett 1971, Chapple and Garofalo 1977) and were crucial to changes in the film industry from the 1950s onwards (Christopherson and Storper 1986). More recently, the importance of independent producers and post-Fordist production methods has been recognised particularly in the film (Wasko 1994, Maltby 1995, ch. 2), television (Veljanovski 1989) and magazine (Driver and Gillespie 1993) sectors. The most notable instance in the UK has been the rise of an independent broadcasting sector, based around organisational changes in British broadcasting. This began with the introduction of Channel 4 (1982). Rather than making its own programmes, the channel functioned right from the start as a 'publisher-contractor'. This trend has continued with further legislation (1990) which required the BBC and ITV networks to contract out at least 25 per cent of their programming to independent producers. Such changes, across each of these industries, have been credited with: media rejuvenation; the vertical 'disintegration' of dominant centralised cultural production companies; a dispersal of power; and better conditions in which individual creativity and diversity can flourish. As such, post-Fordism and independent production networks were praised by neo-liberals (Veljanovski 1989), liberals (Keane 1991) and the Left (Hall and Jacques 1989), each side expressing optimism over a perceived dispersal of media power and greater individual autonomy.

Clearly, changing patterns of media ownership and organisation have important implications for the political economy approach because they challenge the view that the media reinforce structural inequality within society in line with the agenda of wealthy and powerful owners. On the surface, this would seem to lend support to a more pluralist view, which sees journalists and creative entertainment personnel as acting autonomously of the interests of owners. As workers in the cultural industries become more shielded from the interests of owners – through layers of powerful managerial elites and networks of producing organisations – so independence and diversity should flourish. This position thus supports the established liberal view of news journalists and creative artists. Thus, journalists are alternately driven by 'professional codes', 'news values', 'news routines and practices', and 'fourth estate' values (Gans 1980, Tiffen 1989, Schudson 1991) – all of which reflect a wider pluralist world. Meanwhile, in cultural production, as companies struggle to keep pace with the fickle tastes of audiences, musicians and other creative personnel are given a significant degree of autonomy (Frith 1983, Negus 1992) in carrying out their daily work.

Sources, access and news production

Just as researchers have sought to find increased autonomy within news organisations, they have also reappraised assumptions about the news-production process and access to it. This reappraisal has emerged with a series of studies on news sources, 'promotional culture' (Wernick 1991) and journalist–source relations. These have registered a number of subtle shifts away from traditional radical accounts of news production. First, macro descriptions, centring on media ownership and economic power, have been replaced with micro ones emphasising a media that reflect the wider conflict of source organisations in society. Second, earlier radical work on the means by which dominant elites gained superior source access has been challenged by a series of studies focusing on the increased abilities of opposition and 'resource-poor' groups to gain their own access. In other words, attempts to demonstrate elite control of media output have been superseded by an emphasis on a pluralist account of source competition. In fact, a slide towards pluralism has been an underlying feature of many accounts of sources – be they from liberal or radical scholars.

Up until the late 1980s few studies had made significant observations about the role of sources in news production. The most significant research on the subject came in the radical political economy approach of the Glasgow University Media Group (1976, 1980) and the radical 'structural culturist' approach of Hall et al. (1978; see also Golding and Middleton 1982, Chomsky and Herman 1988). Whereas the Glasgow Group tended to explain elite dominance through many of the macro-economic explanations described above, Hall et al. offered an alternative based on a more detailed analysis from the point of view of media–source relations. This study argued that journalists, in their search for 'objective' and 'authoritative' accounts, automatically sought out institutionalised sources. These sources, already legitimated by their power, representativeness and expertise, became the 'primary definers' of news agendas. Opposition sources, and journalists themselves, could only respond to those agendas and frameworks already determined. Thus dominant ideology resulted from the media's 'structured preferences' for the opinions of dominant groups.

The emphasis on elite-source power has been reinforced by a number of more recent studies of political (party and institution) and corporate sources and their 'cultural intermediaries'. This has come from a mixture of media studies, journalism and political communications in the UK (Franklin 1994, Negrine 1994, 1996, Jones 1995, Kavanagh 1995, McNair 1995, Scammell 1995, Rosenbaum 1997, Gaber 1998) and North America (Gandy 1992, Maltese 1994, Stauber and Rampton 1995, Ewen 1996, Hall-Jamieson 1996, Kurtz 1998). All these studies have explored the development of elite sources and their increased interest in managing, and ability to manage the media. All have also identified the rapidly expanding group of 'cultural intermediaries' – professionals whose job it is to promote elite source organisations and improve communications with the media. This group, which includes pollsters, marketing experts, agents and public-relations practitioners, has drawn increasing attention from academic disciplines and the general media.

The new wave of news-source research began with a strong critique of the assumptions that underpinned both 'media-centric' political economy and Hall et al.'s thesis. Schlesinger (1990) pointed out the following problems with Hall et al.'s work: primary definers, being often in conflict, did not speak with one voice; neither did they retain the same levels of access over time, let alone possess equal amounts of access. Similarly, journalists and non-official sources were not always relegated to subordinate positions, but did on occasion challenge official accounts. In effect, the structural-culturist approach, like radical functionalism, gave an overly determinist picture that did not account for change and the 'dynamic processes of contestation in a given field of discourse'. Since then, many researchers have tended towards a combination of pluralist or 'radical-pluralist' alternatives.

Pluralist accounts have developed from several sources. One of these has come from liberal empirical studies of journalists and sources. Many of these (Tiffen 1989, Ericson et al. 1989, Schudson 1991) have explained dominant source access as resulting from the organisational routines and values of news gatherers. Journalists do not simply seek out accredited sources, they are attracted to ones that are close at hand, reliable, well informed and liable to be newsworthy. At the same time Nacos (1990) and Hallin (1994) have explained media attacks on the US government as resulting from 'shifts in elite consensus'. When conflicts among primary definers become too strong, the media reflect those battles and contribute to transfers of power between elites.

These two strands have in turn contributed much to a radical-pluralist synthesis that was most strongly advocated in the work of Schlesinger and Tumber (1994), and Miller (1993, 1994). In their work, on the 'criminal-justice arena' and conflict in Northern Ireland, they emphasised the idea of sources acting in continuous competition for dominance of given media discourses. In this competition, primary definers were not structurally pre-determined, but achieved that status through accumulations and expenditures of different forms of economic and 'cultural capital' (Bourdieu 1984). Under these conditions, non-official sources could gain positive media access by proving reliable, authoritative and routine suppliers for journalists. This process resulted in the rise of institutional legitimacy (a form of cultural capital) that enabled non-official organisations to gain access in spite of institutional and economic disadvantages. By the same logic, official and corporate sources were also shown to often lose authority and legitimacy by proving unreliable and/or divided.

These conclusions were taken further in studies focusing on trade unions, local councils and pressure groups (Curran 1990, Kerr and Sachdev 1992, Anderson 1993, Cracknell 1993, Hansen 1993, Franklin 1994, ch. 6, Deacon 1996, and Davis, ch. 7 in this volume). In many of these accounts, the capacity of opposition and 'resource-poor' groups to gain media access by employing their own 'cultural intermediaries' and using alternative media strategies has been emphasised. Thus, in contrast to many radical accounts that stress the 'public-relations state' (Deacon and Golding 1994) and state–corporate 'propaganda model(s)' (Chomsky and Herman 1988), these studies have contributed to a more pluralist account of media–source relations. Indeed, for several authors (Shoemaker 1989, Scammell 1995 and Miller 1998) such approaches appear to be the only means by which opposition and resource-poor groups can circumvent traditional news routines and gain access that was hitherto denied them.

Impact of new technologies

The same themes of autonomy, access and individual choice have crept into discussions of ICTs (Information and Communication Technologies) and media production. The recent developments of microprocessor, telecommunications and digital technologies have transformed the processes of media production and transmission in the 1980s and 1990s. Thus, older debates, about 'technological determinism' and the part played by technology in either emancipating or repressing the mass of society, have resurfaced. Once again, the main thrust of liberal pluralists and policy-makers alike has been to emphasise a 'techno-utopian' vision of improved prosperity, education, access and, ultimately, greater individual autonomy. In this scenario, technology becomes a determining factor that can overcome the social and economic inequalities that underpin radical political economy descriptions.

Radical approaches towards the impact of new technologies have traditionally been divided. On the one hand, they have been consistently aware
of the impacts of new technology on jobs and management–employee relations, and on the increased ability of governments and corporations to
strengthen their control over the mass media. On the other, they have been
hard pressed to avoid opponents' claims, mostly levelled at the Frankfurt
School, that they are simply 'cultural pessimists', advocates of a 'hypoder-
mic-syringe' model of media production, or simply 'Luddite' (see Webster
and Robins 1986). An additional problem has been that many radicals have
tended to overlook discussions of technology and technological determinism, preferring instead to concentrate on explanations which more traditionally rely on social, political and economic determinants in the
production process. However, there has also been a strong positive advocacy of technology – one that passes through Brecht (1930), Benjamin
(1969) and Enzensberger (1976) – which sees it as a source of enlightenment
and progressive change.

The concerns of liberal and conservative technological determinists have
consistently been to promote ICTs as the means of achieving general human
prosperity. McLuhan (1964), Bell (1976), Toffler (1980) and Sola Pool
(1983) are among those who have written extensively about the great benefits of the new 'information society' and electronic 'global village'. Such
technological optimism has clearly informed more recent discussions concerning autonomy within production and individual access. The transformation from Fordist to post-Fordist organisational structures is very much
related to new technologies. For Piore and Sabel (1984) and Murray (1989),
it is new ICTs which raise skill levels, enable flexible specialisation, and
bring into being weak power structures and producer networks. Jobs are
less rigid and manual, flexibility and employee autonomy higher. Thus individual workers are both more autonomous and gain greater job satisfaction.

Opportunities for access have also appeared to increase. As ICTs become
more mass-produced and cheaper, so the possibilities for individuals to
access public forms of communication and political agendas have grown
(see Downing 1984, and collection in Dowmunt (ed.) 1993). The expansion
of first cable and then digital television, along with cheap production technology, means greater opportunities for low-budget and alternative broadcasting. The clearest examples of this have been in the rise of
community-access cable television in North America (Halleck 1984,
Goldberg 1990) and the BBC's Community Programme Unit in the United
Kingdom (Dovey 1993, Keighron 1993, Dovey (ed.) 1996). Both put the
emphasis on giving individuals and local community groups the means to
produce their own broadcasts for public transmission on programmes like
Video Diaries. Closely related to this is the availability of cheap and light-
weight camcorders which, in addition to being used to produce community
programmes, are an important tool for activist groups and independent
journalists. The cases of Rodney King and Felipe Soltero in the United

States, environmental protesters across Europe, and the plights of people living in East Timor and those involved in Tiananmen Square, have all been highlighted by such video activism. The Internet is another communication means which has been hailed as the new mouthpiece for those lacking public access. The argument put forth is that Internet has enabled dissident voices, from Mexico (Knudsen 1998) to China, as well as independent journalists and activists in North America and Europe, to upset their more powerful oppositions – both by gaining prominent access and through techniques such as net flooding. For authors such as Negroponte (1995), the Internet in effect reconstitutes the Greek agora, subverting orthodox patterns of media concentration and manipulation.

It appears that, in the absence of a consistent and more vocal radical critique, positive technological determinism has been winning the day. A combined wave of positive technological determinism (Negroponte 1995, Turkle 1995, Leeson (ed.) 1996, Pavlik 1996, Poster 1996, Kahin 1997) and technological free-market advocacy (Gingrich 1995, Gates 1996, Dertouzos 1997) has dominated recent discourse. In this overlap of policy-makers, corporate voices and neo-liberal theorists, new technologies have become closely associated with a discourse of prosperity and individual choice. According to this argument, as communication possibilities open up and spectrum scarcity becomes irrelevant, state control becomes unnecessary and no single organisation – private or public – may dominate. Governments, corporations, special interest groups and individuals have thus been placed on a more level playing field in which all may gain access to information and debate and no single entity may gain exclusive control.

Individual autonomy within the production process?

The initial positive accounts of the 'managerial revolution', post-Fordism and independent producers characteristic of the 1980s have, during the 1990s, been replaced by more sober assessment. While resources have been dispersed through networks of organisations and layers of management, has power really been dispersed and have those working in the news and cultural industries been granted greater autonomy? Have the imperatives of the market been any more diluted by the reorganisation of the production process? As the 1990s have progressed, and the full effects of neo-liberal reforms encouraging flexible specialisation and independents have been felt, commentators have become rather more pessimistic in response to these questions. For many, operations may have been dispersed, but power and profits have not. Changes in organisations have been introduced to cut costs and spread risks, not to increase creativity and autonomy. Whoever owns and manages multinational companies, the objectives remain the same. The majority of individual media workers may have found flexibility but they have also found poorer conditions, greater insecurity and fewer rights. In effect, individual autonomy has in fact declined for many people working in the media industries.

Even before the arguments of the 'managerial revolution' had found their way into liberal and post-Fordist descriptions of media production, the thesis had already been criticised by a number of studies (e.g. Barratt-Brown 1968, Nichols 1969, Hill 1981). These studies questioned whether owner values and objectives were different from managerial ones, and found that top managers, owners and large shareholders often moved in similar circles and were tied together by exclusive networks of interlocking directorships. They also found that personal/family ownership of companies was still widespread and that, even where power lay in the hands of shareholders, it was usually a small number of them.

All these points have also been taken up and applied to the cultural industries also. Several authors, most notably Murdock (1982), Chomsky and Herman (1988) and Tunstall and Palmer (1991) revealed the continuing prevalence of family owners and concentrated ownership. Murdock (1982) additionally analysed the limitations of the 'managerial-revolution' thesis as applied to media industries. He drew on a recognised crucial distinction between two forms of control which owners and managers could exert: allocative and operational. Allocative control consists of decisions connected to overall policy-formulation; decisions which included making senior appointments, allocating resources, dictation of editorial lines and product investment lines, and control over the distribution of profits. Operational control, in effect, consists of making effective use of allocated resources and pursuing policy decisions that have already been dictated. Murdock argued that managerial elites, in most cases, had operational rather than allocative control. In other words, they still followed the central aims and objectives laid down by owners. He and other authors (e.g. Evans 1983, Hollingsworth 1986, Curran and Seaton 1997) have since offered a steady supply of examples of owner interference that affected operational control to a high degree.

Equally strong objections have been raised in relation to the rise of post-Fordist networks and independent producers. Gomery (1986) has revisited the Hollywood studio system, Gitlin (1994) the US television networks, Hesmondhalgh (1996, 1998) the record industry, and Robins and Cornford (1992) the British television industry. Each has also noted several negative trends that have resulted from the rise of independents. First, power has very much remained in the hands of the majors in that they maintain control of the money supply and distribution channels. In each case there are a handful of majors/commissioning companies and up to several hundred potential suppliers. This means that the majors, more than ever, are in a position to dictate the conditions of supply. Suppliers, in contrast, operate with little reserve capital and short-term contracts. Many therefore go out of business or, if they become successful, risk take-over by the majors. In each observed case, the evolution of independents and vertical disintegration has been followed by a strong tendency towards 'virtual integration' or 'reintegration'. In contracting out work, the majors also absolve themselves of the overheads, training needs and employment rights associated with direct employment of their workforces. Unionisation among fragmented and dispersed workforces is increasingly difficult to sustain. In effect, the majors have not only increased the flexibility and diversity of the production process, they have cut their costs, reduced employee power and spread their risks.

The losers in these cost-cutting, de-unionisation and risk-redistribution trends are those working in the cultural industries. At the top end there is an extremely well-paid group of film stars, top bands, successful producers, presenters, news readers and so on. But for the vast majority of those employed in the cultural industries, even more than in other industries, flexible specialisation has meant little job security, depressed wages, few employment rights and long hours. Hutton (1996), in a recent critique of the impact of neo-liberal market reforms on British society, identified a developing 30:30:40 division in the labour market. Thirty per cent were unemployed and 30 per cent were in 'insecure employment', being employed on a casual, part-time or self-employed basis. Only 40 per cent were in full-time permanent employment. A brief look at the news industry in Britain demonstrates that the majority of journalists now fit into one of the first two categories. Several national newspapers, and the BBC, have cut the numbers of editorial staff by between a third and a half since the late 1980s. According to Franklin (1997, ch. 3) some 80 per cent of journalists in the UK are now either freelancers, part-timers or employed on contracts of 12 months or less. Under such conditions one can only conclude that journalists and other media workers have very little independence or security and are even less likely to oppose management decisions and editorial lines. Thus the long-term effect of organisational changes has most likely been a decline in the autonomy of media employees.

Sources and the question of access?

While research into source activity has moved the debate into a more pluralist arena, the same research has simultaneously undermined traditional liberal accounts of news production. The first point to make is that all studies of sources, by their very nature, have the effect of making the traditional liberal description of independent 'journalists at work' rather untenable. If news comes out of source supply and media–source relations then it isn't simply the product of an independent 'fourth-estate' media. Under such conditions, liberal-pluralist paradigms must therefore rely on two things: 1) that journalists remain in control of their material and have the upper hand over sources, and 2) that source access remains relatively evenly distributed among different source sectors. However, as much recent work demonstrates, neither of these assumptions can be sustained.

On the first point, both liberals and radicals appear to be moving towards the general opinion that journalists are losing control. Up until the late 1980s the consensus had been that the attempts of either side to manage the other resulted in a see-saw 'tug-of-war', in which sources were slightly stronger but neither side dominated for long (Sigal 1973, Fishman 1980, Gans 1980, Ericson et al. 1989, Tiffen 1989). Ultimately, factors such as source competition, media competition, changing conditions of production and the benefits of media–source co-operation resulted in a closely contested level of equilibrium. However, it has since become apparent that dramatic changes are taking place among both source and media organisations. Such changes, it is suggested, have resulted in a strengthening of the position of source power at a time when journalistic power is seriously under threat. As all the accounts of sources and cultural intermediaries argue, organisations are deliberately targeting the media and investing large sums and hiring personnel to do just that. At the same time journalists are having to produce more with fewer staff and smaller editorial budgets. In Tunstall's (1996) estimation, journalists are now having to produce two or three times the amount of copy they did in the 1960s. These transitions among sources and media outlets have resulted in a significant transfer of political, economic and news-gathering resources – away from journalists and towards sources. Journalists have drifted away from the activities of costly investigative journalism towards reactive news production that relies more on routine source supply. According to the work of Sigal (1973), Fishman (1980) and Gandy (1980), in the United States journalists have for some decades been ever more dependent on the 'information subsidies' supplied to them by sources. These conclusions have been echoed more recently by British scholars (Tunstall 1996, Franklin 1997). As many recent accounts of 'spin doctors' also conclude (Blumler and Gurevitch 1995, Gaber 1998, Rosenbaum 1997), journalists are all too often losing the tug-of-war.

On the second point, it is equally clear that source access is far from equal. In fact, one thing that virtually all studies of news production agree upon, be they liberal (Tunstall 1971, Sigal 1973, Gans 1979, Tiffen 1989 and Blumler and Gurevitch 1995) or radical (Glasgow University Media Group 1976, 1980, Hall et al. 1978, Gitlin 1980, Gandy 1980, Chomsky and Herman 1988, Hallin 1994) is that news has been consistently dominated by sources from government and established institutions. Although non-institutional and 'resource-poor' organisations are becoming increasingly adept at influencing news agendas, there remain several factors which, in theory, will continue to bias access against them.

From a radical political economy perspective, corporate and state sources have massive institutional and economic resource advantages that cannot be matched. The first of these is the power to restrict or enable access to information. The state, and many of its institutions, will always have the political, legal and financial means with which to apply pressure on journalists. Second, institutional and some corporate sources, in spite of elite conflicts and breakdowns, have a de facto legitimacy conferred on them – something that has to be gained by other sources. News values dictate that the public must be informed of the policies and activities of individuals and institutions which, in theory, draw their legitimacy from the support of the public. Linked to institutional resource advantages are economic resource advantages. For Fishman (1980), Chomsky and Herman (1988), and Gandy (1992), source access is linked to financial and human resources and these are clearly unequally distributed. More resources mean more contacts in the media, an increased capacity to produce information subsidies, multiple modes of communication, and continuous media operations. These extreme differences in economic resources mean well-resourced organisations can inundate the media and set the agenda while the attempts of resource-poor organisations become quickly marginalised. This point was made abundantly clear by Miller (1994) in his comparison of Sinn Fein and government communications capabilities in Northern Ireland, by Herman and Chomsky's propaganda model in the United States, and by Jones in his comparison of the National Union of Miners and the National Coal Board during the 1984/5 miners' strike. Thus, institutions are, and are likely to remain, the most common sources for journalists. The opportunities for access may have widened but, equally, elite sources are more able to dominate media content than ever before.

New technologies: from optimism to pessimism

Radical responses to the recent waves of technological optimism have come from a number of directions. For most, the gains have not been offset by the losses. If ICTs have enabled media workers to gain more independence, and individuals to gain more channels of access, they have also enabled those in positions of power to extend that power. Ultimately, if technology has the power to determine social transformations, that power is also directed within existing socio-economic systems. Thus, technology changes the conditions of production, and with it all individuals in potentially positive ways; but it also does so in a way that reflects dominant influences in society.

Many accounts have begun by questioning the liberal assumptions of universal benefit for all arising from the introduction of new technologies. Golding and Murdock (1991), MacKay (1995) and Schiller (1996) have each demonstrated that the ownership and use of new technologies is closely correlated to income. As Miles and Gershuny (1987), Lyon (1995) and Thomas (1995) all argue, ICTs do not determine social relations of power but they do exacerbate them. Thus, social fragmentation and inequality are only likely to increase with new technologies unless policy-makers introduce appropriate legislation that counters such trends. Returning to camcorders and the Internet, both Keighran (1993) and Dovey (ed.) (1996) point out the limitations of community video projects when they are controlled by mainstream broadcasters. Competition for access is high and subject to control by channel producers; audiences are low. The ability of individuals to use camcorders or the Internet is clearly restricted to those with the appropriate educational, cultural and economic resources.

At the other end of the scale, Schiller (1989), Gitlin (1994) and Herman and McChesney (1997) all argue that new communications technologies allow multinational corporations (MNCs) to expand their operations both vertically and horizontally. They have renewed their conviction (see also Schiller 1996, Bagdikian 1997, Mowlanda 1997), first voiced in the 1970s, that international media processes have to be understood as part of a wider process of global capitalist expansion. The ability to transfer information, data flows and finance means that large MNCs may switch between suppliers and transfer their operation bases to alternatives if their requirements are not met. Control of cutting-edge technology, coupled with the convergence of telecommunication and media technologies, also enables large corporations to keep ahead of their smaller independent rivals – ensuring higher production values, wider channels of distribution, and the exploitation of greater economies of scale. Ultimately, the ability, brought by ICTs, to produce cultural goods cheaply and independently is only one part of the equation.

At the site of production, new technologies have similarly been introduced to 'advance particular managerial strategies' which follow 'fundamental capitalist objectives' (Child 1987; see also Braverman 1984) rather than give employees greater autonomy. Job cuts, labour segmentation, 'multiskilling, and contracting out are often the results of technological innovation being imposed at the behest of accountants rather than employees. Thus many of the job cuts in the news industries, from printers to broadcast crews to editorial staff, have been justified by the introduction of new technologies and have frequently worked to centralise production controls.

In addition, it is also clear that cheap technologies do not simply mean wider individual use; they also mean wider use by political (see Barnett 1997) and corporate elites. On the corporate side, many studies have pointed out that ICTs have been introduced to monitor employees at the same time as decentralising and dividing up production. Marx (1990), Sewell and Wilkinson (1992) and Robins and Webster (1993) have all documented the introduction of new surveillance technologies in the workplace. At the corporate production site, video cameras, telephone recordings and computer programs are being used with increasing regularity to monitor the individual work rates and general behaviour of employees. Katz and Tassone (1990), Gandy (1995) and Lyon (1994) have similarly researched the themes of government surveillance. The combination of powerful computer processing, extensive databases and information transfer systems, along with new CCTV networks, has meant that individual actions are increasingly recorded, collated and stored. Individuals and pressure groups may be able to use ICTs to present their alternative accounts and challenge elites but, at the same time, elites have increased their ability to monitor and control individuals.

Conclusion

Clearly, the liberal-pluralist themes of individual autonomy and the dispersal of media power have been found to be problematic. Debates may have moved into alternative areas but the same radical reservations still apply. Under a discourse that emphasises autonomy, diversity and choice, there has also been an increase in inequality, concentrations of power and a socio-economic restriction of choice. Unfortunately, it is the arguments of the liberals that have been voiced in corporate and government proclamations (Veljanovski 1990, Gingrich 1995, Gates 1996) and carried through by policy-makers in recent legislation. Radical arguments have found few takers outside the academy.

However, it must also be acknowledged that these same areas have also provided a number of important challenges to the older assumptions of radical political economy. They have underlined the importance of accounting for the complexities of media power struggles, the dynamics of change and the activities of individuals involved in microprocesses of media production. They have also provided grounds for radical and liberal synthesis and a broadening of accounts concerned with the exercise of media power.

THE MEDIA AS PUBLIC SPHERE

Alongside debates about how media organisations actually work have run continued debates about how media organisations *should* work. The most consistent focus for such evaluations has been the concept of 'the public sphere' (*öffentlichkeit*) developed by the philosopher Jürgen Habermas as, quite simply, 'the sphere of private people come together as a public' (1989a: 27). More specifically, it is a space where private individuals come together – independently of state institutions or economic activity – to engage in rational-critical debate and decision-making about issues that concern them. An obvious example would be the mechanisms of elections and referenda. Later we will consider how far we need to extend our definition of public-sphere activities.

Leaving aside for the moment questions of definition, the basic question arises: do existing media organisations (taken together) operate in the way that the public sphere should operate? Or, more broadly, what do the media contribute to the achievement of a public life that is adequate to the ideal of democratic politics? This is a vast question, which can be analysed on many different scales: although Habermas and many others formulated it on the scale of the nation state, it has become increasingly clear that it needs to be formulated also, perhaps even primarily, on an international scale. We return to the question of the 'international public sphere' later.

Habermas and the public sphere: framing the debate

It remains useful, however, to start out from a consideration of Habermas's original arguments and the criticisms that have been made of them. For, in spite of those criticisms, the underlying question of *democratic adequacy* which Habermas addresses with regard to media organisations remains of central importance.[2] This question has an ethical basis. Put at its simplest, Habermas starts from the principle that we need a democratic public sphere, a space of democratic exchange, based on 'procedures whereby those affected by general social norms and collective political decisions can have a say in their formulation, stipulation, and adoption' (Benhabib 1992: 87). Habermas, in effect, insists that we must evaluate the workings of media organisations and one criterion of evaluation is whether they enable people to debate and decide the issues that affect their lives: in other words, democratic participation.

In *The Structural Transformation of the Public Sphere* (1989a) Habermas offers a historical account of the growth of modern mass media. His position is certainly not an unsophisticated rejection of 'mass media' simply on the grounds that they perform a 'mass' function. His argument rather is that, gradually from the mid-nineteenth century onwards and for a number of reasons, large-scale media (the press, radio and television) caused a deformation, or 'refeudalisation', of the early modern bourgeois public sphere (for a useful synopsis, see Calhoun 1992b). Habermas locates that original model of the public sphere in early modern institutions that developed in the metropolitan centres of, particularly, eighteenth-century Britain: for example, the London coffee-houses where citizens met to discuss issues of the day.

Habermas's analysis of how such institutions *initially* came to function as an effective public sphere is complex: for example, the growth of a literary public sphere (connected with the coffee-houses and associated magazines and journals) and the development of a sphere of private life that was both autonomous from central powerful institutions and separate from the public sphere itself. In this way, Habermas argued, all citizens who met certain entry qualifications (a crucial point, as we will see) could debate public issues freely and on an equal basis; detailed differences in their private circumstances were 'bracketed out'.

Habermas's account of why later historical circumstances, including the development of the mass media, led to the *decline* of this early public sphere is equally complex, but two reasons stand out. First, since the growth of mass media led to the expansion of access to the existing public sphere, inequalities in private circumstances could no longer be bracketed out: the public sphere ceased to be a space for debating the 'common' interest and became instead a site of negotiations between different interest groups. Second, the proper functioning of the public sphere (rational, disinterested debate) came increasingly to be dominated by commercially driven consumption as well as (the first point) by the perspective of the private family realm. Here, Habermas offers a subtle account of the social impacts of the late nineteenth- and twentieth-century welfare state where matters of private good became absorbed in the state's domain. The overall result, according to Habermas, was that the separation between the domestic and the public (which underlay the original bourgeois public sphere) collapsed, and the mass media became in Habermas's phrase 'a secondary realm of intimacy', communicating direct to private individuals in their homes and bypassing the original public sphere entirely.

The weaknesses of Habermas's argument have been noted by many writers (see especially the essays in Calhoun (ed.) 1992a) and acknowledged by Habermas himself (1993). It has been criticised, first, on historical grounds: that an original, fully participatory public sphere, as depicted by Habermas, probably never existed and that his picture of unfettered debate in the London coffee-houses and literary society is an unhelpful idealisation (Schudson 1992); alternatively, that the massification of the media did not have the disastrous impact on public debate that Habermas claims it did (see Curran 1991: 38–46 on the nineteenth-century British press). There have been other major criticisms, influenced by philosophical considerations, which have attacked the very basis of Habermas's position. Even if the bourgeois public sphere did exist as Habermas claims, it was far from being an ideal. On the contrary, it was based upon important *exclusions*: the exclusion of women, the poor, the uneducated, ethnic minorities, and so on (see especially Benhabib 1992, Fraser 1992).

The problem with Habermas's original account, then, is quite fundamental: that by insisting that the ideal public sphere should be based on the bracketing out of 'private' difference (see above), he ignores the social forces that determine *which* differences are bracketed out (the question of 'entry qualifications' again). 'Any public sphere', as Calhoun argues, 'is necessarily a socially organised field, with characteristic lines of division' (Calhoun 1992b: 38; cf. Stallybrass and White 1986: 97–9). There are, accordingly, legitimate conflicts about the basis on which public spheres are formed: who they include and who they do not, and on what terms. Questions about the 'terms' of debate within the public sphere link back to the more direct question of who can participate in that debate. A major feminist critique of Habermas, for example (Benhabib 1992, Fraser 1992) has been that, by over-emphasising the importance of 'rational' debate in the public sphere, he fails to confront the distortions around who has been seen as 'qualified' to take part in 'rational' debate: the historic discrimination against women's right to be considered as 'rational' subjects on the same terms as men. A parallel argument could be developed concerning discrimination based on racial stereotypes. To raise these issues is to question Habermas's argument at a fundamental level.

There is an underlying point here: that we need to analyse the pre-existing social inequalities which influence *how* particular public spheres come to be formed. This point is central to Negt and Kluge's early (1993) attack on Habermas for ignoring the existence and importance of '*counter*-public spheres' (for example, based on working-class cultures).[3] It also underlies Seyla Benhabib's (1992) argument for the need to recognise 'multiple public spheres'. The idea of multiple public spheres raises a difficulty of its own: how are the relations between multiple public spheres to be understood without falling back on the idea of an overarching public sphere where differences are negotiated and the possibility of common interests explored (cf. Garnham 1992)? Even so, it is now clear that Habermas's original account severely underestimated the complexity of the primary question which he raised: how should the mediated public sphere be analysed and evaluated?

Before moving on to consider aspects of this complexity in greater detail, it is worth noting some further criticisms that have been made of Habermas's public-sphere argument. These are important since they are relevant also to the work of other media analysts who have built upon his work (for example, Kellner 1990). Two criticisms in particular are worth bringing out: in different ways, they attack the very basis of all public-sphere arguments.

The first, developed by John Thompson (1993, 1995), is that the whole structure of Habermas's public-sphere argument is out of date. Habermas uses as his reference-point a public sphere based around face-to-face discussion and contact. But surely, Thompson argues, in contemporary societies which are massively complex and dispersed, face-to-face discussion is no longer, even in principle, a possible basis for public discourse? Any contemporary public sphere is necessarily based on communication at a distance, that is, mediated communication. Thompson claims that Habermas's whole argument relies on judging contemporary mass media by standards which were appropriate to much smaller societies, but are now, in the media age, irrelevant. A similar argument has been developed by Paddy Scannell (1989, 1996; cf. Scannell and Cardiff 1991). The mass media, Scannell has claimed, should be understood, not as some defective version of earlier face-to-face public communication, but as the basis for an entirely *new type* of public sphere, based on communication at a distance. The modern media, from this perspective, are understood as enabling the distribution of new forms of 'communicative entitlement' to vast, dispersed populations who have no physical contact with each other.

This argument for the irrelevance of Habermas's model is, however, overstated, since (cf. Curran 1991: 45) it tends implicitly to reproduce a liberal model of the media as an unproblematic space of democratic exchange. Yet it was exactly this liberal model of the media that Habermas's argument challenged. As Nicholas Garnham has put it (in a powerful restatement of the core of the Habermasian argument), *some* notion of 'the reciprocal duties inherent in a communicative space that is physically shared' is necessary even for contemporary societies that are massively dispersed and media-saturated (1992: 367).

A second, and related, criticism is that public-sphere arguments underestimate the positive contribution of the mass media to politics and the public sphere. This is in fact an argument towards which Habermas himself has become increasingly sympathetic. Habermas (1997) no longer holds his earlier view of media audiences as uncritical (Habermas 1989b). He has also reconceived the media and the public sphere in a more optimistic way. The public sphere is now deemed to include civil society, with its infrastructure of self-organised groups, rather than being merely an aggregation of individuals constituted as a public. The role of the media is now conceived as that of communicating the ideas, perspectives and solutions of groups in civil society to the political system, and of staging a reciprocal debate within a reintegrated public. Yet despite this shift (discussed more fully in Chapter 6), Habermas remains pessimistic about the ability of the mass media to fulfil its democratic role in the light of what 'the sociology of mass communication' reveals about the distorting effect of 'administrative and social power' (Habermas 1997: 378).

However, some writers in the sociology of mass communicatin are more sanguine. John Corner (1995: 41–52), in discussing television's relation to politics, aims to reorientate debates about the 'ideological' biases of television towards 'a more direct engagement with the present modes of television-within-politics and politics-within-television' (1995: 43). Corner's argument, in effect, is that, even if there are some negative aspects of television's representation of politics (he is discussing British television specifically), *the net effect* of television's involvement in the coverage of politics is positive. Television, he claims (1995: 44–5), has made possible the popular dissemination of 'regular political information'; television journalism has an increasingly important role in exerting pressure on vested interests (such as the state, the police, and so on); and the sheer vastness and speed of media coverage has reduced the possibility of successful information management by those same vested interests. As the preceding argument about the limits of media autonomy and source pluralism indicates, Corner risks overstating the positive. Even so, his basic point – that the balance sheet of the media's effects on democratic politics is a complicated one – is well made.

Arguments for the countervailing positive effects of the media's operations can be developed at a more specific level also. Scannell and Cardiff (1991) in their historical account of the BBC – developed very much *against* ideological critiques of the mass media, such as Habermas's (Scannell 1988, 1989) – have analysed how, compared with the previous style of public political meeting, the mass media required a more intimate form of address. This form of address gradually came to legitimate the public role of 'ordinary' voices and 'ordinary' ways of speaking. Parallel analyses have been made of more recent forms of talk on television (Tolson 1991, Corner 1995: 51) such as BBC2's *Video Diaries* and the growth of talk shows on controversial issues where 'ordinary people' are encouraged to challenge the positions of 'experts' (Livingstone and Lunt 1994). A variation on such arguments can be developed from particular crisis situations where the media have played a large role in undermining or threatening authoritarian rule (see, for example, Lull 1991, on China).[4]

Detailed arguments based on the positive potential of media outputs could be multiplied, but we need instead to review the general shape of the argument on the mediated public sphere so far. There are powerful arguments against Habermas's original historical analysis of the public sphere. Not only does it exclude some crucial issues about access and representation. It also, at least in its original formulation, takes insufficient account of how mediated communication (that transcends face-to-face contexts) is necessary in contemporary societies. We need also, as Scannell and Corner suggest, to be cautious before rushing to conclude that the overall social impacts of the mass media for democratic politics are negative: there is a large number of issues to be considered on both the positive and the negative sides.

As mentioned at the beginning of this discussion, however, there are fundamental *ethical* issues at stake as well – above all, the issue of democratic participation – and it is here that Habermas's public-sphere argument (even if in a modified form) remains central. It provides an indispensable perspective on the operations of media organisations, since it insists that we continually evaluate the media for what they contribute to our lives *as citizens*, as active participants in the public sphere (Golding 1990). 'Citizenship' is certainly a complex concept in contemporary societies,[5] but we cannot do without it. Nor can 'citizenship' be collapsed into the process of 'consumption'. Satisfying people's right to democratic *participation* involves more than providing ever-wider consumer choice between products.[6]

As noted earlier, some analysis of 'the reciprocal duties inherent in a communicative space' (Garnham) remains vital even in media-saturated societies where the influence of market forces on the media sphere is extensive. The key issue is *how* that analysis should be formulated: just as traditional political economy formulations have been debated and revised earlier in this chapter, so here there is need to complicate and refine related public-sphere arguments. This process of complication is what we now explore: first by looking at specific areas, and then by briefly reassessing the public-sphere formulation as a whole.

Complicating the public-sphere debate

Any current reformulation of the public-sphere argument must take account of a number of factors which, we will argue, have complicated, but not made redundant, the terms of that debate: first, the contributions of fictional material to the contemporary public sphere; second, the globalisation (or at least potential globalisation) of the public sphere in the context of global politics and the massive intensification of cross-border media flows; and, third, the extension of the public-sphere debate to encompass computer-mediated communication, particularly the Internet and the World Wide Web. This section discusses each of these in turn.

Media fictions

Habermas's formulation of the 'public-sphere' concept – and many of the debates around it – has focused on *rational* debate, and a particular, rather narrow definition of what constitutes 'rationality'. Rationality in this context has generally been associated with the formal debate of formal matters, such as how society should be organised and how individuals, groups and institutions should behave. But such formulations exclude more obviously emotive matters which cannot be reduced to rational formulation: identification, imagination, loyalty, even love. Yet these are a vital part of public life and political allegiance. Excluded also are articulations of social issues outside conventional forms of debate: for example, the highlighting of social issues and controversies in television soap operas. It is unhelpful in discussing the mediated public sphere to separate artificially areas of 'fact' (news, documentary, discussion) from areas of 'fiction' (drama, sport, and more generally entertainment) (cf. Curran 1991, Dahlgren 1995). We cannot simply reduce the non-factual aspects of media outputs to 'only entertainment' (Dyer 1992).

The case of television soap operas is particularly interesting since this genre of mass entertainment has consistently been denigrated (on this, see Hobson 1982, Allen 1985, Geraghty 1991). Yet, increasingly, in Britain at least, they have come to be acknowledged not only as entertainment nor even just as important media rituals, but also as spaces where difficult social issues can be broached and debate stimulated: for example, the status of ethnic minorities (and their integration, or otherwise, into mainly white communities), the representation of gay and lesbian relationships (Geraghty 1995). The most recent example is the issue of transsexuality, portrayed by the extremely popular British soap *Coronation Street* since late 1997. This 'public-sphere' function of media fictions has begun to be recognised by the state itself: Britain's Labour government, for example, has asked soap production companies to address issues around drug education in their programmes.

Questions remain, certainly, about the quality of the public 'debate' stimulated through soap plots, let alone about the terms of debate: who is fairly represented, and who is not. But it is clear that fictional spaces such as soap operas can no longer be dismissed as irrelevant to our understanding of the public sphere. On the contrary, they can be crucial to ongoing processes of national and cultural self-definition: for example, in focusing debates and tensions about national and local identity (see for example Miller 1995 on Trinidad, Abu-Lughod 1995 on Egypt). In this broader context, the public-sphere argument is subtly transformed: from being solely about the contents of debate in the public domain to encompassing the media's role in stimulating *private* (as well as public) debate through their prominent influence over contemporary definitions of 'the social' (Hall 1977, Curran 1982).[7] This extends earlier analysis of 'agenda-setting' in the media news (McCombs and Shaw 1972) into the fictional realm.

A similar argument can be made in relation to other non-factual (that is, imaginative) media forms: film, music, and so on. There is only space to discuss music here. Music, perhaps, is the type of 'media fiction' most recognised for its potential to express overt resistance to dominant structures and ideologies (Hebdige 1979, 1987, Garofalo (ed.) 1992, Gilroy 1992, 1993, Lipsitz 1994). This applies to many different musical forms, but one area of popular music in particular has attracted attention: rap music and hiphop. Rap music, in the often cited words attributed to Chuck D, formerly of the group Public Enemy, 'is the CNN black people never had' (quoted in Cross 1993: 206). This is no empty metaphor, and other rap musicians have emphasised how the verbal content of rap was developed in conscious distinction from other musical forms. According to The Watts Prophets (quoted in Cross 1993: 108): 'we realised that disco music was drowning out the spoken word ... we wanted to bring the word back out in front'. While it would be misleading to suggest that rap music has always operated as a counter-public sphere,[8] it has clearly been productive in addressing a number of issues affecting the African-American community in the USA and elsewhere, including 'black-on-black' violence, racism, black nationalism, and so on. Some rap has explicitly attempted to speak out against violence and provide alternative role models for black youth (Rose 1994). And, more generally, rap and hiphop – in various hybrid forms – continue to have a public-sphere function in many countries: for example, in the context of the racial politics of 1990s Britain (the music of Asian Dub Foundation and others).

This argument could be extended to other media (for example, film), but it should already be clear that the public-sphere debate cannot be adequately reformulated without considering fictional forms. Contemporary, highly dispersed societies need not just (factual) news but (fictional) 'images ... of what living is now like' (Williams 1975: 9). Entertainment media, as well as news media, are therefore essential to a democratically adequate public sphere and fundamentally similar issues of access and participation apply to them as they do more obviously in the area of formal, 'rational' debate. Entertainment 'needs to give adequate expression to the full range of cultural-political values in society' (Curran 1991: 34). If so, then expanding our notion of the public sphere to encompass media fictions does not fundamentally alter the terms of the debate. There are of course complexities of detail (for example, how do we formulate the proper boundaries between media fact and media fiction so as not to lose sight of the ethical obligations not to misrepresent fiction as fact?), but these complexities do not alter the basic argument that the public sphere necessarily includes both media facts and media fictions.

The international public sphere

The complications raised by the internationalising of the public sphere are perhaps more fundamental since they change the geographic scale, and therefore the organisational issues, on which public-sphere debates need to focus. Debates about possible 'infrastructures' of the international public sphere add another dimension to the question we started from (how should media organisations work in order to contribute to a public sphere?). In addition, we must ask: what form should, or even can, an international public sphere take?

The question of infrastructure cannot be resolved here, but some consideration of such issues is necessary, if the complexity of public-sphere debates at the international level is to be fully appreciated. What is the role, for example, of non-commercial non-government organisations (NGOs)? How is the role of sovereign states changing – both politically and in terms of their capability (if any) to influence global media flows?

Until quite recently debates concerning the public sphere were formulated in terms of the sovereign nation state. But an exclusively national formulation has now been rendered inadequate by many complex forces, summed up in the term 'globalisation'; whether economic globalisation (Wallerstein 1980) or cultural globalisation (Featherstone (ed.) 1990, Robertson 1992, Sklair 1995). In this context, an important debate has emerged about the form of an 'international civil society' or an international (or even global) public sphere.[9] It is important to maintain here the distinction between the international (or transnational) on the one hand, and the truly global on the other. As has been argued, for example by the geographer Doreen Massey (1994), globalising forces do *not* have identical impacts across the world. They have what she calls a 'power-geometry' which is inherently *uneven*. Any transnational public sphere is (for the foreseeable future at least) unlikely to be equally open to all countries and regions of the world, or at least to be so on the same terms. Given this, Habermas's *ideal* of the public sphere – as a space of free and fully open democratic exchange – remains a crucial reference-point.

There are some reasons to be cautious about the idea of an international public sphere. First, even if there are some institutional structures which may approximate to it (for example, the UN or practices of international NGOs, discussed below), the extent to which they are embedded in social or cultural allegiances that are genuinely transnational (as the idea of an international public sphere would imply) is open to doubt.[10] Even so, there is no doubt we need to work from the starting-point that people can operate in public spheres on a number of different levels (not only national, but international and, of course, local as well). As Braman (1997) has put it, we need to think at the international level of a number of 'interpenetrated' public spheres.

Another reason for caution about what the 'international public sphere' actually means is uncertainty about the continued role of the nation state in any international public sphere. In recent decades the nation state has lost sovereignty upwards to supranational institutions (for example, the UN, the EC, the World Bank and the IMF) and for different reasons downwards to regional ones (Lipschitz 1992, Braman 1995). But at the same time supranational institutions cannot straightforwardly rely on an enforceable legal framework through which to implement political decisions at the international level. As a result, John Keane (1991: 135–40) has argued that, if a global public sphere is to develop, it cannot do so simply through international declarations and statements of governments' intent. An international civil society, he has argued, requires to be 'enriched from below' (Keane 1991: 138), for example by organisations that operate within or across state borders, such as international NGOs (charities, lobby groups, and so on).

At the same time, other writers have argued that the nation state has been made irrelevant by the immense growth of international trade in goods and international consumption of media and cultural products (see for example Strange 1994, Ohmae 1990). The result, they claim, is an effectively border-free world, best understood not in terms of the political structures of nation states, but in terms of the actions of *consumers*, dispersed across the globe. National, that is political, loyalties compete with brand loyalties as the basis for constructing social and individual identities.

Such arguments are, however, exaggerated. Certainly, it is important to acknowledge the 'cultural complexity' (Hannerz 1995) that results from the international flow of goods and cultural products. But we need to ask: what type of collective identity does wearing Nike trainers actually deliver? Are such consumption-based identities really alternatives to identities based on political position or organised social action, and, even if they are taken to be, *should* they be? Such individualistic consumption-based identities may actually work to undermine other socially grounded identities. But, even if they do not, there are strong reasons for doubting whether consumption identities (what you wear, and so on) are even comparable to other new forms of international collective identity (focused around environmentalism, feminism, ethnic connections, religion).[11] The suspiciously easy argument that global consumerism makes redundant the construction of an international political infrastructure – an international public sphere – must be treated with great scepticism.

The role of the state in the construction of an international public sphere – on which older public-sphere debates have focused – is clearly complex. There is a danger of underestimating the continuing role of the state at national and international levels (Hirst and Thompson 1996). The state, none the less, is dependent upon non-state actors in many different and complex ways. We need therefore to formulate these issues in terms of two levels: first the society of states and then 'transnational [civil] society', the web of organisations, groups and individuals pursuing their interests partly through various transnational (but non-state) organisations (Rosenau 1990).

It is worth considering how this transnational society works in more detail, since it is essential to any model of the international public sphere. In fact, it can be argued that it is largely through the existence of international NGOs – the focus which they provide for connections between local individuals and groups – that an international public sphere has come into being (cf. Keane 1991). New political spaces or 'imagined communities' (Anderson 1983) have developed across national boundaries. The global distribution of *media* (and the international *media profile* of NGOs such as Greenpeace and Friends of the Earth) has of course been central to this spread of global loyalties. Four fields of political and media activism can perhaps be mentioned as particularly important: the environment, human rights, the rights of indigenous people and global militarism. As knowledge communities (or 'epistemic communities': Haas 1992), the international NGOs are major participants in the definition of issues at national and international levels, using the media as an essential tool for changing popular attitudes and influencing not just states and supranational institutions, but also transnational corporations. In the absence of strong institutional structures linking nation states,[12] it is NGOs (that is, the large numbers of people across the world who work in them or belong to them) which are at present central in any moves towards the construction of an international public sphere.

The actions of NGOs, however, remain only a small part of wider global cultural flows (Hannerz 1996): fashion, television, films, music, news, financial information, and so on. Whereas in the restricted political arenas in which NGOs deal (the UN, GATT, and so on) it is uncontestable that public-sphere issues such as adequacy of representation, freedom of access and debate apply, this is much less clear in relation to wider global cultural flows. There is international trade in cultural products on a vast scale (with many complex regional and local levels of determination: see, for example, Sinclair et al. 1996), but there *is* no single 'space' which plausibly operates at present as a cultural or public sphere on a global level. Occasional global media events (sporting or political: the World Cup, President Clinton's Grand Jury testimony) seem to focus world attention, but they are hardly sufficient to constitute a permanent public sphere. To extend the public-sphere argument (in a broad sense, which covers both 'fictional' and 'factual' media) to a world scale involves an increase in complexity for which studies of national media provide little precedent. Even so, as we will argue below, that does not mean that the political and ethical concerns underlying Habermas's public-sphere argument are irrelevant on this wider scale. It means only that we have to keep separate (1) the manageable question of how to judge today's global media infrastructure from (2) the much larger, and as yet barely manageable, question of how that global media infrastructure needs to operate. The necessity for this separation of questions will become even clearer when we look at a fast-growing sector of the international public sphere: the Internet.

The Internet

The growth of the Internet and of hyped ideology around its development could change the terms of public-sphere debates. Even though explicit references to Habermas are limited (but cf. Rheingold 1994: 281–9), implicit in this ideology is the idea that the Internet will exacerbate the internationalisation of communication and will give access to information to those in the periphery. It has been suggested that not only does the Internet's basis in existing telecommunications networks make it from the outset an international space, but that more fundamentally it is already structured as a communications space which in principle vast numbers of people worldwide can not only access, but send messages through. Its technology determines that, *in principle at least*, it is a many-to-many medium, not a one-to-many medium. This has suggested to many a radical break from the era of centralised broadcasting. In the words of one of its more cautious proselytisers, the Internet is a medium in which 'every citizen can broadcast to every citizen' (Rheingold 1994: 14). If this is true, perhaps Habermas's public-sphere argument can be revived in something like its original form, electronic media for the first time making possible a genuine public space of exchange which operates at a distance.

The actual position is, however, much more complicated. First, the ideology in question about the Internet, and cyberspace generally, contains its fair share of the mythical and needs to be deconstructed. Second – and this is a crucial point – those positive rhetorics do *not* necessarily advocate anything similar to Habermas's public-sphere argument; on the contrary, they embrace the commercial aspects of the Internet (and particularly the World Wide Web) in a way that is directly at odds with the very basis on which public-sphere arguments can be built. Third, the reality of the Internet (as it is likely to be experienced by its users) may be very different from such rhetorical ideals, and no less determined by the economics of production and distribution than is, say, global satellite television.

In spite of these complexities and uncertainties, the main lines of the argument can already be traced. The best starting-point is to examine the positive rhetoric about the Internet and cyberspace generally: the claims for its potential as a new type of communications space. There is a vast literature here, both popular and academic. Common to most of it is the vision of the Internet as representing a new era in communications, a break with the past, a qualitative change (Kahin and Wilson (eds) 1997: vii). Technological changes (not only the Internet's infrastructure, but the digitalisation of all possible media contents and massive increases in speed and precision of information transmission, for example, through fibre-optic cables) will according to many writers bring major social change (for example, Negroponte 1995). Such technological and social change requires, it is argued, a new way of thinking about communication.

Much of this positive rhetoric tends to essentialize the Internet as a single process or thing, rather than encourage its detailed analysis (Loader 1997: 5). The Internet, it is claimed, will enhance freedom; it is the opening, or 'frontier', onto new possibilities for humanity, which transcend existing social relations. By contrast with existing corrupt forms of 'representative' democracy, the Internet's communication space makes possible a new paradigm of 'direct' democracy, an electronically mediated return to the original Greek paradigm. Internet technology, it is argued, opens up an electronic 'agora' or democratic meeting-place free from territorial, or even social, constraints.

One feature of this ideology is that it tends to operate at some distance from the *actual* social, economic and geographical processes in which new media technologies are embedded. We will return to this point in detail later. That neglect is however combined with a particular broad vision of what the Internet's overall impact on existing social organisation will be. First, building on the point that the Internet's infrastructure (since based on international telecommunications) is intrinsically global (Gore 1994: 7), it is argued that the Internet removes limitations of geography (Negroponte 1995: 165; Johnson and Post 1997: 6). It transforms the existing highly unequal geopolitics of information (Negroponte 1996), empowering individuals and groups on the socio-economic and geographical margins (Poster 1995, Turkle 1995, Johnson and Post 1997). Second, it is argued that the interactivity and decentralisation built into the very technology of the Internet makes it *inherently* democratic, transforming a generation of media couch-potatoes into active on-line producers (Rushkoff 1994, Negroponte 1995, Goodwin 1996). This new cultural productivity, it is argued, cannot be controlled because there is no 'centre' from which to exercise the control; and in any case the volume of information on the Internet makes control impossible even in principle (Johnson and Post 1997). Third, this vision of the Internet democracy is often combined with a rejection of existing political structures, and in particular with anti-statism. The state, it is argued, loses its legitimacy in the on-line world (Johnson and Post 1997: 10) and will slowly wither away (Negroponte 1995: 230, Barlow 1996). To this extent, positive visions of the Internet's political implications resonate with wider claims about the irrelevance of the nation state in global capitalism (see pp. 46–9). Fourth, this vision of social change is reinforced by an even broader claim by some writers: that there is a necessary and beneficial link between global capitalism (as the 'best' system of economic organisation) and the Internet (as the 'best', and most open, communications space). The virtual agora, as in ancient Greece, is both marketplace and meeting-place, without any apparent tension between those economic and political functions.

Given all this, it is not surprising that advocates of the Internet are usually hostile to the idea that the Internet should be regulated by state or quasi-state institutions in any way at all. Shaping the growth of the Internet from the outside in order to make it more democratic is therefore rejected out of hand, even though it is precisely the idea of thinking politically about how the Internet (or other media) *should* operate that is at the heart of public-sphere arguments. The Internet is seen as 'naturally' democratic, an already functioning 'public sphere', which needs no political intervention to ensure that its reality lives up to its ideals. There is no room, or need, for policy intervention, even in principle, on this view. Most positive discourse about the Internet is therefore fundamentally at odds with public-sphere arguments, as previously mounted, whose very basis is the public critique of existing media institutions. There is, then, no consensus that public-sphere arguments are even relevant to the Internet. If a public-sphere argument is to be developed, it must be constructed from first principles.

First, there is the question of access, already discussed. Second, the unequal geographic distribution of Internet hosts and Internet use is not necessarily a temporary imbalance which will automatically be corrected, as history marches on. It parallels the uneven (and historically long-standing) concentration of telecommunications infrastructure in the West, particularly the US (Mansell 1993).

A third issue is that, in terms of how the Internet, and particularly the World Wide Web, will appear to most users, it is the commercial dimension which may be most apparent: that is, either electronic commerce and promotion, or the availability of information such as travel, weather, financial data, which is basic to the functioning of commerce (Schiller 1995, Stallabrass 1995). This indeed was how US Vice-President Al Gore described it in his much-lauded 'Global Information Infrastructure' speech in 1994: '[the Internet] will make possible a global information marketplace, where consumers can buy and sell products' (quoted, Schiller 1995: 17). If so, the 'public-sphere' aspects of the Internet (as an open space for democratic *exchange* of information and debate) may prove less apparent to most users than its purely commercial aspects. This is not merely likely, but virtually *inevitable*, according to radical analysts of global communications. Within that perspective, global media have to be seen as a process of global

domination by a limited number of transnational corporations whose main focus lies in the West (Bagdikian 1992, 1997, Schiller 1996, Herman and McChesney 1997, Mowlanda 1997, McChesney 1998). If so, the Internet, far from constituting an unprecedented 'open' space for communicative exchange, constitutes an unprecedented opportunity for commercial expansion, whereby economies of scale can be exploited to strengthen existing patterns of conglomeration in the global communications industry (Herman and McChesney 1997).

The ideology of the Internet's inherently free and democratic nature fits well with the objective of commercial interests in ensuring that the Internet marketplace remains free from political interference of any sort: this, in effect, is a new version of market-oriented liberalism. This discourse has been massively strengthened by the general global success in the 1980s and 1990s of market liberalism, reflected specifically in relation to the Internet by the US's strongly deregulatory Telecommunications Act of 1996. There are, however, some radical critiques of how the Internet operates and is likely to operate, and of the potential conflicts between its commercial and communicative aspects. Within Internet ideology there is *no space* for debate about how the Internet should operate; it is intrinsically good and interference with it is intrinsically bad. It is only within the second, radical discourse that issues of democracy and power can arise at all even as issues, which explains why such issues are in fact rarely debated publicly (McChesney 1997). Yet such lack of debate arguably puts the whole survival of the public sphere at risk (Herman and McChesney 1997: 198).

To insist on the need for a public-sphere debate in relation to the Internet, the 'information superhighway', and cyberspace generally, involves (as it has in relation to earlier media) contesting market liberalism head on. Market forces are *not* intrinsically 'free', since the 'hidden' costs of advertising and so on are simply passed on to consumers through higher prices. Nor are market forces necessarily the means of maximising freedom of choice in cultural consumption: 'choice is always pre-structured by the conditions of competition' (Curran 1996a: 94), including the cost of market entry, effective access to distribution and differential scale economies. The result of commercial pressures is not necessarily greater choice, but greater homogenisation (see, for example, Blumler 1991). And, in any case, it is *not freedom of consumption* that is the issue in relation to the Internet or any other communication space, but *freedom of expression and debate*: the freedom to speak and the opportunity to listen. Those who praise the Internet cannot have it both ways: the Internet either has the potential to be a genuine space of democratic exchange (a true public sphere), in which case inequalities of power, access and representation must be addressed, or it does not. Excited visions of 'virtual democracy' must at some point be brought to democratic account.

Renewing the public-sphere debate

The terms of the public sphere are in need of radical renewal to take account of a new media world: of vastly increased media outputs (covering both factual and fictional material), greatly intensified cross-border media flows, and (in the Internet) a decentred, or apparently decentred, communications space different from any that has gone before. But that does not mean that the framework of original public-sphere debates can safely be shelved; on the contrary, the expansion of the media universe makes it all the more vital as a reference-point.

A number of media theorists have in recent years sought to develop a revised model of the public sphere (Curran 1991, 1996a, Keane 1991, Dahlgren 1995). Each of them has in different ways sought to distance himself from the idea that the public sphere can only operate through public media institutions. There is a need, Curran has argued, for a 'highly differentiated media system' (1996a: 106) with a private-enterprise sector, a professional sector, a civic sector and a social-market sector distributed around a public-service sector 'core' (Curran 1996a). Dahlgren has similarly argued for the need within the media public sphere for both 'the common domain' (in which the public sector has an essential role) and 'the advocacy domain' (compare Curran's 'civic sector') (Dahlgren 1995: 155–6). This 'multi-perspectival'[13] approach to imagining the public sphere is necessary to reflect the complexity of contemporary societies: the need for private citizens both to be able to express their own views and to come together with others to reach a common view (Curran 1996a: 103–12).

This insistence on institutional plurality in no way involves conceding that issues of *public interest* are of less relevance to contemporary media. Not only does some public institutional involvement in media production remain at the core of these analyses, but the operations of the whole media sector, including the private-enterprise sector, are seen still as matters of central public concern. While acknowledging the practical role of market provision, these models reject entirely the neo-liberal notion that 'the market' is a sphere best left free from public intervention. Indeed the democratic state – viewed in one version of radical political economy as a threat to popular freedom of expression – is viewed in another version as a positive agency for securing media diversity and public access (Curran 1996c, 1998, Humphreys 1996).

Whether this last is accepted or not, there is a public interest in how the media functions (whether at local, national or global levels). There are three public functions of the media which it is helpful to separate (Curran 1996a): first, in giving the public 'access to a diversity of values and perspectives' (Curran 1996a: 103), whether in entertainment or in news and current affairs coverage. Second, the media must function as an agency of representation, enabling the whole range of individuals and groups to express alternative viewpoints, and (conversely) enabling others to hear those viewpoints. Third, the media must assist in society's realisation of its common goals, operating in effect as a common forum for the exchange of views and helping the formulation of decisions. 'Society' is in quotes here, since the argument applies equally to societies on a national scale and to the growing transnational civil society. It is clear that each of these functions can be enhanced by having a plurality of media production, not just a state sector. But, equally important, it is not true that the market is the best means of providing that plurality (Curran 1991, Keane 1991). The neo-liberal equation of 'free markets' with 'free communications' (so prominent, for example, among proselytisers of the Internet or the unfettered global spread of satellite television) is mythical. The same point can be made in terms of the concept of access. Whatever the value of producers' free access to media markets or consumers' free access to media products, those types of 'access' are not equivalent – or even comparable to – 'access' in the sense relevant to public-sphere debates: free access of individuals and groups to the views and cultural productions of their own constituency (i.e. the means of cultural and political self-expression) and free access to participate in shared regional, national or international debate.

This point can be pushed further. The media, as forms of communication at a distance, raise issues of participation (cf. Barbrook and Cameron 1995, Curran 1996c) which are simply not reducible to questions of consumer choice. It is not normally an issue, let alone an issue of public importance, whether you had the opportunity to participate in the production of the clothes you wear. It is an issue, and one of fundamental public importance, what opportunities you had to participate in the representation to others of your living conditions, your opinions, your forms of cultural expression. The latter are fundamentally issues not merely of choice, but of control; they are issues of freedom, which must be addressed at the social level.

That is why the public-sphere debate, initiated in very different circumstances by Habermas, remains of relevance today. It does so, in spite of a number of difficulties which we have noted in this chapter: in particular, the difficulty at the international level of establishing what is the appropriate infrastructure for an international public sphere and by what means and on the basis of what authority transnational media flows should be regulated; and the difficulty (in relation to the Internet) of reaching agreement that public-sphere issues are relevant at all. The public-sphere debate remains important also as a framework, or horizon, for the other areas of research into media organisations discussed in the first two parts of this chapter. For it is the suspicion that the media sphere (on its various levels) does not necessarily operate as it should that is a central motivation for researching how in practice media organisations work.

Notes

1 At the time of writing, the Goldsmiths Media Group consisted of Nick Couldry, James Curran, Aeron Davis, David Hesmondhalgh, Wilma de Jong, Herbert Pimlott and Korinna Patelis.
2 See for example Benhabib (1992), Fraser (1992), Garnham (1992), Dahlgren (1995), McGuigan (1996).
3 For a recent consideration of their arguments, see M. Hansen (1993).
4 Such cases are, however, complex, and do not necessarily provide an argument for the benign influence of large-scale national media. See for example Sreberny-Mohammadi and Mohammadi (1994), an important study of the role of 'small media' in the Iranian Revolution, in helping to topple the Shah's regime, which was supported by the state media.
5 For a recent updating of the debate, see Clarke (1996).
6 To emphasise our role as 'citizens' rather than our role as 'consumers' in this context does not mean neglecting the complexity and symbolic importance of consumption (see especially Miller, 1987).
7 It was precisely Habermas's artificial exclusion of this dimension that made it possible for him to criticise modern media for creating 'a secondary realm of intimacy'.
8 Indeed some aspects of some rap music have been attacked for reinforcing anti-social behaviour: sexism, homophobia, and so on.
9 The significance of the media has often been underestimated in this debate (for example, Luard 1990, Peterson 1992, Bull 1997).
10 See for example, Smith (1990), Peterson (1992), Tomlinson (1997).
11 See generally Beck (1992).
12 As envisaged for example by Sakomoto (1991), Held (1993).
13 Dahlgren (1995: 156), cf Curran (1996a: 106).

References and further reading

Abercrombie, A., Hill, S. and Turner, B. (eds) (1984) *The Dominant Ideology Thesis*, London: Allen and Unwin.

Abu-Lughod, L. (1995) 'The Objects of Soap Opera: Egyptian Television and the Cultural Politics of Modernity', in D. Miller (ed.), *Worlds Apart: Modernity Through the Prism of the Local*, London: Routledge.

Adorno, T. and Horkheimer, M. (1978 [1941]) 'The Culture Industry: Enlightenment as Mass Deception', in J. Curran et al. (eds) *Mass Communication and Society*, London: Arnold/Open University Press.

Aglietta, M. (1979) *The Theory of Capitalist Regulation: The US Experience*, London: New Left Books.

Allen, R. (1985) *Speaking of Soap Operas*, Chapel Hill, NC: University of North Carolina Press.

Allen, R. (1994) *To Be Continued: Soap Operas Around the World*, London: Routledge.

Anderson, A. (1991) 'Source Strategies and the Communication of Environmental Affairs', in *Media, Culture and Society*, 13.4.

Anderson, A. (1993) 'Source–Media Relations: The Production of the Environmental Agenda', in A. Hansen (ed.) *The Mass Media and Environmental Issues*, Leicester: Leicester University Press.

Anderson, B. (1983) *Imagined Communities*, London: Verso.

Anderson, K. and Anderson, A. G. (1993) 'Alternating Currents: Alternative Television Inside and Outside the Academy', *Social Text*, 35, Madison, WI: Coda Press, pp. 56–71.

Ang, I. (1985) *Watching Dallas*, London: Methuen.

Annan (1977) *Report of the Committee on the Future of Broadcasting*, London: HMSO [Cmnd 6753].

Bagdikian, B. (1992) *The Media Monopoly*, 4th edn., Boston: Beacon Press.

Bagdikian, B. (1997) *The Media Monopoly*, 5th edn., Boston: Beacon Press.

Barratt-Brown, M. (1968) 'The Controllers of British Industry', in K. Coates (ed.) *Can Workers Run Industry?*, New York: Sphere.

Barbrook, R. and Cameron, A. (1995) *Media Freedom: The Contradictions of Communication in the Age of Modernity*, London: Pluto.

Barlow, J. (1996) 'Selling Wine Without Bottles: The Economy of Mind on the Global Net', in N. Hershman and G. Leeson (eds), *Clicking In: Hot Links to a Digital Culture*, Seattle: Bay Press.

Barlow, W. (1988) 'Community Radio in the US: The Struggle for a Democratic Medium', in *Media, Culture and Society*, 10.1.

Barnett, S. (1997) 'New Media, Old Problems: New Technology and the Political Process', in *European Journal of Communications*, 12.2, London: Sage.

Barnett, S. and Curry, A. (1994) *The Battle for the BBC*, London: Aurum Press.

Beck, U. (1992) *Risk Society*, London: Sage.

Bell, D. (1976) *The Cultural Contradictions of Capitalism*. New York: Basic Books.

Benhabib, S. (1992) 'Models of Public Space: Hannah Arendt, the Liberal Tradition and Jürgen Habermas', in C. Calhoun (ed.), *Habermas and the Public Sphere*, Cambridge, MA: The MIT Press.

Benjamin, W. (1969) 'The Work of Art in the Age of Mechanical Reproduction', in W. Benjamin, *Illuminations*, tr. Harry Zohn, London: Fontana, 1992.

Berle, A. and Means, G. (1968 [1932]) *The Modern Corporation and Private Property*, New York: Harcourt Brace.

Blumler, J. (1990) 'Elections, the Media and the Modern Publicity Process', in M. Ferguson (ed.), *Public Communication – The New Imperatives*, London: Sage.

Blumler, J. (1991) 'The New Television Market Place: Imperatives, Implications, Issues', in J. Curran and M. Gurevitch (eds), *Mass Media and Society*, London: Arnold.

Blumler, J. and Gurevitch, M. (1995) *The Crisis of Public Communications*, London: Routledge.

Bourdieu, P. (1984) *Distinction*, London: Routledge.

Braman, S. (1995) 'Horizons of the State: Information Policy and Power', *Journal of Communications*, 45.4.

Braman, S. (1997) 'Interpenetrated Globalization: Scaling, Power and the Public Sphere', in S. Braman and A. Sreberny-Mohammadi (eds), *Globalization, Communication and Transnational Civil Society*, Cresskill, NJ: Hampton Press.

Braverman, H. (1984) *Labor and Monopoly Capital: The Degradation of Work in the Twentieth Century*, New York: Monthly Review Press.

Brecht, B. (1930) 'Theory of Radio', in J. Mattelart and S. Siegelaub (eds), *Communication and Class Struggle, Vol. 2: Liberation, Socialism*, New York: International General, 1983.

Bull, H. (1977) *The Anarchical Society: The Study of Order in World Politics*, New York: Columbia University Press.

Burnham, J. (1962 [1942]) *The Managerial Revolution*, Harmondsworth: Penguin.

Calhoun, C. (ed.) (1992a) *Habermas and the Public Sphere*, Cambridge, MA: The MIT Press.

Calhoun, C. (1992b) 'Introduction: Habermas and the Public Sphere', in C. Calhoun (ed.), *Habermas and the Public Sphere*, Cambridge, MA: The MIT Press.

Carey, J.W. (1989) *Communication As Culture: Essays on Media and Society*, Boston: Unwin Hyman.

Castells, M. (1996) *The Rise of the Network Society*, Cambridge, MA: Blackwell.

Chambers, I. (1985) *Urban Rhythms: Pop Music and Popular Culture*, Basingstoke: Macmillan.

Chapple, S. and Garofalo, R. (1977) *Rock 'n' Roll is Here to Pay*, Chicago: Nelson Hall.

Child, J. (1987) 'Managerial Strategies: New Technology and the Labour Process', in R. Finnegan, G. Salaman and K. Thompson (eds), *Information Technology: Social Issues*, London: Hodder and Stoughton/Open University Press.

Chomsky, N. and Herman, E. (1988) *Manufacturing Consent*, New York: Pantheon.

Christopherson, S. and Storper, M. (1986) 'The City as Studio, the World as Back Lot: The Impact of Vertical Disintegration on the Location of the Motion Picture Industry', *Environment and Planning D: Society and Space*, 4.

Clarke, P. (1996) *Deep Citizenship*, London: Pluto.

Corner, J. (1991) 'Meaning, Genre and Context: The Problematics of "Public Knowledge" in the New Audience Studies', in J. Curran and M. Gurevitch, *Mass Media and Society*, London: Arnold.

Corner, J. (1995) *Television Form and Public Address*, London: Arnold.

Cracknell, J. (1993) 'Issue Arenas, Pressure Groups and Environmental Issues', in A. Hansen (ed.), *The Mass Media and Environmental Issues*, Leicester: Leicester University Press.

Crewe, I. and Gosschalk, B. (eds) (1995) *Political Communications: The General Election Campaign of 1992*, Cambridge: Cambridge University Press.

Cross, B. (1993) *It's Not About a Salary: Rap, Race, and Resistance in Los Angeles*, London: Verso.

Curran, J. (1982) 'Communications, Power and Social Order', in M. Gurevitch et al. (eds), *Culture, Society and the Media*, London: Methuen.

Curran, J. (1986) 'The Impact of Advertising on the British Mass Media', in R. Collins, J. Curran, N. Garnham, P. Scannell, P. Schlesinger and C. Sparks (eds), *Media, Culture and Society: A Critical Reader*, London: Sage.

Curran, J. (1990) 'Cultural Perspectives of News Organisations: A Reappraisal and a Case Study', in M. Ferguson (ed.), *Public Communication: The New Imperatives*, London: Sage.

Curran, J. (1991) 'Rethinking the Media as a Public Sphere', in P. Dahlgren and C. Sparks (eds), *Communication and Citizenship: Journalism and the Public Sphere*, London: Routledge, 1991.

Curran, J. (1996a) 'Mass Media and Democracy Revisited', in J. Curran and M. Gurevitch (eds), *Mass Media and Society*, 2nd edn, London: Arnold.

Curran, J. (1996b) 'Welfare vs Free Market: Rival Media Models in the Postcommunist Era', in P. Glenn and O. Soltys (eds), *Media 95*, Prague: Charles University Press.

Curran, J. (1996c) 'Media Democracy: The Third Route', in M. Andersen (ed.), *Media and Democracy*, Oslo: University of Oslo Press.

Curran, J. (1996d) 'Rethinking Mass Communications', in J. Curran, D. Morley and V. Walkerdine (eds), *Cultural Studies and Communications*, London: Routledge.

Curran, J. (1998a) 'Crisis of Public Communication: A Reappraisal', in T. Liebes and J. Curran (eds), *Media, Ritual and Identity*, London: Routledge.

Curran, J. (1998b) 'Newspapers: Beyond Political Economy', in A. Briggs and P. Cobley (eds), *The Media: An Introduction*, Harlow: Longman.

Curran, J. and Seaton, J. (1997) *Power Without Responsibility*, 5th edn, London: Routledge.

Curran, J., Ecclestone, J., Oakley, G. and Richardson, A. (eds) (1986) *Bending Reality: The State of the Media*, London: Pluto.

Dahlgren, P. (1995) *Television and the Public Sphere*, London: Sage.

Deacon, D. (1996) 'The Voluntary Sector in a Changing Communications Environment: A Case Study of Non-Official News Sources', in *European Journal of Communications*, 11.2.

Deacon, D. and Golding, P. (1994) *Taxation and Representation*, London: John Libbey.

Dertouzos, M. (1997) *What Will Be: the Power of Information in the Digital Age*, San Francisco: HarperCollins.

Dovey, J. (1993) 'Old Dogs and New Tricks: Access Television in the UK', in T. Dowmunt (ed.), *Channels of Resistance*, London: BFI and Channel 4.

Dovey, J. (ed.) (1996) *Fractal Dreams: New Media in Social Context*, London: Lawrence and Wishart.

Dowmunt, T. (ed.) (1993) *Channels of Resistance: Global Television and Local Empowerment*, London: BFI and Channel 4.

Downing, J. (1984) *Radical Media*, Boston: South End Press.

Driver, S. and Gillespie, A. (1993) 'Structural Change in the Cultural Industries: British Magazine Publishing in the 1980s', in *Media, Culture and Society*, 15.

Duncombe, S. (1997) *Notes from Underground: Zines and the Politics of Alternative Culture*, New York and London: Verso.

Dyer, R. (1992) *Only Entertainment*, London: Routledge.

Enzensberger, H.M. (1976) 'Constituents of a Theory of the Media', in H.M. Enzensberger, *Raids and Reconstructions: Essays on Politics, Crime and Culture*, London: Pluto Press.

Ericson, R.V., Baranek, P.M. and Chan, J.B.L. (1989) *Negotiating Control: A Study of News Sources*, Milton Keynes: Open University Press.

Evans, H. (1983) *Good Times, Bad Times*, London: Weidenfeld and Nicolson.

Ewen, S. (1996) *PR! A Social History of Spin*, New York: Basic Books.

Fallows, J. (1996) *Breaking the News: How the Media Undermine American Democracy*, New York: Vintage Books.

Featherstone, M. (ed.) (1990) *Global Culture*, London: Sage.

Fishman, L. (1980) *Manufacturing News*, Austin: University of Texas Press.

Fiske, J. (1987) *Television Culture*, London: Routledge.

Franklin, B. (1994) *Packaging Politics: Political Communications in Britain's Media Democracy*, London: Arnold.

Franklin, B. (1997) *Newszak and News Media*, London: Arnold.

Fraser, N. (1992) 'Restructuring the Public Sphere: A consideration of Actually Existing Democracy', in C. Calhoun (ed.), *Habermas and the Public Sphere*, Cambridge, MA: MIT Press.

Frith, S. (1983) *Sound Effects: Youth, Leisure and the Politics of Rock*, London: Constable.

Gaber, I. (1995) 'Driving the News or Spinning Out of Control: Politicians, the Media and the Battle for the News Agenda', inaugural lecture, Goldsmiths College, London.

Gaber, I. (1998) 'The Media and Politics', in A. Briggs and P. Cobley (eds), *The Media: An Introduction*, Harlow: Longman.

Gandy, O. (1980) 'Information in Health: Subsidised News', in *Media, Culture and Society*, 2.2.

Gandy, O. (1992) 'Public Relations and Public Policy: The Structuration of Dominance in the Information Age', in E. Toth and R. Neath (eds), *Rhetorical and Critical Approaches to Public Relations*, Hillsdale, NJ: Lawrence Erlbaum.

Gandy, O. (1995) 'Tracking the Audience: Personal Information and Privacy', in J. Downing, A. Mohammadi and A. Sreberny-Mohammadi (eds), *Questioning the Media: A Critical Introduction*, 2nd edn, London: Sage.

Gans, H.J. (1980) *Deciding What's News: A Study of CBS Evening News, NBC Nightly News, 'Newsweek' and 'Time'*, London: Constable.

Garnham, N. (1990) *Capitalism and Communication: Global Culture and the Economics of Information*, ed. F. Inglis, London: Sage.

Garnham, N. (1992) 'The Media and the Public Sphere', in C. Calhoun (ed.), *Habermas and the Public Sphere*, Cambridge, MA: The MIT Press.

Garofalo, R. (ed.) (1992) *Rockin' the Boat: Mass Music and Mass Movements*, Boston: South End Press.

Gates, B. (1996) *The Road Ahead*, London: Penguin.

Geraghty, C. (1991) *Women and Soap Opera: A Study of Prime-Time Soaps*, Oxford: Polity.

Geraghty, C. (1995) 'Social Issues and Realist Soaps: A Study of British Soaps in the 1980s and 1990s', in R. Allen (ed.), *To Be Continued: Soap Opera from Around the World*, London: Routledge.

Gillett, C. (1971) *The Sound of the City*, London: Souvenir.

Gilroy, P. (1992) *Black Atlantic: Modernity and Double Consciousness*, London: Verso.

Gilroy, P. (1993) *Small Acts: Thoughts on the Politics of Black Culture*, London: Serpent's Tail.

Gingrich, N. (1995) *To Renew America*, New York: HarperCollins.

Gitlin, T. (1980) *The Whole World is Watching*, Berkeley: University of California Press.

Gitlin, T. (1994) *Inside Prime Time*, London: Routledge.

Glasgow University Media Group (1976) *Bad News*, London: Routledge and Kegan Paul.

Glasgow University Media Group (1980) *More Bad News*, London: Routledge and Kegan Paul.

Glasgow University Media Group (1982) *Really Bad News*, London: Writers' and Readers' Publishing Co-operative Society.

Glasgow University Media Group (1985) *War and Peace News*, Milton Keynes: Open University Press.

Goodwin, M. (1996) 'An Ill-defined Act', *Internet World* (June).

Goldberg, K. (1990) *The Barefoot Channel: Community Television as a Tool for Social Change*, Vancouver: New Star Books.

Golding, P. (1990) 'Political Communications and Citizenship: The Media and Democracy in an Inegalitarian Social Order', in M. Ferguson (ed.), *Public Communication*, London: Sage.

Golding, P. and Middleton, S. (1982) *Images of Welfare: Press and Public Attitudes to Welfare*, Oxford: M. Robertson.

Golding, P. and Murdock, G. (1991) 'Culture, Communication and Political Economy', in J. Curran and M. Gurevitch (eds), *Mass Media and Society*, London: Arnold.

Gomery, D. (1986) *The Hollywood Studio System*, Basingstoke: BFI/Macmillan.

Gore, A. (1994) Remarks delivered to the Superhighway Summit, Royce Hall, UCLA, Los Angeles, 11 Jan.

Haas, B. (1992) 'Knowledge, Power and International Policy Co-ordination', *International Organisation*, 46.1.

Habermas, J. (1989a [1962]) *The Structural Transformation of the Public Sphere*, Cambridge: Polity.

Habermas, J. (1989b) *The Theory of Communicative Action, Vol. 2: The Critique of Functionalist Reason*, Cambridge: Polity.

Habermas, J. (1993) *Justification and Application: Remarks on Discourse Ethics*, Cambridge: Polity.

Habermas, J. (1997) *Between Facts and Norms*, Cambridge: Polity.

Hall, S. (1977) 'Culture, the Media and "the Ideological Effect"', in J. Curran et al. (eds), *Mass Communications and Society*, London: Arnold.

Hall, S. and Jacques, M. (1989) *New Times*, London: Lawrence and Wishart/Marxism Today.

Hall, S., Critcher, C., Jefferson, T., Clarke, J. and Roberts, B. (1978) *Policing the Crisis: Mugging, the State, and Law and Order*, London: Macmillan.

Halleck, D. (1984) 'Paper Tiger Television: Smashing the Myths of the Information Industry Every Week on Public Access Cable', *Media, Culture and Society*, 6.3.

Hallin, D. (1994) *We Keep America on Top of the World: Television Journalism and the Public Sphere*, London: Routledge.

Hall-Jamieson, K. (1996) *Packaging the Presidency: A History and Criticism of Presidential Campaign Advertising*, New York: Oxford University Press.

Hannerz, U. (1995) *Cultural Complexity: Studies in the Social Organisation of Meaning*, New York: Columbia University Press.

Hannerz, U. (1996) 'The Global Ecumene', in A. Sreberny-Mohammadi et al. (eds), *Global Media in Question*, London: Arnold.

Hansen, A. (1993) 'Greenpeace and Press Coverage of Environmental Issues', in A. Hansen (ed.), *The Mass Media and Environmental Issues*, Leicester: Leicester University Press.

Hansen, M. (1993) 'Foreword', in O. Negt and A. Kluge, *Public Sphere and Experience: Towards an Analysis of the Bourgeois and Proletarian Public Sphere*, tr. P. Labanyi et al., Minneapolis: University of Minnesota Press.

Hardt, H. (1990) 'Newsworkers, Technology, and Journalism History', *Critical Studies in Mass Communication*, 7.

Harrison, M. (1985) *TV News, Whose Bias? A Casebook Analysis of Strikes, Television and Media Structures*, Reading: Hermitage, Policy Journals.

Hebdige, D. (1979) *Subculture: The Meaning of Style*, London: Sage.

Hebdige, D. (1987) *Cut 'n' Mix Culture*, London: Routledge.

Held, D. (1993) 'Democracy from City State to Cosmopolitan Order', in D. Held (ed.), 'Prospects for Democracy', *Political Studies*, 40.

Herman, E. and McChesney, R. (1997) *The Global Media: The New Missionaries of Corporate Capitalism*, London: Cassell.

Hesmondhalgh, D. (1996) 'Flexibility, Post-Fordism and the Music Industries', in *Media, Culture and Society*, 15.3.

Hesmondhalgh, D. (1998) 'The British Dance Music Industry: A Case Study of Independent Cultural Production', *British Journal of Sociology*, 49.2.

Hill, S. (1981) *Competition and Control at Work: The New Industrial Sociology*, London: Heinemann Educational.

Hirst, P. and Thompson, G. (1996) *Globalisation in Question*, Cambridge: Polity.

Hobson, D. (1982) *Crossroads: The Drama of a Soap Opera*, London: Methuen.

Hollingsworth, M. (1986) *The Press and Political Dissent*, London: Pluto Press.

Humphreys, P. (1996) *Mass Media and Media Policy in Western Europe*, Manchester: Manchester University Press.

Hutton, W. (1996) *The State We're In*, 2nd edn, London: Vintage Books.

Innis, H.A. (1972) *Americanization*, Toronto and New York: McGraw-Hill Ryerson.

Johnson, D. and Post, D. (1997) 'The Rise of Law on the Global Network', in B. Kahin and Neeson (eds), *Borders in Cyberspace*, Cambridge, MA: The MIT Press.

Jones, N. (1986) *Strikes and the Media*, Oxford: Basil Blackwell.

Jones, N. (1995) *Soundbites and Spin Doctors: How Politicians Manipulate the Media and Vice Versa*, London: Cassell.

Kahin, B. (1997) 'Internet and the National Information Infrastructure', in B. Kahin and E. Wilson (eds), *National Information Infrastructure Initiatives: Vision and Policy Design*, Cambridge, MA: The MIT Press.

Kahin, B. and Wilson, E. (eds) (1997) *National Information Infrastructure Initiatives: Vision and Policy Design*, Cambridge, MA: The MIT Press.

Katz, J. and Tassone, R. (1990) 'Public Opinion Trends: Privacy and New Technology', *Public Opinion Quarterly*, 54.1 (Spring).

Kavanagh, D. (1995) *Election Campaigning: The New Marketing of Politics*, Oxford: Blackwell.

Keane, J. (1991) *Media and Democracy*, Cambridge: Polity.

Keighron, P. (1993) '*Video Diaries*: What's Up Doc?', *Sight and Sound*, 3.10, 24–5.

Kellner, D. (1990) *Television and the Crisis of Democracy*, Boulder, CO: Westview Press.

Kerr, A. and Sachdev, S. (1992) 'Third Among Equals: An Analysis of the 1989 Ambulance Dispute', *British Journal of Industrial Relations*, 30.

Knudsen, J.W. (1998) 'Rebellion in Chiapas: Insurection by Internet and Public Relations', *Media, Culture and Society*, 20.3.

Kurtz, H. (1998) *Spin Cycle: Inside the Clinton Propaganda Machine*, Washington, DC: The Free Press.

Leeson, L. (ed.) (1996) *Clicking In: Hot Links to a Digital Culture*, Seattle: Bay Press.

Lipsitz, G. (1994) *Dangerous Crossroads: Popular Music, Postmodernism and the Poetics of Place*, London: Verso.

Livingstone, S. and Lunt, P. (1994) *Talk on Television: Audience Participation and Public Debate*, London: Routledge.

Loader, B. (1997) 'Introduction', in B. Loader (ed.), *The Governance of Cyberspace: Politics, Technology and Global Restructuring*, London: Routledge.

Luard, E. (1990) *Globalisation of Politics*, New York: New York University Press.

Lucas, M. and Wallner, M. (1993) 'Resistance by Satellite: The Gulf Crisis Project and the Deep Dish Satellite TV Network', in T. Dowmunt (ed.), *Channels of Resistance*, London: BFI and Channel 4.

Lull, J. (1991) *China Turned On: Television, Reform and Resistance*, London: Routledge.

Lyon, D. (1994) *The Electronic Eye: The Rise of Surveillance Society*, Cambridge: Polity.

Lyon, D. (1995) 'The Roots of the Information Society Idea', in N. Heap, R. Thomas, G. Einon, R. Mason and H. MacKay (eds), *Information Technology and Society*, London: Sage/Open University Press.

MacKay, H. (1995) 'Patterns of IT Devices in the Home', in N. Heap, R. Thomas, G. Einon, R. Mason and H. MacKay (eds), *Information Technology and Society*, London: Sage/Open University Press.

Maltby, R. (1995) *Hollywood Cinema*, Oxford: Blackwell.

Maltese, R. (1994) *Spin Control: The White House Office of Communications and the Management of Presidential News*, Chapel Hill, NC: University of North Carolina Press.

Mancini, P. and Swanson, D. (1996) *Politics, Media and Modern Democracy*, Westport, CT: Praeger.

Mansell, R. (1993) *The New Telecommunications: A Political Economy of Network Evolution*, London: Sage.

Marx, G.T. (1990) 'The Case of the Omniscient Organisation', *Harvard Educational Review* (Mar./Apr.).

Massey, D. (1994) *Space, Place and Gender*, Cambridge: Polity.

McChesney, R. (1997) *Corporate Media and the Threat to Democracy*, Seven Stories Press.

McChesney, R., Bellamy Foster, J. and Meiskins Wood, E. (eds) (1998) *Capitalism in the Information Age*, London: Sage.

McCombs, M. and Shaw, D. (1972) 'The Agenda-setting Function of the Mass Media', *Public Opinion Quarterly*, 36.

McGuigan, J. (1996) *Culture and the Public Sphere*, London: Routledge.

McLuhan, M. (1964) *Understanding Media: The Extensions of Man*, New York: McGraw-Hill.

McNair, B. (1994) *News and Journalism in the UK*, London: Routledge.

McNair, B. (1995) *An Introduction to Political Communication*, London: Routledge.

McRobbie, A. (1994) *Postmodernism and Popular Culture*, London: Routledge.

Miège, B. (1989) *The Capitalization of Cultural Production*, New York: International General.

Miles, I. and Gershuny, J. (1987) 'The Social Economics of Information Society', in R. Finnegan, G. Salaman and K. Thompson (eds), *Information Technology: Social Issues*, London: Hodder and Stoughton/Open University Press.

Miller, D. (1987) *Material Culture and Mass Consumption*, Oxford: Blackwell.

Miller, D. (1993) 'Official Sources and "Primary Definition": The Case of Northern Ireland', *Media, Culture and Society*, 15.3.

Miller, D. (1994) *Don't Mention the War: Northern Ireland, Propaganda and the Media*, London: Pluto Press.

Miller, D. (1995) 'The Consumption of Soap Opera: *The Young and the Restless* and Mass Consumption in Trinidad', in R. Allen (ed.), *To Be Continued: Soap Opera from Around the World*, London: Routledge.

Miller, D. (1998) 'Promotional Strategies and Media Power', in A. Briggs and P. Cobley (eds), *The Media: An Introduction*, Harlow: Longman.

Morley, D. (1980) *The Nationwide Audience*, London: British Film Institute.

Morley, D. (1992) *Television, Audiences and Cultural Studies*, London: Routledge.

Mowlanda, (1997) *Global Information and World Communication: New Frontiers in International Relations*, 2nd edn, London: Sage.

Mumford, L. (1966) *The Myth of the Machine: Technics and Human Development*, London: Secker and Warburg.

Murdock, G. (1982) 'Large Corporations and the Control of the Communications Industries', in M. Gurevitch et al. (eds), *Culture, Society and the Media*, London: Methuen.

Murdock, G. (1990) 'Redrawing the Map of the Communications Industries: Concentration and Ownership in the Era of Privatization', in M. Ferguson (ed.), *Public Communication*, London: Sage.

Murray, R. (1989) 'Fordism and Post-Fordism' and 'Benetton Britain', in S. Hall and M. Jacques (1989) *New Times*, London: Lawrence and Wishart.

Nacos, B. (1990) *The Press, Presidents, and Crises*, New York: Columbia University Press.

Negrine, R. (1994) *Politics and the Mass Media in Britain*, 2nd edn, London: Routledge.

Negrine, R. (1996) *The Communication of Politics*, London: Sage.

Negroponte, N. (1995) *Being Digital*, London: Hodder and Stoughton.

Negroponte, N. (1996) 'Being Local', *Wired*, 2.1.

Negt, O. and Kluge, A. (1993 [1972]) *Public Sphere and Experience: Towards an Analysis of the Bourgeois and Proletarian Public Sphere*, tr. P. Labanyi et al., Minneapolis: University of Minnesota Press.

Negus, K. (1992) *Producing Pop: Culture and Conflict in the Popular Music Industry*, London: Arnold.

Nichols, T. (1969) *Ownership, Control and Ideology*, London: Allen and Unwin.

Ohmae, K. (1990) *The Borderless World: Power and Strategy in the Interlinked Economy*, New York: HarperCollins.

Pavlik, J. (1996) *New Media and the Information Superhighway*, Boston: Allen and Bacon.

Peterson, M. (1992) 'Transnational Activity: International Society and World Politics', *Journal of International Studies*, 21.3.

Piore, M. and Sabel, C. (1984) *The Second Industrial Divide*, New York: Basic Books.

Poster, M. (1995) 'Cyberdemocracy', Difference Engine, 2, at http://www.gold.ac.uk

Poster, M. (1996) 'Postmodern Virtualities', in T. Robertson et al. (eds), *FutureNatural: nature/science/culture*, London: Routledge.

Radway, J. (1987) *Reading the Romance: Feminism and the Representation of Women in Popular Culture*, 2nd edn, Chapel Hill, NC: University of North Carolina Press.

Rheingold, H. (1994) *The Virtual Community: Finding Connections in a Computerised World*, London: Secker and Warburg.

Robertson, R. (1992) *Globalisation: Social Theory and Global Culture*, London: Sage.

Robins, K. (1995) 'Cyberspace and the World We Live In', in M. Featherstone and R. Burrows (eds), *Cyberspace/Cyberbodies/Cyberpunk: Cultures of Technological Embodiment*, London: Sage.

Robins, K. and Cornford, J. (1992) 'What is Flexible About Independent Producers', *Screen* 33.2.

Robins, K. and Webster, F. (1993) 'I'll Be Watching You', *Sociology*, 27.2.

Rose, T. (1994) *Black Noise: Rap Music and Black Culture in Contemporary America*, Middletown, CT: Wesleyan University Press.

Rosenau, J. (1990) *Turbulence in the World's Politics: A Theory of Change and Continuity*, Princeton: Princeton University Press.

Rosenbaum, M. (1997) *From Soapbox to Soundbite: Party Political Campaigning in Britain Since 1945*, Basingstoke: Macmillan.

Rushkoff, D. (1994) *Cyberia: Life in the Trenches of Hyperspace*, London: HarperCollins.

Sakomoto, Y. (1991) 'The Global Context of Democratisation', *Alternatives*, 16.

Scammell, M. (1995) *Designer Politics: How Elections are Won*, Basingstoke: Macmillan.

Scannell, P. (1988) 'Radio Times: The Temporal Arrangements of Broadcasting in the Modern World', in P. Drummond and R. Paterson (eds), *Television and Its Audiences: International Research Perspectives*, London: British Film Institute.

Scannell, P. (1989) 'Public Service Broadcasting and Modern Public Life', *Media, Culture and Society*, 11.2.

Scannell, P. (1996) *Radio, Television and Modern Life*, Oxford: Blackwell.

Scannell, P. and Cardiff, D. (1991) *History of British Broadcasting, Vol. 1: 1922–1939, Serving the Nation*, Oxford: Blackwell.

Schiller, D. (1981) *Objectivity and the News*, Philadelphia: University of Pennsylvania Press.

Schiller, H. (1989) *Culture Inc: The Corporate Takeover of Public Expression*, New York: Oxford University Press.

Schiller, H. (1992) *Mass Communication and the American Empire*, 2nd edn, Boulder, CO: Westview Press.

Schiller, H. (1995) 'The Global Information Highway', in J. Brook and I. Boal (eds), *Resisting the Virtual Life*, San Francisco: City Lights Books.

Schiller, H. (1996) *Information Inequality: The Deepening Social Crisis in America*, London: Routledge.

Schlesinger, P. (1990) 'Rethinking the Sociology of Journalism: Source Strategies and the Limits of Media-Centrism', in M. Ferguson (ed.), *Public Communication: The New Imperatives*, London: Sage.

Schlesinger, P. and Tumber, H. (1994) *Reporting Crime: The Media Politics of Criminal Justice*, Oxford: Clarendon Press.

Schlesinger, P., Murdock, G. and Elliot, P. (1983) *Televising Terrorism: Political Violence in Popular Culture*, London: Comedia.

Schudson, M. (1991) 'The Sociology of News Production Revisited', in J. Curran and G. Gurevitch (eds), *Mass Media and Society*, London: Arnold.

Schudson, M. (1992) 'Was There Ever a Public Sphere? If So, When? Reflections on the American Case', in C. Calhoun (ed.), *Habermas and the Public Sphere*, Cambridge, MA: The MIT Press.

Schulman, M. (1992) 'Communications in the Community: Critical Scholarship in an Emerging Field', in J. Wasko and V. Mosco (eds), *Democratic Communications in the Information Age*, Toronto: Garamond Press.

Sewell, G. and Wilkinson, B. (1992) 'Someone to Watch Over Me: Surveillance, Discipline and the Just-in-Time Labour Process', *Sociology*, 25.2.

Shoemaker, P. (1989) 'Public Relations Versus Journalism: Comments on Turrow', *American Behavioural Scientist*, 33.

Sigal, L.V. (1973) *Reporters and Officials: The Organisation and Politics of Newsmaking*, Lexington, MA: D. C. Heath.

Sinclair, J., Jacka, E. and Cunningham, S. (1996) *Global Television in Transition*, Oxford: Blackwell.

Sklair, L. (1995) *Sociology of the Global System*, Hemel Hempstead: Harvester Wheatsheaf.

Smith, A. (1990) 'Towards a Global Culture?', in M. Featherstone (ed.), *Global Culture*, London: Sage.

Smyth, D. (1981) *Dependency Road: Communications, Capitalism, Consciousness, and Canada*, Norwood, NJ: Ablex Publishing.

Sola Pool, I. de (1983) *Technologies of Freedom*, Cambridge, MA: Harvard University Press.

Sola Pool, I. de (1990) *Technologies Without Boundaries: On Telecommunications in a Global Age*, Cambridge, MA: Harvard University Press.

Sreberny-Mohammadi, A. and Mohammadi, A. (1994) *Small Media, Big Revolution: Communication, Culture and the Iranian Revolution*, Minneapolis: University of Minnesota Press.

Stallabrass, J. (1995) 'Empowering Technology: The Exploration of Cyberspace', *New Left Review*, 211: 3–32.

Stallybrass, P. and White, A. (1986) *The Politics and Poetics of Transgression*, London: Methuen.

Stauber, J. and Rampton, S. (1995) *Toxic Sludge is Good For You: Lies, Damn Lies and the Public Relations Industry*, Monroe, ME: Common Courage Press.

Strange, S. (1994) *The Retreat of the State: The Diffusion of Power in the World Economy*, Cambridge: Cambridge University Press.

Thomas, R. (1995) 'Access and Inequality', in N. Heap, R. Thomas, G. Einon, R. Mason and H. MacKay (eds), *Information Technology and Society*, London: Sage/Open University Press.

Thompson, J. (1993) 'The Theory of the Public Sphere', *Theory, Culture and Society*, 10.3.

Thompson, J. (1995) *The Media and Modernity: A Social Theory of the Media*, Cambridge: Polity.

Tiffen, R. (1989) *News and Power*, Sydney: Allen and Unwin.

Toffler, A. (1970) *Future Shock*, London: Bodley Head.

Toffler, A. (1980) *The Third Wave*, London: Pan Books.

Tolson, A. (1991) 'Televised Chat and the Synthetic Personality', in P. Scannell (ed.), *Broadcast Talk*, London: Sage.

Tomlinson, J. (1997) 'Global Experience as a Consequence of Modernity', in S. Braman and A. Sreberny-Mohammadi (eds), *Globalization, Communication and Transnational Civil Society*, Cresskill, NJ: Hampton Press.

Tunstall, J. (1971) *Journalists at Work*, London: Constable.

Tunstall, J. (1996) *Newspaper Power: The National Press in Britain*, Oxford: Clarendon Press.

Tunstall, J. and Palmer, M. (1991) *Media Moguls*, London: Routledge.

Turkle, S. (1995) *Life on the Screen: Identity in the Age of the Internet*, New York: Simon and Schuster.

Veljanovski, C. (1989) *Freedom in Broadcasting*, London: Institute of Economic Affairs.

Veljanovski, C. (1990) *The Media in Britain Today: The Facts and the Figures*, London: News International.

Wallerstein, I. (1980) *The Modern World System*, 2 vols, New York: Academic Press.

Wasko, J. (1994) *Hollywood in the Information Age*, Cambridge: Polity.

Wasko, J. and Mosco, V. (eds) (1992) *Democratic Communications in the Information Age*, Toronto: Garamond Press.

Webster, F. and Robins, K. (1986) *Information Technology: A Luddite Analysis*, Norwood, NJ: Ablex Publishing.

Wernick, A. (1991) *Promotional Culture: Advertising, Ideology and Symbolic Impression*, London: Sage.

Williams, G. (1996) *Britain's Media: How They Are Related: Media Ownership and Democracy*, London: Campaign for Press and Broadcasting Freedom.

Williams, R. (1975) *The Country and the City*, London: Hogarth Press.

Williams, R. (1984) 'Drama in a Dramatised Society', in R. Williams, *Writing in Society*, London: Verso.

Winston, B. (1995) 'How Are Media Born and Developed?', in J. Downing et al. (eds), *Questioning the Media: An Introduction*, London: Sage.

Winston, B. (1998) *Media Technology and Society: A History: From the Telegraph to the Internet*, London: Routledge.

MEDIA AS INDUSTRY

|2|

Spectacle, synergy and megamusicals

The global-industrialisation of the live-entertainment economy

JONATHAN BURSTON

The changing nature of live-theatrical production

The economic engine, geographical site, theatrical community and larger social imaginary known as Broadway is being transformed. The corresponding matrix of social, material and ideal constellations we call the West End is also undergoing a similar transfiguration. In each instance, these transformations are indicative of live theatre's very own industrial revolution which, in the late twentieth century, is necessarily transnational in both scope and structure. Though it is somewhat overdue in historical terms, the most profitable portion of commercial theatre sectors not only in the United States and Britain, but also in Canada, Australia and many non-English-speaking countries is playing a frantic game of catch-up, deploying mass-production models that, though long typical of the global cultural industries of cinema, television and popular music, are virtually unprecedented in the history of the theatre. We are witnessing a phenomenon that can only be described as the global-industrialisation of live-theatrical production.

Over 20 short years, practical innovation has combined with rising global consumer demand to transform the field of commercial theatre from an agglomeration of a few discreet, far-flung ecologies into a coherent global cultural industry. This chapter focuses on the theatrical form that, to date, has led these trends: the megamusical. Exemplified by shows such as *The Phantom of the Opera*, *Miss Saigon* and *Disney's Beauty and the Beast*, megamusicals are different in important ways from the merely 'big' musicals that preceded them (*My Fair Lady*, *Guys and Dolls*) or that continue to run in the West End, on Broadway and on tour internationally (*Chicago*, *Grease!*). A large musical does not automatically qualify as a megamusical.

Unlike their predecessors and contemporary close relations, megamusicals are big global business: the capital investments are larger, the markets are bigger, more international and more numerous, and the stakes are higher than ever before in the history of musical theatre. Megamusicals are also produced by a select group of highly capitalised, globally competent and now even transnational players. And, crucially, megamusicals' systems of production are newly and decidedly Fordist: the terms 'franchising', 'cloning', 'quality control' and even 'McTheatre' are now all common in industry parlance.

As a consequence, the working lives of theatrical practitioners across the world of 'legit'[1] have changed profoundly over the last two decades. Reasons for these changes are discoverable in the *commercial, production-based* and *aesthetic* practices typical of megamusicals. Indeed, if an organisational examination of the megamusical phenomenon reiterates any theoretical lesson for media and cultural studies, it is that each of these moments of practice is intimately connected, and none can be considered as discreet from the others if the changes under way within the live-entertainment economy are to be comprehended profitably. We will examine the related elements of theatrical global-industrialisation as they occur in each of these moments. Taken together, they paint a sombre picture of production standardisation, textual homogenisation and rising levels of worker alienation in a sector where such developments were wholly unanticipated. As such they provide an excellent opportunity to problematise recent and important scholarly work (Negus 1992, Frith 1997) that characterises contemporary global entertainment capitalism as a system which regularly provides adequate room for both interpretative agency and cultural diversity.

Commercial aspects of global-industrial transformation

The field of megamusical production is characterised by entry costs that are exponentially higher than those typical of stage-musical production 20 years ago. *Disney's Beauty and the Beast* had upfront costs of approximately US $12 million (Taylor 1995), and Disney's latest Broadway offering, *The Lion King*, has costs estimated upwards of US $20 million (Cox and Evans 1998). Ongoing innovations in technologies of spectacle are largely responsible for raising the sector's entry threshold to such formidably high levels. As a result, the time required for producers to recoup initial production costs has lengthened substantially. A megamusical must enjoy 80 per cent houses for about 3 years if it is to justify its producers' initial investment. These constitute soberingly high stakes, and the rising costs of capitalisation may go some considerable way to explain the recent preponderance of transnational corporations among new producers.

Indeed, the recent arrival of transnational capital in the live-entertainment sector provides one of the best indications of radical industrial change. Along with Disney, new producers of live music-theatricals include Polygram, Universal, News Corporation and Viacom. Transnational entertainment corporations (TECs) are still 'young' producers, but they rightly view the larger field of live-theatrical production – including Las Vegas, Nashville, theme parks, ice shows, and 'quasi-legit' arena-based musical spectaculars – as prime territory for market expansion. Once London megamusical producers Andrew Lloyd Webber (Really Useful Group) and Cameron Mackintosh (Cameron Mackintosh Limited) demonstrated throughout the 1980s how profitable standardised global commercial theatre could be, the entry of TECs into the field in the 1990s was in some respects inevitable. TECs have duly noted the remarkable revenues that legit by itself – that is, *without* the help of the other live-entertainment genres just mentioned – has boasted over the last 20 years. In 1977–8, combined box-office grosses for Broadway and the North American touring circuit stood at only US $209 816 379 (*Variety* 1998). By the end of the 1997–8 season, the numbers had shot to US $1 351 403 718 (Isherwood 1998). This only represents legit growth in North America: worldwide, *Phantom* and *Cats* by themselves have grossed US $2.7 and US $2.2 billion respectively (Cox and Evans 1998).

Even more impressive, these numbers still only represent *early* growth for many of the sector's newcomers. This is because newly established TECs tend to mount live theatricals within product frameworks larger than any given musical. This is done in the hope of stimulating 'synergy' across a given 'brand' or property whose profitability is assumed to depend increasingly on the perpetual redistribution of its content in many different containers. Consider Walt Disney Studios chairman Joe Roth, who in 1996 had reason to look forward to Walt Disney Theatrical's stage musical premiere of *The Hunchback of Notre Dame* in Berlin in 1999:

> A major studio spends to stimulate all of the revenue streams, from merchandising to video to theme parks. Look at [the animated feature] 'The Hunchback of Notre Dame.' It will gross $300 million worldwide, but when you look at all revenue streams that number more than doubles.
>
> (in Bart 1996)

For companies like Disney, the ancillary revenue provided by cast albums, merchandising and television rights affords the necessary incentive to invest in theatrical performance. Theatre is produced not as a stand-alone product, but as part of a given intellectual property's maximal distribution strategy. As TEC theatrical producer John Scher of PolyGram Diversified Entertainment puts it: 'We are an entertainment company, and we are looking for product to feed our systems' (Gubernick 1994). The transplantation of such 'synergistic' attitudes to the global legit ecology has led to a crucial change. Now deploying productions as near-loss leaders for more highly convergent intellectual properties, TECs have concluded that a given the-atrical product's profitability is not a serious concern. So one Disney execu-tive explains to *Variety* that *Lion King's* Broadway strategy does not require the show to make a profit. Rather, under the newly transnationalised con-ditions of theatrical commerce, 'if you break even on Broadway, you're feel-ing OK. You set up Broadway as the marketing point for the rest of the world' both for ancillary products, and for future theatrical productions (Cox and Evans 1998). Broadway production has never enjoyed such advantages of scale before. Older, more conventional producers, whose profitability rode on the particular successes of theatrical productions *qua* theatrical productions, are either running scared, or have resolved to run with the times.

The emergence of a new global theatrical market is marked by additional strategies typical of transnational entertainment capital. These have been taken up not only by the new transnational producers, but by their most rig-orous and ambitious imitators whose origins are more firmly rooted in the-atrical soil. Foremost among them are Cameron Mackintosh Limited and the Really Useful Group – now globally competent corporations in their own right. The initiation of highly routinised systems of commercial man-agement and theatrical production afforded each producer the initial ability to 'go global' in the 1980s. The continued market growth that ultimately demonstrated their success provoked Disney to follow suit by the mid-1990s. And the late 1990s have seen theatrical producers adopting in turn the recently reconfigured business strategies of the TECs. These emphasise both the integration of corporate operations at the different levels of pro-duction, distribution and exhibition, and the consolidation of corporate presence and position *across* related businesses and markets (Herman and McChesney 1997: 70). Such strategies of vertical integration and corporate concentration, respectively, are by no means new to the realm of entertain-ment capitalism. What *is* new, however, is the scale of such enterprise. Responding in part to a 1995 US Telecommunications Act that has 'opened up a Pandora's box of consolidation in the media industry' (Herman and McChesney 1997: 50), media firms are now mobilising within 'a general market situation that is forcing them to move toward being much larger, global, vertically integrated conglomerates' (Herman and McChesney 1997: 53). Those who attempt to buck the trend risk their own extermination in a global entertainment economy that has never more fully promoted restric-tive and anti-competitive business practices.[2]

These same accelerating global pressures are now as prevalent among the front ranks of commercial theatrical producers as they are among front-rank producers in other cultural industries. Yet in recent academic and business-oriented writing on media and popular cultural production, the practical consequences of this new prevalence – namely, the increasing profitability and potential of theatrical production within an ever-more convergent enter-tainment economy – are seriously underemphasised,[3] misreported,[4] or ignored altogether.[5] Such lacunae are ill-timed. Writing of a 1997 alliance of two medium-sized theatre producers[6] anxious to 'bulk up' both vertically and horizontally in order to compete with TECs in the new theatre economy, the *New York Times*'s Rick Lyman flagged the action as 'the most visible sign yet of the seismic shift that has been occurring in recent years in the way theatrical productions are mounted and financed' (Lyman 1997). The seismic shift to which he refers is in fact nothing less than the recent, industry-wide adaptation of the Hollywood studio system to the field of live-theatrical production. In addition to increasing instances of integration and consolidation, then, 'Hollywoodising' changes in theatrical marketing and licensing require our attention.

Because initial investments are deeper and markets are both wider and more differentiated, a megamusical's financial viability has come to rely far more heavily on marketing and publicity than was common before *Cats* (or 'B.C.', as is said in the business). The marketing of Broadway and West End shows (and others of their type in major urban markets around the world) has increased in both size and sophistication as a consequence. Average annual advertising and publicity expenditure for a Broadway musical used to sit between 5 per cent and 10 per cent of annual operating costs, but by 1993 these costs had risen to 15–25 per cent (MCTR 1994). Since then, the arrival of TECs has pushed average marketing costs higher still, and it should not take long before the 1:1 ratio of marketing-to-production expenditure now typical of Hollywood cinema is replicated on Broadway.[7] Indeed, big marketing expenditure has become more crucial to a megamusical's success than either word of mouth or favourable reviews. With Broadway's new level of risk firmly in mind, one New York producer explained to me with chilling logic why undertaking new levels of marketing expenditure and circumventing critical discourse in the press was so important. 'It's *lunacy*', he insisted, 'to spend this kind of money and basically give seventy pricks and ten nice people the opportunity that may help you live or die.'[8] Attempts by megamusical marketers to wrest the job of 'taste-making' away from critics and audiences are essential to the continued success of global expansion. This is a lesson Hollywood learned some time ago. Along with the recent and successful introduction by leading Broadway producers of focus-group research – a marketing initiative as exceptional in the theatre as it is common in Hollywood – steadily increasing marketing budgets provide important examples of an industry-wide re-evaluation of outdated understandings of marketing's *function* as producers strive for increasing economies of scale.

The area of production licensing provides equally illuminating examples of Broadway's recent attempts to attach Hollywood models to theatrical production. One of the megamusical's defining characteristics is a producer's ability to install long and open-ended, 'sit-down' productions in emerging theatrical capitals like Toronto, Sydney, Hamburg, Tokyo or Chicago. Though shows also continue to tour, making short stops in smaller markets, the theatrical 'franchise' has come into being. The term 'franchise' needs to be understood in its most vernacular sense here, as megamusicals are in fact reproduced by a number of methods including direct production, co-production and licensing. Direct production keeps a show being reproduced in a 'hinterland' location entirely under the control of the metropolitan producer. A local producer's purchase of a licence to mount a show, on the other hand, does amount to the acquisition of a limited-time franchise. The licensing agreement attends in the first instance to the crucial matter of 'quality control' and the assiduous replication of production detail. 'We absolutely pack every approval into the local licence', one major producer's licensing chief explained to me, taking pains to describe in addition the systematic vigilance with which head office then ensures the licence is enforced. The end result, though of perplexingly little interest to cultural scholarship to date, has long been a favourite preoccupation of commentators in the arts, leisure and entertainment pages of the press. On the occasion of *Cats*'s astonishing 15-year anniversary in the West End, Rebecca Fowler commented in the *Independent* that *Cats*'s co-producers, Lloyd Webber and Mackintosh,

> franchised the show in much the same way as McDonald's has franchised its method of making and selling hamburgers. In the past there have been shows that have transferred from Shaftesbury Avenue to Broadway. *Cats* took the international marketing of theatre on to a different plane. It created the theatre production as a global product; Andrew Lloyd Webber became a global brand.
>
> (Fowler 1996)

Theatrical 'franchising' has brought about extraordinary transformations in the sector, and more will be said about this in the next section. At this juncture it warrants observing that the scale of this particular commercial innovation by London producers in the 1980s has since been dramatically augmented by Disney. In January 1998 the company announced that it would provide seven multi-million-dollar stage musicals over the next decade to local and foreign licensees, who must choose at least five of them. 'They're just film output deals for stage plays,' explained a senior Disney executive in *Variety*. 'We cut some amazing deals' (Cox and Evans 1998: 78). 'Such deals are common in the movie business,' *Variety* elaborated, 'but rare (if not unheard of) in theater' (Cox and Evans 1998: 78). Even the gathering speed of Broadway reproduction could not match Hollywood's own, until the arrival of genuinely transnational horsepower.

The inauguration of Hollywood-style production package deals as a means of rapid and guaranteed global distribution provides one of the most dramatic examples of the changes under way in the sector as Broadway's particular adaptation of the studio system continues to take root. Many view the adaptation of this and other aspects of the studio system as the logical next step in a field whose costs and revenues continue to escalate and, crucially, whose production credo continues to embrace new levels of performance standardisation. It is to this issue that we now turn.

Production-based aspects of global-industrial transformation

The new high-stakes imperatives of global commercial theatre over the last two decades have both sustained and been induced by new developments inside the theatre itself. With the arrival of megamusicals onto the field of live-theatrical production, highly standardised, 'assembly-line' methods of production have now come to dominate the landscape. As a consequence, the interpretative autonomy of actors and musicians is delimited in megamusicals in a manner otherwise atypical of mainstream theatrical production, and rising levels of alienation among actors, singers, instrumentalists – even among some technicians and management – have taken the sector by surprise. A well-respected theatrical professional in one of the emerging theatre capitals mentioned above described his motivations for joining his first megamusical as its 'resident director'. He told me that he joined the show to work with its internationally prominent creative team, but soon discovered that he actively disliked

> having to be the person who stands there and says, '[male principal], you're six inches too far to the left ... and who trains *endless* [male principals and female principals] to go through the mechanics again ... I would frequently have trouble with the representatives of the choreographer or the musical director 'cause they'd come in and say, 'That person is not *exactly* where they ought to be!'

This resident director soon realised that his ability to encourage the interpretative impulse among his cast was severely limited by automated set and lighting designs licensed in detail by a head office in another city. Further, his responsibilities were configured within an elaborate corporate hierarchy quite unfamiliar to traditional theatre professionals. Reporting frequently to senior managers in New York, he discovered that, like each member of this local theatrical subsidiary, his ability to foster and maintain 'real theatre' was severely constrained by newly globalised systems of live-theatrical reproduction. His dismay over the turn of events was considerable, and exemplary of community sentiment more broadly:

> It no longer is a play any more, it's an *assembly* line! It's a *corporation*. ... It's like you're running a branch plant. ... Well I don't really think you should treat theatre like that. And none of us who went into theatre thought we should treat theatre like that.

The veracity of this last statement is certainly borne out by many performers themselves, for, as difficult as this manager found it to adapt to the new regime, actors and musicians often have more difficulty still. One actor, reproducing a London production in Toronto, confessed to a great sense of *ennui*, even in his capacity as the show's ostensible 'star':

> I'm looking forward to going back to something that you can actually discuss with the director. You know: 'I'd like to move stage *right* here. I don't *feel* right doing this'. And they have a discussion with you ... As opposed to, 'This is the way you *move!*' I mean, there's no discussion.

Significantly, the actor went on to qualify his statement somewhat, suggesting that discussion did occasionally ensue. When it did, however, it was limited to artistic management explaining *why* the actor was required to move, gesture and proclaim in such an unusually prescribed and documented fashion. The regular occurrence of events like these inevitably leads to profound feelings of alienation among a workforce whose collective understanding of its *métier* leaves little room for such experiential categories. The same actor again:

> I always thought it would be interesting to meet with the twelve other [male principals reproducing the show worldwide] and sit down and say, 'Why do you suppose we do all this: move this way and this way and ...?' Maybe it would only be the very original one that would really know. ... The more I do this, the more I'm just, you know, a machine at a factory. You can lie to yourself as much as you want and say: 'You're playing a *character!*' But when it comes down to it, eight times a week, you're – you're a machine.

It is salutary to recall here two of Hesmondhalgh's categories of democratic cultural practice presented later in this volume – namely those of *collaboration* and *co-operation* – and to evaluate the extent to which these practices can be said to operate in megamusical space. Both categories have long been understood as hallmarks of live-theatrical practice, yet they are now residual to the experience of megamusical performers. Instead, categories of *conformity* and of *repetition* have lately become ascendant. Their rise, and collaboration's decline, exposes the poor fit between the conventional dynamics of live-theatrical production and the underlying dynamics of cinema – namely, mechanical reproduction and distribution. The ways in which these mechanised, cinematic dynamics are reinforced by the changing *aesthetic* norms of stage musicals is the next subject we must address.

Aesthetic aspects of global-industrialisation

In the first canonical text in media and cultural studies, 'The Work of Art in the Age of Mechanical Reproduction,' Walter Benjamin proclaimed that 'there is no greater contrast than that of the stage play to a work of art that is completely subject to or, like the film, founded in, mechanical reproduction' (Benjamin 1968: 230). In film acting, he argued, an actor for the first time 'has to operate with his whole living person, yet forgoing its aura':

> For aura is tied to his *presence*; there can be no replica of it. The aura which, on the stage, emanates from Macbeth, cannot be separated for the spectators from that of the actor. However, the singularity of the shot in the studio is that the camera is substituted for the public. Consequently, the aura that envelops the actor vanishes, and with it the aura of the figure he portrays.
>
> (Benjamin 1968: 229)

For Benjamin, technologies of reproduction – namely, cameras and celluloid – maintained critical distinctions between the genres of stage and cinema. But, under late-twentieth-century conditions of transnational theatrical reproduction, Benjamin's observations no longer hold. In megamusicals, a number of forces pertaining to theatrical texts themselves have combined to create in-theatrical environments where an 'inauratic' aesthetic similar to the one he ascribes to cinema now predominates (despite the material presence of performers and audiences in a given moment of time and space). Though the disappearance of an auratic environment need not *necessarily* connote an inauspicious development for those eager to promote democratic forms and relations within media and cultural organisations, we need to consider why, in the instance of the megamusical, it means precisely that.

The corrosive aspects of a widespread 'cinematisation' of theatrical aesthetics reveal themselves in deployments of both scenic and audio technologies. The realm of scenic design provides any number of examples. Technologies of visual spectacle such as helicopters, chandeliers, revolving barricades, flying railway bridges and flying beasts have long been objects of derision among critics of the megamusical genre. One must take care, however, to avoid lapsing into easy, revisionist assessments of visual spectacle's popular value within the stage-musical genre more broadly. Who, after all, can imagine *Peter Pan* without the illusion of flight? Or *A Chorus Line* without the gold sequin tuxedos and those huge revolving mirrors? Contemporary, *megamusical* deployments of automated spectacle, however, frequent in number and voluminous in scale, effectively *overwhelm* actors. And as the frequency and scale of spectacle continues to escalate, so does the displacement of primary responsibility for the production of meaning from actor to prop,[9] rendering individual human performers newly insignificant on the musical stage. Thus the category and practice of what we now may call the fetishised spectacular induces the actor's reification. The dynamics of the fetishised spectacular – wherein ultimately the helicopters become the stars – require that the physical particulars of an actor's interpretation are overawed by the objects of a technological grandiosity that distances actors from their own work, and from their audiences. Such dynamics work well in combination with the standardising imperatives of megamusical 'interpretation' (discussed in the previous section) toward the devaluation of performer skill and an aesthetics of performer interchange-ability. Actors regularly experience this toxic combination of techno-fetishism and interpretative restriction in an especially immediate manner. Automated set and lighting designs require performers to move to very spe-cific places at very specific times, or risk singing in the dark, 'crashing' the show or even getting themselves killed.

Typical megamusical deployments of audio technology likewise reinforce a new, depersonalised aesthetics of performer interchangeability in a num-ber of important ways. Because of their concentrated use of radio micro-phones, megamusicals are rightly understood to have ushered in a new method of sonic production in the stage musical. Radio microphones (or head microphones, or body mikes) are utilised very differently within musical the-atre space than were their antecedents. Instead of being dispersed through-out the stage area as they once were (affording performers with greater opportunities both to project their own sound and to 'blend' it with the sounds of others), a greater proportion of a production's microphones are now taped directly to the bodies of performers. This development has recon-figured altogether the way in which sound is constructed in the musical. As a consequence of higher levels of amplification and a perpetual reprocessing and redirection of performer's sound by audio technicians at the back of the house, a chronic despatialisation – a kind of jettisoning into sonic limbo – of the performer has now become the norm. These same dynamics likewise erad-icate all sense of local particularity from a given performance venue, as the dialogical relationship between a singer's own sound waves and the resonant materials of a particular auditorium is rendered inaudible. Thus a previously 'site-specific' theatre space is transformed into a kind of 'virtual' place. The actor's unique timbre becomes unintelligible and her particular position in time and space substantially devalued. The singing voice becomes 'disem-bodied' (O'Toole 1995, Meola in Burston 1998), a cipher, reduced to a mere sonic manifestation of the megamusical's over-riding industrial logic.[10]

A cautionary note needs sounding at this juncture. Shifts away from a more 'embodied' or traditionally defined 'live-ness' and towards something that is newly and differently fantastical are not reprehensible *per se*. Provocative reconfigurations of 'the real' have always been the theatre's legitimate remit, and exciting mobilisations of recent innovations in audio and visual theatrical technology regularly take place in non-megamusical theatrical space (work by *avant-garde* director Robert LePage immediately springs to mind). It would be a mistake, therefore, to lapse here into either an uncritical essentialism or an undertheorised Romantic conception of the individual author-as-performer. Neither of these positions, in fact, informs my critique here, nor are they generally the motivating forces behind similar critiques volleyed by megamusical performers themselves. In truth, if the megamusical's fantastical shifts effectively eradicate the dialogical qualities normally associated with the actor–audience relationship in mainstream theatrical practice (as they are seen to do by many megamusical performers), and if these shifts in aesthetics are historically proximate to the onset of widespread alienation within a substantial and economically dominant sector of the theatrical workforce, and if, finally, they coincide with a reification of this same workforce through a transformation of theatrical work into a sign of the stage prop (helicopters, chandeliers, etc.) or of the branded souvenir (mugs, key chains, baseball caps), then the critique presented here becomes substantially less conservative than it may first appear.

'Putting it together': synergy and the future of live entertainment

Building on their respective analyses of conditions inside the popular music industry, Simon Frith (1997) and Keith Negus (1992) have recently suggested the need for a theory of entertainment capitalism that properly acknowledges its plasticity. Arguing that music is 'still a mass medium in which unofficial voices may regularly be heard' (Frith 1997: 175), and that the working practices of industry professionals are not determined by commercial imperatives but instead are 'actively made' (Negus 1992: 155), each writer rightly takes issue with earlier work portraying popular-music production as a site of unified and implacable corporate/transnational power and intent. And, as such, each work constitutes an important call for further research into the complex terrain of the cultural industries, characterised as it is by different forms and logics across multiple localities, and by manifold relations within highly differentiated organisational hierarchies. Indeed, in light of Frith and Negus, the example of the megamusical demonstrates how highly differentiated various sectors of the cultural industries can be. A hybrid of the theatre, cinema and even the popular-music sectors (Burston 1998), the megamusical, as both form and industry, nevertheless displays ominously few examples of the kinds of space for agency that Frith and Negus each delineate.[11] It remains essential, therefore, for new research to continue analysing the *specific* conditions, times and spaces of any given instance of popular cultural production.[12] The megamusical phenomenon suggests that neither Frith's model, nor that of Negus, is necessarily transferable to other areas of organisational activity within contemporary entertainment capitalism.

To date, media, communications and cultural studies have provided scant insight into the burgeoning cultural industry that is the global live-entertainment economy. But as that landscape continues to expand so must the scope of our research into mass forms of popular culture. In fact, the megamusical has merely formed the *vanguard* of the forces of change across the wider sector, and the box-office totals cited earlier (p. 71) constitute only a fraction of the revenues now being generated worldwide by commercial live-theatrical production each year.

Consider the extraordinary developments in the United States's fastest-growing city, Las Vegas. In Vegas, the annual portion of tourist revenue generated by expenditure on live entertainment (as opposed to gambling) has increased dramatically over the last decade as show production budgets have expanded more than *ten-fold* (spectaculars that used to cost US $6 million to produce can now cost upwards of US $60 million). Opulent new venues continue to come on line every year, their frequency only matched by an astonishing number of new hotel rooms. 'Synergy'-led strategies have prompted even larger developments in the Vegas economy as a consequence. Entertainment corporations, hoping to benefit from the city's already-existing live-production infrastructure, are now collaborating with municipal and state governments in a startlingly comprehensive plan to turn the city into a major television, cinema and multimedia centre that will compete with Hollywood and New York (*Variety* 1997a: 31–55).

Predictions made in the 1980s by both scholars and pundits about the coming of electronic 'cocooning' have, at best, anticipated a short-term trend: audiences in Canada, Britain and the US are now leaving their televisions and VCRs to return to *all kinds* of public entertainment venues in numbers no one in the 'virtual' nineties ever expected to see again (*Business Week* 1994, Saunders and Mitchell 1997). As we have seen, however, live-theatrical spaces have themselves undergone significant kinds of virtualisation in the meantime, and the megamusical has played a starring role in this process. Fetishising deployments of new technologies of audio-visual spectacle have effectively diminished the value of human performers on the musical stage. This trend has worked in combination with substantial, new, Fordist restrictions on individual interpretative agency to create a new theatrical aesthetics of performer interchangeability. As a result, we have begun to discern the features of the prototypical 'virtual' actor in live-theatrical settings (see Burston 1998). Future enquiries into fast-converging entertainment forms should be mindful of these current conditions of production and their implications. So, for instance, we need to think through the ways that new megamusical norms may serve to sanction the fast-approaching perfection of *genuinely* virtual actors – 'vactors', as they are sometimes known, or 'synthespians' – by companies like Industrial Light and Magic, Media Lab and Pacific Data Image (Sand 1994, Stalter and Johnson 1996).

Here, and in the previously mentioned instances of megamusical practices, it behoves us to recall the fundamental wisdom that, when constructing viable theories of production (cultural and otherwise), the *social uses* of technologies often take analytical precedence over the technologies themselves. Particular *deployments* of technology are usually more problematic than technology as such. Even with such caveats in mind, however, current corporate thinking regarding the possible applications of synthespian technology is not encouraging. In 1995 Industrial Light and Magic's Steve Williams had this to say about the benefits that producers will reap from the impending arrival of practical and affordable digital technologies of performer simulation: 'You don't have to pay a [virtual] actor. There will be no drug addictions or delays. [Virtual] actors will be on the set every day' (Mazurkewich 1995). One may also assume that union complications will likewise become a thing of the past. More recently, Williams commented at an animators' forum that 'it was all just a matter of time' before 'blood actors' will face actors 'who only exist in a digital medium'.[13] We need to consider, then, the *ethical* as well as the aesthetic implications of the coming era of the synthespian in cinematic, televisual and even live-theatrical production.[14] Despite their extraordinary scope, the combined commercial, production-based and aesthetic manifestations of global-industrial change have arrived unexpected in the live-theatrical sector. But, as we rocket into our highly convergent, technologised entertainment future, neither scholars, critics, practitioners nor fans can afford to remain surprised by the onset of change for much longer.

Notes

1 The term 'legit' historically connotes traditional theatre fare and excludes burlesque, circuses, Vegas-type revues, etc. Contemporary legit productions are undertaken by established producers, within union contracts, in large theatres.
2 For an entertainment-industry analysis of the pro-conglomerate climate produced by the 1995 US Telecommunications Bill, see Peers and Wharton (1996).
3 In a recent business monograph on the newly revivified Disney Corporation, Grover (1997) mentions the activities of Walt Disney Theatrical only twice, and only in passing.
4 Wasko (1997) incorrectly identifies the Palace Theatre, where *Disney's Beauty and the Beast* is now playing, as a Broadway house purchased by Disney. Disney's sole Times Square 'purchase' to date is its long-term lease of the New Amsterdam Theatre, where *The Lion King* is now firmly ensconced and likely to run forever. Indeed, in a 1996 piece entitled 'Understanding the Disney Universe', Wasko fails to describe adequately the sum and import of Disney's theatrical ambitions (notwithstanding the fact that the outlines of the Disney theatrical strategy were clearly visible in the pages of the industry press as early as 1994).
5 In their otherwise excellent analysis of the size, breadth and significance of top media corporations' current holdings, Herman and McChesney (1997) fail to report on their theatrical properties. Once again, this is despite the attention many corporations have lavished on their respective live-theatrical operations for a number of years.
6 Pace Theatrical Group and Jujamcyn Theaters. This alliance fell apart with Pace's subsequent purchase by emerging stage giant SFX Entertainment.
7 See Frith (1997). Tasker (1996) argues that marketing budgets on Hollywood blockbusters now regularly come in higher than their production budgets, and her observations are now regularly borne out in the industry press. See, for example, Grove (1999).
8 This chapter draws on research undertaken from 1994 to 1998 in London, New York and Toronto featuring over 100 interviews with industry professionals. Here and below, italics indicate spoken emphasis.
9 See King (1991) for an illuminating discussion of similar dynamics of signification operating in film.

10 A longer treatment of these arguments is available in Burston (1998).
11 See Hesmondhalgh (1996, 1999) for new and important arguments against conceptualising excessive organisational plasticity within the popular music industry itself.
12 Though Frith (1997) is entitled 'Entertainment', in the main the essay attends to matters relevant to the study of popular music.
13 Animation master class sponsored by the Canadian Consulate General, New York, 25 January 1999.
14 See, for example, Argy (1998).

References

Argy, S. (1998) 'Virtual celeb technology', *Variety*, Los Angeles supplement, 16–22 Nov.

Bart, P. (1996) 'The Mouse Fights Back', *Variety*, 30 Sept.–6 Oct.

Benjamin, W. (1968) 'The Work of Art in the Age of Mechanical Reproduction', in Hannah Arendt (ed.), *Illuminations: Essays and Reflections*, New York: Shocken Books, pp. 217–52.

Burston, J. (1998) 'Theatre Space as Virtual Place: Audio Technology, the Reconfigured Singing Body, and the Megamusical', *Popular Music*, 17.2: 205–18.

Business Week (various authors) (1994) 'The Entertainment Economy. America's Growth Engines: Theme Parks, Casinos, Sports, Interactive TV', 14 Mar.

Cox, D. and Evans, G. (1998) 'B'way Rules Rewritten to Heed "Lion's" roar', *Variety*, 22 Dec. (1997)–4 Jan (1998).

Fowler, R. (1996) 'How "Cats" Conquered the World', *Independent*, 30 Jan., p. 13.

Frith, S. (1997) 'Entertainment', in J. Curran and M. Gurevitch (eds), *Mass Media and Society*, 2nd edn, London, pp. 160–76.

Grove, C. (1999) 'Marketing Mania', *Variety*, Columbia Pictures 75th Anniversary Supplement, Jan. 1999.

Grover, R. (1997) *The Disney Touch: Disney, ABC and the Quest for the World's Greatest Media Empire*, Chicago: Irwin Professional Publishing.

Gubernick, L. (1994) 'Hollywood Angels', Forbes, 153.11 (23 May).

Herman, E.S. and McChesney, R.W. (1997) *The Global Media: The New Missionaries of Global Capitalism*, London: Cassell.

Hesmondhalgh, D. (1996) 'Flexibility, Post-Fordism and the Music Industries', *Media, Culture and Society*, 18: 469–88.

Hesmondhalgh, D. (1999) 'Indie: The Institutional and Aesthetic Politics of a Popular Music Genre', *Cultural Studies*, 13.1: 34–61.

Isherwood, C. (1998) 'B.O. Boom Belies B'way Blues', *Variety*, 8–14 June.

King, B. (1991) 'Articulating Stardom', in C. Gledhill (ed.), *Stardom: Industry of Desire*, London: Routledge, pp. 167–82.

Lyman, R. (1997) 'Two Powerhouses of the Theater Meld Broadway and the Road', *New York Times*, 9 June.

Mazurkewich, K. (1995) 'The Great Canadian Cartoon Conspiracy', *Take One*, (Canada), 7 (Winter): 4–11.

MCTR (Ministry of Culture, Tourism and Recreation, Ontario, Canada) (1994) *Evaluation of the Provincial Entertainment Tax Impact on Commercial Theatre*. Prepared by Coopers & Lybrand Consulting.

Negus, K. (1992) *Producing Pop: Culture and Conflict in the Popular Music Industry*, London: Arnold.

O'Toole, L. (1995) 'Theater is Discovering a New Voice', *New York Times*, 22 Jan.

Peers, M. and Wharton, D. (1996) 'D.C. Greenlights Goliaths: Telecom Bill Sets Stage for the Big Guys to Get Bigger', *Variety*, 5–11 Feb.

Sand, K. (1994) 'Enter the Digital Actor', *Journal of the British Actors' Equity Association* (Oct.).

Saunders, D. and Mitchell, A. (1997) 'It's Party Time Again (the Death of Cocooning', *Globe and Mail* (Toronto), 13 Sept.

Stalter, K. and Johnson, T. (1996) 'H'wood Cyber Dweebs are Raising the Dead', *Variety*, 4–10 Nov.

Taylor, K. (1995) 'A Vastly Overblown Beauty', *Globe and Mail* (Toronto), 9 Aug.

Tasker, Y. (1996) 'Approaches to the New Hollywood', in J. Curran, D. Morley and V. Walkerdine (eds), *Cultural Studies and Communications*, London: Arnold, pp. 213–28.

Variety (1997a) Special Las Vegas edn, 11–17 Aug.

Variety (1997b) 'The Global 50: Merger Mania Shuffles Rankings', 25–31 Aug.

Variety (1998) 'Road Grosses', 25–31 May.

Wasko, J. (1997) 'Understanding the Disney Universe', in J. Curran and M. Gurevitch (eds), *Mass Media and Society*, 2nd edn., London: Arnold, pp. 348–68.

|3|

The political economy of the Internet

KORINNA PATELIS

The development of the Internet in the West has been attended by a hyped ideology (Internetphilia) that sees in the Internet the cure for a number of ills besetting contemporary society. This hegemonic approach to the changes the Internet engenders extends to all aspects of life, from academia to finance to politics. It has essentially framed the way we perceive and talk about the Net, marginalising any approach that does not subscribe to the rosy technological deterministic view of our inevitable free-market future. Though some have pointed to the metaphysical, speculative and futuristic nature of the discussions involved (Barbrook and Cameron 1996, Hacker 1996, Sardar 1996), the lack of systematic critique[1] and the holistic nature of the dogma in question has led to an unprecedented move towards deregulation in communication and to the uncritical introduction of e-commerce on-line. The Internet has become a symbol for global free-market capitalism. In opposition to the existing paradigm, this chapter will show that socio-economico-political factors determine on-line communication and largely control the future of the Internet. Consequently, the regulation of Internet-related industries is of paramount importance if the Internet is to have any public-service function.

Internetphilia has been announcing the inevitable arrival of a whole new era, one whose features are dramatically different, whose qualities and mechanisms cannot be understood with past methods of analysis. It constantly perpetuates the notion of a clear break with the past. The motor engine of such newness is purely technological; it is a change in essence, a qualitative change (Kahin and Nesson 1997: vii) which in turn installs a new mode of producing, distributing and consuming information. The underlying theme is the transition from analogue to digital information; the ability to store information in combinations of one and zero is the key to the new era (Gore 1994, Negroponte 1995: 11–20). The basic qualities possessed by digital technology are newness and dynamism. Everything is new,[2] everything is in constant fast movement. What is new today will be old tomorrow because the digital injects all aspects of society with dynamism. Dynamism destroys power by making it temporary.[3] Consequently everything will be transformed continuously, nothing will be stale, no structures will prevail. No knowledge will be diachronic, no policy definite, no question permanent; therefore our understanding of knowledge has to change. The digitalisation of technology is causing changes in society as a whole, changes which cannot be understood, addressed or dealt with if a new philosophy is not installed.

The constant reference to time and the up-to-dateness of knowledge labels those critical of technopia 'anachronistic', their understanding of the technological change 'poor'; they are 'digitally homeless' (Negroponte 1995: 7). Through this process alternative perspectives are silenced and Internetphilic authors assume the position of cyber-visionaries. Internetphilia argues that Internet communication will enhance freedom.[4] Freedom is what the virtual frontier stands for; the value that is prioritised over any other. However, the freedom in question is the negative idea of freedom, meaning freedom from external restrictions (as opposed to a positive idea of freedom[5]). Internetphilia is fixated upon the idea that the Internet is free, a sovereign entity above existing relations, above society. Freedom from reality is what virtuality in the age of the Internet stands for, and freedom from reality means freedom from any social, economic or political micro or macro process, culture included. The Internet substitutes for the structured confined system of corrupt representative democracy an inherently free paradigm for direct democracy. To be a Netizen and participate in this delocalised agora is a natural right in the digital world – one free from territoriality and social constraints. Freedom to act in the Internet means freedom to speak. Freedom of expression – virtually the symbol of cyber-freedom – is what Netizens campaign for.

It is further maintained that the Internet is global (Gore 1994a: 7) because it annuls distance and thus removes the limitations of geography (Negroponte 1995: 165, Johnson and Post 1997: 6), transforming the geopolitics of information, i.e. the unequal access to information across the globe due to geographical location (Negroponte 1996a).[6] Geography is redundant, as is geo-power. Consequently, the Internet will empower individuals inhabiting the social margins and the institutions and countries of the socio-economic periphery[7] (Poster 1995, Turckle 1995, Johnson and Post 1997). It will subvert the current power structure by transforming citizens across the globe from orthodox media couch-potatoes to active producers of on-line information (Goodwin 1996). Such empowerment is further enabled by the fact that technically the Internet is decentralised: it has no centre[8] and thus cannot be technically controlled (Negroponte 1995, Barrett 1996, Caruso 1996, Gates 1996, Volkmer 1996, Froomkin 1997, Johnson and Post 1997, Schwartz 1997). In any case, the sheer volume of information passing through makes it impossible to exercise any control over it (Johnson and Post 1997). The idea is that the technical impossibility of regulation and control cripples nation-state power (Caruso 1996: 57). This and Internetphilia's concern with individual freedom mean that Internetphilia is inherently anti-statist (Chapman 1995, Poster 1995, Barlow 1996, Gidary 1996, Heilemann 1996, Kline and Burstein 1996, Negroponte 1996, Steele 1996, *Economist* 1996, 1997a, Volkmer 1996, Abrams 1997, Froomkin 1997, Johnson and Post 1997, Kahin 1997, Neuman *et al.* 1997, Rapp 1997, Rodriguez 1997, Browning 1998). The state is portrayed as an inefficient anachronism, a bureaucratic enemy of freedom, its presence unnecessary for the proper functioning of the Internet. The state loses its legitimacy in the on-line world (Johnson and Post 1997: 10); it ought to and will slowly wither away as cyberspace becomes wider and wider (Negroponte 1995: 230, Barlow 1996a).

This faith in the Internet is shared by Internetphilia's advocates, who come from all aspects of life and vary in their focus. In academia and journalism one can distinguish, first, a liberal-populist approach concerned with individual freedom and the Internet as the marketplace of ideas (Negroponte 1995, Froomkin 1997, Dyson 1998); the most recent advocates of such an approach are market determinists (Barlow 1996, Tapscott 1996, *Economist* 1997, Huber 1997, Kahin 1997, Rosseto 1997: 244, Schwartz 1997, Solomon 1998). Second, one also finds a more postmodernist approach, analysing how Internet communication frees the subject from the ontological curse of modernity (Poster 1995, Turckle 1995, Reid 1996, Renan 1996). In politics, the Clinton administration in the US and the Bangeman approach in the EU[10] have been the key proponents of the liberalisation of communication in the name of convergence (Clinton 1992, 1998, Clinton Administration 1993, 1995, 1997, Gore, 1993, 1994, 1994a, CEC 1994: 8,15, 1997, KPMG 1996, Bangeman 1997, 1997a, Papas 1997: 5). In business, too, the exploitation of the digital moment has been inevitable (Gates 1996, Hammond 1996, Henning 1997).

Internetphilia articulates in two ways. Though these are not neatly separated, the first, whose central tenets are analysed above, refuses to accept that there is private property in the on-line world line (Barlow 1996: 172, Negroponte 1995: 59) or that property affects the on-line world (Turckle 1995). The Internet is constructed as an inherently anarchic system, juxtaposed to the current property system. Internetphilia's second articulation, currently hegemonic, shares these features, but is also characterised by a celebration of the existing private-property system, a market determinism which, with the announcement of convergence, is naturalised as the only way for the future of public policy. In short the Internet and the market are presented as essentially similar entities, inseparable and self-regulatory.

Internetphilia's second articulation developed in response to the Internet's incipient commercialisation. The Internet was now viewed as commercialised:[11] 'it has gone corporate', mainstream (Andrews 1994, Lohr 1994, *Economist* 1996, Miller 1996: 23–4, Henning 1997: 17–18, Hudson 1997: 11–37, Noam 1997, Schwartz 1997: 15, Sassen 1998). In the face of such commercialisation any claim that the Net transcends material relations was no longer sustainable. In replacement came a celebration – a bold asser- tion which typifies the way in which the Internet and private property are discussed, namely, that the Internet gives rise to a whole new financial envi- ronment, a new economy. It is a 'digital economy' based on abundance rather than scarcity; a market where supply equals demand and prices are set at the lowest optimum level; where oligopolies are avoided owing to low market-entry costs; where market dysfunctions are history and diversity is guaranteed. This market is a producer and consumer paradise. Its hallmark is dynamic competition (Gilder 1996: 5).

In the world of bits, there is no packaging, there is no distribution (they are automatic). Marginal costs are abolished, in consequence of which economies of scale no longer yield a competitive advantage. Whereas differ- ential pricing is difficult in an atom economy, it is a matter of an extra click in the bit economy. Such characteristics lead to an increase in network effi- ciency. This is the market driven by demand. For, if the necessary condition for market efficiency is that the marginal willingness to pay equals marginal cost (Varian 1996, Negroponte 1997), price on the Net equals marginal willingness to pay. In other words, demand sets prices and instead of scarcity of supply the Web economy 'exhibits a scarcity of demand' (Schwartz 1997: 2). Demand can finally get its revenge, it can obtain the power it always deserved, for this is the market of the people[12] (Negroponte 1997a: 112). In other words, traditional market conditions that can lead to exploitation are based on scarcity. If the Internet is the perfect market, then capitalism is the perfect system, for no inequalities will be produced. In Bill Gates's words (1996: 207):

> Capitalism, demonstrably the greatest of the constructed economic systems, has in the past decade clearly proved its advantages over the alternative systems. As the Internet evolves into its broadband, global interactive network, those advantages will be magnified. Product and service providers will see what buyers want a lot more efficiently than ever before and consumers will buy more efficiently. I think Adam Smith would be pleased.

If the market cannot be dominated, no company can have increasingly large profits and attempts to colonise cyberspace are doomed to fail (Bloomberg News 1997, Kantor 1998).

Through the notion of the new economy, the market and the Internet are constructed as essentially similar entities; the Internet bears a fundamental resemblance to the market. Indeed, it becomes a metaphor for it. As Kahin (1997: 184) puts it:

> Then again, the market itself has never moved this fast. Within a growing investment community, the Internet is seen not only as the once and future NII, but as a vast frontier for innovation and

enterprise. It is at once physical, logical and institutional, an organic mesh of unfathomable richness and vitality. It bears an eerie resemblance to the marketplace itself – which, with the coming of the electronic commerce, it promises to electrify in a reciprocal embrace.

Given the virtues of the new economy, why deprive the world of the opportunity for the Internet to install an environment of competition and act as a democratiser in other areas of economic activity apart from communication? In setting up this argument Internetphilia places e-commerce at the centre of the agenda. If the Internet is an economy of abundance, then the buying and selling of goods other than communication should not jeopardise e-communication (Hagel and Armstrong 1997: 16). Gradually, the Internet is defined not solely as a communications medium, but also as a delivery platform, an infrastructure/technology on which many applications can be run as the users fancy (Lehr 1998, Solomon 1998).

Given the prospect of using the Net for both e-commerce and e-communication, as well as any other application, how does one regulate it? And in the face of such a perfect digital economy why should one regulate it? The promises of the new economy have strengthened the anti-statist basis of Internetphilia. The anti-statist campaign launched for the CDA is accompanied by a hegemonic conviction that the Internet is not, cannot be and should not be regulated. The theme which facilitates Internetphilia's quest for minimum regulation and the free market is convergence. What is put forth is that telecoms, a liberalised industry, and broadcasting, more or less regulated, are converging into one technology. It is not sound to have two different regulatory paradigms for the same technology. A liberalised paradigm is better able to deal with the ever-mutating technological change as well as with the multifunctional nature of the Net. In short if different applications are to cohabit on-line then only a liberalised regulatory regime can deal with them. In public policy, convergence is the core of Internetphilia's second articulation.

Internetphilia's two articulations are very similar: for the first, a distinction between production and consumption on-line does not exist. For the latter, a distinction between production and consumption on-line can be made, but it is insignificant since the power relationship between the two has been subverted by the perfect market.

The backlash

There is a tendency to perceive Internetphilia as an ideology that is now going through a backlash, the expression of the Internet's adolescence, a hype cured by the medium's maturation (Bettig 1997, Hudson 1997, Noam 1997, Sassen 1998). Such an approach is misleading. First, it does not make any chronological sense since Internetphilic literature is on the increase.[13]

Second, it is itself Internetphilic since it reflects the notion of constant change. Third, it underestimates the centrality of Internetphilia's second articulation for the business world; the Internet has become virgin economic territory for every entrepreneur. Fourth, it is blind to the fact that public policies, echoing and promoting the above central claims, are being instituted and implemented at the same time as authors are speaking of a backlash. Internetphilia differs from the hyped ideologies that attended the rise of cable TV, for example, in that it brings about dramatic policy changes in the regulation of communications technologies: the Telecommunications Act of 1996 and the Green Paper on Convergence were unprecedented moves towards deregulation in the history of mass communication. The backlash scenario undermines how central public policy has been in promoting the Internetphilic agenda. The neo-liberal policy framework set by Internetphilia in the name of technological determinism has urged governments across the world to adopt a US-based liberal framework for the regulation of e-communication. Any sporadic backlash against such an agenda has been labelled anachronistic or protectionist. A whole neo-liberal way of perceiving communication has been dictated in the name of technology. The Internet's symbolic power in promoting state-capitalist development and resurrecting bankrupt free-market policy is on the increase. With the arrival of e-commerce such power has consequences that extend to areas other than communication. There is no backlash against the Internet's symbolic power. Finally, the notion of a backlash does not recognise how central the introduction of e-commerce is in affecting the whole nature of the Internet. E-commerce alters the function of the Internet from a communication medium to a delivery platform. Its terrestrial equivalent would be to introduce 500 new TV shopping channels and argue that this would not affect the function of TV.

The introduction of e-commerce on-line needs to be criticised. It has not been sufficiently criticised because backlash and criticism have one more shortcoming. They reduce all objections to access, and hence an 'info-rich and info-poor' analysis stands as the only opposition to Internetphilia (Bettig 1997, Sussman 1997: 171). Though access is an important issue, centring on access for critique leaves the impression that it is the lack of infrastructure and access that is stifling the digital democracy. But such a standpoint reflects the Internetphilic tenets which should be overcome. The uneven spread of the Internet's development is recognised in OECD reports, EU official documents, global information infrastructure documents, etc. An access-centred critique is formalist, it makes no normative claims and defends no ideal function for the Internet; it merely restates that the individual should have access to the Internet. There is no discussion of Internet content. The content could be anything.

To produce a fruitful critique one has to comprehend that it is not Internetphilia's level of euphoria that is problematic, it is not that the correct questions have been set and Internetphilia merely gives the wrong answers. It is that the questions are wrong. What does demand for Internet access mean? Access to what? And access for what purpose? Why should the advocators of free-market capitalism be given the right to hegemonise a medium and define its whole nature? Why is the market more inherently similar to the Net than to the radio? Why should e-commerce and e-communication co-exist – even if compatible? Do we put stores in our schools, though we may accept that this would not intervene in the learning process? Why is it taken for granted that the ideal is an Internet the uses of which are decided by the individual? And who has accepted a priori that there is a sovereign entity such as the abstract individual to determine such access?

Internetphilia's philosophical basis can be criticised on the same grounds as many neo-liberal dogmas: a faith in the abstract individual (Marx 1968: 29), an unfounded conviction that the individual is detached from the social, that it is sovereign (MacIntyre 1981, 1988, 1990, Sandel 1982, Walzer 1983, Taylor 1990a), and a belief in negative liberty founded upon the tautology that man, being born free, ought to be free. In addition, it can be argued that Internetphilia is a technological deterministic dogma. It can also be argued that it naturalises and reifies the market and the Net. Furthermore, Internetphilia exhibits an unjustified faith in direct democracy. It is also blind to the fact that scarcity is a not a technologically dictated phenomenon but an economic reality. Thus, no matter what the technology in question, there is no such thing as an economy of abundance, since economic goods are by definition scarce.

Continuity in the digital world

The way in which we perceive of the questions central to understanding e-communication has drastically to change. To achieve this, it is necessary to mend the carefully constructed ruptures with the past and posit 'power' as a central concept in our understanding of the Internet. Internetphilia dislocates the Internet from economic, historical and social conditions, leaving its audience confident that knowledge of the virtual world does not assume an understanding of such conditions. It establishes an analytical framework marked by virtual-communication essentialism, a tendency to describe and analyse the Internet in a historical, institutional and above all economic vacuum, the central assertion being that even if there is an Internet economy such an economy is novel and different. This in turn skilfully renders redundant any concerns related to financial inequality, public function and pluralism. In order, then, that any paradigmatic shift be possible, it is imperative that it be attended by an understanding of on-line communication as physically located within current socio-economic power structures and therefore as framed by material factors.

The current picture of the Internet is in striking contrast to Internetphilic claims. Inequalities in Internet development and the nature of the development in question mirror rather than subvert state-capitalist power structures. This is no surprise, given that there has been no attempt to develop the Internet in any other fashion. The Internet did not develop in a economic vacuum, it is part of a wider context and economic environment. As a communication medium it is enabled by a combination of technologies the production of which has been commodified for at least a decade – the infocommunication sector valued at US $1.3 trillion (Herman and McChesney 1997). Estimates of the Internet's participation in this economy vary. According to Forrester Research, Internet activity generated revenue of over US $2.2 billion in 1995; ActivMedia claims that reported on-line revenues reached US $21.4 billion in 1997, while Forrester's estimate is US $14.4 billion. Estimates of what revenue the Internet will be generating by 2001 vary from Forrester's US $45.4 billion dollars (Forrester 1995) to Gates's own prediction of US $13–15 billion by 2001; ActivMedia projects this figure to US $1.234 billion in 2002.[14] Thus the Internet is a commodified medium: the exchange value of on-line communication is prioritised over its other values. There are three main ways in which such prioritisation takes place, each generating significant revenues. First, the commodification of access: the internet service-provision market is now worth US $8.4 billion (AOL alone has 13 million subscribers and is worth US $2 billion). Second, the commodification of Internet navigation tools and search engines (Yahoo's revenues alone were US $30 206 000 in the first quarter of 1998). Third, advertising: Web advertising revenue grew by 28 per cent to US $169.8 million in the third quarter of 1997 (Cowles/Simbanet 1997).

For the sake of clarity the Internet economy can be divided into infrastructure and content as shown in Figure 2.1. Such a distinction (though false) makes it clear that the Internet is physically located; this means its function is totally dependent upon Internet infrastructure. The two parts of the Internet economy exist in a hierarchy; without the infrastructure there can be no on-line activity or content (OECD 1997). Internet infrastructure is the production and distribution of the on-line world, distribution being of paramount importance. Connectivity, bandwidth and hardware are for the

THE CONTENT	Broadcasters, Web-casters, on-line content providers, Web-site designers, database providers, advertisers, governments, on-line users?
THE INFRASTRUCTURE	Search engines, navigation tools, ISPs Hardware, software and server industries public telecommunication operators

Fig. 3.1   The Internet economy

Internet what transmission reception, clearness and TV sets are for television broadcasting; and they are scarce. Speed, stability and security are factors that make up connectivity.

The infrastructure/content distinction moreover routes e-communication
into older industries, old-fashioned markets with well-established players.
This has to be reflected back to the notion of an 'economic break with the
past'. Routing Internet industries into older industries undermines the
notion of a totally 'new economy', a virgin market, uncontaminated by the
monopolies of old media, where 'everybody gets to have a go'; the Internet
is inevitably determined by older economies and industries.

There is, of course, convergence in the Internet economy. A more accurate term for describing this phenomenon is 'vertigal integration'. ISPs are
being bought by telecoms companies, search engines are launching joint
ventures with telecoms and ISPs (MCI and Yahoo), broadcasters and telecoms (LineOne, the joint venture of BT and News Corporation). Since infrastructure determines content, vertical integration or synergies are instigated
and benefit companies that are part of the Internet infrastructure.

It is precisely because infrastructure determines content that the Internet
cannot be said to be hyper-geographical or hyper-economical. There is an
Internet architecture, a geo-economy that determines e-activity. Such a geo-
economy constitutes a series of inequalities which determine not only who
uses the Internet but above all the way in which the Internet is used. Not all
connections to the Internet cost the same or share the same speed or bandwidth; not all uses of the Internet are growing at the same speed; not all subscriptions allow the same activity; not all content has the same chance of
being viewed.

Mapping Internet inequalities

In 1997 Network Wizards figures showed only 15 countries in the world
with more than 100 000 hosts registered under their own domain name[15]
(Network Wizards 1997). All of these are in the West, which leaves 128
countries with fewer than 100 computers connected. Similarly the *OECD
Communication Outlook* places 92 per cent of all Internet hosts in the
OECD area. From Network Wizard statistics one can deduce that at least
60 per cent of these hosts are in the US (Kahin 1997: 156). There were no
host computers in the Honduras in 1995 and merely 400 in 1997. Today
there are 45 000 users in Jamaica (Foga 1998). There are 500 hosts in
Morocco, none in some central African countries. Basic indicators also
show that Europe is far behind in cyberspace. There were a total of 4.38
million hosts in the EU at the end of 1997, an increase of 140 per cent from
the previous years, but still very low if one considers the total estimated
number of hosts worldwide. Discrepancies between EU countries are dramatic. There were 2.7 hosts per 1000 habitants in Greece and only 0.2

domain names; 17.0 per 1000 in the UK – both countries being far from Finland's 95 per 1000 (ESIS 1998). Such discrepancies show the exact opposite of what Internetphilac claims: the geo-economical periphery is not centred in the virtual world.

Profiles of the average user reconfirm these inequalities. CommerceNet Nielsen found that Internet access in the United States and Canada was up by 50 per cent, from 23 million estimated users in August–September 1996 to 34 million by April 1997. A Find/SVP and Jupiter Communication survey found that 14.7 million households in the US were on-line (a figure that had doubled from previous years), while International Data Corp estimated that 20 per cent of American households were on-line (IDC 1998). Jupiter estimates that 3.7 million households are on the Net in Europe and 3.4 in the Asia Pacific Rim. Similarly, PC Meter market research estimated that 11 per cent of the total of 98.8 million households in the US had Internet access (up from 4.4 a year earlier). Surveys estimating the number of US users vary from Morgan Stanley's low estimate of 8 million to Wirtin Worldwide's projection of more than 35 million.[16] The Internet is like a tree out of whose trunk branches keep growing all the time. The way this tree grows is not accidental; it is dictated by international economico-political structures. Demand for backbone capacity towards a given country results in a more centralised network, which makes connections to this country faster and more capacious, which in turn increases demand. There is a main Internet backbone, a central intercontinental network to which smaller networks are connected. The US is at the centre of the majority of these connections.[17] As R. Hagen, director of Internet engineering at MCI, notes, 'If you were to squint at a map of the global Internet infrastructure, all lines would roll into the US, that's not a good way to build a network' (Evagoras 1997: 7). So if, for example, an information packet had to be transmitted from Buenos Aires to Lima it would have to go via Washington or Portland (MIDS 1997).

Internet backbones are made up of capacity owned by the world's PTOs (OECD 1996: 1); since businesses lease lines from PTOs and users use phone lines to establish dial-up connections,[18] the world's PTOs are obviously the first gatekeepers of the on-line world.[19] This relationship between telecommunications infrastructure and the on-line world is of importance; it means that to a large extent telecom capacity and infrastructure will determine Internet usage growth (thus access) and the network's architecture. If one considers the central features of the global telecoms infrastructure, a great deal about the state of the Internet is revealed. For example, 68 per cent of the world telecom infrastructure serves the needs of 16.8 per cent of the world's population (which equals the percentage of the global population living in the OECD area) (OECD 1997: 10). This could explain why 82 per cent of Internet hosts are in the OECD area. Furthermore, the US is disproportionately significant for global telecoms: five of the seven most important routes pass through the US (Cable and Distler 1995: 10). US companies dominate the world telecom market (Mansell 1993).

A country's existing telecommunications infrastructure is thus paramount for the growth of Internet usage both in providing capacity to ISPs and in providing users with domestic lines for dial-up usage (OECD 1997). Infrastructure includes connection type (analogue, digital, using fibre-optic wire), capacity and speed, as well as the public or private character of telecommunications. To give an example, Montenegro, a recently established democracy, has one telecom carrier responsible for regulating the provision of its telecommunications; all telecom lines linking Montenegro with the rest of the world have to pass through the former Yugoslavia's capital, Belgrade. Owing to limited capacity, not enough bandwidth can be leased to ISPs. The telecom carrier also refuses to give a mobile telecom licence to Global System Mobile Communication, a company trying to provide Montenegro with wire-less connections to the Internet. Thus, Montenegro remains outside cyberspace[20] for political and bandwidth reasons.

In addition, connection bandwidth varies significantly across the globe and with it the speed of transmission. Most US backbone parts are of 622 Mbits or higher, a bandwidth which places the US at the centre of the infrastructure architecture. India has 10 Mbits of Internet capacity amd Russia has 40, which in part explains the low Internet penetration rates encountered in those countries (Evagoras 1997). In Europe there are few 2-Mbit bandwidths, in consequence of which such bandwidths are too expensive to lease to business, which may explain why Europe lags in digital business ventures and why European countries are struggling to keep up with bandwidth demand (OECD 1996). The network-stability problems caused by bottlenecks and limited bandwidth are huge.[21]

Dedicated connections of high speed that accommodate large information flows (514 Kbs and higher) are not available to the average user. The most common connection to the Internet is 28.8 Kbs, available to 39.0 per cent of users, followed by 14.4 Kbs – the latter being the typical speed for 25.5 per cent of users (Kantor and Neubarth 1996: 48). If one compares these with, say, the 44.736 Mbps enjoyed by IBM users sending information around the IBM network (part of the US backbone), one comprehends that bandwidth is not infinite in cyberspace; bandwidth is a 'private good', not allocated on an equal basis. At a very basic level, bandwidth variations mean that not all users have the same distribution system at their disposal – for without bandwidth there is no distribution of content. Thus, even if one produces on-line content, it is useless without the bandwidth to transmit it. If one wanted to send an information packet of 680 MB from Atlanta to Las Vegas it would take 53 hours more than would a packet sent by the Mr Hagen quoted on p. 93 (even if one were an MCI subscriber). This means that Mr Hagen has more power in on-line communication, since he can more effectively and quickly transmit and receive content. Dependence on bandwidth means that the Internet is by definition not an environment of abundance. As usage increases, available bandwidth becomes the most important private good on-line. In fact, traffic charging is becoming customary.[22]

Setting the bandwidth problem aside, the cost of Internet access varies significantly with financial development and geographical position. According to the OECD the Internet tariff basket, which represents the price of a monthly subscription plus the pstn charge (peak rate) for 20 hours on-line per month, reveals dramatic discrepancies in access pricing: a Mexican going on-line at peak time would have to pay four times what a Canadian would, with a British user having to pay something less than the Mexican but at least three times what an American would pay (OECD 1997).

Business use versus commercial use

A further dimension of inequality in the manner in which the Internet is developing concerns the growth of business access and use compared to consumer access and use. Figures show that the former is by far outgrowing the latter. This means that growth in business use does not automatically bring growth in consumer use. ActivMedia estimates the growth rate in business connections to the Internet at 15 per cent per month and the growth rate of consumer access at 50 per cent per year. Similarly, according to the OECD, approximately two-thirds of Internet traffic consists of internal data transfers within corporations (OECD 1996).

Comparing domain names confirms such conclusions. Figure 2.2 shows Internet hosts as registered by domain name. In December 1991 there were fewer than 500 000 commercial host computers,[23] while educational hosts

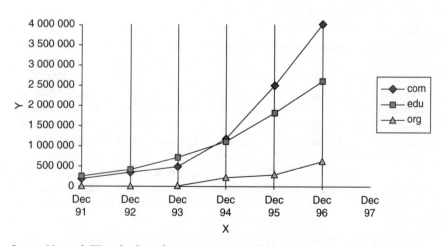

Source: Network Wizards (data after 1996 are not available)

Fig. 3.2 Internet hosts by domain name

were leading the way. In December 1996, at an estimated 4 million, commercial hosts were by far in advance. The number of educational hosts had also grown – but not to the same extent – to 2.5 million. Should this developmental difference not be thought conclusive, a look at the number of organisation hosts[24] ought to convince. Moreover, there were 1.3 million businesses on-line in 1996, a number that may go up to 8.0 by 2001. Eighty-two per cent of Fortune 500 companies were connected to the Internet in 1996, while the remainder had dial-up connections and 100 per cent of large companies had Internet connection (Forrester 1996). Furthermore, in 1996 Forrester projected that the number of Web-sites in large companies would quadruple in 2 years from an average of 2.5 (Forrester 1996a). Further evidence comes from the WWW. According to ActivMedia research the number of commercial Web-sites rose from 600 in September 1994 to 95 000 in July 1996. The number of commercial Web-sites listed in Yahoo (Web business directory) grows by 19 per cent per month.

E-commerce and e-communication

Increase in business use goes hand in hand with e-commerce, the introduction of which essentially shifts the function of the Internet from a commodified medium for communication to a supermarket, a shift which is celebrated rather than questioned. There were 4000 cybermalls in 1997, grouping smaller and larger firms (Flisi 1997). IDC surveyed 175 large companies to find that 46 per cent of them were planning to install e-commerce technology on their Web-sites (NUA 1997), while 100 per cent of companies interviewed by Forrester were accepting orders through the Net, 41 per cent use the Internet to confirm payment and 38 per cent to confirm delivery. Sixty-seven per cent of the companies interviewed by Forrester were engaged in Internet commerce to take the lead. Business-to-business trade was expected to reach US $8 billion in 1997, a 100 per cent rise from 1996; this figure is expected to rise to US $327 billion in 2002 (Forrester 1997). Anderson Consulting predicts that the on-line grocery shopping market will grow to US $60 billion in the next 10 years. The White House estimated that commerce on the Internet could total US $10 billion at the turn of the century (White House 1997). ActivMedia estimates that e-commerce revenue will reach US $1.2 trillion by 2001 (ActivMedia 1998). According to a survey conducted in 1997, 5.6 million people, that is 15.5 per cent of on-line users, have used the WWW to purchase a product or service; similarly, 73 per cent of WWW surfers search the Web for product information prior to purchase (Nielsen Media 1997).

For electronic commerce to be possible a number of factors have to be safeguarded, the achievement of which requires significant changes. These are security, speed and copyright; in *Wired*'s words, 'no privacy no trade' (Davies 1998: 135). Security is the necessary first step for electronic commerce, and encryption is iron-clad security. There is also the question of how e-communication and e-commerce are regulated, for they have traditionally belonged to different regulatory paradigms (Hartman 1998). Consequently, even if one disagrees with the political objections directed against the introduction of e-commerce, it is clear that e-commerce and e-communication cannot easily co-exist. If one reflects upon Figure 2.1 and contemplates what e-commerce would mean for the Internet economy, one comprehends that it would allow the introduction of non-communication firms to the infrastructure of the Net – and, as we have seen, infrastructure determines content.

ISPs: structuring the on-line experience

Internet service providers are the second gatekeepers of the on-line world. At a very basic level their charging policy regulates on-line activity economically. Thus, charging a different rate for Internet access and for Web hosting created the notion of the on-line consumer and producer. Were it not for ISPs charging extra money for putting information on-line, such a distinction would not have so easily become pervasive. The notion of an on-line audience and of on-line ratings was the inevitable result. Moreover, all ISPs have codes of conduct, sets of rules that Net users have to adhere to, and which can have detrimental effects on content. Filtering content is also becoming popular with academic providers.

In addition to such direct control, ISPs also exercise control via their promise to structure the on-line experience, to morph the Web, an intention made clear in their marketing and advertising campaigns. In those, despite the fact that the Internet is constructed as a vast frontier to be explored, each company promises to transform the chaos into a pleasure dome of knowledge. In short, what is being sold is structuration. Providers promise to make the Internet a safe and structured experience; to put it in LineOne's words, 'Is there a way to cut through the jungle?', or in AOL's words, 'We organise the Web for you'. What is also promised is that such structuration will be customised by taking into account the individual user's needs. Microsoft's campaign perfectly encapsulates this double promise: 'Where do you want to go today?'. The myth of the Internet as a chaotic landscape is the ultimate marketing tool, for it allows big companies to present themselves as performing a twofold indispensable function in the on-line world: structuration and customisation. It is the ultimate marketing technique because it portrays the on-line company as performing a vital function, as an institution which aids the individual to exercise autonomy on-line. Hyping this double function relieves companies of the need to account for synergies and vertical integration, which are presented as beneficial for the customer, as control of ever larger aspects of cyberspace becomes a factor adding to the company's performance.

Portal sites are a perfect example of how this ethos extends from ISPs to content providers. The task of portal sites is not solely to provide new content but to organise existing content, pointing the user to appropriate resources. They are thus the gateway to the Internet experience, particularly for new users, since switching can prove costly. Those in favour of a commercialised Internet portray the function of portal sites as merely operational, in the words of M. Pareth, a Goldman Sachs analyst, 'portals are services that aggregate reoccurring amounts of traffic and provide different sets of functionality to that traffic' (Goldman Sachs 1998: 3). By mobilising the marketing ideology presented above it is maintained that portal sites, by providing users with the mediation that is necessary for the Internet to function at all, provide a service that is vital to the user. However, what they are in fact doing is performing a function vital for the further commercialisation of the Internet by customising content and categorising Web pages – which is not to the user's but to the companies' benefit. In this way they channel attention, for channelling attention and aggregating traffic is what they are supposed to achieve. They are the starting-point for many consumers and accordingly knowingly structure what the user can do on-line.

Software and navigation tools

The importance of software in structuring and forming information cannot be comprehensively covered within the constraints of this chapter. It is enough to state that software is value laden and as such can contribute to structures which project certain contents over others. Search engines too are acquiring increasing power in cyberspace. They mediate the on-line experience by pointing to available content. Yahoo alone mediates approximately 30 million experiences a month. Such mediation should not be taken lightly, because as a result of it not all content receives equal exposure. It is now becoming customary to pay search engines to promote certain material, while search engines are also increasingly suggesting content to be accessed.

Signposting

The above analysis neatly separates Internet-related industries, masking the fact that it is in the interplay of infrastructure and content that a more comprehensive perception of power on-line can be found. The manner in which the industries and inequalities described above intertwine, overlap and mix constitutes the most important formation of on-line power: signposting. Understanding consumption or use on the Internet as occurring when the user views/uses a Web page is mistaken, because it ignores that it is the totality of and interaction between the different parts which define and form the on-line world that structures and shapes the on-line experience (consumption). And it is in the ability to determine such intersection and interaction that on-line power lies. In brief, it is through the interplay between the five industries that constitute the Internet experience – telecommunications, internet service providers, software, search engines and on-line broadcasters – that users' attention is structured; users are signposted to use the Internet in certain ways.

Conclusion

This rather gloomy picture of the Internet is not meant to evoke Marxist cynicism, but to provide the basis for a radical reconceptualisation of the Internet, to restore questions concerning social equality, the public good and cultural sovereignty to the research agenda. The Internet could be more than a delivery platform. It could also be more than a digital vehicle for individual use and gratification. But for this to occur at all the current naive paradigm of pseudo-liberal individualism has to be replaced by a vision of what the Internet ought to be. The environment in which the Internet is developing constitutes an urgent reason for the revitalisation of public-service media arguments. It returns abandoned justifications for public intervention and the funding of communication to the centre of debate. It brings questions concerning the public interest back into the heat of the discussion agenda. A public-service Net is needed to reverse the current commercialisation trends. It is only if we are not scared to utter the word 'public' that we can start debating a way out of the neo-liberal agenda. The Internet can provide the base for a renewal of the public-service tradition. The objective of this chapter is not to sketch what such a public-service Internet would be but to open up the debate, shifting questions away from market determinism.

Notes

1 There has been some criticism; see Papageorgiou (1996), Robins (1996), Auletta (1997).
2 One could not even begin to summarise the documents in which the newness of digital era emerging is underlined. To all the authors, politicians and governments sited as Internetphilic throughout this chapter one could add Tapscott (1996: 7), Henning (1997).
3 There is a classic moment in which this notion of newness and the currency of knowledge is taken up by Negroponte himself when interviewed by the *Financial Times*. Commenting on *Being Digital*, Negroponte says 'Don't you think it is a little bit old? ... as much as I like to think I understood how fast all this was going to move I don't think I did' (Griffith 1998).
4 Once again references to freedom are too many to cite; for a typical example see Gore (1994: 2).

5 For a distinction between negative and positive freedom see Berlin (1969); for a critique of this distinction see Allison (1981); for a critique of the concept of negative liberty see Taylor (1990).

6 In the fifth-anniversary issue of *Wired*, Negroponte renews his faith in the transforming power of the Net, arguing that the third world will no longer be the third world since the Net leverages latecomers in the developing world (Negroponte 1998). A similar point is made by Barlow (1998).

7 Typical of this is Negroponte's story of how he logged on from the small Greek island of Andros or the story of Marc Warren, a man who was born in a little village outside Maine and decided to build a BBS (Conway 1996).

8 Developed by the US Department of Defense as a decentralised computer system. According to some it was developed to survive a nuclear catastrophe by enabling the fail-safe transmission of information via a new message-packaging system (Negroponte 1995: 233). The Internet is indestructible since part of this network of networks is bound to survive (one cannot destroy all of the computers in the US). The idea, conceived by L. Robert in 1963, is of a network with no central computer (Lyon and Hafner 1996). The Net is a network of computers, each of which communicates separately with many others rather than via one central computer. So, by virtue of there being more than one route for the transmission of information from computer A to computer B, if information were to be lost in communication many other routes would still exist.

9 The Republican opposition has been enthusiastic too (see Gingrich 1995: 55).

10 Though the Bangeman approach in EU infocommunication policy is a definite Internetphilic component, EU policy as a whole cannot be characterised as Internetphilic. It is marked by a tension between social and economic prosperity; it was also late to introduce electronic commerce, has recognised Europe's lag in cyberspace (CEC 1996, EHLSG 1997: 10, ESC 1998: para. 1.2), and has not assumed a hegemonic role in the 'digital revolution'. It consequently differs from the US, a difference that cannot be analysed within the constraints of this chapter (see Patelis 1999, 1999a for details).

11 For an example of how this is reflected in the popular press see *Guardian*'s story on the commodification of pornographic Web surfing and the cover story of *Net* magazine titled 'The End of the Free Ride'.

12 For a graphic portrayal of what this demand-led markets looks like in a demand/supply chart see the classic Internetphilic graphs in Hagel and Armstrong (1997: 25). Some authors have gone so far as to suggest that in the digital economy markets function so well, matching demand and supply to such an extent, that the distinction between them is increasingly difficult to make. In Tapscote's words: 'as mass production is replaced by mass customisation producers must create specific products that reflect the requirements and tastes of individual customers, in the new economy consumers become involved in the actual production process' (Tapscott 1996: 62).

13 The sale of the NSF backbone to commercial companies which marks the commercialisation of the Net occurred in 1994, long before all the Internetphilic documents referred to in this chapter were published.

14 This is not only the Forrester research prediction but that of the US government as well (Clinton Administration 1997: 2).

15 There are complications to this argument. Strictly speaking a host need not be registered with an address reflecting its geographical location. For example, the host computers used for IBM's headquarters in Singapore might be registered under ibm.net. As much as this is important, it does not affect public access to the Net, and should mostly be taken into account when measuring geographical location of business.

16 According to *Internet Magazine* the average US user had a salary of $59 000 – dou-

ble the US average of $20 690 (Kantor and Nuebarth 1996: 47). Similarly, Georgetown survey found that 84.4 per cent of users reside in the US, that 38 per cent of them are female, that the average user is a white (87 per cent) 35-year-old male. Eighty-one per cent have had a college education, 50 per cent have a degree of some sort.

17 For example, 65 per cent of all Singapore Internet traffic passes through the US.

18 I have chosen to exclude Internet communication via wireless telephony since this is not a technology used by a substantial number of users.

19 According to the OECD the Internet is a prime reason for the rise in demand for new telephone lines: 18 million in 1995 (OECD 1997: Ch.1). Revenue from leased lines has also increased, partly due to demand for Internet access, representing 5 per cent of the public telecoms market at US $26 billion (OECD 1997).

20 This information was revealed in an interview with the chief executive officer of GSMC.

21 In an attempt to evaluate these, MIDS issues an 'Internet weather forecast', mapping delays and bottleneck problems around the Internet (MIDS 1997).

22 To take an example, JANET, Britain's central and largest education-related server and network, at one time did not charge educational institutions' servers for usage. But, as traffic has increased by some 200 per cent and 300 per cent in the last years, charges have been introduced. Charges will directly reflect usage and only usage of the JISC national service will not be charged. Any other usage will be at 2 pence per Megabyte including VAT and it is estimated that about 23 institutions will have to pay £30 000 or more, raising a total of £2 million – 11 per cent of the JISC networking budget. This is merely an example of what is increasingly happening on a larger scale.

23 I know there is a problem with defining what a commercial site is but for the time I will define a commercial site as any host computer whose owners have registered it as commercial and thus whose address ends in com.

24 Organisation host is defined as a host that belongs to a non-profitable organisation promoting non-profitable causes.

References and further reading

Abrams, F. (1997) 'Clinton vs. the First Amendment', *New York Times*, 30 Mar., Sec. 6 Magazine, p. 42.

ActivMedia (1998) *The Real Numbers Behind Net Profits*, report available at www.activmedia.com.

Alison, L. (1981) 'Liberty: A Correct and Authoritarian Account', *Political Studies*, 60.4.

Andrews, E. (1994) 'MCI to Offer One Stop Shopping on the Internet', *New York Times*, Mar., 21 Sec. D Financial Desk, p. 2.

Auletta, K. (1997) *The Highwaymen: Warriors of the Information Superhighway*, New York: Random House.

Bangeman, M. (1997) 'Europe and the Information Society: The Policy Response to Globalisation and Convergence', speech delivered in Venice, 18 Sept.

Bangeman, M. (1997a) 'A New World Order for Global Communication', speech delivered at Telecom Interactive 97 International Telecommunication Union, Geneva, 8.

Barbrook, R. and Cameron, A. (1996) 'The Californian Ideology' available at hyperlink http://www.wmin.ac.uk/mmedia/hrc/ci/calif5.html, repr. in D. Hudson, *Rewired: A Brief and Opinionated Net History*, Indianapolis: Macmillan Technical Press, 1997.

Barlow, J. (1996) 'Selling Wine Without Bottles: The Economy of Mind on the Global Net', in Leeson, L.H. (ed.), *Clicking In: Hot Links to a Digital Culture*, Seattle: Bay Press, also available on-line at http://www.eff.org/pub/Publications/John-Perry-Barlow/HTML/idea-economy-article.

Barlow, J. (1996a) 'Jackboots on the Infobahn', in P. Ludlow (ed.), *High Noon on the Electronic Frontier: Conceptual Issues in Cyberspace*, Cambridge, MA: MIT Press.

Barlow, J. (1998) 'Africa Rising', *Wired*, 6.1 (Jan).

Barrett, N. (1996) *The State of Cybernation: Cultural, Political and Economic Implications of the Internet*, London: Kogan Page.

Berlin, I. (1969) *Four Essays on Liberty*, Oxford: Oxford University Press.

Bettig, R. (1997) 'The Enclosure of Cyberspace', *Critical Studies in Mass Communication*, 14: 138–57.

Bloomberg News (1997) 'Internet Firms Gather in a Blue Period', *International Herald Tribune*, 10 Mar., p. 11.

Browning, J. (1998) 'Power to the People', *Wired*, 6.1 (Jan.).

Cable, V. and Distler, C. (1995) *Global Superhighways: The Future of International Telecommunication Policy*, London: The Royal Institute of International Affairs.

Caruso, D. (1996) 'The Idealist,' in Brockman, J. (ed.), *Digerati: Encounters with the CyberElite*, San Francisco: HardWired.

CEC (Commission of the European Communities) (1994) *Europe and the Global Information Society: Recommendations of the Bangemann Group to the European Council*, Brussels: European Commission, 26 May.

CEC (1996) *Communication from the Commission to the Council and the Parliament on 'Standardisation and the Global Information Society: The European Approach'*, Brussels: COM(96)35.

CEC (1997) *Green Paper on the Convergence of the Telecommunication, Media and Information Technology Sector and the Implications for Regulation Towards an Information Society Approach*, Brussels: COM(97)623.

Chapman, B. (1995) 'Individuals, Not Governments, Should Shape Internet's Future', available at http://www.discovery.org/lawnetcolum.html.

Clinton Administration (1993) *The National Information Infrastructure: The Administration's Agenda for Action*, Washington, DC, 15 Sept., available on-line at http://www.whitehouse.gov.

Clinton Administration (1995) *The Global Information Infrastructure: A White Paper*, prepared for the White House Forum on the Role of Science and Technology in Promoting National Security and Global Stability.

Clinton Administration (1997) *A Framework for Global Electronic Commerce*, Washington, DC, 1 July, available at http://www.whitehouse.gov/WH/New/Commerce/about-plain.html.

Clinton, B. (1992) 'The Economy', speech delivered at Wharton School of Business, University of Pensyl., 16 April.

Clinton, B. (1998) Remarks delivered at the Technology 98 conference, Carlton Ritz Hotel, San Francisco, 26 Feb.

Conway, L. (1996) 'Wiring the Maine Line', *Wired*, 4.7 (July).

Cowles/Simbanet (1997) Electronic Advertising and Marketplace Report, Stamford, CT.

Davies, A. (1998) 'No Privacy No Trade', *Wired*, 6.8 (Aug.).

Dyson, E. (1998) *Release 2.0: A Design for Living in the Digital Age*, New York: Broadway Books.

ESC (Economic and Social Commitee of the European Union) (1998) 'Draft Opinion of the Section for Industry, Commerce, Craft and Services on the Green Paper on the Convergence of the Telecommunications, Media and Information Technology Sector, and the Implications for Regulation', Brussels, available on the ispo server www.ispo.cec.cec.be.

Economist (1996) 'Why the Net should Grow Up', *Economist*, 19 Oct.

Economist (1997) 'In Search of the Perfect Market: A Survey of Electronic Commerce', *Economist*, 10 May.

Economist (1997a) 'Hands off the Internet', Economist, 5 July.

EHLSG (European High Level Strategy Group) (1997) 'Internet in Europe', discussion paper for the ICT for the Global Standards Conference, Building the Global Information Society for the 21st Century, available at www.ispo.cec.be.

ESIS (1998) 'The Information Society Developments in the EU: Basic Indicators', available at www.ispo.cec.be.

Evagoras, A. (1997) 'World Wide Weight', *Internet Magazine*, Sept.–Aug.

Evagoras, A. (1997a) 'Data Flow to and from the US', e-mail to K. Patelis posted on 23 Oct.

Flisi, C. (1997) 'Web Malls and Branding', *International Herald Tribune*, sponsored section, e-business: retail, Oct., p. 15.

Foga, N. (1998) 'Changes in the Jamaican Legal and Regulatory Framework in Light of the Convergence of Telecommunications, Media and Computing and the Growth of the Internet', paper presented at ITS 1998, 21–4 June, Stockholm.

Forrester (1995) *The Internet Economy*, Massachusetts: Forrester Research. Available at http://www.forrester.com.

Forrester (1996) *Computing Strategies: Everyone Gets The Net*, Massachusetts: Forrester Research. Available at http://www.forrester.com.

Forrester (1996a) *Telecom Strategies Report: Web Hosting For Hire*, Massachusetts: Forrester Research. Available at http://www.forrester.com.

Forrester (1996b) *Media and Technology Strategies Internet Advertising Vol.1 Number 1*, Massachusetts: Forrester Research. Available at http://www.forrester.com.

Forrester (1997) *Business and Trade and Technology Strategies: Sizing Intercompany Commerce*, Massachusetts: Forrester Research. Available at http://www.forrester.com.

Forrester (1997a) *What Advertising Works*, Massachusetts: Forrester Research. Available at http://www.forrester.com.

Froomkin, M. (1997) 'The Internet as a Source of Regulatory Arbitrage', in B. Kahin and C. Nesson (1997), *Borders in Cyberspace: Information Policy and the Global Information Infrastructure*, Cambridge, MA: MIT Press.

Gates, B. (1996) *The Road Ahead*, New York: Penguin.

Gidary, A. (1996) 'A Magna Carta for the Information Age', available at http://www.discovery.org/magnacart.html.

Gilder, G. (1996) 'The Freedom Model of Telecommunications', available at http://www.pff.org/pff/amciv/ac-april/ac495gg.htlm.

Gingrich, N. (1995) *To Renew America*, New York: HarperCollins.

Golding P. (1996) 'World Wide Wedge: Division and Contradiction in the Global Information Infrastructure', in D. Daya Kshan (ed), *Electronic Empires: Global Media and Local Resistance*, London: Arnold, 1998.

Goldman Sachs (1998) 'Technology: Internet New Media', report, New York: Goldman Sachs (July).

Goodwin, M. (1996) 'An Ill-defined Act', *Internet World* (June).

Goodwin, M. (1996a) 'Witness to History', *Internet World* (Sept.).

Gore, A. (1993) Remarks, at the National Press Club, 21 Dec.

Gore, A. (1994) Remarks, as delivered to the Superhighway Summit, Royce Hall, UCLA, Los Angeles, 11 Jan.

Gore, A. (1994a) Remarks, as delivered to the International Telecommunication Union, 21 Mar., available on-line.

Griffith, V. (1998) 'Fast Forward for the Cyber-evangelist', *Weekend FT*, 25/26 Apr., pt. III.

Hacker, K. (1996) 'Missing Links in the Evolution of Electronic Democratization', *Media, Culture and Society*, 18: 213–32.

Hagel, J. and Armstrong, A. (1997) *Net Gain: Expanding Markets through Virtual Communities*, Boston: Harvard Business School Press.

Hammond, R. (1996) *Digital Business*, London: Hodder and Stoughton.

Hartman, T. (1998) 'The Marketplace vs. the Ideas: The First Amendment Challenges to Internet Commerce', presented at the ITS 1998, Stockholm, 21–4 June.

Heilemann, J. (1996) 'Big Brother Bill', *Wired*, 4.10 (Oct.).

Henning, K. (1997) *The Digital Enterprise*, London: Century Business Books.

Herman, E. and McChesney, R. (1997) *Global Media: The New Missionaries of Capitalism*, London: Cassell.

Huber, P. (1997) *Law and Disorder in Cyberspace*, Oxford: Oxford University Press.

Hudson, D. (1997) *Rewired: A Brief and Opinionated Net History*, Indianapolis: Macmillan Technical Press.

IDC (International Data Coorporation) (1998) '1996 World Wide Web Survey of Home and Business Users', report.

IRAG (Interim Report of an Advisory Group) (1997) 'The Future of the Internet: What Role for Europe', available at www.ispo.cec.be.

Johnson, D. and Post, D. (1997) 'The Rise of Law on the Global Network', in B. Kahin and C. Nesson (eds), *Borders in Cyberspace*, Cambridge, MA: MIT Press.

Kahin, B. (1997) 'The US Information Infrastructure Initiative: The Market, the Web and the Virtual Project', in B. Kahin and E. Wilson (eds), *National Infrastructure Initiatives: Vision Policy Design*, Cambridge, MA: MIT Press.

Kahin, B. and Nesson, C. (1997) *Borders in Cyberspace: Information Policy and the Global Information Infrastructure*, Cambridge, MA: MIT Press.

Kantor, A. and Neubarth, M. (1996) 'Off the Charts: The Internet 1996', *Internet World* (Dec.).

Kantor, P. (1998) 'Online Entertainment Crashes', *Variety*, 4–10 (May).

Kline, D. and Burstein, D. (1996) 'Is Government Obsolete', *Wired*, 4.1.

KPMG (1996) Public Issues Arising from Telecommunications and Audiovisual Convergence, report for the EU (contract number 70246), Sept.

Lehr, W. (1998) untitled paper presented at the ITS 1998, Stockholm, 21–4 June.

Lohr, S. (1994) 'Outlook '94: The Road From Lab to Marketplace', *New York Times*, late edn, 3 Jan., Sect. C.

Lyon, M. and Hafner, K. (1996) *Where Wizards Stay Up Late: The Origins of the Internet*, New York: Simon and Schuster.

MacIntyre, A. (1981) *After Virtue*, London: Duckworth.

MacIntyre, A. (1988) *Whose Justice Which Rationality?*, London: Duckworth.

MacIntyre, A. (1990) *Three Rival Versions of Moral Enquiry*, Oxford: Blackwell.

Mansell, R. (1993) *The New Telecommunications: A Political Economy of Network Evolution*, London: Sage.

Marx, K. (1968) *Selected Works*, New York: International Publishers.

MIDS (1997) 'Latin America Connection Map', available at www.mids.org.

Miller, S. (1996) *Civilizing Cyberspace: Policy, Power, and the Information Superhighway*, ACM Press.

Noam, E.(1997) 'An Unfettered Internet? Keep Dreaming', *New York Times*, late edn, 11 July, Editorial Desk, p. 27.

Negroponte, N. (1995) *Being Digital*, London: Hodder and Stoughton.

Negroponte, N. (1996) 'Being Local', *Wired*, 2.1.

Negroponte, N. (1996a) 'Pluralistic not Imperialistic', *Wired* (Mar.).

Negroponte, N. (1997) 'Pay Whom Per What When Part One', *Wired UK* (Feb.).

Negroponte, N. (1997a) 'Pay Whom Per What When Part Two', *Wired UK* (Mar.).

Negroponte, N. (1998) 'The Third Shall be First', *Wired*, 6.1.

Network Wizards (1997) 'Host Count', available at http://www.nw.com.

Neuman, R., McKnight, L. and Solomon, R. (1997) *The Gordian Knot: Political Gridlock on the Information Highway*, Cambridge MA: MIT Press.

NielsenMedia/Commerce Net (1997) *Internet Demographics*, survey, New York City.

NUA (1997) 'The Internet Review 1996: A NUA Synopsis of the Internet', available at www.nua.com.

OECD (1996) *Information Infrastructure Convergence and Pricing: The Internet*, OEDE/GD (96) 73, Paris.

OECD (1997) *Communications Outlook*, OECD/GD Vols 1 and 2, Paris.

OECD (1997a) *Information Technology Outlook*, OECD/GD, Paris.

OECD (1997b) *Global Information Infrastructure: Global Information Society (GII-GIS): Policy Recommendations for Action*, OECD/GD (97) 138, Paris, on-line at NUA site posted to NUA mailing list.

Papageorgiou, G. (1996) 'Class Society in Cyberspace' ('I taxiki kinonia ston kiber-noxoro'), *Eleytherotipia*, 19 Aug.

Papas, S. (1997) 'Digital Television: 500 Channels of Junk Video?', speech by Director General Spyros Papas at the 4th Annual CEO Summit on Converging Technologies, 3 June.

Patelis, K. (1999) 'What's Regulation Got to Do With It?', *Mute*, 12.

Patelis, K. (1999a) 'Beyond Internetphilia: Regulation, Public Service Media and the Internet', paper presented at the International Broadcasting Symposium, Manchester, 24–5 Mar.

Poster, M. (1995) 'Cyberdemocracy', *Difference Engine Vol. 2*, available at http://www.gold.ac.uk.

Poster, M. (1996) 'Postmodern Virtualities', in G. Robertson et al. (eds), *FutureNatural: Nature/Science/Culture*, London: Routledge.

Progress and Freedom Foundation (1994) 'Cyberspace and the American Dream: A Magna Carta for the Knowledge Age', available at http://www.pff.ogr.

Ramsay, M. (1997) *What's Wrong with Liberalism? A Radical Critique of Liberal Political Philosophy*, Leicester: Leicester University Press.

Rapp (1997) 'Sanitizing the Internet? No Way', *New York Times*, Sec. 13LI Long Island Weekly Desk, p. 16.

Reid, E. (1996) 'Text-based Virtual Realities: Identity and the Cyborg Body', in P. Ludlow (ed.), *High Noon on the Electronic Frontier: Conceptual Issues in Cyberspace*, Cambridge, MA: MIT Press.

Renan, S. (1996) 'The Net and the Future of Being Fictive', in Leeson (ed.), *Clicking In: Hot Links to a Digital Culture*, Seattle: Bay Press.

Robins, K. (1996) 'Cyberspace and the World We Live In', in Doney (ed.), *Fractal Dreams: New Media in Social Context*, London: Lawrence and Wishart.

Rodriguez, F. (1997) 'Letter sent to DFN, Organisation that is Censoring xs4all Webserver Protest,' e-mail posted to Netime mailing list, 17 Apr.

Rosseto, L. (1996) 'Response to the Californian Ideology', available at http://www.wmin.ac.uk/mmedia/HRC/ci/calif2.html.

Rosseto, L. (1997) 'What Kind of a Libertarian: An Interview', in D. Hutson, *Re-wired: A Brief and Opinionated Net History*, Indianapolis: Macmillan Technical Publishing.

Sandel, M. (1982) *Liberalism and the Limits of Justice*, Cambridge: Cambridge University Press.

Sardar, Z. (1996) 'alt.civilizations.faq. Cyberspace as the Darker Side of the West', in Z. Sardar and J. R. Ravetz (eds), *Cyberfutures: Culture and Politics on the Information Superhighway*, London: Pluto Press.

Sassen, S. (1998) 'Losing Control: Sovereignty in the Age of Globalisation', public lecture given at the London School of Economics, 12 Feb.

Schwartz, E. (1997) *Webonomics: Nine Essential Principles for Growing your Business on the WWW*, New York: Broadway Books.

Solomon, R. (1998) 'Cutting the Gordian Knot', paper delivered at the ITS 1998, Stockholm, 17 June.

Steele, S. (1996) 'Taking a Byte Out of the First Amendment: How Free Is Speech in Cyberspace?' *Human Rights*, 23 (Spring).

Sussman, G. (1997) *Communication Technology and Politics in the Information Age*, London: Sage.

Tapscott, D. (1996) *The Digital Enterprise: Promise and Peril in the Age of Networked Intelligence*, New York: McGraw-Hill.

Taylor, C. (1990) 'What is Wrong with Negative Liberty', in D. Miller (ed.), *Liberty*, Oxford: Oxford University Press.

Taylor, C. (1990a) *Sources of the Self*, Cambridge: Cambridge University Press.

Turckle, S. (1995) *Life on the Screen: Identity in the Age of the Internet*, New York: Simon and Schuster.

Varian, H. (1996) 'Differential Pricing and Efficiency', *First Monday*, 14, 60.4.

Volkmer, I. (1996) 'Universalism and Particularism: The Problem of Cultural Sovereignty and Global Program Flow', available at http://ksgwww. harvard.edu/iip/volkmer.html and repr. in B. Kahin and C. Nesson (eds), *Borders in Cyberspace*, Cambridge, MA: MIT Press.

Walzer, M. (1983) *Spheres of Justice*, New York: Basic Books.

White House (1997) 'Press Release: Text of the President's Message to Internet Users', 1 July.

|4|

Alternative media, alternative texts?

Rethinking democratisation in the cultural industries

DAVID HESMONDHALGH

The radical wing of media and cultural studies has been unrelentingly critical of media organisations. Terms with negative connotations abound: conglomeration, commodification, the concentration of symbolic power in too
few hands. Undeniably, all these processes are features of the contemporary
media landscape. But students often complain that they are rarely given a
sense of what positive goals they might argue for, in calling for reform and
critique of the mass media. What forms might more democratically organised media take?

In fact, one positive concept has been dominant in the political economy
of culture in recent years: the public sphere, the ideal of a space of communication where people can participate equally, regardless of background,
and where reason, rather than power, will determine the outcomes of discussion (Habermas 1989 [1962]). While still a central issue in current
debates, the concept is tottering, close to collapse under the accumulated
weight of criticism. A particularly damaging critique has come from femi-
nists. Even those feminist writers who are sympathetic to the idea have worried that, as a model for mass communication, as well as in historical reality,
the bourgeois public sphere comes alarmingly close to a kind of gentlemen's
club (e.g. Fraser 1992).[1]

While recognising the very rich contributions made to media theory by
work on the public sphere, this chapter attempts to construct a positive
model of media democratisation which draws on a different theoretical
legacy often sidelined by those who have tried to apply Habermas's idea to
contemporary mass communication (and which has been even more marginalised by much cultural-studies writing). This is a tradition which focuses
more closely than the public-sphere model on the emancipatory possibilities

of organisational and technological innovation in the media. While nearly always critical of media organisations, it may also serve as a much-needed source of positive, idealistic thinking in an age of defeatism and miserable pragmatism. This legacy of writing often takes the work of Bertolt Brecht and Walter Benjamin as a starting-point, and examines how existing media structures might be radicalised through activism. Although it has roots in interwar German Marxian writing, the tradition is upheld principally among radical writers based in North America (e.g. Kellner 1985, Wasko and Mosco (eds) 1992, Downing 1995). The term I will use for this body of writing is *alternative media activism* (AMA). Emerging from attempts at intervention in media practice, it sometimes lacks the methodological rigour of theoretical work in other traditions. It is often prone to the criticism that it invests new technologies with too great a transformational potential. Nevertheless, the writings of Brecht, Benjamin and their later followers provide fertile ground for thinking about how the media might be changed for the better. In this brief survey, I will use this literature to outline some of the key goals of a radical media practice, as formulated by AMA writers. The aim is to lay out some criteria by which we might judge the success or otherwise of those cultural producers who attempt to bring about a democratic transformation of the way in which cultural texts and artefacts are produced and distributed. None of these criteria is uncontroversial or unambiguous, and I want to register debates and doubts about these terms, while retaining them as normative concepts. Reflecting my own research interests, I shall mainly draw here on examples from the music industry, but will refer throughout to other cultural industries too.[2]

The AMA literature has an additional advantage over scholarly work which has drawn on the idea of the public sphere and over much recent analytical work on the media in general. The critical-political economy tradition has enormously emphasised informational content over media form, and has tended to value cognitive and rational modes of thought over the aesthetic, the emotional and the affective (see McGuigan 1998 for a similar argument). Judged as a whole, the political economy approach, for all its strengths, can perhaps be fairly accused of treating entertainment as merely a *distraction*, a diversion from what it sees as the most desirable goal of mass communication: the activism of the concerned, rational, participatory citizen. Entertainment, according to this view, gets in the way of the kinds of serious public-affairs programmes which citizens might watch more of, were there not so many other, more trivial options available to them.

There is an essential point which must not be lost here. Citizens need to be informed about public life and good journalism can undoubtedly promote the pursuit of social justice and the abuse of social power. But it is vitally important too that issues of form and aesthetics are not dismissed, and that entertainment is not treated as though it must always be inferior to the presentation of information. Today, people in 'advanced' industrial societies are bombarded by the images, sounds and words of the entertainment industries every day of their lives. Any normative model of media democratisation will need to pay close attention to the aesthetics of entertainment. Only by understanding the enormously powerful affective role of such texts can we grasp the politics of contemporary culture.

To ignore issues of aesthetics has another unfortunate consequence besides this failure to address changing reality. It also serves to sideline the concerns of those who work within media organisations. For creative workers in such organisations constantly have to ask themselves what are ultimately aesthetic questions: how do we get our message across to audiences? what pleasures do we provide? what innovations might we bring about? how can we mark our work as different from that of our rivals? In my view, the AMA literature offers a much greater awareness of the politics of aesthetics than its rival intellectual traditions, but rather than treating the aesthetic as a realm autonomous of the dynamics of production, as in much cultural-studies work, AMA is concerned (though not always satisfactorily) with the relationship between the organisation of media production and the political-aesthetic nature of the product.

This dual concern with both process and product determines the structure of what follows. I begin with ways in which it might be possible to conceive of the democratisation of the means of cultural production (sections 1–4). I then move on to concepts which the alternative media literature has generated to discuss the transformation of the form and content of cultural products (5–6). As will become clear, the relationships between democratisation of the means of production and democratisation of the political-aesthetic nature of texts are too complex to define in a simple, programmatic manner. But the nature of such links needs to be interrogated rather than ignored.

1 Participation and access

One of the most widely cited texts in the AMA tradition is a brief passage by Brecht about radio, first published in 1932. These comments envisage the transformation of the medium from an apparatus of 'distribution' to one of 'communication' (Brecht 1978 [1932]: 52). The value appealed to here is a long-standing belief that widespread participation is at the heart of democratic activity, because it provides a check on the power of representatives, elected or otherwise. Much of the AMA literature has stressed the desirability of widening access in restrictive and exclusive media, in order to make available new voices, new experiences, and perspectives which would normally be excluded from the specialised, professional world of mainstream production. The most discussed example is the public-access television movement in the US (Kellner 1985, Boddy 1990, Anderson and Goldman 1993). Many of these AMA writers follow Brecht in looking to new or developing technologies as the means for greater participation.

The notions of access and participation can be woolly ones. For some activists, participation seems to be an end in itself. But the 'self-realisation'[3] of participants is not a sufficient criterion for judging the successful democratisation of a medium. Communication consists of more than just the sending or encoding of messages. The audiences for cultural artefacts and performances also need to be considered. How are these audiences reached? With what effect on the communication? What do audiences make of the performance or artefact in question? We need, then, to look at access to the *distribution* of cultural goods, as well as to their *production*.[4] To give one example of these issues from the music industry, there is evidence that large numbers of unskilled entrants (musicians and record-company staff) came into the music business market after punk and dance became prominent in British musical-cultural life, in the late 1970s and late 1980s respectively. But only where networks of retail and distribution were formed (see Hesmondhalgh 1997 on one such network, based around Rough Trade Records) was it possible for these new entrants to gain access to the higher levels of promotion and publicity needed to 'participate' on a scale which gained sustained national attention. To put all this simply, it is one thing for cheap technology to allow someone to make a record in her/his bedroom; it is quite another to sell that record to someone you have never met, who lives 300 miles away.

In examining access and participation, we also need to take account of the range of discourses in operation in a particular type of cultural work. Many musicians and music-industry entrepreneurs, for example, tend to speak disparagingly of professionalism, and choose to work in the music industry because it does not appear to have developed a set of professional codes. This has fed into the emphasis on deskilling in post-punk and in dance music culture, and has arguably encouraged access and participation. But there is also widespread admiration, often among the very same musicians and record-company workers, for processes of long-term aesthetic development which are possible only with professionalisation. Many enthusiastic amateurs find themselves having to learn professional skills 'on the job' in order to match the more established companies and entrepreneurs in a competitive market. These innovators then have to negotiate their own professionalisation, leading to many conflicts in 'alternative' media organisations over the extent to which an original democratising vision has been abandoned (see Hesmondhalgh 1999 for a study of such conflicts in indie/alternative rock).

The dynamics of the television industry offer a contrasting example. The costs of entry into this highly restricted world of production mean that 'alternative' television (as outlined for example by Boddy 1990) operates very much on the fringes of broadcasting institutions: rarely publicised, minimally resourced and hardly watched. There is a very strong professional discourse within television which places a high value on technical 'finish'. Training takes years and experience is hard to come by, even with the recent proliferation of channels across the world. It is very difficult to get to appear on television, whether in a paid capacity or in order to present a viewpoint. It is even harder to appear on your own terms, without being considerably constrained by the very tight presentational conventions of television. In Brecht's terms, then, television is hardly a medium of communication at all, rather it is one almost entirely of distribution. It would be foolhardy to predict that the proliferation of channels in the new broadcasting environment of the late 1990s and early twenty-first century will improve this situation. Many of the channels to which it will be possible for higher numbers of people to gain access, in terms of appearing or having their voices and opinions heard, will be confined to low-prestige, low-audience sectors, at least for the foreseeable future.

2 Collectivism, collaboration, co-operation

Today, there is still a widespread conception of cultural creativity which sees it in its highest form as the product of individual labour. Writers have pointed out the empirical inaccuracy of this image, and have shown that even the most seemingly individual, autonomous forms of fine art are the product of many individuals working together (e.g. Becker 1982, Wolff 1993). To value collaboration means taking an unfashionable attitude towards the politics of work. Increasingly, there is an assumption among even liberal and left-oriented professionals that meritocratic workplaces offer greater satisfactions and rewards than workplaces where the emphasis is on equality. In presenting this model of democratisation, however, I want to operate from a different assumption: that people operate better where there is a minimum degree of hierarchical control, and where there are high levels of equality of responsibility, opportunity and reward. An ideal is collaboration with genuine equality. This is never achieved in practice, in capitalist societies riddled with class, gender and ethnic divisions. However, the nearer particular moments come to this ideal, the more successful I think we should assume them to be in terms of democratisation, other things being equal.

Democratic and equal collaboration within a particular working situation is not progressive in itself, however. Many institutions operate with a high degree of internal democracy, but work as part of broader systems which are intensely hierarchical and exclusive. Prime examples would be the fellows of Oxbridge colleges, or professional partnerships of lawyers, accountants and doctors. Co-operation, then, is an external as well as an internal matter. The competitive nature of the cultural industries, and the celebration of enterprise which is often to be found within them, militate against systems of inter-firm co-operation. Nevertheless, there have been notable instances of *networks* of creative workers, entrepreneurs, technicians and others which served to overcome at least some of the cut-throat mentality of market thinking. In many instances, such networking has been carried out within the logic and mentality of the market: that is, it was done merely in order to achieve competitive advantage over firms outside the network. But there are cases where such connections have been forged specifically in order to transform the competitive nature of the cultural marketplace, and to create alliances against what were perceived to be hegemonic industrial, political and aesthetic forms. Herman and McChesney (1997: 200) offer some instances, such as the World Association of Community Radio Broadcasters (AMARC) or the Global Alternative Media Association (GAMA).

It is important not to romanticise collaboration. The practical difficulties involved in day-to-day collaboration on a piece of cultural work often go beyond those involved in networks based on occasional phone and e-mail contact. Some sociologists have suggested that music is particularly prone to collaboration in a whole range of expressive situations (Becker 1982), including the recording studio, as decisions are made about how best to communicate with an audience (Hennion 1990 [1983]). This is not to deny, as any musician will testify, that musical collaboration is riven with conflict. The point is that certain forms of musical practice defy the widespread conception of cultural labour I referred to above, which sees it as dependent, at its best, on individual talent or genius. Once recordings are introduced into the commercial system of circulation, however, this complex division of labour is effaced. Companies rely on the name of a musician to allow audiences to identify the likely sound of a particular recording. Thus, even though the recording might be a relatively collaborative act, involving the producer/sound mixer, engineer, record-company A&R representatives, the artist's manager, and so on, the final product is mainly credited to the musician or group who act as the public 'face' of the recording. This problem of authorship is also evident in the history of the cinema, where for many years there was a very strong division between commercial, entertainment cinema on the one hand and 'art' cinema on the other. In the latter branch, films were (and, to some degree, still are) identified with particular directors, or 'auteurs'.[5] As with the star system in the recording industry, a complex division of labour is here masked under the cloak of individualism.

So, in the world of the cultural industries, to what extent is co-operation and collaboration (rather than merely a complex division of labour) possible? Crucial aspects to consider here are *company size* and *ownership*. Much of the general literature on co-operative work suggests that democratic decision-making becomes more difficult as a firm grows (e.g. Rothschild and Whitt 1986: 91–5). One writer has suggested that workplace egalitarianism becomes impossible when general meetings of staff exceed the size where everyone could feasibly make a contribution (Russell 1985). Here we return to the qualified norm of participation suggested in the first section above. Small firms are places where owner-managers can maintain tyrannical domination over staff, with the right to hire and fire, unchecked by unionised labour. Some socialists have rejected claims for the progressive potential of smaller working units because they make collective action by labour more difficult. Others have quite rightly questioned the degree to which small cultural producers can be seen as evidence of a new, more democratic era in media production (e.g. Sparks 1994) or of a flexible, post-Fordist economy characteristic of 'New Times' (e.g. Aksoy and Robins 1992). But more benign owner-managers can produce an atmosphere of collaboration within and across firms, which, as some writers on co-operatives have pointed out, makes their companies more collaborative than co-operatives collectively owned but dominated by core personalities (Rothschild and Whitt 1986). Small workplaces are all too often riven with conflict and lost friendships, but they are also places of potential equality and co-operation.

Ownership too is a vital area of analysis in looking at cultural producers, of whatever size. In media and cultural studies, the main arena for debates on the importance, or otherwise, of ownership and control has been the sociology of journalism, particularly concerning the freedom of journalists to make decisions about their work independently of the interference of owners (e.g. Tunstall 1971, Hall et al. 1978, Curran 1990). Such work suggests that there are no fixed rules about how control is operated in cultural production companies. But, following Graham Murdock's important borrowing of the distinction between 'allocative' and 'operational' control from organisational sociology (Murdock 1982), I take it as axiomatic that the ultimate power over decisions about how the firm operates, particularly in matters of long-term 'allocative' strategy, rather than in everyday issues of 'operational control', lies with its owners. Company policy towards employees is inevitably compromised by the search for profit, though it is surely less compromised in some small companies, where enlightened owner-managers effectively manage the company for relatively little profit, than by the absolute obligation to produce profit for shareholders to be found in entertainment corporations. In summary, ownership, control and company size are important factors to investigate in discussing collaborative and co-operative aspects of the 'democratisation' of cultural production. Yet these have been strangely neglected in recent work on the production of culture.

3   Status and rewards

The low degree of democratisation in the cultural industries is manifested not only in inequalities in the power to make decisions affecting processes and outcomes, but also in unequal distribution of status and rewards available to cultural workers. The neglect of this issue in the sociology of culture has been remarkable. Many books exist on film, recording, broadcasting and publishing, and yet few make reference to the working conditions and financial recompense available to the people working in these industries.

Such issues have been absolutely central to the sociology of work in general, so why have they been marginalised in the study of *cultural* work? It may be that the sociology of culture has been unconsciously influenced by analyses which view creative artistic work as autonomous: the very form of analysis which it has often sought to critique. Another likely explanation is that the sociology of work often examines the type of waged work which prevailed in western societies from the industrial revolution until the 1980s. Creative professionals, by contrast, are often rewarded by copyright payments, and make their living by contracting themselves to a number of different organisations over their career. Given that much work is taking this more 'flexible' form (though that word masks the insecurities and anxieties surrounding such working conditions) perhaps the study of remuneration and status in the cultural industries can provide a template by which to look at changes in other sectors.

A rare analysis of the conditions of cultural workers is provided by Bernard Miège (though see also Gray and Seeber 1996 on labour relations in the arts and entertainment industries). In particular, Miège notes the reliance of cultural firms on the existence of 'vast reservoirs of under-employed artists' (Miège 1989: 72) and the generation, accentuation and use by such companies of 'contradictions' between various professionals in the cultural industries. These include contradictions between authors; between artists and other members of the artistic professions; and between authors and performers (Miège 1989: 87-93). Miège also notes the 'vitality of small "independent" companies' in providing 'greater independence' for artists to create their works, and a means of 'avoiding the leonine clauses' of contracts with major corporations (Miège 1989: 90). Miège is unusual, then, in recognising the democratising potential to be found in small cultural producers.

The relationship between the commercial company and its creative artists is at the heart of the notion of democratisation in the cultural industries. In the music industry, this relationship is embodied in the contract between the two parties. There are three main types of contract that a musician might sign: management, publishing and recording. Publishing and recording deals generally take the following form. The musicians agree to render their services exclusively to the company for a specified period and in certain specified territories. In return, the company will normally make commitments to promote the work of the artists. The musicians are paid an advance and then, when such an advance has been recouped via sales, they are paid a royalty. The long history of dubious contracts and career-breaking rip-offs cannot be told here.[6] But two main areas of general controversy can be identified, relating to the standard advance-royalty/exclusivity contract between musicians and company.

The first area concerns the financial rewards available for artists. The advance is essentially a loan against money which the musicians' recordings will make. Repayment is 'cross-collateralised' against costs such as recording and touring. In many cases, the advance is never recouped and musicians can be in debt to their record company for many years. Many young bands enter into this system unaware of the difficulties of recouping the substantial advances that they initially welcome. The level of royalty rate is set in the initial contract as a certain percentage of retail sales. Generally, the level of the royalty rises as the artist makes more records – the justification for this is that the company has to invest more resources initially, in order to establish the artist's career. In most contracts, however, costs are still recoupable against royalties – in other words, artists pay for their recording and for many promotional expenses out of their earnings. Yet the company retains the lion's share of the money and retains control of copyrights – increasingly, the source of much of the wealth in the cultural industries.

The second area of controversy relates to the artistic autonomy of artists and the level of commitment shown by a company to an artist's output. A particularly important issue in the music business in recent years has been the restraints on artists brought about by the long-term nature of the recording and/or publishing contract. Although established star names are able to negotiate relatively high royalty rates, many contracts remain very long-term in nature – and this is actually a disadvantage for the artist. Normally, the company has a right to exercise an option or a series of options to retain the artist's services. The standard contract is asymmetrical, however, in that the artist must fulfil certain criteria if s/he wants to be retained by the company, but s/he cannot choose to leave. These criteria will usually include sales – which are dependent on the efforts of the record company. A danger for the artist in being held to a long-term contract is that the sympathetic staff who signed her/him may leave the label, to be replaced by personnel with little interest in her/his work; the other is that any change of direction by a musician may receive an unsympathetic reception from the record company.[7]

At various independent record companies associated with the punk genre, new ways of dealing with artists were developed which challenged the standard arrangements in the music industry. Deals with musicians were often on a 50-50 basis, rather than the usual single-figure percentage royalty rates. Long-term contracts were rejected in favour of deals based on personal trust. The aim of such deals was to be as 'musician-centred' as possible. Contracts were avoided on the grounds that the standard contracts were loaded in favour of companies and that if the personal trust between musicians and companies broke down there was no point in pursuing the relationship anyway. These companies generally favoured record-by-record deals, which gave artists the freedom to move on to other companies, should they so wish. The 50-50 deals meant that payment rates for musicians were enormously higher than the single-figure percentage royalty rates common even for established bands on major labels. If a band could achieve high sales on such a deal, they would make a great deal of money.

In the end, the post-punk rebellion was unsuccessful; and many musicians became disenchanted with the lack of promotion which such small companies could provide. But the punk intervention serves as an example of attempts to transform the apparatus of *commercial* cultural production. All too often, the literature on 'alternative media' is confined to very small, marginal interventions, operating so far outside most people's experience of popular culture that they are known only to small groups of activists and intellectuals. Here, however, activism took place actually in the field of commercial entertainment production itself.

4   Decentralisation

Some progressive forms of cultural policy, often under the influence of the AMA literature, orient themselves towards the geographical decentralisation of media industries.[8] Although decentralisation is not a sufficient condition for democratisation, there are reasons for thinking it is a necessary one. In Britain, for example, nearly all the principal media industries are heavily concentrated around London and south-east England. In spite of the efforts of cultural regulation over the last 40 years, television has become heavily centralised too (Robins and Cornford 1992). One of the progressive aims of public-service broadcasting was to ensure provision for the regions, but for the London-centred British audio-visual media such regional bases are often considered to be 'backwaters', nightmare postings to be endured rather than learned from. Few British cities have developed successful internal markets able to sustain jobs and develop skills at a local level. Such centralisation may well encourage aesthetic standardisation, whereby distinctive regional ways of experiencing the world, and of representing that experience, are marginalised.

Alongside the centralisation of talent and resources within a particular nation state, the international centralisation of cultural production also needs to be stressed, in thinking about how the media might be democratised on a global level. Because of the international domination of English as the language of business and popular culture, Britain and the USA are at the 'core' rather than the 'periphery' of many media industries. But this is of little consolation to those cultural workers within Britain and the USA who have been unable to gain access to centralised resources from their regional bases.

Different dynamics of decentralisation and centralisation can be observed in the music industry. Music is in itself relatively decentralised as a form of expression, partly because its instruments are often portable, and relatively inexpensive. Certain skills can be self-taught, or passed on from person to person. Technologically and commercially mediated music, in the modern world, is to be found everywhere. There are many examples, then, of the growth of local recording and live 'scenes' in numerous different genres. But opportunities for building careers around music, and for communicating on a wider scale than the local, remain unevenly distributed. In Britain, for example, the growth of a scene around a particular city is soon dissipated as musicians and other creative personnel are lured away to London for more money and greater recognition.

5 Mobilisation

Sections 1–4 of this chapter represent a programmatic statement about the undemocratic nature of contemporary cultural production and a typology of it how it might be democratised. I have referred in passing to how this undemocratic state of affairs might be transformed in practice by cultural activism. These are transformations which, in my view, would be desirable in any form of work. But the cultural industries are different from other industries because they are concerned with the production of signifying systems, of aesthetic and informational objects. How might we think about the democratisation of *texts*? In a classic work of alternative media activism, Hans Magnus Enzensberger lists 'mobilisation' as one of the key features of a democratic media system (Enzensberger 1974: 113). This refers to the way cultural products can encourage a critical attitude towards social and artistic conditions, and can initiate action in response to those conditions. Mobilisation is a potentially useful concept here in drawing links between aesthetic strategies and other levels of analysis of media organisations: discursive, technological, industrial, legal. But, as with the concepts already discussed, I want to signal my caution in using this term.

The main problem with the concept of mobilisation as a way of fusing attention to textual aesthetics and to social relations is that it risks collapsing aesthetics into the notions of access and participation discussed above. This is the case in Walter Benjamin's often-cited but, in my opinion, over-rated essay, 'The Author as Producer', a starting-point for much AMA literature. Having pointed out the importance of aesthetic strategy as well as political inclination, Benjamin then defines progressive formal innovation in terms of its capacity to mobilise other cultural producers (although he never uses the German word for 'mobilisation'): '*An author who teaches writers nothing, teaches no one.* What matters, therefore, is the exemplary character of production, which is able first to induce other producers to produce, and second to put an improved apparatus at their disposal' (Benjamin 1978 [1934]: 233, original emphasis). But then the 'improved' nature of this apparatus is defined chiefly by reference to the fact that it makes consumers into producers. So the second example of 'what matters' sounds very much like the first. As is often the case in his writing, the example Benjamin gives is of Brecht's epic theatre which, by drawing on elements of the new arts of film and radio, and by stripping theatre down to its 'primitive elements', turned the passivity of theatrical musicians, writers and critics into something more active. Brecht provides cultural performances which supposedly mobilise audiences and which do so, at least partly, by engaging with popular forms. It is apparent too, from other key works of Benjamin (most notably 1973 [1936]) that these popular forms are interesting to him because they offer technological innovations which potentially provide new ways of understanding the world.

Benjamin's call for cultural producers to address not only issues of form and content, but also their position in a production 'apparatus', is important. This is a form of cultural politics preferable to those versions of cultural studies which stress the activity of *audiences* as a sufficient means for judging the effectiveness of the aesthetic strategies and formal innovations adopted by producers (e.g. Fiske 1987). However, Benjamin's conception of the importance of form in 'The Author as Producer' is limited. Technique, Benjamin implies, is good where it encourages participation; and participation is valuable for its own sake. This reduces the problem of the political aesthetic as to whether technique produces more art by more people. Participation is an essential part of any democratic model of cultural production, but here it seems to be portrayed as an end in itself. This merely defers the question of what makes for a radical political aesthetic, rather than answering it.

Another problem with the concept of mobilisation is that it carries with it connotations of a view which sees the best art as that which brings about activism in support of a political cause. Although I think it is important to maintain, against an aestheticist position, art's ability to suppress or promote awareness of prevailing social conditions, I do not believe that creative expression can be judged purely on the basis of its political efficacy in this way.[9] It must be possible to pursue a broader notion of what 'good' cultural production might involve than that occasionally found on the far left, where films, songs, books and so on are sometimes judged more or less entirely on the basis of whether or not they bring forward the date of the socialist revolution. For that view downplays the psychological, emotional and private resonances of cultural expression too much. As Wolff (1993) observes, it fails to recognise the specificity of the aesthetic realm. The widespread feeling among people of liberal and socialist views that an exclusively political reading of culture is insufficient and unsatisfactory has led to a crisis in the 1990s in the notion of the political aesthetic and I return to these issues in the next section.

In spite of its drawbacks, I still think the notion of mobilisation might be useful. From the vantage-point of the 1990s, perhaps it is possible to put forward a more fully developed conception of mobilisation, by combining its connotations of participation with the idea of working collaboratively and collectively. This is stressed more intermittently than other concepts, such as access and co-operation, in the AMA literature, but it is an essential component of any more fully developed politics of cultural production. So, in order to develop the concept further, we might ask: what kind of participation is encouraged by the radical text? Does it genuinely involve a reaching out towards the creativity of others, an attempt to temper one's own individual vision of what constitutes 'good' cultural work by taking into account the very different notions of value which might be produced in other communities, from other points of view? By asking these questions, it might be possible to update the concerns of the German interwar Marxists to take more fully into account recent debates about cultural difference and respect for the 'Other'.

6   Quality, diversity and innovation

The three main ways in which commentators have attempted to develop a systematic language concerning aesthetics in media theory have been via the notions of quality, diversity and innovation.

The difficulties surrounding the term *quality* in television discourse are well established, and indicate some of the problems of developing political-aesthetic criteria for judging media texts, in particular popular cultural texts. The term was for many years associated with the application of aesthetic criteria derived from the literary novel and from the theatre (i.e. from 'high' culture forms) to television. As Corner (1995: 168–71) suggests, the specific properties of television make the use of such criteria inappropriate for use in public debate about the merits or otherwise of the medium: it is, in spite of the rise of narrowcasting, a heterogeneous medium; it uses many other forms besides the single piece of fiction characteristic of theatre and cinema; and it addresses people in their everyday lives, as a 'relaxant' rather than as a special event. While this makes it a powerful medium, it also means that individual television programmes are less 'dense' in symbolic meaning than other expressive forms. Reacting against the dismissal of television characteristic of much public debate, media and cultural studies in the 1970s and 1980s therefore tended to shun the word 'quality', preferring political analysis to moral-aesthetic evaluation. But, by the late 1980s, media and cultural studies writers started to argue for the restoration of issues of evaluation and quality in political debates about television, partly as a means of defending public-service broadcasting against neo-conservative 'deregulation' (see Brunsdon 1990, Mulgan 1990). Nevertheless, problems with the term 'quality' persist. Is it possible to make general statements about what constitutes good television, or good cinema, or good popular music? Or should each popular genre be judged only on its own terms – that is, according to the expectations of value which the genre implicitly sets up? There is little sign of a resolution to these issues and some political economy writers have resorted to the concept of *diversity* as a means by which to assess the level of democratisation in a medium at the level of outcome. There is a tendency in such literature for diversity merely to be stated as a goal (e.g. Murdock 1990: 81–2) or for dubious statistical measurements to be used, making reference to an industry's own marketing classifications as the basis for a typology of genre (e.g. Christianen 1995).

A richer tradition, which in many respects runs in parallel with the AMA literature I have discussed above, is the Marxian analysis of the politics of aesthetic strategies (e.g. Bloch *et al.* 1980). The dominant strand of such writing has seen formal *innovation* as the basis of a progressive political aesthetic. The most impressive and forbidding attempt to develop such an aesthetic was that of Theodor Adorno. Like many other modernists, Marxist and otherwise, Adorno saw art as radical where it subverted traditional, established forms. But Adorno was careful to distinguish between the 'pseudo-individualisation' characteristic of most commodified cultural production (see Adorno 1990 [1941]) and the authentic innovation provided, in his view, by 'autonomous' art, which could offer a critique of a whole society (the 'totality') through experiments in the formal language of a particular artistic medium (Adorno 1976). Adorno and other critical modernists' focus on formal innovation has come under attack from postmodernist cultural theory, which is less concerned with the need for innovation and (to cut a long story short) more with the undermining of authority through parody, irony and self-referentiality. An interesting intervention in this respect has been made by Georgina Born. From a position sceptical of both modernism and postmodernism, Born (1987: 64–8) has criticised efforts to apply modernism's notion of shock and negation as social critique to popular culture, on the grounds that such efforts universalise modernism's strategies, making them trans-historical and cyclical, rather than recognising them as the product of very specific conjunctions of art and politics. But, if a modernist, avant-garde notion of innovation is no longer applicable, this raises the question of what democratising political-aesthetic strategies are appropriately imaginable for now or for the near future. Postmodernist aesthetics aims at developing new models, but as Born and others (e.g. Goodwin 1991) have shown, it often makes premature claims about the changing nature of contemporary cultural production, for example the degree to which 'high' and 'low' cultural forms have collapsed into one another. Again, we see evidence here of a crisis in the notion of the political aesthetic, and of the difficulty of talking about the democratisation of *texts*.

In calling for recognition and analysis of the aesthetic realm, there is a danger of *idealism* (in one of its philosophical senses, rather than in the everyday sense of an unpragmatic pursuit of ideals): of attributing too much autonomy and explanatory power to the role of ideas and consciousness. Adorno and other modernists were perhaps guilty of this. In Adorno's work, good art is attributed with enormous powers of social change; and bad culture is symptomatic of the most fundamental flaws in societies. In spite of the dangers of such idealism, it is still important to recognise the provisional effectiveness of cultural products in asking audiences to reflect on, resist and challenge prevailing political conditions. I say 'provisional' because there are no fixed laws for what constitutes progressive aesthetic practice. As Janet Wolff puts it:

The conditions under which art may be effective, politically and historically, are determined both by the nature of cultural production at that moment, and its possibilities, and by the nature of contemporary society, and in particular of its general ideology.

(Wolff 1993: 85)

This effectivity is a matter not only of the cognitive content of cultural products, of the 'message' behind the narrative of a film, or the words of a song. It also concerns issues of form, which are often much more difficult to talk about. As film-makers, musicians and television personnel find new forms (new sounds, styles, editing techniques, visual sensibilities, modes of address) which provide new pleasures for audiences, they raise questions about cultural change. At its most powerful, the arrival of a new style can bring about a sense of alliance between people relatively marginalised in the unequal world of contemporary capitalism. While the work of translating such feelings into concrete action for social change might still be difficult, such emotions are none the less significant. So we need the concepts of mobilisation, quality, diversity and innovation as potential guides for assessing aesthetic democratisation, but we need to move beyond them in order to develop clearer and fuller ways to think about aesthetics after modernism.

Towards a model

I have briefly outlined six categories which, although they employ ambivalent and controversial terms, might be used as a normative basis for looking at democratisation in the cultural industries. I need hardly point out that the six categories of factor would interact in complex and unexpected ways. Reduced to its bare bones, however, the model works in something like the following way. An industry, sector, organisation or firm is democratised where:

1 participation and access are widened;
2 producers are more likely to act collaboratively and co-operatively than competitively and in circumstances of hierarchical control;
3 there is a greater equality of reward, opportunity and conditions for creative workers;
4 resources and talent are spread more widely and relatively evenly across geographical space;
5 the texts produced and circulated promote the adventurous and critical participation of consumers, encouraging them to produce as well as receive;
6 high-quality, diverse, innovative and adventurous texts emerge from such participation.

Unless I felt that the current situation in the cultural industries was relatively undemocratic, an examination of these issues would hardly be worth undertaking. There is a surprisingly widespread view among those who work in the media that the current state of things is more or less satisfactory. This can perhaps best be summarised in the comments of one industry insider at a music-industry conference I once attended, to the effect that there was no need for local or central government to fund any cultural activity, as the free market ensured that anyone with talent would eventually, given enough perseverance, 'make it'. But who decides who has the talent? And shouldn't cultural expression be about more than a handful of well-rewarded stars and a vast pool of under-paid strugglers? The music-industry insider comment reveals the need to think carefully and systematically about the nature of media organisations today.

I have also argued that, in examining such issues, process and product need to be considered in tandem. In exploring media democratisation, the provisional effectiveness of aesthetics I mentioned above can never be understood in isolation from the social and institutional conditions of cultural production. A particularly difficult challenge will be to explore the relationship between such conditions and the results which cultural producers create from such conditions. Do attempts to democratise the way that the media are produced and distributed result in 'better' media texts? Do alternative media organisations produce alternative media texts? The simple answer is: not necessarily. There is no simple correlation between democratic forms of production and 'good' oppositional texts.[10] The vast resources of the most hierarchical and exploitative corporations allow them to sign up talented and highly motivated people to produce brilliant, funny, powerful films, TV shows and records. It is important not to dismiss the pleasures of *Seinfeld* or the Fugees (both produced and distributed by major corporations) as mere exploitation and appropriation. Hence my arguments above for the need to think through issues of entertainment aesthetics. But more inspiring is the triumph of those who manage to produce moments of creative excitement and adventure from 'outside' that system, against the odds, and often with disregard for the accumulation of wealth and status which might be available elsewhere.

Notes

1 A very useful survey of debates about the public sphere is provided by Thompson (1993). See also Calhoun (ed.) (1992).
2 There is no space here to deal with important questions concerning whether information technology has democratised the media and cultural industries, in particular about whether the Internet has democratised mass communication. But I hope to provide a framework which other, more qualified commentators might be able to use in order to consider such questions with clarity.
3 The term used by political philosopher Jon Elster to criticise the notion of 'participatory democracy' (cited in Hagen 1992).

4 The importance of distribution to understanding power in the cultural industries is a vital insight of the political-economy approach to mass communications (see in particular Miège 1989 and Garnham 1990). Sociology of culture has also paid significant attention to distribution (e.g. Becker 1982).

5 Where the directors of commercial, entertainment cinema were identified, it was often retrospectively by cinema obsessives and critics, rather than as part of the promotion of a film.

6 Some important developments in contractual law in the entertainment industry are surveyed by Greenfield and Osborn (1994); and, in a journalistic account, by Garfield (1986).

7 This was a central issue in Panayioutou versus Sony Music Entertainment (UK) Limited – the George Michael case. Michael tried unsuccessfully to argue in this important dispute with his record company that his long-term contract with Sony was a 'restraint of trade' under European law.

8 See, for example, the recommendations of the report on Greater Manchester, by the Centre for Employment Research (1989).

9 This, in my view, is a problem in the work of some of the US-based inheritors of German Marxism's analysis of culture, for example Douglas Kellner's readings of 'media culture' (Kellner 1995).

10 Born (1993: 285) makes a similar point when she writes that 'institutional alterity does not produce aesthetic difference or political dissent, just as inhabiting the institutional mainstream does not completely preclude them'.

References

Adorno, T. (1976) *Philosophy of Modern Music*, New York: Seabury Press.

Adorno, T. (1990 [1941]) 'On Popular Music', in S. Frith and A. Goodwin (eds), *On Record*, New York: Pantheon.

Aksoy, A. and Robins, K. (1992) 'Hollywood for the 21st Century: Global Competition for Critical Mass in Image Markets', *Cambridge Journal of Economics*, 16: 1–22.

Anderson, K. and Goldson, A. (1993) 'Alternating Currents: Alternative Television Inside and Outside the Academy', *Social Text*, 35: 56–71.

Becker, H. S. (1982) *Art Worlds*, Berkeley: University of California Press.

Benjamin, W. (1973 [1936]) 'The Work of Art in the Age of Mechanical Reproduction', in *Illuminations*, London: Fontana.

Benjamin, W. (1978 [1934]) 'The Author as Producer', in *Reflections*, New York: Schocken.

Bloch, E., Lukacs, G., Brecht, B., Benjamin, W. and Adorno, T. (1980) *Aesthetics and Politics*, London: Verso.

Boddy, W. (1990) 'Alternative Television in the United States', *Screen*, 31.1: 91–101.

Born, G. (1987) 'On Modern Music Culture: Shock, Pop and Synthesis', *New Formations*, 2: 51–78.

Born, G. (1993) 'Afterword: Music Policy, Aesthetic and Social Difference', in T. Bennett, S. Frith, L. Grossberg, J. Shepherd and G. Turner (eds), *Rock and Popular Music*, London: Routledge.

Brecht, B. (1978 [1932]) 'The Radio as an Apparatus of Communication', in J. Willett (ed. and trans.), *Brecht on Theatre*, London: Eyre Methuen.

Brunsdon, C. (1990) 'Problems with Quality', *Screen* 31.1: 67–90.

Calhoun, C. (ed.) (1992) *Habermas: Critical Debates*, Cambridge, MA: MIT Press.

Centre for Employment Research (1989) *The Culture Industry: The Economic*

Importance of the Arts and Cultural Industries in Greater Manchester, Manchester: Centre for Employment Research, Manchester Polytechnic.

Christianen, M. (1995) 'Cycles in Symbol Production? A New Model to Explain Concentration, Diversity and Innovation in the Music Industry', *Popular Music*, 14.1: 55–94.

Corner, J. (1995) *Television Form and Public Address*, London: Edward Arnold.

Curran, J. (1990) 'Culturalist Perspectives of News Organizations', in M. Ferguson (ed.), *Public Communication: The New Imperatives*, London: Sage.

Downing, J. (1995) 'Alternative Media and the Boston Tea Party', in J. Downing, A. Mohammadi and A. Sreberny-Mohammadi (eds), *Questioning the Media*, 2nd edn, London: Sage.

Enzensberger, H. M. (1974) *The Consciousness Industry*, New York: Seabury Press.

Fiske, J. (1987) *Television Culture*, London: Methuen.

Fraser, N. (1992) 'Rethinking the Public Sphere: A Contribution to the Critique of Actually Existing Democracy', in C. Calhoun (ed.), *Habermas: Critical Debates*, Cambridge, MA: MIT Press.

Garfield, S. (1986) *Expensive Habits*, London: Faber and Faber.

Garnham, N. (1990) *Capitalism and Communication*, London: Sage.

Goodwin, A. (1991) 'Popular Music and Postmodern Theory', *Cultural Studies*, 5.2: 174–90.

Gray, L. S. and Seeber, R. L. (1996) *Under the Stars: Essays on Labor Relations in Arts and Entertainment*, Ithaca, NY and London: Cornell University Press/ILR Press.

Greenfield, S. and Osborn, G. (1994) 'Sympathy for the Devil? Contractual Constraint and Artistic Autonomy in the Entertainment Industry', *Media Law and Practice*, 15: 117–27.

Habermas, J. (1989 [1962]) *The Structural Transformation of the Public Sphere*, Cambridge, MA: MIT Press.

Hagen, I. (1992) 'Democratic Communication: Media and Social Participation', in J. Wasko and V. Mosco (eds), *Democratic Communications in the Information Age*, Toronto: Garamond Press.

Hall, S., Critcher, C., Jefferson, T., Clarke, J. and Roberts, B. (1978) *Policing the Crisis*, Basingstoke: Macmillan.

Hennion, A. (1990 [1983]) 'The Production of Success: An Anti-Musicology of the Pop Song', in S. Frith and A. Goodwin (eds), *On Record*, New York: Pantheon.

Herman, E. S. and McChesney, R. W. (1997) *The Global Media*, London: Cassell.

Hesmondhalgh, D. (1997) 'Post-punk's Attempt to Democratise the Music Industry: The Success and Failure of Rough Trade', *Popular Music*, 16.3: 255–74.

Hesmondhalgh, D. (1999) 'Indie: The Aesthetics and Institutional Politics of a Popular Music Genre', *Cultural Studies*, 13.1: 34–61.

Kellner, D. (1985) 'Public Access Television: Alternative Views', *Radical Science Journal*, 16: 79–92.

Kellner, D. (1995) *Media Culture*, London and New York: Routledge.

McGuigan, J. (1998) 'What Price the Public Sphere?', in D. Thussu (ed.), *Electronic Empires*, London: Arnold.

Miège, B. (1989) *The Capitalization of Cultural Production*, New York: International General.

Mulgan, G. (ed.) (1990) *Questions of Quality*, London: British Film Institute.

Murdock, G. (1982) 'Large Corporations and the Control of the Communications Industries', in M. Gurevitch, T. Bennett, J. Curran and J. Wollacott (eds), *Culture, Society and the Media*, London: Methuen.

Murdock, G. (1990) 'Television and Citizenship: In Defence of Public Broadcasting', in A. Tomlinson (ed.), *Consumption, Identity and Style*, London: Routledge.

Robins, K. and Cornford, J. 'What is "Flexible" About Independent Producers?', *Screen* 33.2: 190–200.

Rothschild, J. and Whitt, J. A. (1986) *The Cooperative Workplace*, Cambridge: Cambridge University Press.

Russell, R. (1985) *Sharing Ownership in the Workplace*, Albany, NY: SUNY Press.

Sparks, C. (1994) 'Independent Production: Unions and Casualisation', in S. Hood (ed.), *Behind the Screens*, London: Lawrence and Wishart.

Thompson, J. B. (1993) 'The Theory of the Public Sphere', *Theory, Culture and Society*, 10.3: 173–89.

Tunstall, J. (1971) *Journalists At Work*, London: Constable.

Wasko, J. and Mosco, V. (eds) (1992) *Democratic Communications in the Information Age*, Toronto: Garamond Press.

Wolff, J. (1993) *The Social Production of Art*, 2nd edn, Basingstoke: Macmillan.

|5|

Broadcasting deregulation in Turkey

Uniformity within diversity

DILRUBA ÇATALBAŞ

In the course of the 1990s the private broadcasters which beamed their signals from various European countries paved the way for a completely new phase in Turkish broadcasting. Ironically, absolute state control over the airwaves was replaced by total anarchy which lasted for 4 years. Nearly a decade later the Turkish broadcast-media sector seemed to have achieved a precarious stability. However, similarly to the situation in the country itself, contradictions continue to co-exist in the audio-visual system: freedom goes hand in hand with heavy supervision of broadcasts; fierce competition disguises extensive cross-ownership and concentration; the abundance and diversity of new outlets nurtures uniformity and mediocrity in programming.

This chapter is an attempt to assess the impact of privatisation on television programme provision and news and current affairs broadcasting in its early years and critically evaluate its heritage up to the present day. In doing so, it also briefly explores the political, economic and social background against which these changes have happened in order to reveal the complexity of the interactions between wider changes in society and media. It argues that although Turkish audiences today have alternatives to the public broadcaster, TRT, the diversity and quality of television programme supply continue to be restricted by market forces because the mainstream channels follow the successful formula and provide very similar schedules, conspicuously lacking distinction and imagination. It also contends that the ideological plurality and diversity brought about by privatisation are accompanied by certain malignant tendencies such as sensationalisation, trivialisation and commercialisation which affect particularly main evening newscasts.

Deregulation à la Turque

With the launch of the first ever Turkish private channel, Star, on 1 March 1990, the 60-year-old state monopoly in Turkey came to an abrupt end. The successful launch of Star by Magic Box Inc. proved the ineffectualness of the laws protecting the state monopoly in the age of satellites. The fact that Magic Box was partly owned by the son of the late President Turgut Özal led to a widespread conviction that the *de facto* privatisation of broadcasting had the implicit support of the then Motherland Party government. Özal himself had commented during an interview in 1990 that the existing broadcasting legislation in Turkey did not outlaw satellite channels (*Cumhuriyet*, 13 May 1990). Thus, electronic media suddenly became one of the most promising fields of investment for Turkish entrepreneurs. Soon a host of local channels owned by local businessmen and municipal authorities opened the way for localisation and decentralisation of broadcasting. Municipal authorities in the three largest provinces, Istanbul, Izmir and Ankara, controlled by the Social Democratic Populist Party (SDPP), were among the pioneers. Initially, local governments used their resources to relay signals from private channels into their constituencies, thus immensely helping new media to increase their area of penetration. Later, a large number of municipal authorities began to introduce their own radio and television stations. Local authorities, which promoted their initiatives as a step forward for pluralism, had to face severe attacks concerning political and financial accountability. Private channels, however, were criticised because of their unashamedly profit-oriented attitude. Private television channels which disobeyed all regulations and violated the rules on copyright and advertising claimed that as satellite broadcasters they were not obliged to abide by Turkish laws. However, these allegedly 'foreign' channels were aiming directly at Turkish audiences and drawing their advertising revenues from Turkey. They also made use of the cable networks of a state institution, the Post Telegraph Telephone Company, PTT, and even set up their own transmitters on Turkish soil. Hence, although the privatisation of Turkish broadcasting was initiated by the satellite ventures, it was through the support of the municipal authorities and the PTT that it became an irreversible process. By November 1994 there were 372 television stations in Turkey, including 11 national ones, and more than 1500 radio stations (*Yeni Günaydin*, 21 Nov. 1994).

This abrupt and chaotic transformation deeply shook TRT, resulting in the loss of not only its central position but also a significant proportion of its viewers and advertising revenue. By the mid-1990s, TRT was suffering from a deep financial crisis and seemed unable to compete with its commercial rivals. The proliferation of new outlets also caused anarchy in the airwaves and completely crippled the legislation. As policy-makers appeared unable or unwilling to make the necessary legal amendments, the politics of broadcasting in Turkey came to be determined by the politicians' attitudes to day-to-day developments.

Posterior legalisation

For 3 years private media in Turkey operated in a completely illegal, or as some commentators put it, extra-legal fashion. What happened in Turkish broadcasting resembled the similarly chaotic transformation of Italian broadcasting. In Turkey as well

> (i)t was not so much statutory law but the dynamics of the broadcast-ing markets that pushed the developments along. Law had to step aside or be modified when it was seen as a hindrance to the expansion of this market.
>
> (Hoffmann-Riem 1992: 153)

Nevertheless, the privatisation of the Italian electronic media had been based on the ruling of the Constitutional Court in 1976 which had acknowl-edged the right of private investors to set up local stations (Mazzoleni 1992). In Turkey, however, the Constitutional Court ruled that no institu-tion other than TRT should be allowed to broadcast unless the relevant clauses of the 1982 Constitution and of Broadcasting Law No. 2954 were amended.[1] In other words, the new players in Turkey did not have any legal pretext but were encouraged by the blossoming advertising market and the increasing popularity of private media. Their confidence was also bolstered by the statements of politicians promising to 'legalise' them. Even though the very existence of private media was a clear violation of the constitution and of the broadcasting law, politicians did not hesitate to appear on private television and radio stations. Moreover, despite their illegality, at least in broadcasting law, private companies were extended generous public subsi-dies. In addition to the direct transfer of financial resources, these compa-nies were also permitted a 30 per cent investment reduction and immunity from import taxes.

Although there appeared to be a broad agreement among the major polit-ical parties that the privatisation of broadcasting, already a *de facto* devel-opment, was not only inevitable but also desirable, Article 133 of the 1982 Constitution which safeguarded the state monopoly could not be changed until 8 July 1993. However, it was not before 13 April 1994 that the polit-ical parties finally came to an agreement on the new broadcasting law, No. 3984. During the 4-year-long proceedings there were intensive speculations and lobbying attempts by private media interests and advertisers who were fiercely critical of the provisions concerning ownership and advertising restrictions. Law No. 3984 stated that one company could not own more than one television station at the same time. While the maximum amount of shares which could be possessed by the same person or by a foreign investor was limited to 20 per cent, advertising airtime was restricted to 15 per cent of daily transmission hours and 20 per cent of any one hour.[2] Other contested features of the new law concerned the composition and funding of the Radio and Television Supreme Council which was formed as the new supervisory body of broadcasting. Law No. 3984 asserted that the supreme council would be composed of nine members, five of whom would be chosen by parliament from among the 10 candidates put forward by the government. The remaining four would be chosen from among eight candidates proposed by the opposition parties. This settlement, which did not include other democratic institutions, created a supreme council prone to political favouritism. Furthermore, private media spokespersons condemned the stipulation that TRT and the private channels pay 4 per cent of their monthly advertising revenues to the supreme council. From the day of its approval, Law No. 3984 has often been subject to calls for amendments by private media interests, journalists' associations and political parties.

Politics and broadcasting

The privatisation of Turkish broadcasting was as much the outcome of the prevalent political and economic spirit, which favoured the strengthening of a free-market economy and the expansion of democratic rights and freedoms, as of satellite technology. The roots of the political, economic and social conditions which influenced the evolution of Turkish broadcasting in the 1990s go back to the previous decade, in which the military take-over on 12 September 1980 was a turning-point. The two interrelated processes that distinguished this decade were the constitutional change effected by the military regime in 1982 and economic restructuring carried out by the subsequent civilian governments of the Motherland Party (Heper 1990a).

On 6 November 1983, at the end of the first elections following the 1980 coup, the Motherland Party of Turgut Özal emerged as the single most important political party in Turkey. The MP government pursued an economic programme which advocated a greater reliance on market forces. The stabilisation and structural adjustment achieved by the previous military government, in which Özal had been responsible for the economy, was successfully continued after 1983 by a period of liberalisation and acceleration of economic growth (Önis 1991). However, although the MP government invariably declared its support for privatisation, it did not attempt to abolish the state monopoly over broadcasting. The post-1980 regime had introduced some new provisions in Law No. 2954 that consolidated the influence of government over the state broadcaster. MP's enthusiastic exploitation of this opportunity seriously irritated opposition parties. Especially after the annulment of its autonomous status in 1971, TRT has always been caught in the cross-fire between government and opposition. When they are in the opposition, politicians argue that the impartiality of TRT cannot be realised unless its autonomy is restored. But they forget their promises when they assume power.

The second MP government, 1987–91, responded to calls for the privatisation of broadcasting by proposing an expansion in independent programme production (Hürriyet Vakfı 1988). Although MP governments gave only half-hearted support for privatisation of broadcasting, they actively encouraged growth and technological development in telecommunications and broadcasting. In 1990 the Turkish PTT became the first among its counterparts in 24 OECD (Organisation for Economic Cooperation and Development) countries to spend 80 per cent of its revenues on new investments (Geray 1993). In the 1990s PTT embarked on another venture to launch the first ever Turkish satellite, TÜRKSAT, by 1994. The PTT was confident that the TÜRKSAT project, which included two communications satellites, 'would enter Turkey among those countries which use the technologies of the 21st century' (PTT Genel Müdürlügü 1993). It was also planned that TÜRKSAT should be used for telecommunications and broadcasting links with the central Asian republics. At the beginning of the 1990s Turkey, exhausted by the negative attitude of the European Union towards its application, had been searching for new political and commercial alliances. The newly independent Turkic states of central Asia were seen as a natural area of expansion. In parallel with the progress achieved in telecommunications a similar development also took place in broadcasting. Prior to the introduction of private satellite channels, the major turning-points for Turkish television were the introduction of colour broadcasting in 1982 and the inauguration of a second channel on 6 October 1986. By 1993 TRT was broadcasting seven television services, including TRT-INT and TRT Avrasya (Eurasia). It was argued that TRT-Avrasya was designed to advertise the Turkish model of westernisation and to show the peoples of the central Asian republics 'how a unified world of Muslim Turks can be successful if they look to the West' (Aksoy and Avci 1992).

The liberal economic policies pursued by the MP throughout the 1980s not only opened up the Turkish economy to the world markets but also produced 'new mental images, desires, aspirations and motivations' (Abadan Unat 1991: 180). Özal promised the Turkish people a big leap so as to 'skip a generation' in the race to catch up with the developed economies of the world. Although the liberal economic policies of the MP governments fostered westernisation, there was also a contradictory development: the encouragement of religion first by the military and later by the MP government created an environment in which Islamist groups started to flourish in both cultural and economic spheres. In addition to the rise of political Islam, another problem which would put its stamp on the 1990s was emerging Kurdish nationalism and the armed struggle of the Kurdistan Workers' Party (PKK) in south-east Anatolia. However, the most important shortcoming of Turkish democracy in the 1980s was that the MP 'was interested in *economic* and not *political* restructuring in the sense of bolstering the civil societal elements' (Heper 1990b). During the two terms of MP government, political and civil rights remained considerably restricted. Increasingly from the second half of the 1980s, however, the MP had to face growing pressures for the expansion of democratic freedoms. Opposition parties, prior to the general elections in November 1991, promised the Turkish electorate a more democratic and transparent political system and a more 'free-speaking' Turkey. They advocated the privatisation of broadcasting to enhance pluralism, competition and quality. However, a probably more important reason for broadcasting becoming one of the principal themes of the 1991 elections was the emergence of Star and the tacit approval it received from the MP in return for favourable coverage of the government.

The two terms of Motherland Party rule were ended by the general election in October 1991, resulting in a coalition government of the True Path Party (TPP) and the SDPP. The new government, led by Süleyman Demirel, came into office in an atmosphere of hope and tolerance. Since it represented a consensus of centre-right and centre-left views, it appeared more capable of bringing Turkey a much-needed political liberalism. The coalition protocol promised to pass a constitutional amendment to abolish the state monopoly over broadcasting and restore the supremacy of law. However, it was during the term of Demirel's government that anarchy on the airwaves reached its climax. Consequently, on 22 January 1993, the minister of the interior demanded the closure of all illegal private radio and television stations. As soon as the decision was announced it caused a wave of panic, particularly among small radio stations (*Cumhuriyet*, 1 Feb. 1993). A concerted public campaign by private radio to present itself as the victim of a non-democratic act was clearly an embarrassment for a government which had promised democratisation and freedom. In the end, the minister of the interior declared that the government did not wish to close down the present broadcasters but to prevent prospective entrants until the legal framework was drawn up (*Cumhuriyet*, 4 Feb. 1993). However, it soon became clear that this U-turn was only a short-term victory for private media. When the minister of transport demanded the suspension of all illegal broadcasts by 1 April 1993, the government seemed ready to implement its decision at all costs. It was believed that the decision had been taken under pressure from the National Security Council, which perceived the emerging ethnic and religious radio and television broadcasts as a threat to the unity and integrity of Turkey. Like the previous decision, this one was also met by widespread protests in which the opposition parties, including the Motherland Party, vigorously took part.

The controversial suspension of private media in Turkey was soon overshadowed by an unexpected change of blood within the upper echelons of Turkish politics. As a result of the sudden death of Turgut Özal on 17 April 1993, Süleyman Demirel was elected a month later, on 16 May, as the new president. With Demirel's move to presidential office, Tansu Çiller became the first woman prime minister of Turkey. On 8 August 1993, Article 133 of the 1982 Constitution was amended to abolish the state monopoly over broadcasting, as Çiller had promised prior to her election as the new leader of the TPP. Another important problem that the Çiller government had to tackle was the Kurdish one, or the south-east problem as it was officially defined. Under mounting popular and military pressure, in March 1994 the Çiller government annulled the parliamentary immunities of five pro-Kurdish Democracy Party (DEP) deputies on charges of separatism. On 16 June 1994 the DEP was closed down by the Constitutional Court. It was within this atmosphere that the new broadcasting law was finally passed by the Turkish parliament on 13 April 1994. More than a year later, on 23 July 1995, the Çiller government amended 16 different articles of the 1982 Constitution, thus allowing societies, trade unions, professional organisations, university staff and students to engage in politics (Economic Intelligence Unit 1995). However, even these constitutional changes could not prevent the demise of the government in September 1995 when the new leader of the social democrats, Deniz Baykal, decided to withdraw from the coalition. Baykal had replaced Karayalçin as a result of the merger between the SDPP and the Republican People's Party (RPP) under the name of the latter. In the early elections on 24 December 1995, the pro-Islamist Welfare Party gained the largest share of the votes cast, making it the senior partner in the coalition government with Çiller's TPP. This government, which came to power on 28 June 1996, attracted the hostility of the secular elite and the army because of its tolerance to Islamist groups and religious symbols such as headscarves. Its relations with the mainstream media seemed equally troublesome due to substantial coverage of allegations concerning the sources of Mrs Çiller's wealth and the WP's Bosnian aid appeal (*Milliyet*, 19 Nov. 1996). The coalition partners attempted to discipline media by restricting the lavish promotion campaigns of newspapers and by proposing a new press law which aimed to curb and prosecute 'false' news. Moreover, Necmettin Erbakan, the leader of the WP, used the controversial Clause 25 of Law No. 3984[3] to ban a television broadcast on the conditions of hunger strikers in a prison (*Hürriyet*, 18 July 1996). The dissolution of the government in June 1997 opened the way for another right- and left-wing coalition between the MP and the Democratic Left Party (DLP) with the support of some smaller parties. On 16 January 1998 the WP was dissolved by the Constitutional Court on the charges that it had acted against the principles of the secular republic. As WP deputies regrouped within the newly established Virtue Party, the controversy over political Islam and the future of secularism and democracy in Turkey was aggravated.

From bureaucratic despotism to ratings populism

The arrival of private media, with their colourful, bright, fast-moving images, live satellite transmissions, sophisticated computer graphics, modern CNN-like news studios and young and attractive personalities, revolutionised Turkish television. For years TRT had pursued a programming policy in accordance with the ambiguously defined principles laid out in Law No. 2954, which aimed to protect and enhance national culture, tradition and language. This high-brow paternalistic formulation fostered centralisation and cultural elitism, which led to the exclusion of certain popular cultural expressions (such as Arabesque music, melancholic tunes played by a mixture of traditional folk and western instruments) and a cautious and sometimes narrow-minded treatment of television content. From the outset, private media achieved a decisive break from TRT conventions in every respect. Their broadcasts displayed a much more liberal attitude towards what TRT had always tried to ration and control: sex, violence and bad language. Some imported erotic shows, such as *Tutti Frutti* and *Playboy*, were accompanied by a new phenomenon called 'red dot' (soft porn) films. Between 15 November and 15 December 1992, Show TV alone broadcast 700 minutes of erotic programmes, which accounted for 8.1 per cent of all its entertainment broadcasts (Cankaya 1993). However, the exploitation of sex was not always explicit. In relation to the employment of more feminine and sensuous women presenters, the general co-ordinator of Star said: 'The more women there are in a programme the more revenue it brings' (*Milliyet*, 11 Apr. 1993). While devising their broadcasts the new channels were inspired by their Italian and American counterparts which they admired as 'colourful' and 'full of vitality'. These qualities, they insisted, 'should not be denied to Turkish audiences' (*Milliyet*, 11 Apr. 1993). In a very short time their policy paid off. In 1992 the combined audience share of four private channels in Istanbul was 70.8 per cent, while five TRT channels had only 24 per cent (Sahin and Aksoy 1993). The general co-ordinator of Star in 1993 claimed that, 'the reason why Star was so popular with the audience was that it was not despotic' like TRT (*Milliyet*, 11 Apr. 1993).

The unprecedented increase in the number of new outlets greatly increased the demand for television programmes to fill in the schedules. This brought about an influx of low-quality, low-budget programming around mass-viewing entertainment formats such as music programmes and game shows. In their music programmes private media provided ample room for both pop music and Arabesque. Other forms, such as classical music and Turkish folk, however, seemed to be almost completely left to TRT, which reluctantly softened its attitude towards Arabesque in the face of increasing competition. The majority of game and quiz shows, on the other hand, were domestically produced versions of western programmes, such as *Wheel of Fortune* (*Milliyet*, 28 Dec. 1992), *The Price is Right?* (*Cumhuriyet*, 8 Mar. 1993) and *Family Fortunes*. These game shows, which give away not only cash prizes but also consumer goods and brand-new cars, have higher audience ratings than many news and current affairs programmes. Another disturbing consequence of the inability of the home market to meet the increasing demand was the abundance of foreign programmes, particularly films and endless repeats. Nevertheless, it did not take long for private media to discover that, although foreign programmes were considerably cheaper, domestic productions yielded higher ratings. The cheapest and most cost-effective way of filling in the schedules with domestic productions proved to be broadcasting Turkish movies. In a matter of a couple of years private television channels recklessly consumed most of the 70-year-old film stocks of Turkish cinema. Soon intensifying competition for audience ratings forced private channels to make more investment in in-house productions, most of which turned out to be low-budget comedies, talk shows, reality-based programmes and more recently soap operas. Documentaries and cultural and educational programmes, on the other hand, were hardly given any space. Ali Kirca, the director of ATV news, argued that we

> would not be able to see classical music broadcast on private television because no private television would take a programme which has such low ratings on the TRT and knowingly broadcast it. However, the state would broadcast this, thus, we have an equilibrium.[4]

Increasing pressures for audience maximisation not only augmented the amount of entertainment but also fostered a trend in the direction of infotainment which particularly affected sports programming. Private televisions reinforced the tradition of sports reporting on Turkish media to focus first and foremost on football. But they did this in a much more marketable fashion. Programmes such as *Goal Show, Third Half* and *Stadium* were among the successful examples of football shows in which well-known commentators chatted with their studio guests while the audience were entertained by showmen and musicians. This format was later replaced with football-paparazzi programmes such as *Tele Vole* which cover the private lives of famous football personalities and celebrities. Paparazzi programmes, when they first appeared, caused great controversy for invading privacy and violating journalistic ethics by using hidden cameras. However, the most significant innovation that private media brought to factual programming was reality shows which attracted serious criticism for broadcasting bloody and gruesome pictures of victims with little consideration of their impact on viewers, especially children. Following the success of the first reality-based programme, *Immediately (Sicagi Sicagina)* of Show TV, all mainstream channels, with the single exception of TRT, began to produce similar programmes. In December 1994 six among the top 25 news programmes were reality shows. Haluk Sahin explained the success of reality shows in Turkey as being linked to the prevalence of some serious social problems: the 'malfunctioning of jurisdiction and sanction systems'; 'distrust of bureaucracy by the public'; 'diminishing trust of the state'; and 'ineffective public conscience'. Sahin claimed that ordinary people, who felt themselves powerless against all these, wanted to draw attention to their problems and even use the media as a mechanism to punish and humiliate.[5] During the late 1990s the reality-based programmes largely disappeared from screens, but most of their features were incorporated into evening newscasts.

Although the bulk of the new channels were generalist in character, there were other types such as subscription television (Cine 5) and all-music channels (Kral TV, Number One TV, Genc TV, Eko TV). In parallel to the enlargement of the domestic pop-music market in the 1990s, music channels provided opportunities for many talented young VJs and directors to enter the television industry. More recently, a CNN-like round-the-clock news channel, NTV, which used to be owned by Cavit Çaglar, the proprietor of regional Flash TV, gained genuine acclaim with its quality news and current affairs programmes and documentaries. Another strand included Islamist channels, such as Samanyolu TV (STV), Kanal 7 and Mesaj TV. Despite also being generalist channels, Islamist stations at the outset took up a more conservative broadcasting policy than their liberal rivals, accusing the latter of 'destroying national identity and culture' through 'products of the western mentality' (*Zaman*, 30 Dec. 1994). However, as competition intensified Islamist channels had to soften their stance. The complete renewal in 1998 of the programming and outlook of TGRT, a moderate nationalist-Islamist channel, was a clear indication of the determination of the Islamist media not to be marginalised. However, in contrast to the apparent tabloidisation of news programmes on main-stream private media, Islamist channels, particularly Kanal 7 and STV, remain committed to serious and informative news and current affairs programmes as well as documentaries.

It is true, though not necessarily for ideological reasons, that the main-stream private media caused real moral panic in Turkey concerning the impact on young people and children of numerous programmes containing sex, violence and bad language. As far as children's programming was concerned, private media almost completely relied on foreign cartoons to fill up the early morning hours. In February 1993 the number of cartoons broadcast by 10 television channels, including two public stations, was 144 (*Cumhuriyet*, 4 Feb. 1993). Meanwhile, private channels made little effort to produce children's educational programmes. Another controversy surrounding the private media concerned their use of language which was, for some, informal and accessible, but for others was uneducated and vulgar. The extensive employment of English words and expressions, as well as poor use of the Turkish language, inflamed a long-lasting debate over the degeneration of language and culture in the media.

As private media consolidated their position, TRT's response to competition was slow and did not go beyond some modest adjustments, such as organising its channels around different themes and relaxing its supervision of programmes and of the codes for advertisements.

'Speaking Turkey'

The arrival of private media which broke TRT news traditions of lengthy and uncritical coverage of politics and excessive protocol reporting, created a new atmosphere of freedom and openness. News and current affairs programmes and studio discussions on private channels soon captured the attention of audiences and gained the respect of commentators. Apart from a few incidents which demonstrated the fragility of the consensus over no-go areas, news programmes on private television channels were largely tolerated by the government and state bureaucracy.[6] This led to unprecedented 'taboo bashing' and stretching the boundaries of the permissible (Sahin and Aksoy 1993). All news and current affairs programmes, which competed for the top of the ratings, were claiming that they chose topics that none of their rivals dared. Television stations promoted their news teams as 'young', 'dynamic' and 'fearless'. With regard to the changing nature of television news reporting, journalists working for private media were talking about the empowerment of journalists, while dealing with wrongdoing, fraud and political, social and legal injustices. Ugur Dündar, a famous television journalist, claimed that television journalism became 'a new horizon of the press and a new front-line in the struggle for the freedom of the press' (*Hürriyet*, 23 Dec. 1993).

The current affairs programmes and studio debates which dealt with controversial topics were commended for breaking down official dogmas and relativising national identity and culture (Sahin and Aksoy 1993). Official taboos had prevented TRT from dealing with certain social and political issues, such as the Kurdish problem and secularism, in any way that might challenge the views of the political establishment. Haluk Sahin attributed the success of news programmes on private channels to the restraints endured in the days of the TRT monopoly.

> With private television channels becoming widespread in Turkey, this suppressed potential has exploded. Many issues, which had been seen as taboos due to the TRT's being a state television, jumped onto the screens. . . . Homosexuals came on screens and debated. The term Kurd was first mentioned on screen. The municipal governor of Urfa, known as an enemy of secularism, was interviewed. . . . All these taboos were demolished. Instead of them, a new freedom and dynamism came, and it was proved that the country would not sink even if these things were talked about.[7]

The relativisation of national identity and culture, however, involved emerging ethnic and cultural variations as well as differences in terms of religious convictions and social-group aspirations within Turkish society, which, since the formation of the republic in 1923, was encouraged to perceive itself as a unified entity: a one-nation, one-culture society. Critics argued that the function of TRT had been to maintain and advance this 'official' vision by suppressing the 'real' differences within Turkish society. TRT, Aksoy and Avci (1992) argued:

> has until very recently, monopolised the task of promoting and secur-
> ing the continuation of the national, Turkish culture, defined within
> the framework of Kemalist principles. What should be emphasised,
> however, is that this task has been carried out by means of exclusion,
> censorship and political partiality.

The disintegration of this unitary, official identity into a variety of diverse identities is welcomed as a positive change in the overall cultural climate of Turkish society. It is argued that private media could also influence the future of the whole democratic system in Turkey by becoming 'diagnosis and treatment points' for the elimination of anti-democratic tendencies.[8]

Although they sometimes showed significant differences from each other in terms of their formats and ideological orientations, the current affairs programmes and studio discussions broadcast by private channels in the early years of privatisation did provide access to a greater range of political perspectives than TRT. For instance, in relation to the Kurdish problem they included speakers from a diverse spectrum, including Kurdish politi-cians, socialists and Islamists (Çatalbaş 1996). The most important of the recurrent themes the programmes dealt with were: government strategies in combating terrorism; the role of the army in the region; the bases and for-eign links of the PKK campaign; the issue of democratic reforms, such as education and television broadcasting in the Kurdish language; the alleged connections of the DEP with the PKK; the social and historical grounds of the Kurdish problem in Turkey; the dangers of a possible polarisation between the Turkish and Kurdish communities; the issue of separation; and the deficiencies of Turkish democracy. However, how these themes were portrayed and debated changed considerably, particularly in studio discus-sion programmes, in which a multiplicity of competing opinions was gener-ally present, depending on the political inclinations of the participants. First, there was the conservative approach which saw the Kurdish issue as a prob-lem of terrorism. This view was adopted by a large section of the state appa-ratus and by the extreme nationalists. Nevertheless, sometimes the discourses of some government ministers and officials challenged this view: official ideology in Turkey is 'by no means monolithic, nor even a particu-larly coherent set of ideas' (Schlesinger et al. 1983). The moderate approach was in favour of differentiation of the Kurdish problem from the PKK and concern over national security. This view could be found in a diverse polit-ical spectrum, including the liberals, the Kemalist left and the Islamists. However, the Islamists rejected the nationalist dimension completely as they were in favour of 'Islamic brotherhood' policies. Although they recognise Kurdish ethnic identity, Islamists are opposed to the PKK and its Marxist-Leninist ideology. The third view, which was espoused by socialists and pro-

Kurdish participants, however, saw the Kurdish insurgency as the struggle of an oppressed nation. Not surprisingly, the most passionate and provocative criticisms of the handling of the problem by the Turkish state came mainly from DEP members and other pro-Kurdish speakers, as well as Islamists and socialists like Dogu Perinçek of the Turkish Workers Party (TWP). Thus, there was considerably more room for critical views to be aired on private stations than on the public broadcaster. Private stations considerably broadened the ideological framework and allowed a genuine debate between different perspectives on the Kurdish problem to be conducted over the nation's airwaves. In their programmes certain speakers, such as DEP deputies, openly challenged the official view which defines the Kurdish issue as merely a law-and-order problem. These speakers argued that the PKK phenomenon has its roots in state policies which prevented the political and cultural expression of Kurdish ethnic identity and demanded a political solution to the problem.

Perspectives of this kind seemed missing from TRT's current affairs programmes, which relied on the major parliamentary parties and the state bureaucracy, thus remaining within the official line. Moreover, some of its current affairs programmes seemed to openly defend and propagate the conservative statist position which perceives Kurdish insurgency as a national-security issue which can only be resolved by military victory over the secessionist (Çatalbaş 1996). Thus, in relation to the Kurdish issue, probably the most important political problem in the history of the republic, TRT failed to represent the full range of views in Turkish society. Owing to its dependency on the state, TRT seemed unable to respond to the new atmosphere of freedom and openness. This is mainly because the legal framework and political culture in which TRT operates demands that its programmes reinforce rather than question the official ideology. As Bülent Çapli observed, it was always considered that 'the Turkish television system held an important responsibility in maintaining political stability and national unity' (Çapli 1994).

Although the inclusion of private media in factual programming was largely welcomed as a positive step towards the democratisation and liberalisation of broadcasting, increasing competition and commercialisation gave rise to certain undesirable tendencies. To begin with, news programmes on private channels began to run after sensational stories and, in doing so, showed little respect, if any, for the individual's right to privacy and the right to reply for parties whose names and credibility suffered as a result of their programmes. Moreover, the private media were sometimes accused of completely violating the principles of journalistic ethics, abusing their powers to further the interests of their parent companies and to attack their rivals. This became particularly evident in what was called the 'media wars' between Hürriyet and Sabah, the two biggest press groups, and Star in 1993. In the cases of Hürriyet and Sabah, the television channels with which these two papers were affiliated, Show TV and ATV, also became involved in the conflict. The tone of the accusations became so degrading that the Society of Turkish Journalists warned these companies that 'swear-words instead of ideas, aggression instead of criticism, campaigns to mock private lives instead of news, and attacks against family honour and pride under the name of commentary cannot be accepted' (*Cumhuriyet*, 6 Oct. 1993).

Furthermore, private channels were criticised for attempting to influence the course of justice by acting like judges themselves and for 'instigating mass protests against the decisions of the courts' (*Milliyet*, 8 Jan. 1994). This was seen as a dangerous development of a 'media law' in which people were tried and found guilty by public opinion before their case was heard in the courts.[9] When they were broadcasting from abroad, private media did not give any right of reply to the parties whose sentence was determined by the telephone polls. The most widely debated example of this was Star's coverage of Nurettin Sözen, the former SDPP municipal governor of Istanbul, in relation to a corruption scandal in the Istanbul Water Company (ISKI) (*Hürriyet*, 29 Jan. 1994). Another forceful criticism of the journalistic practices of private television was that they sometimes exaggerated and distorted the facts for the sake of sensationalism. One specific incident on 9 April 1994, which involved Star and another private channel, TGRT, was a cause for concern. On that day both television channels reported that thousands of Muslims in Gorazde had been killed as a result of a chemical attack by the Serbs and encouraged their audiences to take part in demonstrations in Ankara and Istanbul (*Hürriyet*, 12 Apr. 1994). According to press reports, the majority of the demonstrators were Islamists, who were particularly sensitive to the Bosnian conflict and were in favour of the active military involvement of Turkey in Bosnia. In the event neither the claims of chemical attack nor the number of casualties was confirmed. Star and TGRT were accused by the professional associations of journalists and by other private channels of 'irresponsible broadcasting' and 'provocation' (*Milliyet*, 12 Apr. 1994).

Moreover, there were significant divergences on private channels between different genres in terms of their ideological plurality and openness. Schlesinger et al. argue that news bulletins are 'more "closed" forms of presentation' than the documentary form, as they tend to be 'rendered in a style that conceals the process of selection and decision which lies behind the reporting, and which allows little room for comment and argumentation' (1983: 36). News programmes on private channels, in contrast to those on TRT, opted for a shorter format and employed novel techniques such as the short cartoon segment of ATV's main evening newscast, called 'Our City', which presents Turkey as a Wild West town to stimulate interest. The prevalence of crime, accident and human-interest stories which took up a sizeable portion of the newscasts on private stations was an indication of 'popular' or 'tabloid' journalism (Dahlgren and Sparks 1992). There were also indications that newscasts on private channels tended to reflect corporate attitudes and political dispositions more than some other genres, like current affairs programmes and studio discussions. This seemed especially so when it came to matters concerning nationalist values and institutions and the commercial interests of the media companies themselves. An analysis of the main evening newscasts of seven major television channels, including TRT-1, revealed that, as far as the reporting of controversial political issues was concerned, the news programmes of private broadcasters did not always challenge official definitions (Çatalbaş 1996). For instance, in relation to the Kurdish problem the newscasts on private television were not very different from those on TRT. The Kurdish problem generally appeared in newscasts in the form of routine reports on the clashes between the Turkish security forces and the outlawed PKK in the south-eastern provinces. Dealing with one of the bloodiest conflicts in the republic's history, these reports generally informed the audience about the location of the battles as well as the casualties on both sides. The factual information used within the reports was generally based on statements made afterwards by the security forces and by local governments in the provinces involved. Moreover, some private television channels, such as Star, HBB and TGRT, seemed to be actively supporting the official discourse by conveying openly patriotic and emotional messages. Thus, as Mehmet Ali Birand, a well-known journalist and television producer, argued, they seemed to be extending to society and the state a 'bribe of nationalism and the flag'.[10]

Furthermore, private television channels appeared more inclined to exploit the human-interest angle than TRT. Contrary to the official, straightforward tone of TRT news, the narrative of news stories on private channels often included subjective and sentimental expressions, and capitalised on dramatic and/or entertaining properties. With these features, private television news sometimes came very close to the populist style of tabloid newspapers. However, the populism did not stop at style but affected content as well. Ufuk Güldemir, who worked for both Show TV and Star as chief news editor, said: 'If Neslihan Yargici [a famous fashion designer] calls Aczmendis [an Islamic fundamentalist sect] sexy and that is what the public is talking about, it also enters our news. . . . The TRT's news programmes reflect the state's agenda but my bulletins reflect the public's' (*Show Dergi*, 2 July 1995). Similarly, news reports on private channels sometimes conveyed closed messages as they tended to approach issues from their own political position. The most prominent private stations, such as ATV, Show TV, Kanal D and Star, all have a western, liberal, free-market ideology. Some others, like HBB, Kanal 7 and Samanyolu TV, have a more conservative nationalist and Islamist character. Aside from their political inclinations, the broadcasts of private channels also seemed to be influenced by their ownership and by their dealings with other powerful economic and political groups in society. For instance, the underrepresentation of certain interest groups, such as workers' unions, indicates an inclination on the part of some commercial channels, such as Star, to suppress certain issues which may not necessarily be compatible with their corporate ideology. The owners of Star, the Uzan family, are known for their dislike of unions and actively discourage their staff from joining them.

Another cause for concern in relation to news programmes on private media was the excessive number of commercials. Thanks to their consistent and large audience following, news programmes were seen as one of the moments when commercial opportunities could be maximised. Subsequently, due to legal restrictions, overt advertising within news programmes was replaced by more covert forms such as product placement, split-screen commercials and news reports about the products or activities of certain well-known brands.

Reflections for today

Today, the Turkish television system has three tiers, unequally matched in vigour: a battered public broadcaster, TRT; affluent national private broadcasters; and marginalised local private media. Despite their 'immaturity' compared to TRT and despite being completely outnumbered by local channels, national private media are the main axis of the system which determines the rules of the game. The majority of national private channels are integrated into large holding companies which, in addition to their involvement in newspaper and magazine publishing and distribution, have stakes in a diversity of businesses (Nebiler 1995). The ownership of these holding companies tends to be concentrated in the hands of a few, such as Dogan and the Medi Group, which control around 70 per cent of newspaper sales and a large proportion of television advertising through their joint venture, BIMAS, which sells commercial airtime for Kanal D and ATV. Extensive cross-ownership and concentration provide media companies with considerable power to further their other economic interests and to negotiate certain privileges with the politicians.

The most important influence on the broadcasts of private channels is their inherently commercial, profit-seeking nature. Private media are driven more than anything by ratings, which create and legitimise a 'competitive ethos' that defines the success of programmes simply in terms of audience ratings. Today, Turkish television, particularly in prime time, appears to be completely invaded by game shows, soap operas and football-paparazzi programmes characterised by excessive commercialisation. The result is homogenisation of programming around entertainment and infotainment. Under the influence of the 'competitive ethos' newsmen also continuously monitor and try to beat their rivals' figures (Ehrlich 1995). Competition for ratings compels private media to adopt audience-maximisation techniques, with disturbing consequences such as sensationalised, trivial and shallow reporting and populism. As the number of serious current affairs programmes and studio debates diminishes, mainstream channels seem to prefer softer and less demanding but highly rated topics. Main evening newscasts display entertaining properties which come in different forms, such as lengthy coverage of celebrities, the funny and the bizarre. The transformation of Turkish television news has some ambivalent features; as Daniel C. Hallin has observed in the case of American networks: 'If the news agenda has been democratised in certain ways, it has been trivialised in others, with more attention to stories like celebrity trials and beached whales' (1994: 177).

Another important point which must be borne in mind in relation to the private media is the seemingly more cautious attitude they adopted after the approval of the new broadcasting law. Under increasing pressure from the Radio and Television Supreme Council, which has draconian powers to temporarily suspend broadcasts, the management of private stations sometimes interfered openly with their current affairs programmes. For example, in October 1994, as a result of a warning from the council, Star management cancelled a specific episode of *Camera Lens (Objektif)* in which one of the most controversial issues in the early history of the republic, the Independence Courts, was debated (*Cumhuriyet*, 28 Oct. 1994). The supreme council also issued a warning to Show TV in August 1995 for broadcasting a special edition of *32nd Day (32. Gün)* which contained an interview with a militant from Dev-Sol, the major left-wing armed group in Turkey (*Hürriyet*, 2 Aug. 1995).

In addition to the allocation of all national and regional frequencies, Law No. 3984 also assigns to the supreme council responsibility for supervising radio and television broadcasts, helping enforce the right to reply and determining the necessary organisational, financial and technical prerequisites. However, despite the clear requirements of Law No. 3984, private stations in the early years of privatisation openly violated certain provisions (*Hürriyet*, 2 Feb. 1994). Therefore, in 1994 the Radio and Television Supreme Council issued 41 warnings to 12 television stations and one radio station.[11] The majority of the cautions were prompted by the use of telephone lotteries. Others, however, were given because broadcasters, according to the council, had failed to 'respect the law, be just and impartial in their broadcasts' and their broadcasts had 'degraded or humiliated persons or institutions beyond the limits of criticism'.[12] For a long time the warnings issued by the supreme council seemed largely ineffective. However, a number of events in late 1995 proved that the council was willing to use its extensive powers. With an unexpected decision on 27 November 1995, the supreme council informed the then prime minister, Tansu Çiller, that the director general of TRT and his administrative council were dismissed. The council stated that the decision was taken as a result of a government programme broadcast on 30 October 1995 (*Hürriyet*, 28 Nov. 1995). A committee of lawyers, convened by the council, concluded that the programme had violated Law No. 3984 which states that broadcasters must 'provide an equality of opportunities for democratic groups and political parties'. The council had previously warned TRT because of the breach of the same clause by another government programme.[13] As far as TRT was concerned, this decision of the supreme council signified a phenomenal change. Prior to the establishment of the council, the appointment and dismissal of TRT's director generals had remained within the power of the Council of Ministers, except for a brief period of 'autonomy'.

However, TRT was not the only broadcaster which felt the zeal of the supreme council. Private channels also were given harsh sentences. The supreme council ordered the closure of Star for three days in November 1995 as a result of the failure of this channel to broadcast a statement by Prime Minister Çiller, as ordered by the Ankara Court of Justice, in reply to the allegations made against herself. Since then the temporary suspension of television channels by the supreme council, although fiercely criticised for being severe and anti-democratic, has become a usual punishment for private media.

Not all decisions of the supreme council were caused by infringements of the programming requirements. However, as the growing authority of the supreme council demonstrated, the editorial freedom of the broadcast media cannot be considered in isolation from the legal framework of broadcasting, freedom of the press and freedom of speech in Turkey. Although Article 28 of the 1982 Constitution states that 'the press is free and shall not be censored', there are a number of provisions which make it an offence to write or print 'any news or articles which threaten the internal or external security of the state or the indivisible integrity of the state with its territory and nation, which tend to incite offence, riot or insurrection, or which refer to classified State secrets'.[14] These restrictions are also translated into a number of laws. According to research carried out by the Turkish Press Council, there are 152 laws which limit press freedom in Turkey (*Milliyet*, 3 Apr. 1995). Similarly, although Article 31 of the 1982 Constitution forbids 'restrictions preventing the public from receiving information or forming ideas and opinions' through the mass media other than the press, Article 13 allows legal constraints 'with the aim of safeguarding the indivisible integrity of the State with its territory and nation, national sovereignty, the Republic, national security, public order, general peace, the public interest, public morals and public health'.[15] Recently, an anti-terrorism law has also imposed certain limitations on freedom of expression and the press, particularly in relation to separatist activities.

Concluding remarks

The 1990s have been a decade of phenomenal changes for the Turkish audio-visual media. As a result of private television channels becoming an integral part of the broadcasting landscape, the deficiencies of TRT, namely its political partiality, insufficient professionalism and cultural elitism, became more evident. In their current affairs and studio discussion programmes the private channels did bring to the Turkish public sphere the openness and plurality that it had lacked for many years. However, the impact of privatisation was not always altogether positive. To begin with, the news programmes of mainstream private channels exhibit symptoms of tabloidisation, sensationalism, populism and commercialisation. Furthermore, they pursue an extremely commercially minded, down-market programming regime. In other words, market forces play an important role in determining not only what is to be broadcast, but what is not to be broadcast, especially in prime time. As the new broadcasting order fosters extensive cross-media ownership and concentration, there is a real danger in Turkish television that 'the tyranny of the market may replace or supplement governmental pressures' (Randall 1993).

In conclusion, the contribution of the private channels to the liberalisation and democratisation of broadcasting in Turkey, however real, must be considered within the larger context of their overall programming policies and the political and legal boundaries of the new broadcasting order. In the same way, the liberating and democratising potential of the market should be weighed against the extent to which the private media have become a powerful economic sector closely linked with other economic and political power groups.

Notes

1 Constitutional Court Ruling No. 1990/8, 18 May 1990. See also Bülent Serim, 'Hukukun Üstünlügüne Saygi' (Respect for the Supremacy of the Law), *Cumhuriyet*, 15 Feb. 1993; Mehmet Akat, 'Radyo-TV ve Anayasanin 133. maddesi' (Radio-Television and Article 133 of the Constitution), *Cumhuriyet*, 19 Apr. 1993.

2 *Radyo ve Televizyonlarin Kurulus ve Yayinlari Hakkinda Kanun No. 3984 (The Law on the Establishment and Broadcasts of Radio and Television Stations No. 3984)*, published in Official Newspaper, No. 21911, 20 Apr. 1994.

3 Clause 25 of Law No. 3984 gives the prime minister or the minister he or she appoints the right to ban a specific broadcast which is considered a threat to national security and public order.

4 Ali Kirca, interview with author, 24 Nov. 1993.

5 Haluk Sahin, interview with author, 3 Dec. 1993.

6 The trial of two producers, late Erhan Akyildiz and Ali Tevfik Berber, by the Military Court on charges of disseminating anti-military feeling provides a good illustration of this situation. These two journalists were taken to the court because they broadcast in their programme, *Antenna*, on 8 December 1993, interviews with members of the association of the opponents of war. On another occasion, Mehmet Ali Birand, a famous journalist and producer of *32nd Day*, was taken to the court on charges of providing propaganda for the PKK and insulting the army. The charges were based on a specific episode broadcast on 16 November 1992, in which Birand interviewed Osman Öcalan, the brother of PKK leader Abdullah Öcalan.

7 Haluk Sahin, interview with author, 3 Dec. 1993.

8 Osman Ataman, director of the Association of Radio and Television Owners and Broadcasters, interview with author, 22 Dec. 1993.
9 For the arguments on this matter see Altan Öymen, 'Medya Yargiçlari', 6 Jan. 1994, 'Linç Hukuku', 7 Jan. 1994, *Milliyet*; Hasan Pulur, 'Divan-i Harpten Divan-i Medya'ya', 8 Jan. 1994, *Milliyet*. The statement of Yekta Güngör Özden, director of the Constitutional Court, 11 Sept. 1994, *Hürriyet*.
10 Mehmet Ali Birand, interview with author, 19 Dec. 1994.
11 Information is provided by the Radio and Television Supreme Council.
12 *Radyo ve Televizyonlarin Kurulus ve Yayinlari Hakkinda Kanun No. 3984 (The Law on the Establishment and Broadcasts of Radio and Television Stations No. 3984)*, published in Official Newspaper, No. 21911, 20 Apr. 1994.
13 According to Clause 35 of Law No. 3984, the supreme council has the power to dismiss TRT's director general and administrative council if programmes which violated the law continued to be broadcast.
14 *1982 Anayasasi (The Constitution of the Republic of Turkey)*, 1982, published by the Directorate General of Press and Information, Ankara, 1982.
15 *1982 Anayasasi (The Constitution of the Republic of Turkey)*, 1982, published by the Directorate General of Press and Information, Ankara, 1982.

References and further reading

Abadan Unat, N. (1991) 'Market Research and Public Opinion Polling in Turkey as an Agent of Social Change', in M. Kiray (ed.), *Structural Change in Turkish Society*, Bloomington, IN: Indiana University Press, pp. 179–92.
Ahmad, F. (1985) 'The Transition to Democracy in Turkey', *Third World Quarterly*, 7.2 (Apr.): 221–7.
Ahmad, F. (1993) *The Making of Modern Turkey*, London: Routledge.
Aksoy, A. and Avci, N. (1992) 'Spreading Turkish Identity', *Intermedia*, 20. 4–5: 39–40.
Alemdar, K. and Kaya, R. (1993) *Radyo Televizyonda Yeni Düzen*, Ankara: TOBB.
Alpay, S (1993) 'Journalists: Cautious Democrats', in M. Heper and A. Öncü (eds), *Turkey and the West: Changing Political and Cultural Identities*, London: Heinz Kramer, I.B. Tauris and Co., pp. 69–91.
Avery, R. K. (1993) *Public Service Broadcasting in a Multichannel Environment*, London: Longman.
Aziz, A. (1989) *Elektronik Yayincilikta Temel Bilgiler*, Ankara: TRT Basim ve Yayin Müdürlügü.
Çagdas Gazeteciler Dernegi (1993) *Devlet ve Basin*, Ankara: ÇGD Yayinlari, No. 6.
Çagdas Gazeteciler Dernegi (1994) *Basin Güncesi*, No. 9, Haziran, Ankara: ÇGD Yayinlari.
Cankaya, Ö. (1990) *Türk Televizyonunun Program Yapisi (1968–1985)*, Istanbul: Mozaik Basim ve Yayincilik.
Cankaya, Ö. (1993) 'Türkiye'de Televizyonculugun Gelisimi ve Bugünkü Durumu', *Marmara Iletisim Dergisi*, No. 2.
Çapli, B. (1994) 'Turkey', in J. Mitchell, J.G. Blumler, P. Mounier and A. Bundschuh (eds), *Television and the Viewer Interest*, London: John Libbey, pp. 135–46.
Çatalbaş, D. (1996) 'The Crisis of Public Service Television: Turkish Television in the 1990s', unpub. PhD thesis, London University.
Collins, R. (1993) 'Public Service versus the Market Ten Years On: Reflections on Critical Theory and the Debate on Broadcasting Policy in the UK', *Screen*, 34.3: 243–59.

Curran, J. (1990) 'Culturalist Perspectives of News Organizations: A Reappraisal and a Case Study', in M. Ferguson (ed.) *Public Communication: The New Imperatives*, London: Sage, pp. 114–34.

Curran, J. (1991a) 'Rethinking the Media as a Public Sphere', in P. Dahlgren and C. Sparks (eds), *Communication and Citizenship*, London: Routledge, pp. 27–57.

Curran, J. (1991b) 'Mass Media and Democracy: A Reappraisal', in J. Curran and M. Gurevitch (eds), *Mass Media and Society*, London: Edward Arnold, pp. 82–117.

Curran, J. and Seaton, J. (1991) *Power Without Responsibility*, 4th edn, London: Routledge.

Dahlgren, P. and Sparks, C. (1992) *Journalism and Popular Press*, London: Sage.

Dodd, C. H. (1990) *The Crisis of Turkish Democracy*, 2nd edn, London: Eothen.

Economic Intelligence Unit (1995) *Country Report: Turkey, Third Quarter*, pp. 10, 11.

Ehrlich, M. C. (1995) 'The Competitive Ethos in Television Newswork', *Critical Studies in Mass Communication*, 12.2: 196–212.

Ferguson, M. (ed.) (1990) *Public Communication: The New Imperatives*, London: Sage.

Finkel, A. and Sirman, N. (eds) (1990) *Turkish State Turkish Society*, London: Routledge.

Fiske, J. (1992) 'Popularity and the Politics of Information', in P. Dahlgren and C. Sparks (eds), *Journalism and Popular Culture*, London: Sage, pp. 45–63.

Garnham, N. (1983) 'Public Service versus Market', *Screen*, 24.1: 6–27.

Garnham, N. (1986) 'The Media and the Public Sphere', in P. Golding, G. Murdock and P. Schlesinger (eds), *Communicating Politics*, Leicester: Leicester University Press, pp. 37–54.

Garnham, N. (1994) 'The Broadcasting Market and the Future of the BBC', *Political Quarterly*, 65.1: 11–19.

Geray, H. (1993) 'Turkey's Communications Boom', *Turkish Review* (Spring), Ankara: Directorate General of Press and Information.

Golding, P. (1994) 'Telling Stories: Sociology, Journalism and the Informed Citizen', *European Journal of Communication*, 9: 461–84.

Halevy-Etzioni, E. (1987) *National Broadcasting Under Siege*, London: Macmillan.

Hall, S., Connell, I. and Curti, L. (1976) 'The Unity of Current Affairs Television', in *Working Papers in Cultural Studies*, No. 9, CCCS, University of Birmingham.

Hallin, D. C. (1994) *We Keep America on Top of the World: Television, Journalism and the Public Sphere*, London: Routledge.

Heinderyckx, F. (1993) 'Television News Programmes in Western Europe: A Comparative Study', *European Journal of Communication*, 8: 425–50.

Heper, M. (1990a) 'The Executive in the Third Turkish Republic, 1982–1989', *Governance*, 3. 3.

Heper, M. (1990b) 'Turkish Democracy Reconsidered: Illusion Breeding Disillusion?', in H. Korner and R. Shams (eds), *International Aspects of Economic Integration of Turkey into the European Community*, Hamburg: Hamburg Institute of Economic Research, pp. 17–46.

Heper, M. (1991) 'Introduction', in M. Heper and J. M. Landau (eds), *Political Parties and Democracy in Turkey*, London: I.B. Tauris and Co.

Heper, M. and Öncü, A. (eds) (1993) *Turkey and the West: Changing Political and Cultural Identities*, London: Heinz Kramer, I.B. Tauris and Co.

Hoffmann-Riem, W. (1992) 'Trends in the Development of Broadcasting Law in Western Europe', *European Journal of Communications*, 7: 147–71.

Hultén, O. and Brants, K. (1992) 'Public Service Broadcasting: Reactions to Competition', in K. Siune and W. Treutzschler (eds), *Dynamics of Media Politics*, The Euromedia Research Group, London: Sage, pp. 116–28.

Hürriyet Vakfı (1988) *Çagdas Gelismelerin Isigi Altinda Devlet Medya Iliskileri*

(Relationship Between State and Media in the Light of Contemporary Developments, No. 10, Istanbul.

Keane, J. (1991) *The Media and Democracy*, Cambridge: Polity.

Kellner, D. (1990) *Television and the Crisis of Democracy*, Boston: Westview Press.

Livingstone, S. and Lunt, P. (1994) *Talk on Television: Audience Participation and Public Debate*, London: Routledge.

Mango, A. (1994) *Turkey: The Challenge of a New Role*, Westport: Preager, with the Center for Strategic and International Studies, Washington DC.

Mazzoleni, G. (1992) 'Italy', in Euromedia Research Group, *The Media in Western Europe*, London: Sage, pp. 123–42.

McQuail, D. and Siune, K. (eds) (1986) *New Media Politics: Comparative Perspectives in Western Europe*, London: Sage.

Murdock, G. (1990a) 'Television and Citizenship: In Defence of Public Broadcasting', in A. Tomlinson (ed.), *Consumption, Identity and Style*, London: Routledge, pp. 77–101.

Murdock, G. (1990b) 'Redrawing the Map of the Communications Industries: Concentration and Ownership in the Era of Privatization', in M. Ferguson (ed.) *Public Communication: The New Imperatives*, London: Sage, pp. 1–15.

Murdock, G. (1992) 'Citizens, Consumers and Public Culture', in M. Skovmand and K.C. Schrøder (eds), *Media Cultures: Reapprasing Transnational Media*, London: Routledge, pp. 17–41.

Mutlu, E. (1987) 'Yayincilik Sistemlerinde Çogulculuk Yönsemesi ve Türkiye', *A.Ü. Basin Yayin Yüksekokulu Yilligi, 1986–1987*, pp. 201–20.

Nebiler, H. (1995) *Medyanin Ekonomi Politigi: Türk Basininda Tekellesme ve Basin Ahlakinin Çöküsü (The Political Economy of the Media: Monopolisation in Turkish Press and the Collapse of the Journalism Ethic)*, Istanbul: Sarmal Yayinevi.

Önis, Z. (1991) 'Political Economy of Turkey in the 1980s, Anatomy of Unorthodox Liberalism', in M. Heper (ed.), *Strong State and Economic Interest Groups: The Post-1980 Turkish Experience*, Berlin: Walter de Gruyter.

Özbudun, E. (1988) *Perspectives on Democracy in Turkey*, Ankara: Turkish Political Science Association.

PTT Genel Müdürlügü (1993) *TÜRKSAT Milli Haberlesme Uydulari Sistemi (TURKSAT National Communication Satellites System)*.

Randall, V. (1993) 'The Media and Democratisation in the Third World', *Third World Quarterly*, 14.3: 625–46.

Richeri, G. (1985) 'Television from Service to Business: European Tendencies and the Italian Case', in P. Drummond and R. Paterson (eds), *Television in Transition*, London: BFI, pp. 21–35.

Rowland, W. and Tracey, M. (1990) 'Worldwide Challenges to Public Service Broadcasting', *Journal of Communication*, 40.2: 8–26.

Rowland, W. and Tracey, M. (1991) 'Public Service Broadcasting: Challenges and Responses', in J. G. Blumler and T. J. Nossiter (eds), *Broadcasting Finance in Transition*, Oxford: Oxford University Press, pp. 315–34.

Sahin, H. (1979) 'Ideology of Television: Theoretical Framework and a Case Study', *Media, Culture and Society*, 1.2 (Apr.): 161–9.

Sahin, H. (1981) 'Broadcasting Autonomy in Turkey: Its Rise and Fall, 1961–1971', *Journalism Quarterly* (Autumn): 395–400.

Sahin, H. (1991) *Yeni Iletisim Ortami, Demokrasi ve Basin Özgürlügü*, Istanbul: Basin Konseyi.

Sahin, H. and Aksoy, A. (1993) 'Global Media and Cultural Identity in Turkey', *Journal of Communication*, 43.2: 31–41.

Schlesinger, P. Murdock, G. and Elliott, P. (1983) *Televising 'Terrorism': Political Violence in Popular Culture*, London: Comedia Publishing Group.

Seaton, J. (1994) 'Broadcasting in the Age of Market Ideology: Is it Possible to Underestimate the Public Taste?', *Political Quarterly*, 65.1: 29–38.

Sunar, I. and Sayari, S. (1991) 'Democracy in Turkey: Problems and Prospects', in G. O'Donnell, P. C. Schmitter and L. Whitehead (eds), *Transition from Authoritarian Rule*, Baltimore: The Johns Hopkins University Press.

Tachau, F. and Heper, M. (1983) 'The State, Politics, and the Military in Turkey', *Comparative Politics*, 16.1: 17–35.

Tracey, M. (1977) *The Production of Political Television*, London: Routledge.

PART

III

MEDIA AS BATTLEFIELD

|6|

The killing of Brazilian street children and the rise of the international public sphere

SONIA SERRA

In the age of global markets, supranational polities and ubiquitous media, there is a complex web of institutions responsible for representing different publics and collectives and for mediating between states and peoples. Among them, civil-society organisations and social movements, alongside the press, have taken a special role, becoming essential elements for the rise of deliberative democracy. Transcending the boundaries of nation states, non-governmental organisations and global media redefine the public space and change the character of political life. In this scenario, emergent practices of global governance and networking challenge notions of national sovereignty and cut across top-down relations between states, markets and citizens.

The rise of the international public sphere calls for a new framework, embedded in the relationship between media institutions and polities, which can better account for these new forms of representation and mediation. In this context, the role of international media, which have tended to be viewed either through the positive lens of developmentalism or the negative frames of dependency theory and media and cultural imperialism, requires reassessing. Media sociology also needs to address how local–global interactions affect the production of news.

This chapter has two main objectives. First, it argues that Habermas's revised concept of the public sphere offers a powerful model for considering the new roles of the media in bringing issues into the public arenas of post-liberal societies, provided that it is extended to better address the new configurations mentioned above. Second, it fleshes out this theoretical enterprise by providing an empirical illustration of the operation of the international public sphere. This is done by examining the emergence of the issue of the killing of street children in Brazil on the international scene and the national political agenda. The chapter shows that intermedia relations between domestic and foreign journalists, as well as the networking strategies and public-relations efforts of indigenous NGOs, assisted by multinational agencies such as the Catholic Church, Amnesty International and UNICEF, were catalysts of significant changes in press coverage and public policy.

Habermas, the public sphere, civil society and social movements

Thirty years after the publication of *Structural Transformation* (Habermas 1989 [1962]), the German thinker offered another version of the concept of the public sphere, which revises some of his premises and represents a significant improvement. However, if his early work elicited numerous positive and negative responses (e.g. Scanell 1989, Garnham 1990, Kellner 1990, Thompson 1990, Curran 1991a, Dahlgren 1991, Holub 1991, articles in Calhoun 1992b, Peters 1993), his more recent attempts to re-envisage the public sphere have not yet received due attention, at least in the English-speaking world.

This later account, as outlined predominantly in *Between Facts and Norms* (Habermas 1997 [1992]) – one of his most recent commentaries on the matter available in English at the time of writing – is a highly elaborated model which has benefited from scholarly critique of his previous work and is also informed by the historical developments which have taken place over the period. It condenses and refines important developments of his thinking presented in his later works (e.g. Habermas 1992a, 1992b, 1994) but the scope of the dynamics of his model, as he himself recognises, still needs to be extended to 'go beyond our limited focus on national societies and ... take in the international order of the world society' (Habermas 1997: 444).

For the purposes of this chapter some points in this revision are especially relevant: the concept of civil society, the new role of social movements and the actual performance of the media in the rise of issues in public arenas. A reworking of the notion of civil society plays a central role in this revised concept of the public sphere. Habermas (1997: 367) now defines civil society as 'composed of those more or less spontaneously emergent associations, organisations, and movements that, attuned to how societal problems resonate in the private life spheres, distil and transmit such reactions in amplified form to the public sphere'.

The public sphere is defined as a social space between the political system, on the one hand, and the private sectors of the lifeworld and functional systems, on the other. It is a network for communicating facts and opinion; an arena for the detection, thematisation, problematisation and even dramatisation of problems which must be processed by the political system. It functions as a 'sounding board' and stimulates influential opinions.

A focus on the innovative force of social movements, which he had neglected in his previous work (Calhoun 1992b), also plays an important part. But, distinct from authors who regarded social movements which transcend nation-state schema as the path to radical socialist transformation (e.g. Frank and Fuentes 1990), and the alternative to liberal electoral democracy in the form of participant civil democracy (e.g. Frank 1993), Habermas believes that they cannot overcome the political system, but can only have an indirect impact on its self-transformation.

As Habermas (1997) observes, citing Cohen and Arato, social movements perform both an offensive and a defensive role. Offensively they attempt to bring up new issues, solutions and values, to produce broad changes in public opinion, to shift the parameters of institutional political will-formation, and to exert pressure on legislative, juridical and administrative systems in favour of certain policies. Defensively, they seek to preserve and amplify the associative structures of public influence and to generate counter-institutions and alternative publics. They contribute, then, to extending and radicalising existing rights.

Habermas's later notion of the public sphere is elaborated within the framework of a proceduralist deliberative democracy. Deliberative politics depend on the interplay between informal processes of public opinion and formal democratic procedures of will-formation developed in constitutional states, in such a way that problems discovered and thematised by informal 'weak' publics in the unregulated public sphere are dealt with in formal 'arranged' representative publics such as parliaments. (For the notions of weak as opposed to strong publics see Fraser 1993.)

A pluralist public sphere, with active voluntary associations and social movements with grass-roots bonds, relatively unsubverted by the effects of power and based on a political culture which is sufficiently separated from class structures, as well as a political system porous and receptive to influxes from the periphery, appears to be the way to reconcile participatory democracy with representative democracy. In Habermas's formulation, Tocqueville's early question – does the existence of voluntary associations alter the shaping of public discourse? (Wuthnow, 1991) – receives a positive answer.

Reversing centre–periphery flows

Habermas's later writings emphasise that democracy has to be recast from a theory of communication. To explain how communicative power can be converted into political power Habermas (1997) starts from Bernard Peters's model, which describes the circulation of power in constitutional democracies as having a centre–periphery axis and containing two main explanatory elements: the system of 'sluices' and a two-tiered mode of problem-solving – one for routine operations and the other for extraordinary situations. According to the model, in the centre of the political system are the complexes of administration, parliamentary bodies and the courts. At the edges of the administrative complex, as an *inner* periphery, there are institutions with functions delegated by the state, such as universities, professional associations and foundations. On the outer periphery there are different types of 'customer' and 'supplier' groups, which include private organisations, business associations and labour unions on the one side, and public interest groups on the other. The 'real periphery', Habermas (1997: 355) says, is constituted by voluntary informal opinion-forming associations which 'belong to the civil-social infrastructure of a public sphere dominated by the mass media'.

The communicative flows which originate on the periphery have to pass through the sluices of democratic and institutional procedures of the parliamentary complex or the courts, and to persuade authorised members of the political system, before they can be transformed into political power. A significant feature of the model is the possibility that in cases of conflict the established patterns of the usual routine mode of operation of the political system are supplanted by a different mode. In this case, following a 'consciousness of crisis', there is an increase in public attention and an intensified search for solutions.

For this to happen, Habermas introduces two further assumptions: first, that the periphery has sufficient capacities not only to detect but to interpret and present the problems in a way that is original and attention-grabbing, and thus can disrupt the routines; and, second, that it has occasion to exercise them, in the sense of social integration. In routine modes, the initiative in agenda-setting and policy-making lies with the centre of the political system, but as Habermas (1997: 381) argues the great issues of the last decades were not initiated by central powers. Instead, they were brought up by intellectuals, concerned citizens, radical professionals and self-proclaimed advocates.

On this view, before problems are formally considered by the political system, they face a public struggle for recognition, which sometimes includes incessant campaigning and sensational demonstrations. For civil society and social movements to perform their role and a liberal public sphere to develop, certain conditions have to be met – most particularly democratic constitutional guarantees and the climate of a liberal political culture. Alongside this there must be a rationalised lifeworld and a contained media power. Freedom of assembly, association and expression, a protected private life, a political system which operates with freely organised political parties and general elections, and a democratically regulated media system are prerequisites for liberal public spheres, which cannot flourish under authoritarian conditions.

None the less, even under democratic conditions one of the most difficult issues remains how social inequalities affect access, inclusion and performance in the public sphere, which reflects both systemic and individual asymmetries. In principle, the public sphere is characterised by open accessibility and equality. The only prerequisite for inclusion is the capacity for public use of reason. The force of the best argument is to prevail over status or power, and historically it was indeed envisaged as a liberating defence mechanism against absolutism (Gomes 1997).

In practice, it has been shown (and Habermas himself does not deny this) that the public sphere has always been constrained by social status, patriarchalism and other forms of discrimination, which are increasingly reinforced by the selective pressures of the media. Radical critics of Habermas such as Fraser (1993: 27) argue that an 'adequate conception of the public sphere requires not merely the bracketing, but rather the elimination, of social inequality'.

Another significant issue in Habermas's later writings is his answer to such criticism. Habermas argues that constitutional guarantees and the absence of exclusion mechanisms grant a potential for self-transformation of the public sphere. He further argues that civil society is expected to neutralise such inequalities, since autonomous associations act as advocates for subordinate groups and campaign for neglected issues. In doing so, such associations help to preserve an openness to divergent opinions and to guarantee a representative diversity of voices. This, in turn, means that counter-knowledge can be produced and countervailing forces can be unleashed.

However, Habermas also argues that it is only through their controversial presentation in the media that issues can reach the larger public and thereby shape the public agenda. In Habermas's (1997: 307) new analysis, the media do not simply select which issues and voices gain publicity in the public sphere, but also take on significant roles of institutional mediation and social integration. They channel currents of public communication which 'flow through different publics that develop informally inside associations', and they perform the unique role of bringing together readers, listeners and viewers scattered across different areas of the globe in complex societies. The mass media thus enlarge the public sphere, which becomes more inclusive the more the audience is widened. This perspective indicates that the public space in contemporary societies must be seen as a 'highly complex network that branches out into a multitude of overlapping international, national, regional, local, and subcultural arenas' (Habermas, 1997: 373). The case study presented in the following sections enables us to observe the operation of the international public sphere in a concrete setting.

The killing of street children in Brazil

From the mid-1980s in Brazil, killings of poor youths by the police and death squads escalated. Nevertheless, these did not provoke public outrage, as protests against the murders were silenced by primary definitions, mainly provided by the police and the courts, which justified the killings by emphasising the criminal behaviour of the youths. These were reproduced by the press, which drew on cultural and social prejudices against street children, reinforced by the attempt to create a moral panic about their involvement with drug-trafficking. However, in the early 1990s the killing of street children in Brazil became the subject of numerous press reports and television documentaries all over the world, shocking international public opinion.

The issue provoked debates in foreign parliaments and questioning in foreign offices. Human-rights groups in several countries pressed their own governments to condemn the problem and push the Brazilian government into action. Intergovernmental bodies such as the European Parliament passed resolutions threatening economic sanctions and sent a delegation to discuss the matter with authorities and NGOs. The French government also sent an envoy. Personalities such as Pope John Paul II, the late Princess of Wales, the British prime minister John Major and the Nobel Peace Prize winner Adolfo Esquivel, who visited the country at the time, all met street children to manifest their concern about the problem, and some made strong statements condemning Brazilian society and authorities. The United Nations also sent a special envoy to assess what the government was doing to solve the problem, which had turned into a serious diplomatic embarrassment for the Brazilian government (Câmara dos Deputados 1992: 220).

The 'extermination of children' also became an obligatory subject for journalists and policy-makers in Brazil. A new law which radically changed the legal framework for dealing with the problem was enacted, a National Plan to Combat Violence against Children was launched by the president, and a Parliamentary Commission of Inquiry (CPI) to investigate the killings was set up in Congress. Many other substantive, deliberative and individual measures followed (see Protess et al. 1991 for classification). Also, many new child-protection groups were formed, and new programmes for street children were started. The spotlight on the plight of street children activated international solidarity and increased the flow of funds for NGOs dealing with them. In countries such as England, groups were formed to campaign about the problem.

The international scandal had negative consequences as well. For instance, the focus on such violence contributed to a sharp decline in tourism in Rio (*El País*, 22 Sept. 1990, *Le Monde*, 28 Feb. 1992, *Jornal do Brasil*, 24 Mar. 1991). In addition, international support for human-rights activists further angered the death squads and their supporters, who persecuted the defenders of street children. Youths who had been protected by human-rights activists and featured in stories in the foreign and domestic media were killed.

The issue of the killing of street children in Brazil is thus a dramatic example of the operation of the international public sphere. It offers significant evidence for discussing models of the rise of issues in public arenas, and for reassessing the role of the international media in contemporary societies. This chapter summarizes the findings of a larger research project which analysed 5 years of press coverage of Brazilian newspapers and weeklies, and also that of influential outlets in the international press, such as the *New York Times*, *Le Monde*, *El País*, the *Guardian*, *Time* and *Newsweek*. Its arguments are based on several interviews conducted with: a) national journalists and correspondents for the foreign outlets, and the main international news agencies; b) representatives of Brazilian and international NGOs and religious organisations; c) parliamentarians, judges and state officials. The project aims to understand why the violence against poor and mainly black children and adolescents took so long to become a matter of public concern, and how this was eventually achieved. Here, the main question is: which factors contributed to the rise of the issue of the killing of street children on the media and policy agendas?

Context and contest

Escalating murders

The first and most obvious explanation, as provided by some journalists, was the rise of the problem itself. Although some scholars influenced by a symbolic interactionism model rightly argue that social problems are not mere reflections of objective conditions (Hilgartner and Bosk 1988, Hansen 1991), changes in reality cannot be neglected. Indeed, statistics later produced indicated a sharp increase in the rate of murders among other causes of deaths of youths, especially those between 15 and 17 years of age (Pinto 1991). Although this was not a sufficient explanation, it was certainly the worsening of the problem which led to a 'crisis consciousness' in the periphery.

From early 1987, or even before, frequent blatant killings of youths at the hands of the police led poor communities to stage their protests by blocking roads or rioting, as they struggled to call attention to these arbitrary deaths. These actions initially proved counterproductive, because the disorderly communities were then regarded as the cause of the problem. None the less these cries from the periphery reverberated and were heard by voluntary associations, advocacy groups, bishops, concerned journalists and academics and left-wing politicians.

Civil-society mobilisation

The second important factor was the increasing mobilisation of civil society. As already commented, civil-society organisation is a prerequisite for the functioning of the public sphere (see also Dahlgren 1995) and this was only possible because of changes in the political climate in Brazil. During the transition to democracy and the rebirth of the public sphere in the 1980s, several secular and religious voluntary organisations dedicated to defending the rights of 'minors' were formed. From 1985 they were articulated in the National Movement of Street Children (MNMMR), which was organised with the support of UNICEF, the Catholic Church and even liberal state officials (Swift 1991).

In the context of constitutional reform, the movement campaigned for changes in policies for children and adolescents, and submitted a proposal for a new Statute for Children and Adolescents, which was deeply opposed by law-and-order sectors. From mid-1988 the children's movement started to survey and expose the killings. In May 1988 Bishop Dom Mauro Morelli and the local section of the MNMMR in a violent town on the Rio periphery promoted a 33-hour vigil to protest against the killing of youths who had been assisted by the Pastoral. The protest act was covered by the main papers in Rio (*Jornal do Brasil*, 3 May 1988, *O Globo*, 5 May 1988) and resulted in an editorial condemning the killings in *Jornal do Brasil* (6 May 1988), as well as investigative stories about the lives of street children (e.g. *Jornal do Brasil*, 10 May 1988). But there was still no public outrage, no response from the authorities and no follow-up in other media outlets.

In this same month, the head of ASSEAF – an association of former inmates of the government foundation for needy minors and young offenders – contacted the Geneva-based United Nations consultative body, Defence for Children International (DCI), asking for assistance to expose the problem in Brazil and abroad. This INGO supported an exhibition of pictures of violence against Brazilian youths in Europe, and funded the first survey on killings of children and adolescents on the outskirts of Rio, which was conducted by a pool of Brazilian NGOs, including a university centre – NEPI.

In early July, organisations linked to the Catholic Church, ASSEAF and a child advocacy group from another town on the Rio periphery organised a political meeting in the Brazilian Bar Association in Rio, to condemn the killings in the area and to announce that Defence for Children International had commissioned a survey on the deaths of children and adolescents. Ivanir dos Santos, the head of ASSEAF, stressed that the impunity of the crimes had brought NGOs together to seek support from international organisations. They expected that the results of the survey would have international repercussions, and that this would work as an element of pressure on the Brazilian government (*O Dia*, 7 July 1988). In August, during the general assembly of the MNMMR, participants staged a protest to condemn the murder of 100 street children linked to the movement in the previous 2 years. The assembly decided to elect the fight against the killings as a priority, together with pressure to guarantee constitutional rights (MNMMR/ IBASE/NEV-USP 1991).

In September, in order to call attention to the problem of the killings of minors and make public the results of the ASSEAF/DCI survey, the organisations held a public protest and a show in a central square in Rio, with the presence of intellectuals, artists and a representative of DCI. The investigation highlighted 306 murders of youngsters less than 18 years old by death squads between January 1987 and July 1988 in the outlying areas of Rio. However, this warranted just short news reports in Brazilian papers such as *O Estado de São Paulo* (28 Sept. 1988), which simply stressed the possible consequences of the handing of the report to an international organisation. Again, there was no follow-up.

One year after the national NGOs had started to publicise the killings of street children abroad, the issue started to gain more prominence in the international media. In early May a *Newsweek* special report (1 May 1989) produced in Brazil and other countries highlighted the issue of the violent lives and deaths of street children as a global problem, in line with UNICEF's 1989 State of World Children report. That month the Rio section of the MNMMR, which was one of the main sources in the *Newsweek* story, invited foreign journalists to a press conference to denounce the killing of street children in Rio by 'extermination groups' funded by merchants. The MNMMR co-ordinator, Maria Tereza Moura, said that they had got tired of crying out to the domestic press (personal interview).

Moura's claims were reproduced in a large feature in *Le Monde* (18 May 1989) following the unusual murder of a young black slum boy whose body was found, not on the outskirts of Rio, but in the smart borough of Ipanema. He was wrapped up in a carpet with a note which read: 'I killed you because you did not study and did not produce anything, and I am going to kill those kids who do not study and do not respect nature'. Then the Permanent Committee for the Defence of Children and Adolescents was created, bringing together voluntary associations for street children and other more influential civil-society organisations, including the independent research institute IBASE.

Another important initiative by the NGOs was the organisation of a national conference in the capital of the country, in September 1989, at the time of the campaign for presidential elections. The second meeting of the MNMMR was a big event which gathered around 750 street children and 200 street educators. At the opening of the conference a public protest was staged to denounce the killings, with the participation of national human-rights groups and international organisations such as the United Nations, the Organisation of American States, UNICEF and DCI. The preliminary results of a national survey on violent deaths of children and adolescents produced by sections of the MNMMR co-ordinated by IBASE were released.

In addition, around 500 street children invaded the national Congress, while a session was being held, to protest against the killings and demand investigation of the connections of the police with the death squads and approval of the statute bill. This forced parliamentarians and representatives of the federal government to respond publicly to the indictments, and a few also engaged in the campaign. However, within two months the issue was absent from plenary discussions in parliament and no effective government actions were registered to combat the problem.

The meeting of the street children attracted foreign television networks such as the Japanese RBS, the Italian RAI and the state channel in Spain, in addition to news agencies such as Reuters, EFE and France-Press. It generated a report in the *Guardian* (27 Sept. 1989) and a news in brief in *El País* (29 Aug. 1989). During the conference, the issue of violence against street children was also promoted in the Brazilian newspapers, from the crime section to national newsdesks and political columns. But, after the event, killings of poor youths continued to be routinely reported in the press, while clashes between law-and-order sectors and children's protection groups in Rio reached critical levels.

None the less, the understanding that the killing of street children was a big issue aroused the interest of influential journalists such as Gilberto Dimenstein – a political columnist who was editor-in-chief of the bureau of *Folha de Sao Paulo*, the largest-selling Brazilian newspaper. Dimenstein conducted an investigative report on the killings, which was carried by *Folha* on 18 March 1990, and also published a book, which was sponsored by UNICEF and a national foundation of toy manufacturers (ABRINQ). The book was launched in April 1990 in the hall of the Congress, and further raised awareness of the issue in Brazil and abroad (*Guardian*, 21 Apr. 1990).

Another report was launched by the centre for the co-ordination of marginalised populations – CEAP – in May 1990, and the NGOs continued to promote gatherings and demonstrations such as the street marches organised by the Catholic Church-based Sao Martinho foundation, to mobilise street children and society in relation to the problem and to call for approval of the statute.

These organisations, together with radical politicians, concerned journalists and academics, had produced a counter-discourse which challenged received ideas about street children and dominant definitions of their murders. They had been able to initiate a public controversy in the Brazilian media and society and to broaden support for the cause among the more enlightened sectors of society. By mid-1990 more influential voices were starting to resonate in the public sphere, and the first administrative responses – such as the opening of 200 inquests about extermination groups in Rio (*Jornal do Brasil*, 8 Apr. 1990) and the creation of a special group in the police to hunt down justice-makers in São Paulo (*Guardian*, 18 May 1990) – were initiated.

None the less, the efforts of national civil society to sound the cries from the peripheries initially provoked little public outrage and no substantive reactions from the political system. As the *Guardian* correspondent remarked, 'it was only the international response to the crescendo of condemnation about the killings by the National Movement of Street Children that jolted the authorities out of their indifference' (Rocha 1991: 15).

International pressure

The third and most significant factor which explains the rise of the issue in the media and policy arenas is the placing of the problem in the international agenda, and the national repercussions of international pressure. This was especially catalysed by Amnesty's campaign in the international media, which led to increased media attention in Brazil and abroad and pushed the government to respond.

However, it is important to note that the international pressure was initiated by domestic organisations, since the publicising of the problem abroad was a strategy deliberately pursued by organisations in the street children's movement, who believed that raising international awareness was necessary for at least two main reasons. First, it was necessary because street children's issues had to be perceived as a global problem since their roots and solutions were related to the world order. Second, and perhaps even more important, it was recognised that in relation to issues such as these only international public opinion could push the government, the press and larger society to respond. As one participant argued,

> for the international condemnation to produce effects it was necessary that there were organised sectors in civil society to amplify it, and to react to government responses. Otherwise the government would just respond with a rhetorical discourse justifying the problem. (personal interview with Wanderlino Nogueira Neto, FORUM DCA)

In April 1990, 2 years after the production of the first survey funded by DCI, figures on the killings collected by the Brazilian NGOs were handed to Amnesty International by the MNMMR. In June 1990 the international human-rights organisation joined the campaign against the killings of poor youths in Brazil. Amnesty's campaign was launched with publication of a report on police brutality, which also contained data collected by the Brazilian NGOs on the killings of street children (Amnesty International 1990a), followed by documentaries, press conferences and international press releases, and the publicising of the issue in its newsletters and annual reports (e.g. Amnesty International 1990b, 1991). Amnesty also lobbied in parliaments in the United States, England and many other countries, and in intergovernmental bodies such as the United Nations and the European Parliament. Additionally, it launched mass appeals and brought direct pressure to bear on the Brazilian authorities.

Preliminary work has demonstrated that Amnesty International's revelations represented a turning-point in the development of the issue (Serra

1993, 1996). The Brazilian president ordered full investigation of Amnesty's indictments, although the problem was a responsibility of the governments in the states. The president also sanctioned the new statute, which was passed in Congress despite the opposition of powerful groups in the judiciary, the army, the police and business associations.

The law was the result of a long debate in the Brazilian public sphere, but the pace of reform was influenced by international condemnation of the killings. Approval of the new policy was also facilitated by the fact that it incorporated principles of the proposed International Convention on the Rights of Children and was sponsored by UNICEF. Presidential support aimed at responding to international pressure on the one hand, and, on the other, showing concern to place children's rights high on the agenda for the forthcoming United Nations Children Summit.

The external pressure, which led the federal government to publicly support the reformers, provoked a further division between the elites but changed the balance of power in favour of the organisations around the street children's movement. These were represented in the national commission established in December 1990 to deal with the problem, which was equally composed of government sectors and civil-society organisations. The Parliamentary Commission of Inquiry (CPI) to investigate the killings, which had been demanded by the street children movement since 1989, was finally installed in the Chamber of Deputies in mid-1991. The impact of international pressure on the political system is further confirmed by the deputy Benedita da Silva, who stated that even after the invasion of congress by the street children and the launching of Dimenstein's book in the hall of the Congress, she spent a whole year trying to obtain approval for the setting-up of the CPI (personal interview, May 1994). The deputies were only sensitised after the repercussions of Amnesty International's allegations and especially after sensationalist documentaries and other television programmes screened abroad shocked international public opinion and outraged Brazilian newspapers.

The importance of the international coverage for the domestic press was also indicated by the CPI, which concluded in its final report that 'the Brazilian press only moved the issue from the police pages to the political pages after the foreign press did so' (Câmara dos Deputados 1992: 18). This raises other significant questions, which require further comment. What were the respective roles of the foreign and national media? What were the most important sources for the domestic and foreign press?

Difference and deference

Theoretical models of the public sphere and empirical studies have shown that different media play different roles in the public space (Curran 1991b, 1996, 1998, Sparks 1991, Dahlgren 1995, Wolsfeld 1997), since they are governed by different selection principles, reach different audiences and have different political standings (Cracknell 1993). In the context of the international public sphere the variation is even greater, since some constraints on news production might pull domestic and foreign journalists in opposite directions. In the case we are examining here journalists and their organisations did not respond to the problem, nor to pressures from readers and sources, in the same way, at the same time and with the same impact.

The liberal newspaper *Jornal do Brasil*, for instance, was one of the first quality dailies to give a hearing to cries from the periphery, to investigate the problem and to advocate political solutions to the killings of street children. It also provided pre-publicity and what was usually favourable coverage to the domestic NGOs' efforts. Its initial coverage already contained the main themes used by the sectors in defence of children to frame the issue, such as the need to combat the impunity of the killings, social indifference in relation to deaths of the poor, and the characterisation of street children's offences as strategies of survival (see e.g. *Jornal do Brasil*, 6 May 1988). However, although the paper was an important source for the Brazilian elite, civil society and foreign correspondents despite its small readership, this earlier coverage did not provoke public outrage and further responses from other newspapers or policy-makers. The paper highlighted the international repercussions of the issue as a way to nudge the Brazilian media and society a step further towards addressing the problem.

The conservative *O Estado de São Paulo*, by contrast, initially resisted the definition of the problem offered by the more radical NGOs and only gave prominence to the issue in terms of its possible negative consequences, especially after a resolution of the European Parliament indicated that the killing of street children could result in economic sanctions against Brazil. The paper started to investigate the killings with the aim of contesting the figures and frames presented by the NGOs and some foreign outlets. However, such investigative stories did contribute to a better understanding of the problem, led to a change in the paper's own reporting of the issue and provoked responses from the authorities in the state (*O Estado de São Paulo*, 4 Aug. 1991, 6 Aug. 1991, 7 Aug. 1991).

The leading weekly *Veja*, which responded more to the concerns of its wide middle- and upper-class readership, and whose initial stories mostly concerned the street children as a threat to society (e.g. *Veja*, 29 May 1991, 18 Sept. 1991), took a longer time to become sensitised to the issue. *Veja* continued to ignore the problem even after it had reached the headlines in its foreign counterparts such as *Time* (17 Sept. 1990) and *Newsweek* (24 Sept. 1990). However, its later coverage showed that a larger sector of Brazilian society was finally responding to the national and international pressure, and it therefore contributed to raising awareness of the problem (*Veja*, 27 Nov. 1991).

There were also significant differences in the foreign outlets' attention to the problem and their respective impact. For instance, newspapers such as the *Guardian* and *Le Monde* were among the first to respond favourably to the national NGOs' claims, and to carry features on the problem. Their stories influenced policy-makers, civil society and other media in their respective countries, with some repercussions in the Brazilian media and society. The *New York Times* was less receptive to the NGOs' definitions (e.g. 13 Nov. 1990), but its reports after Amnesty's revelations had a much larger impact that was not restricted to the United States and Brazilian society and media. They also triggered a flurry of worldwide coverage (e.g. the Canadian *Globe and Mail*, 19 Nov. 1990, 20 Nov. 1990, 21 Nov. 1990, the Jamaican *Sunday Gleaner*, 18 Nov. 1990, the Yugoslav *Borba*, 19 Nov. 1990) because, as journalists and scholars acknowledge, the most powerful media, with the largest reach, help to set the agenda and define reality for the less powerful ones (Reese 1991, Shoemaker and Reese 1996). Among these, *The Times* has a special media-agenda-building role (Hess 1996).

Television programmes broadcast in countries such as Britain, the United States, France and Italy, and later the coverage by global media networks such as CNN, which followed the international press reports, brought the problem to the attention of a wider audience at a world level, prompted the indignant protests of viewers, and resulted in further cross-national exchanges between groups in civil society and in global public opinion bringing pressure to bear on the authorities. Reports of these reactions in the Brazilian press contributed to a broadening of concern over the issue in Brazilian society, and as a consequence to wider coverage in more market-led media outlets.

Most national journalists interviewed, including *Veja*'s Brazil news editor, confirmed that the international press reports had wide repercussions in the domestic press. This was also evidenced by the impact of stories about foreign media coverage of the killings in Brazil, written by Brazilian correspondents based in central countries (see, for example, 'Deaths of Children: A Scandal on British TV', *O Globo*, 30 Jan. 1991, 'Deaths of Children in Brazil Shock British People', *O Estado de São Paulo*, 31 Jan. 1991). Nonetheless, these also provoked indignant reactions among some sectors of the press, who complained that they reflected vested interests and top-down pressure on the country from central foreign powers ('False Picture', *O Globo*, 30 Jan. 1991).

However, both analysis of the press coverage and interviews with domestic and foreign journalists are in keeping with studies which argue that the local press is the basic source for foreign correspondents (Hess 1996). For instance, Roberto Gazzi, the city editor of *O Estado de São Paulo*, recalled that, when the NGOs publicised the issue, foreign correspondents telephoned the paper for confirmation. All the foreign correspondents interviewed were of the opinion that in Brazil there were quality newspapers and news weeklies with high standards of journalism and confirmed that they counted on the domestic press as a fundamental source.

Textual analysis and statements made by journalists revealed that the national media was a source not only of information but also of frames, and an indicator of national opinion. Correspondents and stringers such as Mac Margollis of *Newsweek*, John Maier of *Time*, Aldo Gamboa of *UPI*, Claire de Oliveira of *France Press* and Ricardo Soca of *El País* stressed the importance of the national press in setting the agenda for foreign correspondents and said they usually waited for the reaction of the domestic press. This was denied by *Le Monde*'s correspondent Hautin-Guiraud. Nonetheless, killings of poor youths initially had no salience as a social problem and a political issue and warranted only brief crime news reports in the main Brazilian outlets, although pictures of the youngsters' bullet-riddled bodies appeared daily on the front pages of more sensationalist popular newspapers.

Jan Rocha of the *Guardian* claimed that, although the national press was a very important source, most of her information on the specific problem came through direct investigation in the field and from her close contacts with the Catholic Church and local and international human-rights groups. In fact, the British correspondent was one of the first foreign journalists to mention the problem (e.g. *Guardian*, 20 Aug. 1986). Rocha criticised the selective reporting of the Rio press for highlighting crimes in the smartest areas and relegating murders on the outskirts to 'bottom-of-the page footnotes' (*Guardian*, 4 June 1987: 10).

There were important differences in the press coverage of the killings which could be related to differences in journalist's motivations, including their professional commitments, their place in civil society and their personal histories and links with the social movement. Some journalists who acted as advocates for the issue, such as Tim Lopes of *Jornal do Brasil* and Gilberto Dimenstein of *Folha*, later played an important role as activists. In so doing, some were motivated by a sense of citizenship or humanitarian and moral values; others simply felt this was a potentially newsworthy story, likely to interest foreign editors. Thus, changes of correspondents, who have a licensed autonomy (Curran 1990), sometimes resulted in changes in their paper's reporting, although there were also variations related to specific editorial policies of both national and international news organisations.

However, there were broader influences related to the socio-economic structure and the geopolitical position of Brazil (marked by the experience of slavery and colonialism), which accounted for significant differences in the news value attributed to the issue by the domestic and foreign press respectively. On the one hand, as Brazilian journalists themselves acknowledged, for a significant part of the elite press in Brazil killings of poor youths were not considered newsworthy – either because, as Roldão Arruda of *O Estado* pointed out, they 'were so used to the problem that they could not see it' or because they 'closed their eyes' as this was not part of the interest of their readers, as Paulo Leite of *Veja* admitted. In such an unequal society as Brazil, the low social status of the victims and historically and ideologically constructed images of street children as societal threats, alongside popular acceptance of practices of retaliation, help to explain why the deaths were initially regarded as 'natural' and blamed on the victims themselves. Rhetorical devices which identified the *trombadinhas* (young pick-pockets) as bandits deserving punishment or as guilty victims had become part of the repertoire of the primary levels of public-opinion formation, and of the 'discursive reserve' (Ferguson 1998) of journalists.

On the other hand, as foreign journalists claimed, this was the type of issue that the international media were used to looking at, either because 'on purely journalistic grounds it was a strong story', as Stephen Powell of Reuters commented, or because of 'an unthinking bias' against a country such as Brazil. In the words of Margollis, Brazil 'is seen most when it is worst'. Killings of street children generate stories which 'activate existing chains of cultural meaning' (Hansen 1991: 453) and reaffirm cultural images of Third World countries as places of barbarism, which selective coverage in western media has helped to construct and reinforce (Dijk 1989, Philo 1993).

National and foreign journalists, the NGOs and government sectors all complained of stereotypical coverage in the international media, which was also reflected in the themes mostly present (brutality, impunity, corruption, social indifference) or absent (foreign-debt connections, unjust international relations, domestic government efforts). In contrast, traditional mistrust among the international media of authorities in less developed countries (e.g. Miller and Beharrell 1998) contributed to the fact that in the international coverage NGOs were more represented than official sources (Serra 1996). If the latter usually enjoyed privileged access to the domestic press, while not always receiving favourable coverage, the same did not happen in the foreign press. Brazil's sensitivity to outside pressures, as James Brooke of the *New York Times* pointed out, was also influenced by its position in the world scenario.

Nevertheless, the international pressure exerted on the Brazilian government by human-rights organisations such as Amnesty International was only effective because they had gained publicity in the national and international media. Foreign-press attention also had the significant effect of increasing coverage in the Brazilian press and legitimating the claims of domestic NGOs, contributing to a change in the balance of power between sectors for and against the reforms.

The responses of policy-makers and the media were differentially affected by their standing in relation to the status of the different actors. Collective actors in opinion-forming associations have unequal opportunities to influence media content in relation to corporate actors and political elites, and in order to do this, as Habermas (1997 [1992]) has argued, they may need sponsors with more material or organisational resources or influence. National and international press coverage reflected hierarchical differences between the NGOs. Amnesty's statements had a much greater and more immediate effect than the national NGOs' revelations and those of other international organisations. An analysis of a sample of the foreign coverage showed that the event that received most coverage was Amnesty International's statement in September 1990 (Serra 1996).

As Habermas comments, in the struggle to influence public opinion and acquire political power in the public sphere, the reputation of the actors comes into play. Well-known groups such as Amnesty International and office-holders who have already acquired political influence enjoy accreditation. But, as this chapter shows, by getting together and establishing links with organisations with more influence at the centre, especially central global powers, peripheral groups can gain access to the international public sphere and influence the national political system. None the less, Habermas also admits that even accredited groups need to dramatise their claims and also produce convincing propositions to capture media attention and sensitise the actors in the political system and the general public.

Debate and drama

The contest between the law-and-order groups and the reformers also involved attempts to manage the news by creating media events and newsworthy frames. On the one side, the police and the minors' courts released statistics of escalating crime by youths, provided the media with sensational images of spectacular operations to chase drug-traffickers in the slums, and fed the press with dramatic stories of violent young criminals. On the other side, the NGOs produced dramatic figures of the killings, and to a certain extent the media appeal of the campaign conducted by the NGOs and especially Amnesty International was related to their efforts to change primary definitions by challenging these representations with frameworks suggesting 'innocent children versus cruel authorities' and 'wicked killers versus brave defenders of street children'.

The street children's movement also staged highly emotional protests, promoted street marches and large meetings and tried to create an impact with political demonstrations, giving advance warning to the press. These were not just 'pseudo events' (Boorstin 1967) to make the news, but political facts in their own right, as well as interactive forms and means of communication aimed at better organising and articulating the movement and raising consciousness among the media and the public.

If the dramatisation of the issue was part of the struggle for public recognition of the problem, there were also more discursive forms of publicity. The NGOs conducted surveys and issued informative reports and books. Participants on the different sides of the dispute also wrote analytical articles and gave interviews which were carried by the press. There was a certain ambivalence in the press as a result of this cross-fire between different camps. But the Brazilian press, which approached the issue from its own perspectives and interests, also carried independent investigative stories which produced important knowledge, contributed to opinion formation and further informed the children's advocacy groups. Journalists were subjected to unequal pressures and were exposed to alternative discourses, but they also reacted critically to the contradictory frames. Quantitative and qualitative changes in the coverage over time were the result of the public debate, which also raised the consciousness of journalists, even if this debate was both emotionally influenced and rationally oriented, and was structured by power.

Many studies point to the mediatisation of contemporary public life and argue that public-relations techniques have become prerequisites for successful intervention in public debate and policy-making (e.g. Deacon and Golding 1994, McNair 1995). However, these analyses lead to different conclusions about the public sphere. Some authors who investigate forms of political communication such as electoral campaigns contend that the media have been transformed into a simulacrum and argue that the contest in the public space merely reflects the symbolic manipulation of spectacular images, which replaces the content of discourses and political action. Nonetheless, research with pressure groups indicates that their preference for the quality media still 'conforms to a largely implicit model of a rational public sphere' (Schlesinger and Tumber 1994: 103). In the campaign for approval of the Statute for Children and Adolescents in Brazil, the successful public-relations work of UNICEF also included talks with journalists and involved feeding them with substantive information for their enlightenment on the issue.

In the case examined here, news-management techniques and discursive capacities were important tools for the political actors involved, but these included more interactive and political forms as well. It is demonstrated here that the success of the social movement of street children was especially dependent on their articulation in transnational networks with access to the media and intergovernmental bodies.

Such networks have reciprocal influence and exchange resources, knowledge, information and ideas, which enhance their legitimacy and effectiveness (Mainwaring and Viola 1984, Scherer-Warren and Krischke 1987). Their grass-roots bonds facilitate their role as warning sensors for social problems. Their capacity and resources for building alliances, lobbying parliaments, dramatising issues to sensitise the media and public opinion, and pressurising governments, enable them to raise new issues in the political agenda and influence the public debate. As Fernandes (1995) notes, NGOs are key elements for 'planetary citizenship' because of their dual characteristic of local insertion and international connection.

Conclusion

Several authors have called attention to important transformations in public life, taking place at a global level, which demand a rethinking of theories of the press, these being traditionally posed within the framework of single nation states. The increase in direct or virtual exchanges between civil societies and transnational social movements across borders, the growing impact of supranational legal and political organisation, the globalisation of the media and the formation of world public opinion, which pointed to the rise of an international public sphere, became significant issues in this debate (e.g. Garnham 1990, Gurevitch et al. 1991, Keane 1991, 1992, Mattelart and Mattelart 1992, Frederick 1992, Serra 1993, 1996, Mattelart 1994, Ferry 1995, Sreberny-Mohammadi 1996). However, little empirical work has been done on the dynamics of the international public sphere, and what little there has been mostly ignores the connections between this and the operation of the national media and national political processes.

The historical reconstruction of the rise of the issue of the killing of Brazilian street children presented in this chapter reverses this flow of analysis by focusing on the mobilisation of national civil society, the international outcry and the subsequent repercussions in Brazilian society, media and the political system. It clearly shows that the formation of the international agenda and its repercussions in the national arena involved complex mediation and representations and top-down, bottom-up and cross-wise relations between pressure groups, authorities, civil societies and the media at the local, national and transnational levels.

This chapter argues that the international public sphere is not a monolithic unit and, although hierarchically organised, can represent a defence mechanism for groups outside the structure of power. The chapter demonstrates that peripheral groups can influence the definition of issues that are debated in the media and dealt with by the political and administrative system via the international public sphere. It thus supports and extends Habermas's arguments outlined above.

Cobb, Ross and Ross, quoted in Habermas (1997: 380), argue that the 'outside initiative model' of agenda-building, in which a group outside government enunciates a grievance and tries to broaden support from other groups in society in order to pressurise policy-makers to deal with the problem, is 'likely to predominate in more egalitarian societies'. None the less, in this example, which involved one of the most inegalitarian societies (Brazil) and one of the most marginal groups (street children), this was made possible by the mobilisation of international civil society and the publicising of the issue in the international media, with knock-on effects in the domestic media and the national political system. This empowered the local children's defence groups, and helped to neutralise the powerful constraints represented by social inequalities.

As seen, this was a deliberate strategy pursued by the street children's movement, which understood the importance of appealing to international public opinion and the world media to influence national policy-making. As Hallin (1998) and others (e.g. Castells 1997) note, this association of local movements with global public opinion is becoming increasingly common. In contemporary societies there are obviously distinct paths to reform, but this further demonstrates the importance of considering the broader framework of the international public sphere, and a more adequate elaboration of notions of international civil society and global public opinion for any model of the media's role in the rise of issues in public arenas.

References

Amnesty International (1990a) *Beyond the Law: Torture and Extrajudicial Execution in Urban Brazil*, London: Amnesty International Publications.

Amnesty International (1990b) *Amnesty International Report 1990*, London: Amnesty International Publications.

Amnesty International (1991) *Amnesty International Report 1991*, London: Amnesty International Publications.

Boorstin, D. J. (1967) 'The Reign of Pseudo-Events', in A. Fontenilles and J. Marty, *The Mass Media: Communications et Relations Sociales*, Paris: Dunod.

Calhoun, C. (1992a) 'Introduction: Habermas and the Public Sphere', in C. Calhoun (ed.), *Habermas and the Public Sphere*, Cambridge, MA: MIT Press.

Calhoun, C. (1992b) *Habermas and the Public Sphere*, Cambridge, MA: MIT Press.

Câmara dos Deputados (1992) *Comissão Parlamentar de Inquérito-CPI: Destinada a Investigar o Extermínio de Crianças e Adolescentes – Relatório Final*, Brasília: Diário do Congresso Nacional.

Castells, M. (1997) *The Power of Identity*, Vol. II of *The Information Age: Economy, Society and Culture*, Oxford: Blackwell.

Cracknell, J. (1993) 'Issue Arenas, Pressure Groups and Environmental Agendas', in A. Hansen, *The Mass Media and Environmental Issues*, Leicester: Leicester University Press, pp. 3–21.

Curran, J. (1990) 'Culturalist Perspectives of News Organizations: A Reappraisal and a Case Study', in M. Ferguson (ed.), *Public Communication*, London: Sage, pp. 114–34.

Curran, J. (1991a) 'Rethinking the Media as a Public Sphere', in P. Dahlgren and C. Sparks (eds), *Communication and Citizenship*, London: Routledge, pp. 27–57.

Curran, J. (1991b) 'Mass Media and Democracy: A Reappraisal', in J. Curran and M. Gurevitch (eds), *Mass Media and Society*, London: Arnold, pp. 82–117.

Curran, J. (1996) 'Rethinking Mass Communications', in J. Curran, D. Morley and V. Walkerdine (eds), *Cultural Studies and Communications*, London: Arnold, pp. 119–65.

Curran, J. (1998) 'Newspapers and the Press', in A. Briggs and P. Cobby (eds), *The Media: An Introduction*, Harlow: Longman pp. 81–96.

Dahlgren, P. (1991) 'Introduction', in P. Dahlgren and C. Sparks (eds), *Commmunication and Citizenship*, London: Routledge, pp. 1–24.

Dahlgren, P. (1995) *Television and the Public Sphere: Citizenship, Democracy and the Media*, London: Sage.

Deacon, D. and Golding, P. (1994) *Taxation and Representation*, London: John Libbey.

Dijk, T. A. Van (1989) 'Structures of Discourse, Structures of Power', in J. Anderson (ed.), *Communication Yearbook 12*, London: Sage.

Ferguson, R. (1998) *Representing 'Race': Ideology, Identity and the Media*, London: Arnold.

Fernandes, R. C. (1995) 'Elos de uma Cidadania Planetária', in *Revista Brasileira de Ciências Sociais*, 28.10: 15–37.

Ferry, J. (1995) 'Las Transformaciones de la Publicidad Política', in J. Ferry, D. Wolton et al., *El Nuevo Espacio Publico*, Barcelona: Gedisa, pp. 13–27.

Frank, A. G. and Fuentes, M. (1990) 'Civil Democracy: Social Movements in Recent World History', in S. Amin et al., *Transforming the Revolution: Social Movements and the World-System*, New York: Monthly Review Press, pp. 139–80.

Frank, A. G. (1993) 'Marketing Democracy in an Undemocratic Market', in B. Gills, J. Rocamora and R. Wilson (eds), *Low Intensity Democracy: Political Power in the New World Order*, London: Pluto Press, pp. 35–58.

Fraser, N. (1993) 'Rethinking the Public Sphere: A Contribution to the Critique of Actually Existing Democracy', in B. Robbins (ed.), *The Phantom Public Sphere*, Minneapolis: University of Minnesota Press, pp. 1–32.

Frederick, H. (1992) 'Computer Communications in Cross-Border Coalition-Building: North American NGO Networking Against NAFTA', *Gazette. The International Journal for Mass Communication Studies*, 50: 217–241.

Garnham, N. (1990) *Capitalism and Communication: Global Culture and the Economics of Information*, London: Sage.

Gomes, W. (1997) 'Esfera Pública Política e Media: Com Habermas, Contra Habermas', *Compós 1997*.

Gurevitch, M., Levy, M. R. and Roeh, I. (1991) 'The Global Newsroom', in P. Dahlgren and C. Sparks (eds), *Communication and Citizenship*, London: Routledge, pp. 195–216.

Habermas, J. (1989 [1962]) *The Structural Transformation of the Public Sphere: An Inquiry into a Category of Bourgeois Society*, Cambridge: Polity.

Habermas, J. (1992a) 'Further Reflections on the Public Sphere', in C. Calhoun (ed.) *Habermas and the Public Sphere*, Cambridge, MA: MIT Press, pp. 420–61.

Habermas, J. (1992b) 'Concluding Remarks', in C. Calhoun (ed.), *Habermas and the Public Sphere*, Cambridge, MA: MIT Press, pp. 462–79.

Habermas, J. (1994) *The Past as Future*, interview by M. Haller, Cambridge: Polity.

Habermas, J. (1997 [1992]) *Between Facts and Norms: Contributions to a Discourse Theory of Law and Democracy*, trans. W. Rehg, Cambridge: Polity.

Hallin, D. (1998) 'Broadcasting in the Third World: From National Development to Civil Society', in T. Liebes and J. Curran (eds), *Media, Ritual and Identity*, London: Routledge, pp. 153–74.

Hansen, A. (1991) 'The Media and the Social Construction of the Environment', *Media, Culture and Society*, 13.4: 443–58.

Hilgartner, S. and Bosk, C. (1988) 'The Rise and Fall of Social Problems: A Public Arenas Model', *American Journal of Sociology*, 94.1: 53–78.

Hess, S. (1996) *International News and Foreign Correspondents*, Washington DC: Brookings Institution.

Holub, R. (1991) *Jurgen Habermas: Critic in the Public Sphere*, London: Routledge.

Keane, J. (1991) *The Media and Democracy*, Cambridge: Polity.

Keane, J. (1992) 'The Crisis of the Sovereign State', in M. Raboy and B. Dagenais, *Media, Crisis and Democracy*, London: Sage, pp. 16–33.

Kellner, D. (1990) *Television and the Crisis of Democracy*, Boulder, CO: Westview Press.

Mainwaring, S. and Viola, E. (1984) 'New Social Movements, Political Culture and Democracy: Brazil and Argentina in the 1980s', *Telos*, 61: 17–52.

Mattelart, A. (1994) *Comunicação Mundo: Historia das Ideias e das Estratégias*, trans G. J. de Freitas Teixeira, Petrópolis: Vozes.

Mattelart, A. and Mattelart, M. (1992) *Rethinking Media Theory*, Minneapolis: University of Minnesota Press.

McNair, B. (1995) *An Introduction to Political Communication*, London: Routledge.

Miller, D. and Beharrell, P. (1998) 'AIDS and Television News', in D. Miller, J. Kitzinger, K. Williams and P. Beharrell (Glasgow Media Group), *The Circuit of Mass Communication: Media Strategies, Representation and Audience Reception in the AIDS Crisis*, London: Sage.

MNMMR/IBASE/NEV-USP (1991) *Vidas em Risco: Assassinatos de Crianças e Adolescentes no Brasil*, Rio de Janeiro.

Peters, J. D. (1993) 'Distrust of Representation: Habermas on the Public Sphere', *Media, Culture and Society*, 15: 541–71.

Philo, G. (1993) 'From Buerk to Band Aid: The Media and the Ethiopian Famine', in J. Eldridge (ed.), *Getting the Message: News, Truth and Power*, London: Routledge, pp. 104–25.

Pinto, L. (ed.) (1991) *Exterminio de Crianças e Adolescentes*, Rio de Janeiro: CBIA.

Protess, D. et al. (1991) *The Journalism of Outrage: Investigative Reporting and Agenda Building in America*, New York: Guildford Press.

Reese, S. D. (1991) 'Setting the Media's Agenda: A Power Balance Perspective', in J. Anderson (ed.), *Communication Yearbook 14*, London: Sage, pp. 309–40.

Rocha, J. (1991) 'Introduction', in Dimenstein, *Brazil: War on Children*, London: Latin America Bureau, pp. 1–15.

Scannell, P. (1989) 'Public Service Broadcasting and Modern Public Life', *Media, Culture and Society*, 11: 135–66.

Scherer-Warren, I. and Krischke, P. J. (1987) *Uma Revolução no Cotidiano?: Os novos Movimentos Sociais na America Latina*, São Paulo: Brasiliense.

Schlesinger, P. and Tumber, H. (1994) *Reporting Crime: The Media Politics of Criminal Justice*, Oxford: Clarendon Press.

Serra, S. (1993) 'Multinationals of Solidarity: International Civil Society and the Issue of the Killing of Street Children', International Association for Mass Communication Research conference paper, Dublin, June.

Serra, S. (1996) 'Multinationals of Solidarity: International Civil Society and the Killing of Street Children in Brazil', in S. Braman and A. Sreberny-Mohammadi (eds), *Globalization, Communication and Transnational Civil Society*, Creskill, NJ: Hampton Press, pp. 219–41.

Shoemaker, P. J. and Reese, S. D. (1996) *Mediating the Message: Theories of Influences on Mass Media Content*, Harlow: Longman.

Sparks, C. (1991) 'Goodbye, Hildy Johnson', in P. Dahlgren and C. Sparks (eds), *Communication and Citizenship*, London: Routledge, pp. 59–74.

Sreberny-Mohammadi, A. (1996) 'Globalization, Communication and Transnational Civil Society: Introduction', in S. Braman and A. Sreberny-Mohammadi, *Globalization, Communication and Transnational Civil Society*, Creskill, NJ: Hampton Press, pp. 1–19.

Swift, A. (1991) *Brazil: The Fight for Childhood in the City*, Florence: UNICEF.

Thompson, J. B. (1990) *Ideology and Modern Culture: Critical Social Theory in the Era of Mass Communication*, Cambridge: Polity.

Wolsfeld, G. (1997) *Media and Political Conflict*, Cambridge: Cambridge University Press.

Wuthnow, R. (ed.) (1991) 'The Voluntary Sector: Legacy of the Past, Hope for the Future?', in R. Wuthnow, *Between States and Markets: The Voluntary Sector in Comparative Perspective*, Princeton, NJ: Princeton University Press.

7

Public-relations campaigning and news production

The case of 'new unionism' in Britain

AERON DAVIS

This chapter argues that the news production process is being increasingly influenced by the activities of professional public-relations practitioners. This influence has spread far beyond the confines of Westminster and party politics and has become increasingly sophisticated in its methods. Where once 'outsider' organisations attempted to gain coverage with press releases, news conferences and demonstrations, now they attempt to monitor and subtly alter news values and journalist routines. The example taken here is the British trade-union movement which, during the 1990s, has widely adopted professional PR practices and personnel as an alternative means of influencing corporate and political decision-making. Despite the reservations expressed by many scholars – that PR has limited results, especially for non-institutional and 'resource-poor' groups – unions have actually achieved some notable successes. After introducing the debates and some of the details of trade-union PR in the 1990s, most of this chapter will be taken up with a case study of the communication unions' successful campaign against Post Office privatisation in 1994.

As a number of recent studies have demonstrated (see Chapter 1), sources have increasingly begun to use the media as an alternative means of achieving political and economic influence. Despite the growing academic and media interest in source–media relations and the art of the 'spin doctor', little serious research on public relations itself has emanated from UK media studies departments. In 1993 *Media, Culture and Society* (15.3) produced a special issue on the topic; but media sociology has since failed adequately to investigate the subject, either empirically or theoretically. Most of the existing literature has been concerned with the formal political process: governments, political parties and the electoral process – in other words, how institutional elites, with a high level of access, professionally manage their media relations. How non-institutional source organisations, from large multinational corporations to small single-issue pressure groups, use PR to gain access and set agendas, remains under researched. Those studies choosing to focus on sources (Ericson et al. 1989, Anderson 1993, Hansen 1993, Miller and Williams 1993, Miller 1994, Deacon and Golding 1994, Schlesinger and Tumber 1994, Manning 1998) have all been based on research at the end of the 1980s and early 1990s. As such, all were completed before the recent and widespread adoption of professional PR. As a result most (Miller 1994 and Manning 1998 being the exceptions) have not been particularly concerned with separating the practice of PR from its source ties. Public relations has simply been regarded as an extension of the existing resources and media relations of an interest group or organisation. Professional PRPs (public-relations practitioners) themselves – those working outside formal politics – have largely been ignored, and detailed case studies and evaluations of public relations in action are barely in evidence.

The British trade-union movement is one such sector where circumstances have led organisations to adopt professional PR methods as a means of influencing the political and industrial spheres. During 18 years of Conservative government many traditional means of union influence were eroded (see accounts in Bassett and Cave 1993, Taylor 1994 and McIlroy 1995). Government legislation and changing patterns of employment, have combined steadily to erode union membership and union density since 1979. Representation at government level has been severed and industrial action severely restricted by anti-union legislation. In seeking the political centre ground the Labour Party has similarly distanced itself from the unions – reducing their voting power and neglecting many of their policy concerns. In two decades unions have thus become significantly smaller and financially poorer, have been strongly deterred from strike action and have been denied much of their former institutional legitimacy. The decline in political influence and strike activity has been followed by a similar reduction in coverage of industrial relations and union affairs (see Manning 1998, ch. 6). By all accounts, unions can no longer be included among the ranks of the 'primary definers', as determined by Hall et al. (1978) in the 1970s. Not only do they have to struggle to get media access but they must work to obtain favourable coverage in spite of a negative media image built up over decades.

Unions have generally been slow to adopt professional public-relations methods and personnel. For many unionists (Beckett 1977, TUC 1979, Douglas 1985, Myers 1986) and radical media sociologists (Glasgow University Media Group 1976, 1980, Beharrell and Philo (eds) 1977, Douglas 1986, Hollingsworth 1986) in the 1970s and 1980s, the media were inherently hostile to the cause of labour and, as a result, industrial action naturally produced negative reports of unions. Despite many commentators (see Adeney and Lloyd 1986, Jones 1987, Verzuh 1990) arguing that much union industrial action in the 1980s, particularly the 1984/5 coal strike, was hampered by poor communications, little changed before the 1990s. Manning's 1988 survey of the 37 largest unions revealed that only seven of them had a full-time press officer – little different from the Glasgow Group's (1976) own findings a decade earlier.

In contrast, my own research (see Davis 1998) found that union communications were transformed in the second half of the 1990s.[1] A survey completed in 1997 found that two-thirds of all unions employ at least one part-time person to deal with public relations and only 9.3 per cent stated that they had 'no PR function'. Unison, the largest union, had 33 communications staff and all but one of the larger unions (those with over 100 000 members) had a communications department with between two and eight practitioners. The TUC was itself relaunched in 1994 as a 'campaigning and public affairs organisation'. The newly created 'Campaigns and Communications Department' employed a staff of 10 and was set up with the advice of Burson-Marsteller, the largest PR consultancy in the world. The survey also found that 63.4 per cent of all unions employed staff with journalistic and/or PR experience and 55 per cent offered specialist communications training for staff and local branch members. A quarter of unions employed PR consultancies and 57.4 per cent employed other consultancies such as lobbyists or press-cutting agencies. 76.6 per cent of unions stated that their communications budgets had increased, relative to overall union budgets, during the 1990s – half of those, substantially.

Union activists and radical media sociologists alike have, however, remained cautious about the usefulness of public relations as a means by which unions may influence media output and elite decision-making. Even more recent radical pluralist accounts of source–media relations (see especially Schlesinger and Tumber 1994, Miller 1994 and Manning 1998) have expressed reservations about the ability of all non-institutional and resource-poor groups to have more than a temporary or minor effect on news production. These reservations are summarised as follows:

1 Because of corporate and state ownership, media organisations are inherently hostile to unions and the Left generally.
2 Journalist news routines and news values (also described as 'dominant ideology') mean that unions will always be reported negatively in industrial relations coverage.
3 Journalist news routines and news values (or dominant ideology) mean that reporters will tend to skew coverage, and therefore agendas, towards those dictated by institutional and elite sources.
4 Elite sources have much greater economic resources with which to support PR operations; which means, in comparison to unions, they can use more sophisticated equipment and employ large groups of professional PRPs at all times.
5 Elite sources naturally have a level of authority and legitimacy (or 'cultural capital') that comes with their position and means that their input will be given greater weighting and credibility than unions and other 'outsider' sources.

However, continuing union faith in public-relations methods, coupled with a number of PR victories, defies this scepticism. A survey by Mitchell (1997) found that the 'most effective' form of political activity for unions (from a choice of seven options) was thought to be public-relations campaigning (38 per cent). Protests and strikes were fourth, with only 13 per cent of unions regarding them as 'most effective'. My own survey found that, 'compared to the 1980s', 76 per cent of unions believed 'union access' to the media had increased and 79 per cent thought that media coverage was 'more favourable'. 67.4 per cent also expected continued increases in funding, relative to union budgets, in their communications activities over the next 5 years. Interviews with union communications staff (Davis 1998) also revealed many examples of successful or partially successful campaigns within the previous decade – most of which remain undocumented. These include: the ambulance drivers' dispute in 1989 (see Kerr and Sachdev 1992, Manning 1998); BIFU's (banking union) successful blocking of the Lloyds take-over of Midland Bank in 1992; the UCW's (communication workers) prevention of Post Office privatisation (Cockerell 1997); BALPA (airline pilots) and the TGWU's successes against British Airways in 1996 and 1997; and the ongoing 'Fat Cats' campaign (1992 to time of writing), initiated by the GMB against directors' salaries. Other campaigns, while not succeeding, did manage severely to embarrass the incumbent Major government and many corporations. These include: the TUC-inspired attack on pit closures in 1993; the POA's (prison officers) attempts to halt prison privatisation and undermine Group 4 in 1993; the teachers' unions' campaign against education cuts in 1995; and ASLEF and the RMT's 'Save Our Railways' campaigns (1992 to time of writing) to block rail privatisation and embarrass train operators. Such campaigns not only caused political difficulties, they also ensured that such subjects remained high on the new Labour government's legislative agenda.

In each of these cases, union PRPs had aided unions in developing a wide range of methods for bypassing many of the obstacles described above. Using professional public relations, unions have managed to find ways of overcoming economic resource deficits, negative reporting and legitimacy gaps. In contrast to the hostile relations of the 1970s and 1980s they have attempted to build up their media contacts and develop positive media profiles. They have hired consultants and trained up voluntary labour (members) to bridge the resources gap. Rather than use the traditional arguments about pay and jobs they have argued the public-service case and attacked the failings of government ministers and 'greedy' corporate executives – citing them as the cause of any problems. They have made up for lack of authority and legitimacy by voicing their arguments through alternative third-party elites. All these methods, in fact, contributed to the successful campaign by the communication workers' unions to disrupt government plans for Post Office privatisation in 1994. They are described in some detail in the case study that follows.

CASE STUDY: THE UNION OF COMMUNICATION WORKERS VERSUS POST OFFICE PRIVATISATION, 1994

This study looks at how a very successful PR campaign, carried out by the Union of Communication Workers (UCW), contributed to the failure of the government to privatise the Post Office in 1994.[2]

Events were set in motion on 15 July 1992, when Michael Heseltine, president of the Board of Trade, unexpectedly announced that Parcelforce would be privatised. Two weeks later the government declared it would be reviewing all postal services and thus signalled its intention to privatise the whole of the Post Office. After 2 years of delays, Heseltine announced (19 May 1994) the forthcoming publication of a green paper – 'The Future of Postal Services' – on the issue. This presented three options: greater commercial freedom for the Post Office within the public sector, a complete privatisation, and the government's 'preferred option' of a partial (51 per cent) privatisation. The paper, published at the end of June, gave a three-month consultation period, after which the government would announce future legislation. Post Office management, led by Bill Cockburn (chief executive) and Michael Heron (chairman), also came out in favour of the 51 per cent option. They had been campaigning for 2 years for more freedom from government and, following the events of June and July, they also began an extensive campaign. On 12 July, when MPs voted by 305 to 273 in favour of a motion supporting the 51 per cent privatisation, the government's long-running privatisation programme looked set to continue.

The unions' campaign, led by the UCW,[3] had begun preparing to defend the Post Office's public-sector status even before the 1992 announcement. Their campaign began to accelerate during the early months of 1994 and moved quickly into operation over the summer. After several months of media campaigning and lobbying, in which the Labour Party and many other interest groups entered the debate, the government's plans suddenly began to look doubtful. Between the end of the consultation period (30 Sept. 1994) and the start of November, when legislation was being finalised for the Queen's Speech, Heseltine and the DTI looked increasingly desperate. On 2 November, with the cabinet divided, Ulster Unionists refusing to support the government, and up to 20 Conservative MPs threatening rebellion, cabinet plans for the Post Office were shelved. The strength and ingenuity of the union's campaign was cited as being the main cause of government defeat in a number of campaign reviews in the *FT*, *Standard*, *Independent*, *Guardian* and *PR Week* (all on 3 Nov. 1994). *PR Week* described the UCW communications team as:

> prime examples of a new generation of union professionals using communications tactics more familiar to big business ... a devastatingly

effective team galvanising the union's most useful weapon – its 160,000 members – and in the process becoming the first union ever to defeat a government privatisation.

An examination of the media profiles of each of the principal organisations involved suggests that communication campaigns played an important part in the government's decision-making process. The content of coverage overall was significantly more favourable to the unions and critical of Heseltine/the DTI. Most of the time the unions were presented quite neutrally, scoring a small positive average (between 0 and 0.09) for all papers except the *Daily Express*. The overall rating for Post Office management was slightly negative, with only the *Daily Express* and *Sun* newspapers offering positive overall coverage. The DTI and Heseltine had the most negative coverage, with an overall average below –0.5. The *Mirror* and *Today* were extremely negative and even *The Times* and *FT*, the least critical, scored –0.12. This picture was not uniform throughout the period. For the first 10 weeks (see Figure 7.1), the DTI/Heseltine appeared to be struggling but in contention. After that they rarely managed to obtain neutral coverage and came out extremely badly in the last 7 weeks. The Post Office remained fairly consistent during the first 14 weeks, faced very neg-

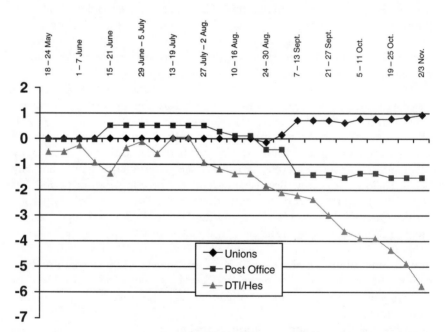

Fig. 7.1   Cumulative favourability rating of organisations in broadsheet press coverage, 18 May to 3 November 1994
Sample: 283 articles.

ative coverage at the start of September, and never recovered from there. The unions maintained neutrality, gaining positive coverage after week 15.

However, any initial overview of events makes this claim appear to be rather exaggerated – a case of spin doctoring on behalf of the spinners themselves. To begin with, the economic and communications resources of the Post Office and DTI easily outmatched those of the unions. The Post Office had a turnover in 1994–5 of £5.88 billion, 190 000 employees (PO business briefs), and some 460 'communications staff' (Post Office 1997a, 1997b). The Post Office campaign was extremely thorough and was commented upon frequently by journalists (*FT*, 20 May 1994, *The Times*, 12 Aug. 1994, *Telegraph*, 12 Aug. 1994). Articles in the *Telegraph* (28 Aug. 1994) and *The Times* (8 Sept. 1994) estimated that £1.8 million had been spent on the campaign by the end of August.[4] Heseltine and the DTI had the might of the Government Information Services and Conservative Party press machine behind them. The COI directory for January 1994 lists 67 communications staff as working in the DTI. In answer to a commons question (November 1994), the DTI declared that just over £1.6 million had been spent on consultancy for the project alone.[5] Heseltine and other ministers (notably Edward Leigh, Patrick McLoughlin and Tim Eggar) evidently attempted to promote the privatisation options vigorously. In contrast, the UCW had a total staff of 120 and an annual accounts expenditure of £12.5 million. The three unions between them had a handful of 'communications staff' in total. They claim to have spent £500 000 on their campaign – most of it during six months in 1994.

A brief inspection view of the content analysis makes the claims of the union communications team appear more questionable still. As expected, government and business sources did dominate news output. Unions and other anti-privatisers did appear to do well in terms of being cited in articles (see Table 7.1). The Labour Party (16.5 per cent) and the unions (14 per cent) figured rather more than members of the DTI (10.4 per cent) and other government figures (5.2 per cent). The most cited groups were, in fact, Post Office management (18.7 per cent) and Conservative Party rebels (18.7 per cent). This, unfortunately, gives a rather distorted account. The contributions of the Labour Party and the unions were, more often than not, little more than single quotes in the middle or at the end of an article, i.e. simply used to offer 'journalistic balance' within articles framed by other organisational contributions. However, if the same material is looked at in terms of article content and actors' contributions (see Table 7.2), the results are strongly skewed in favour of the DTI (20.7 per cent), other government sources (19 per cent), and Post Office managers (15.6 per cent). Labour (11 per cent) and the unions (12.6 per cent) are some way down, with Conservative rebels (8.5 per cent) contributing least. This picture becomes more skewed still when looking at the number of times groups are not mentioned at all. The views of Heseltine and the DTI are discussed in or contribute to 89 per cent of articles. Post Office management are included in 56

Table 7.1   Actors cited in press coverage (per cent)

	Pro-privatisation	Anti-privatisation	Others
DTI/Heseltine	10.4		
Government			5.2
PO management	18.7		
Unions		14	
Labour		16.5	
Other organisations			12.1
Conservative rebels		18.7	
Public/postal workers			4.4
TOTAL	29.1	49.2	21.7

Source: 364 citations

Table 7.2   Actors contributing to press coverage (per cent)

	Pro-privatisation	Anti-privatisation	Others
DTI/Heseltine	20.7		
Government			19
PO management	15.6		
Unions		12.6	
Labour		11	
Other organisations			11.3
Conservative rebels		8.5	
Public/postal workers			1.2
TOTAL	36.3	32.1	31.6

Source: 564 contributions

per cent of stories. The unions are only mentioned in 37 per cent. The public and postal workers have negligible input, with 4.4 per cent of citations and 1.2 per cent of contributions. Thus, as in virtually all earlier studies of media content (e.g. Sigal 1973, Hall et al. 1978, Gans 1979, Chomsky and Herman 1988, Tiffen 1989, Hallin 1994), the substance of coverage proved to be very much oriented towards institutional sources.

It might therefore be concluded that the unions' campaign was not particularly relevant. They had comparatively few economic and human resources. Their contribution to news articles was fairly small. They were never reported with any great authority and they rarely seemed to set news agendas. On the other hand, at that time, the government was deeply unpopular and had a small parliamentary majority. The cabinet was split between 'consolidators' and 'radicals', and the DTI, Treasury and Post Office management were in frequent disagreement. It could in fact be argued that the unions' campaign was victorious because: a) the institutional elites were in conflict (thus echoing the findings of, for example, Miller 1994 and Hallin 1994); and b) the media were simply reflecting popular opinion of government policy (thus confirming a classic liberal perspective of the fourth estate media). If any credit is to be given to the unions' communications campaign several questions need to be answered. How did they: 1) overcome their economic and communication resource deficits; 2) manage to put across convincing and authoritative arguments with little institutional authority or legitimacy; and 3) manage to alter reporting patterns and set news agendas and interpretive frameworks?

Overcoming resource inequalities

The unions made up for their lack of economic, communication and institutional resources by making use of their network of members and hiring external consultants. The CMA had 14 000 members and the UCW 160 000 members – spread over 100 branches across the UK. This membership was a vital part of the campaign and worked hard to promote the union message in the regions – through the local media, town councils, local events and in letter-writing to MPs. Media training was given and campaign packs were circulated to all branch representatives. All campaigning was carefully planned through campaign headquarters with communication being maintained to branches through regular 'special branch circulars'. This closely co-ordinated media and letter-writing campaign worked consistently over the summer and was used to maximum effect at particular pressure points. UCW sub-group letters frequently commented on membership activity (for example, 25 Aug. 1994): 'Activity by branches is frenetic. Millions of leaflets have been distributed. Rallies are being organised every weekend and countless initiatives are being pursued in relation to local petitions.'

Although the unions did not have the media profile of their opponents they had spent a lot of time building up contacts. The union employed its first full-time media and campaigns officer, Daniel Harris, in 1990. Communications budgets increased under the new general secretary, Alan Johnson, and extra communications and research staff were taken on after 1992. As Daniel Harris (interview) explained:

> I built up a long-term rapport with the media ... This filtered through to the national press. For 3 years I was putting out press releases and talking to people ... Through all the period, from a very drip drip drip approach we were getting good stories about local postmen in ... It was a long slow build-up of quotes and stories always giving the union the moral high ground.

The unions also made up for their lack of professional communications staff and media contacts by hiring a number of consultants. The most controversial of these was Lowe Bell Political, headed by a principal adviser to Margaret Thatcher and the Conservative Party – Tim Bell. They supplied a team of four to work part-time on the campaign from July 1994 onwards. The team advised on strategy, brought access to Conservative MPs and numerous connections with the right-wing press. At the other end of the spectrum, Keith Bill of Union Communications was employed to run the pressure group PPS (Protect our Postal Services) from March 1993, and also offered access to union-friendly media. Thus media access across the spectrum of local and national titles was achieved.

Access to institutional information was gained by hiring external consultants – thereby overcoming some of the disadvantages associated with 'outsider' groups. Connect Public Affairs was hired in August 1992 to keep the unions updated on parliamentary and government affairs. David Lane, an ex-director of Royal Mail International, was also hired over the summer of 1994. He and members of the CMA provided detailed information on Post Office and DTI plans for privatisation. As correspondence with each of these groups indicated, the unions had advance warning of every important committee or cabinet meeting, as well as details of all Post Office campaign plans. It was this information that allowed the unions to begin early preparations, time media exposure and public campaigns appropriately, and come up with counter-arguments to every government or DTI statement.[6]

Overcoming primary definition: third-party endorsement, official sources and experts

Arguably the most important factor in the media campaign was the unions' use of third-party endorsement. As Lowe Bell strategists explained (Lowe Bell 1994):

> Winning is all that matters – not how much the UCW is in the news ... the campaign must encourage submissions independently of the unions' case but which support its central arguments. It is vital that this process does not look like a union-inspired lobby.

The unions developed their strategy accordingly and, through a mixture of lobbying, public campaigning and polling, they galvanised opposition from a range of sources. In effect, they bypassed the need for institutional legitimacy and direct access. Instead they gained a voice by using the legitimacy and access possessed by other sources: the public, 'economic experts', politicians and assorted 'neutral' user groups.

The 'voice of public opinion' was aired frequently by the commissioning and publishing of opinion polls. Over 10 different polls, conducted mostly on behalf of the UCW, found their way into the national press – often providing the basis for a headline story. In the content analysis, 16 articles featured a MORI poll in the story, and poll results were mentioned with great frequency by all anti-privatisation campaigners. The unions also set up Protect our Postal Services (PPS), in March 1993, in order to organise and promote localised public responses that were 'not under the UCW banner'. The group was made up of a number of charities and pressure groups with an interest in postal services. These included the National Federation of Women's Institutes, ACRE, RADAR, Help the Aged and the National League for the Blind and Disabled. Although the unions had minimal direct contact with the PPS board, the two were closely connected. Keith Bill, of union communications, was the secretary of PPS and was part of the UCW sub-group campaign committee. As a UCW sub-group letter (1 July 1994) illustrates, the two were closely co-ordinated: 'Once they [the PPS] have seen the green paper they will adopt a position and campaign vigorously on what is likely to be a platform remarkably similar to our own (aimed at keeping the Post Office together).'

A second block of 'neutral' third-party endorsement was built up from user groups and other interested parties. The main targets were the Mail Users Association (MUA), the Post Office Users National Council (POUNC) and the National Federation of Sub-Postmasters (NFSP). All three were lobbied and had informal talks with the unions. A UCW sub-group circular (25 Aug. 1994) comments: 'As already reported, the Mail Users Association are on course to produce a helpful response to the green paper . . . We are also working hard to influence the POUNC response.' Following a drawn-out lobbying battle for the support of the NFSP, the NFSP leadership also agreed to meet with the UCW. It was later reported in a sub-group letter (14 Sept. 1994) that 'following our discussion we are now guaranteed a positive message from the NFSP nationally'.

The degree of accord between the UCW and its allies becomes apparent in the press releases and submissions to the DTI that followed. The union (POUC) response to the green paper (September 1994) reads: 'Ownership is itself not the most important issue facing the Post Office' (p. 3); 'If the government is genuinely committed to ensuring that the whole of the Post Office remains a British success story, it will keep it together and give it genuine commercial freedom in the public sector' (p. 29). These comments can be compared with a number of other organisational press releases issued at the time: PPS (27 July 1994) – 'There is a viable alternative . . . That is give the Post Office public sector commercial freedom – the Freedom to Deliver'; POUNC (30 Sept. 1994) – 'The postal users watchdog has told government that it is unable to endorse any of its proposals and it has urged that consideration be given to keeping all three post office businesses together'; Colin Baker of the NFSP (30 Sept. 1994) – 'It [the Federation] does not see ownership as a critical issue. However should separation and privatisation take place, the Federation has many concerns'. These submissions and releases all found their way, in some form, into the national press. 'Customers Unsure of Need for Change' (1 July 1994), 'Post Office Watchdog Raps Sell-Off Plans' (30 Sept. 1994), 'Sub-Postmasters Seek Sale Pledge' (1 Oct. 1994), were some of the headlines to emerge in the *FT* as a result.[7]

MPs provided another means of official source access to the media. Just as sources can supply an 'information subsidy' to various media outlets, so they can do the same for MPs who are prepared to promote a source's position. In this case the unions and their hired consultants provided detailed briefs and drafted speeches and motions for three different political party groups: the Labour Party, Ulster Unionists and rebel Conservative MPs. Although running its own campaign, the Labour Party was in close contact with the unions throughout, making use of much of the unions' research and campaign materials. Both argued for increased 'commercial freedom within the public sector' and used the same arguments concerning VAT, closures of rural post offices, loss of the second delivery, international comparisons, etc. Peter Hain MP, the most vocal Labour critic after Robin Cook, had previously worked for the UCW. He remained in regular contact with them and asked several parliamentary questions in accordance with union strategy. Union correspondence (David Lane, 30 Oct. 1994) also shows that the unions were in frequent contact with both the Conservative rebels and the Ulster Unionists, offering briefings and organising their resistance, even during last-minute meetings with Heseltine. Jim Lester, a prominent rebel who was sponsored by the CMA union, proposed a well-publicised early day motion which was immediately signed by seven conservative rebels (with 12 more to follow). This motion was itself penned by the UCW and simply supported the unions' position: '. . . welcomes the publication of a report by London Economics . . . and therefore supports the parts of the green paper which retain the Post Office as an integrated organisation in the public sector, endowed with greater commercial freedom' (Hansard, 19 Oct. 1994).

One of the most skilful PR moves by the UCW was to get free-market economists to argue their case for them. Advice from all the union's PR consultants was for the union to present a credible 'alternative white paper' at the end of the consultation period. This would be produced by 'a reputable business school, preferably using a consultant that is a known Tory sympathiser' (Lowe Bell presentation). Eventually, London Economics, a 'Thatcherite' think-tank run by a former adviser to Norman Lamont (Bill Robinson), was commissioned to write a report that would argue the unions' case. The conclusions of the report (London Economics 1994: 79) stated:

> evidence suggests that there is no reason to believe that, simply by transferring the Post Office to the private sector, the company and the public will benefit from significant gains than would be the case if the Post Office remained publicly owned . . . We propose an alternative model of a publicly-owned, commercially free Post Office.

The report was, predictably, taken up and given wide coverage. Clearly, if even 'Thatcherite economists' were against privatisation, then the government appeared stranded.

If we now review the figures for actors' contributions, it transpires that many of the 'other organisations' (see Tables 7.1 and 7.2), frequently presented as neutrals, are actually 'union allies'. These allies contributed substantially to press articles during the period. 'Rebels' were cited 68 times.

Other cited 'allies', not already mentioned, included David Lane, the Liberal Democrats, Lowe Bell and Age Concern. The contributions of these others amounted to 40 citations and 59 organisational contributions. If we re-evaluate the total for organisational contributions, in terms of those for and against the government's preferred option, Table 7.2 is reshaped as below (see Table 7.3). What transpires is that the media contributions of the unions and the Labour Party could not alone match those arguing for privatisation. If union allies, including rebels, are added, media output is more influenced by anti-privatisers. Significantly, many of these contributions appeared in the last five and a half weeks of the campaign when media interest was consistently high and government legislation was being finalised. During this period there occurred an unrelenting media barrage (101 items) from supposedly neutral parties coming out against privatisation. The favourability rating of Heseltine and the DTI correspondingly took a sharp downturn.

Table 7.3   Actors contributing to press coverage (per cent)

	Pro-privatisation	Anti-privatisation	Others
DTI/Heseltine	20.7		
Government			19
PO management	15.6		
Unions		12.6	
Labour		11	
Other union allies		10.5	
DTI allies (CBI, IoD)	0.9%		
Rebels		8.5	
Public/postal workers			1.2
TOTAL	37.2	42.6	20.2

Source: 564 contributions

The union campaign: setting agendas, dividing oppositions and the creation of negative news

In spite of having less direct input into news output, union tactics did much to set media agendas and interpretative frameworks. This involved continually pursuing media-friendly lines of argument, encouraging divisions among the pro-privatisation lobbies and countering each opposition proposition. In stark contrast to the 1970s and early 1980s, the unions managed to avoid media scrutiny and to make their institutional opponents appear confused, untrustworthy and even illegal in their actions.

From the start, the unions worked hard to avoid the media pitfalls of earlier union campaigns. Industrial action was never threatened, the jobs issue was minimised and positive alternatives to privatisation were offered. As Chris Proctor (interview, 2 June 1997) explains:

We didn't concentrate on traditional trade-union interests. We lost 100 000 jobs in the BT privatisation and the job issue certainly worried our members. But we took the view that we lost that because demos and strikes were inherently bad news from a PR point of view. So the whole thing wasn't save our jobs but save your Post Office and protect your services ... We justified the fact that people liked the Royal Mail. Ideas really struck a chord. Just the issue of the Queen's head and the possibility that it wouldn't be on stamps any more. It seemed almost unpatriotic to privatise the Post Office. Julia came up with the idea that people liked their local postmen. We realised that we had 160 000 members; that we had 160 000 ambassadors that we could use.

At each union's annual conference, motions were passed that condemned privatisation but rejected strike action – something that was never an issue during the campaigns. Returning to the media content analysis, the jobs question was also clearly minimised. Out of 283 articles, the issue of jobs makes the headline in only six pieces (2 per cent) and is only mentioned in 14 articles altogether (less than 5 per cent in total). To avoid accusations of intransigence, the unions campaigned, not against change, but for a positive alternative of greater commercial freedom within the public sector, as in the cases of the BBC and BP (see Economists Advisory Group 1993).

At the same time opposition campaigns were undermined by dividing oppositions and initiating negative stories. Half-way through the campaign the UCW derailed Post Office management's campaign. A UCW sub-group circular (25 Aug. 1994) reports:

As you will be aware the Post Office has launched a huge internal and external communications campaign. We aim to produce reliable figures to demonstrate how much this will cost them – it will be a good news story. Certainly it is unprecedented for public servants to act in this way during a privatisation debate.

Articles about Post Office management expenditure duly appeared in the *Telegraph* (28 Aug. 1994) and *The Times* (8 Sept. 1994). As a result the Post Office campaign was widely criticised by many papers on grounds of expense and legality. A MORI poll of Post Office managers, conducted for the CMA in August, was also released to the press in September. This showed that 76 per cent of managers were actually in favour of the public-sector option and that the higher levels of Post Office management were isolated. Post Office managers were themselves given the 'fat cat' tag and accused simply of seeking personal gain from any potential share sale. The favourability profile of Post Office management consequently suffered a large dip in September and Post Office contributions to articles subsequently declined drastically.

Government divisions and backbench fears were also exploited and privatisation was made to seem unworkable. UCW and allied arguments consistently made the government's particular proposals for privatisation appear to be in conflict with either the public interest or the requirements of the Treasury. First it was demonstrated that complete privatisation was unworkable because cross-subsidisation was essential for maintaining the rural network of post offices – many of which were in marginal Conservative constituencies. When a 51 per cent privatisation was proposed to safeguard these elements, the anti-privatisation lobby argued that it made more economic sense for the Post Office to be kept together, whether private or public. Eventually, when Heseltine was making a last-minute attempt at a compromise, involving a 40 per cent privatisation, it was pointed out that this would bring in less revenue for the Treasury than 3 years' worth of the existing EFL (external financing limit) formula. The unions' own preferred option, of more commercial freedom within the public sector, was not a possibility because the Treasury would not have accepted the loss of all of its potential Post Office revenues.

All these positions were vigorously argued, locally and nationally, in an effort to divide the Conservatives and isolate Heseltine. Polls, press releases and opposition statements continued to be released and published on important decision-making days for the government and Conservative Party. In addition, the UCW specifically targeted all potential backbench rebels, Conservative MPs in marginal seats and key cabinet waverers. In each case the addresses of local Conservative Party associations, Conservative councillors and MPs were supplied to branches to organise local mail campaigns. As a special branch circular (14 Oct. 1994) informs:

> The next two weeks will be crucial. We have identified a group of Cabinet Ministers and Government Whips upon whom we want to bring maximum pressure. The best way this can be done is for them to receive a large postbag from their own constituents. To this end we have produced a special leaflet for delivery in their constituency. It is vital this leaflet is delivered early in the week commencing 17th October 1994.

Several statements, released to the press at the time, speak of Conservatives opposing privatisation on account of the mail they received.[8] As one anonymous Conservative MP said (*Independent*, 28 Oct. 1994), 'I don't oppose privatisation but I have had a big mailbag of letters objecting. I think the government should pause.' Conservative voters, MPs and local party workers were then polled after several months of being confronted with local press and letter-writing campaigns. The negative results were released accordingly – many in full-page adverts in *The Times* and the *Telegraph* (12 Oct. 1994) – at the time of the Conservative Party conference. By the time Heseltine addressed the October conference he already appeared isolated from many cabinet colleagues, local party members and activists. In the weeks that remained before the final cabinet meeting divisions continued and it became impossible to unite all parts of the party behind any single option.

Conclusion

This widespread adoption of professional public relations by organisations in society thus offers up some interesting questions for further research by media and communications scholars.

Clearly, in spite of their disadvantages, the unions managed to gain access for their arguments and affect media agendas significantly. Essentially they did this by making use of their membership and utilising a number of professional PR techniques – ones employed more commonly by corporate and political elites. At the heart of these techniques lies a thorough understanding of news values and journalist routines. If, for example, journalists seek out 'experts' and research, in an effort to be objective, then professional PRPs attempt to use, or even create, such sources. If journalists tend to report negative news, then professional PRPs attempt to dig up negative stories that focus on their oppositions. If particular journalists favour certain types of story and format, and are likely to need to fill some space on a Monday, then PRPs will attempt to supply those types of story, in that format, on a Sunday. A process that began with the press release and news conference has become much more sophisticated. Thus it must be asked: where does PR end and journalism begin? What does this mean for the notion of objective and independent journalism?

For some, it means that a more level playing field on the PR/media battleground has been created – one in which 'outsider' groups may obtain access and influence. In addition to actively interpreting media texts, individuals may participate in and contest their creation. However, although non-institutional and resource-poor groups can, on occasion, make significant impacts on news output during campaigns, one must ask how the unequal distribution of professional communications resources affects the wider production of media texts. What effect does the occasional victory by such groups have on long-term media discourses shaped by consistently high levels of elite access? What happens to those groups who don't have even the minimal amounts of economic and cultural capital required to gain coverage?

On another tack, what does the adoption of PR and media-oriented campaigns mean for those organisations that use this approach? Does this development entail organisations being 'incorporated' into media frameworks rather than arguing for clear ideological positions? Does this mean, as is the case with much media speculation over 'spin doctors', communicators dictating to policy-makers?

Some might conclude that these questions simply demonstrate the further evolution of postmodernism: a world where experts and authority are ethereal, where ideology has no sound basis, and where truth and objectivity have long since been lost. In effect, PR entails individuals and organisations further contesting and undermining the very means by which individuals attempt to rationally develop social norms. However, this conclusion all too easily ignores the power struggles evidently taking place. As the political-economy tradition observes, such struggles involve the use of political and economic resources to affect media outputs in order to gain control over additional political and economic resources. How then does one combine these two very different traditions and perspectives? How does one develop a political economy of public relations and promotional culture?

Notes

1 The research involved: 1) a postal survey of all 74 TUC affiliated unions from which 54 (73 per cent) usable responses were received; 2) a series of 21 semi-structured interviews with union PRPs and general secretaries across 19 different unions. See Davis (1998) for a full explanation of methods.

2 The research involved the accumulation of information on source organisations and their campaigns through campaign documents and eight semi-structured interviews with participants. This was compared to the results of an extensive content analysis of the national press during the six months in which the campaigns were most intensive. The newspaper analysis looked at a total of 283 articles from 10 different national daily newspapers. The period selected began on the day of the cabinet meeting on 18 May 1994 and ended with the cabinet meeting that rejected all options on 3 November 1994. The breakdown between papers was as follows: the *FT* – 51, *The Times* – 51, the *Guardian* – 45, the *Telegraph* – 40, the *Independent* – 34, *Today* – 15, the *Mirror* – 15, the *Daily Express* – 11, the *Daily Mail* – 11, the *Sun* – 10. For each article, all quoted individuals and all organisations which had their positions/arguments stated, were recorded. Lastly, the three principal groups – the unions, Post Office managers, and Heseltine/the DTI – were each given a favourability rating of minus two to plus two for each article. Zero denoted either no mention or a neutral presentation. Minus one represented a negative impression of a group and/or policies associated with it; plus one, a positive impression. Minus two represented an outright attack on that group; plus two, an outright endorsement.

3 The principal union involved was the UCW whose membership was mostly postal workers. The National Communication Union (NCU) and Communication Managers Association (CMA) played supporting roles. Together, they made up POUC – The Post Office Unions Council.

4 This figure, which was put out by union sources, was probably exaggerated. The campaign was, however, extensive and included: private meetings with 150 MPs; at least three mailouts to all 190 000 postal workers, explaining events and putting the case for privatisation; regional briefing meetings and weekly updates for 12 000 managerial staff; a hotline number for employees and members of the public to call; a glossy document and promotional video, arguing the case for privatisation, sent to all post and sub-post offices, 'opinion formers' and 'decision makers'; and a high-profile media and advertising campaign in the national press (interview with James Lindsey, 24 June 1997).

5 It should, however, be noted that the campaign by civil servants in the DTI was likely to have been low-key because, according to DTI officials (interviews 16 June 1997 and 24 June 1997), no legislation had yet been declared.

6 Consultancy fees and MORI polls accounted for approximately a fifth of union campaign expenses. The vast majority of the money was spent on printing and distributing campaign materials.
7 The Periodical Publishers Association (PPA), Readers' Digest and the National Consumer Council also eventually adopted positions that, if not entirely in accord with the unions, were critical of the government's attempts to break up the Post Office.
8 Julian Critchley MP (*The Times*, 24 Aug. 1994), Peter Emery MP (*Telegraph*, 8 Sept. 1994) and John Taylor MP (*FT*, 3 Oct. 1994).

References and further reading

Access Opinions Ltd (1994) *Post Office Privatisation: A Survey of MPs* (May).

Adeney, M. and Lloyd, J. (1986) *The Miners' Strike: Loss Without Limit*, London: Routledge and Kegan Paul.

Anderson, A. (1993) 'Source–Media Relations: The Production of the Environmental Agenda', in A. Hansen (ed.), *The Mass Media and Environmental Issues*, Leicester: Leicester University Press.

Bassett, P. and Cave, A. (1993) *All for One: The Future of the Unions*, London: Fabian Society.

Beckett, F. (1977) 'Press and Prejudice', in P. Beharrell and G. Philo (eds), *Trade Unions and the Media*, London: Macmillan.

Beharrell, P. and Philo, G. (eds) (1977) *Trade Unions and the Media*, London: Macmillan.

Bill, K., Interview 19 June 1997 (director of Union Communications and secretary for PPS campaign).

Central Office of Information (1994) *The IPO Directory: Information and Press Officers in Government Departments and Public Corporations* (Jan.).

Chomsky, N. and Herman, E. (1988) *Manufacturing Consent*, London: Pantheon.

Cockerell, M. (1997) *A Word in the Right Ear*, BBC2 documentary (19 Jan.).

Connect Public Affairs Ltd correspondence with UCW, 21 Aug. 1992, 26 Nov. 1992, 30 Nov. 1992, 2 Dec. 1992, 9 Feb. 1993, 22 Feb. 1993, 29 Mar. 1993, 16 Apr. 1993, 6 May 1993, 21 Apr. 1994, 10 June 1994, 31 May 1994.

Davis, A. (1998) *Trade Union Communications in the 1990s: A Report for the TUC and its Affiliate Unions*, TUC.

Deacon, D. and Golding, P. (1994) *Taxation and Representation*, London: John Libbey.

Department of Trade and Industry (1994) *The Future of Postal Services: A Consultative Document*, green paper (June), Cmnd 2614, London: HMSO.

Department of Trade and Industry, interviews with anonymous sources, 16 June 1997 and 24 June 1997.

Douglas, D. (1985) *The Role of the Media in the Great Coal Strike of 1984/1985*, Doncaster: ASP.

Douglas, S. (1986) *Labor's New Voice: Unions and the Mass Media*, Norwood, NJ: Ablex Publishing Corporation.

Economists Advisory Group (1993) *Commercialisation of the Post Office: How to Secure Financial Independence without Risking Service Quality* (Aug.).

Ericson, R. V., Baranek, P. M. and Chan, J. B. L. (1989) *Negotiating Control: A Study of News Sources*, Oxford: Oxford University Press.

Gans, H. J. (1979) *Deciding What's News*, London: Constable.

Glasgow University Media Group (1976) *Bad News*, London: Routledge.

Glasgow University Media Group (1980) *More Bad News*, London: Routledge.

Glasgow University Media Group (1982) *Really Bad News*, London: Routledge.

Hall, S., Critcher, C., Jefferson, T., Clarke, J. and Roberts, B. (1978) *Policing the Crisis: Mugging, the State, and Law and Order*, London: Macmillan.

Hallin, D. (1994) *We Keep America on Top of the World: Television Journalism and the Public Sphere*, London: Routledge.

Hansen, A. (1993) 'Greenpeace and Press Coverage of Environmental Issues', in A. Hansen (ed.), *The Mass Media and Environmental Issues*, Leicester: Leicester University Press.

Harris, D. Interview 18 June 1997 (formerly media and campaigns officer for UCW, 1990–6).

Hollingsworth, M. (1986) *The Press and Political Dissent*, London: Pluto Press.

Jones, N. (1987) *The Media and Industrial Relations: The Changing Relationship*, Warwick Papers in Industrial Relations, No. 18, Warwick: Warwick University Press.

Kerr, A. and Sachdev, S. (1992) 'Third Among Equals: An Analysis of the 1989 Ambulance Dispute', *British Journal of Industrial Relations*, 30.2.

Labour Party, campaign pack (1994), including: model letter to local newspapers, briefing, model resolution to local councils, sticker, model press release, model letter to Michael Heseltine, sticker, petition forms, Robin Cook statement.

Lane, D., correspondence with UCW and MPs, 10 July 1994, 12 July 1994, 14 Aug. 1994, 17 June 1994, 9 Sept. 1994, 30 Oct. 1994.

Lindsey, J., Interview 24 June 1997 (corporate public relations manager for the Post Office).

London Economics (1994) *The Future of Postal Services: A Critique of the Government's Green Paper* (Sept.).

Lowe Bell (1994) 'The Freedom to Deliver: Enterprise and Efficiency for the Post Office in the Public Sector', presentation.

Manning, P. (1998) *Spinning for Labour: Trade Unions and the New Media Environment*, Aldershot: Ashgate.

McIlroy, J. (1995) *Trade Unions in Britain Today*, Manchester: Manchester University Press.

Miller, D. (1994) *Don't Mention the War: Northern Ireland, Propaganda and the Media*, London: Pluto Press.

Miller, D. and Williams, K. (1993) 'Negotiating HIV/AIDS Information: Agendas, Media Strategies and the News', in J. Eldridge (ed.), *Getting the Message*, London: Routledge.

Mitchell, N. (1997) *The Conspicuous Corporation: Business, Publicity, and Representative Democracy*, Ann Arbor: University of Michigan Press.

MORI polls: Attitudes to the Postal Service, Oct. 1991; Attitudes to the Postal Service, Dec. 1992; Attitudes to the Post Office, March 1994; Attitudes to the Post Office, April 1994; Post Office Managers Survey, Aug. 1994; Sub Post Offices Survey, Aug. 1994; Tory Backbenchers, Oct. 1994.

Myers, N. (1986) 'Union World', in J. Curran, J. Ecclestone, G. Oakley and A. Richardson, *Bending Reality*, London: Pluto Press.

National Federation of Sub-Postmasters (1994) 'Response to the Consultative Document on the Future of Postal Services', 30 Sept.

Post Office (1994) *The Future of Postal Services: The Need for Change*.

Post Office (1997a) *The Post Office Business Briefs* (Feb.).

Post Office (1997b) *The Post Office Communications Directory* (Feb.).

Post Office Users National Council (1994) *The Future of Postal Services: POUNC Report on Government's Green Paper*.

Press releases: Emery, Sir Peter (Conservative MP for Haniton) 5 Sept. 1994; National Federation of Sub-Postmasters 30 Sept. 1994; Protect your Postal Services, 27 July 1994; Post Office Users National Council, 30 Sept. 1994.

Proctor, C. Interview 2 June 1997 (campaigns and media officer with the CWU).

Protect our Postal Services (1994) 'PPS Submission on the Government's Green Paper on the future of Postal Services' (Sept.).

Protect our Postal Services, correspondence with UCW and draft documents, 11 Mar. 1993, 8 Apr. 1993, 17 June 1993, 30 June 1993, 19 July 1994.

Schlesinger, P. and Tumber, H. (1994) *Reporting Crime: The Media Politics of Criminal Justice*, Oxford: Clarendon Press.

Sigal, L. V. (1973) *Reporters and Officials: The Organisation and Politics of Newsmaking*, Lexington, MA: D. C. Heath.

Taylor, R. (1994) *The Future of the Trade Unions*, London: André Deutsch.

Tiffen, R. (1989) *News and Power*, London: Allen and Unwin.

Trades Unions Congress (1979) *Media Coverage of Industrial Disputes January and February 1979: A Cause for Concern*.

Union of Communication Workers (1994) correspondence with NFSP and Sub-Postmasters, 12 Aug.

Union of Communication Workers (1994) 'Stand By Your Post: Campaign Brief'.

Union of Communication Workers, correspondence, strategy documents and minutes of UCW sub-group committee meetings on privatisation issue, 21 Jan. 1992, 27 Oct. 1992, 29 Oct. 1992, 21 June 1993, 19 July 1993, 20 Sept. 1993, 18 Oct. 1993, 20 Dec. 1993, 2 Feb. 1994, 21 Feb. 1994, 16 May 1994, 22 May 1994, 19 June 1994, 29 June 1994, 1 July 1994, 25 Aug. 1994, 14 Sept. 1994.

Union of Communication Workers, special branch circulars, 2 Feb. 1994, 24 Mar. 1994, 28 Mar. 1994, 20 Apr. 1994, 29 Apr. 1994, 18 May 1994, 19 May 1994, 15 June 1994, 29 June 1994, 4 July 1994, 3 Aug. 1994, 11 Aug. 1994, 30 Aug. 1994, 15 Sept. 1994, 12 Oct. 1994, 14 Oct. 1994, 26 Oct. 1994, 2 Nov. 1994, 30 Nov. 1994.

Union of Communication Workers, campaign materials (1994), including: posters, postcards, leaflets, stickers, balloons, sample complaint letters, sample news releases and speakers' briefs.

Union of Communication Workers (1994) 'Post Office Review: The Effects on Northern Ireland' letter to Northern Irish MPs, 2 Aug. 1994.

Verzuh, R. (1990) 'Changing Images: British Trade Union Communication Under Thatcherism', unpub. postgraduate thesis, Warwick University.

8

Mainstreaming the margins

The transformation of Marxism Today

HERBERT F. PIMLOTT

The alternative media have had a spectacular lack of success in reaching out beyond the radical ghetto. Studies have highlighted a number of recurring themes such as limited audiences, lack of professionalism, insufficient finances, or general ineptitude (e.g. Downing 1984, Landry *et al.* 1985, Chippindale and Horrie 1988). However, when this record is broken, the exception provides a unique opportunity to gain a fuller understanding of the possibilities and the problems of the alternative media. This chapter examines one such exception, *Marxism Today* (MT),[1] which, despite being published by a marginal political organisation, the Communist Party of Great Britain (CP), during the hegemony of the New Right in the 1980s, gained access to the national public sphere. After providing a background sketch of *Marxism Today*'s first 20 years, the chapter will examine the period of its transformation, 1977–91, thematically: the struggle for its autonomy and ideas; finances; production; contributors and readers; distribution; and national press coverage.

Background

Marxism Today was launched in 1957 to try to win over a new generation of intellectuals to 'Marxism',[2] especially after the massive exodus of members after the crisis of 1956, the Hungarian Uprising and Khrushchev's 'secret speech', and to help develop the party line. To underline the importance of the journal symbolically, John Gollan, the CP general secretary 1956–75, was appointed as MT's first editor. However, James Klugmann, a loyal party intellectual and deputy editor, was the *de facto* editor until he succeeded Gollan officially in 1962; he remained in post until Martin Jacques took over in 1977.

Klugmann's editorship was a conventional one as he piloted *Marxism Today* along the party line during its first two decades; as the party line changed and opened up to different ideas, so too did the journal. Controversial articles were often circulated among members of MT's editorial board (MTEB), in order to help make decisions as to their suitability for publication. Controversial contributions were also circulated among leading members in the relevant party bodies: for example, a controversial article about the CP's industrial strategy would have been referred to the economic committee or the industrial organiser. Appointed by the leadership, the editor exercised control on behalf of the party and was supported by an editorial board, which also oversaw the editor and functioned as a representative body of a cross-section of thinking and members, including leading party officers and intellectuals, many of whom were already represented on political (PC) or executive committees (EC).[3]

While opinions which were viewed as beyond the acceptable parameters of debate were refused publication, these boundaries were not static and began to expand after 1967 when the CP adopted a more open line on religious, cultural, scientific, artistic and ideological questions (Executive Committee, Communist Party of Great Britain 1967) and a more independent, and cautiously critical, stance on the USSR. Even as political and economic matters remained closely scrutinised for deviations from the party line, by the mid-1970s there was pressure to open up the CP's thinking in these areas from the 'reformist' wing of the party: Gramscians, Eurocommunists, revisionist Marxists, etc.

The rise of organised factions within the CP during the 1970s led to two increasingly irreconcilable wings, 'reformist' and 'traditionalist',[4] neither of which could command a majority of the membership, which struggled to influence party ideology and strategy and to control the various party bodies. Gordon McLennan, general secretary 1975–89, and the leadership managed a balance between the two wings by throwing their weight behind one or the other of these groupings: the bulk of the membership, the 'centrists', looked to the leadership for guidance. While this may have been an effective day-to-day strategy for managing these disparate elements, it was ultimately to cost the party its ideological and organisational cohesiveness. However, it was within this shifting balance of fortunes that Jacques had to negotiate MT's transformation.

The production of *Marxism Today* remained a party affair. Klugmann oversaw the process and was responsible for most of the editorial work, with some help from a few party workers and with occasional help from board members with proofreading and sub-editing. The printing and typesetting of *Marxism Today* was carried out by Farleigh Press, the CP's printing press, and distribution via party branches and bookshops and subscriptions was handled by the CP's agency, Central Books. The purpose for publishing MT was not dependent upon it making money, as with commercial periodicals, because its role was discussing the CP's political work: MT had begun as a sub-section of the CP's press and publicity department. As long as MT was published for an internal audience, there was little need to change its production and distribution arrangements. There was also little need to think about its cultural form (format, design, layout, writing style), despite occasional complaints from some party members (e.g. Alce 1977).

Between 1957 and 1977, MT's sales varied between 2500 and 4000, with very occasional special issues, such as the 20th anniversary issue of 1956, selling in excess of 5000 or more. However, against a variable party membership of between 25 000 and 34 000 during the same period, this represents a variation in its reach of between 16% at best and 7% at worst.[5] MT's future looked bleak in 1977 as the decline in its immediate audience, party membership, increased; although party membership overall had been declining since the early 1960s, there had been an influx of white-collar workers, women and intellectuals between 1967 and 1977. Other party publications, such as the *Morning Star*, the CP's daily newspaper and most public face, and *Comment*, the internal party affairs bulletin, were also facing financial pressures and declining readerships. The leadership had a much greater interest in these two publications, because of their greater frequency, higher circulation and directly political, promotional roles, than in MT, which was of peripheral interest because it was seen as a 'talking shop' for intellectuals.

Struggle for autonomy

The role of the editor was key to the periodical's success because he was solely responsible for its production.[6] Appointed as editor in September 1977, Martin Jacques implemented changes slowly, not just because of limited resources, but also because any change had to be negotiated with and agreed by the leadership, though they were more concerned about additional costs. Jacques's position on the EC enhanced his ability to negotiate with the leadership, as he acquired the requisite skills and contacts for lobbying for MT's autonomy and outmanoeuvring its critics. He had good relationships with some of the leadership, including McLennan, and kept them informed of the changes he wanted to effect, even as the leadership expressed little interest in MT.

Reflecting the leadership's cautious, political thinking and its lack of interest (many board members rarely attended), the MTEB had gradually atrophied during Klugmann's editorship, as its role in overseeing the journal was minimised. As part of the reformist wing, Jacques hoped to use his position to help change the CP's thinking and eventually become part of a new leadership which would remake the party. This meant that Jacques had to change the MTEB's composition and resist attempts by traditionalists to have a greater say over MT. In 1979 he was able to make some small adjustments to the board, including a few sympathetic intellectuals, such as Eric Hobsbawm. After the reformists suffered some setbacks at the 1979

National Party Congress, Jacques had to move cautiously until the defeat of the *Morning Star* and other traditionalists; it was not, therefore, until 1986 that a major recomposition and expansion of the MTEB took place, which included non-CP members, such as Stuart Hall.

However, Jacques changed the board's role into that of a 'think tank': intensive sessions were spent developing and debating ideas and analyses (although the editor was not committed to publishing anything unless he wanted to or it was politically expedient to do so).[7] Jacques made a clear separation of functions between the MTEB and MT's editorial collective, a small group of people he had assembled to help out with the monthly production and distribution process: 'brainstorming' and producing the periodical. It was not appropriate for the MTEB, which only met every two or three months, to attempt to dictate what articles should go into the journal or how it should be produced, though they could make suggestions.

The other institutional frameworks necessary for MT's autonomy were in place by 1984, but the recurring internal threat from factions which sought to overthrow the leadership and seize control of the party absorbed time and resources, and forced the leadership and MT into an alliance. The traditionalists, however, were divided among themselves; the most important faction was grouped around the *Morning Star*, which brought the internal tensions into open warfare after their attempt to get rid of Jacques in 1982 over an MT article which mildly criticised trade unions. Although the leadership was not entirely happy with the article, they were much more angry with the ways in which Tony Chater, the editor of the *Star*, and Mick Costello, the industrial organiser, had publicly attacked a party publication without the knowledge or approval of the leadership. This internal struggle over the CP's direction, strategy and leadership was eventually lost by the traditionalist forces. However, by 1985 the bitter internal struggle drove out large numbers of party members from all sides, and the loss of the *Star*, which split from the party, and the closure of various party publications, meant that MT was the CP's only success story.

Drawing upon the support of the leadership and backed by its public success, Jacques was able to outmanoeuvre his critics, who after the purge of traditionalists in 1985 began to include those who had been close to MT's political project but disliked its aloofness from the party. By 1988 Jacques was redefining MT's role in order to maintain its autonomy from those, such as the grouping of former Eurocommunists led by Nina Temple who took over the leadership in 1989, who wanted the magazine to work more closely with the CP, in line with its original subtitle, 'the theoretical and discussion journal of the Communist Party'.

During the course of his editorship, Jacques continually hammered home MT's importance in reaching an audience outside the party. This was something the CP had promoted and which MT, to all intents and purposes, was doing. It tried to reach out to other groups, especially feminist, ethnic and social movements, as the party's programme claimed was necessary. The two most important concepts were the 'broad democratic alliance' (BDA) and the 'war of position' because they committed the CP to seeking an alliance with progressive groups and to a political-ideological campaign to establish the BDA as a counter-hegemonic force to displace Thatcherism. This was what MT was attempting to do.

MT's ideas had challenged the orthodoxies of left beliefs, and the twin analyses of the crisis of the labour movement and the hegemony of Thatcherism, initiated by Eric Hobsbawm (1978) and Stuart Hall (1979) respectively, had been remarkably prescient. The controversial nature of these ideas, which drew considerable criticism from much of the left, actually seemed to further their circulation. However, 10 years later MT developed the 'New Times' project which sought to try to move away from only providing criticism of the left's thought into developing a new analysis which could make sense of the rapid changes in the economy, society and culture in the second half of the twentieth century.

A final analysis of MT has to recognise that it also promoted a new approach to culture, especially popular culture and lifestyle, which had been traditionally dismissed by the left as a legacy of capitalist ideology. This approach drew upon and helped popularise British cultural studies as well as influencing MT's conception of 'popular politics', which recognised the importance of such events as Band Aid in reaching a much wider audience than the left was traditionally able to do through its publications and activities.

Organisation of production

There are two basic models for the alternative press: 'Bolshevik' and 'Comedia' (Khiabany 1997). In the Bolshevik model, the parent organisation oversees and controls the editing, production and distribution of the paper because of the crucial role it plays in the party's political work. The party also pays for the paper as part of the price of political work because the structures of the capitalist marketplace inhibit the distribution of socialist ideas. The Comedia model, however, suggests that many problems of the alternative media can be solved by taking advantage of the marketplace. There is an obvious tension between the two models which is evident in the hybrid model that MT became.

Under Klugmann, MT had functioned with up to five people at times helping out and with occasional help from board members, but 'hot-metal' printing (typesetting articles in lead) and the process of circulating controversial articles among board members and the EC required time and whole issues were often prepared months in advance. However, this began to change under Jacques as the production process became better organised and disciplined, which led, for the most part, to the most efficient use of human, financial and technological resources, evident in the consistently high production values and the introduction of new technologies, such as phototypesetting.

With only one part-time editorial assistant, Jacques organised an editorial collective, composed of volunteers, to carry out all the necessary production tasks. Changes to the layout, design and format of MT were planned and introduced, and, rather than relying on leading party members to send in articles, MT made great efforts to find the most knowledgeable people to contribute articles on their areas of expertise (for free). As MT's success brought in increased advertising and sales revenues, it was able to hire more staff and re-invest in technology, promotion and other aspects of production and distribution.

The large numbers of volunteers drawn to MT had to be organised into separate collectives to take responsibility for the various production and distribution tasks necessary for the marketplace: publicity, design, advertising, etc. They were overseen by Jacques and his staff. The production of MT was not allowed to be 'amateurish' and volunteers were expected to do their best; those who proved themselves were given further responsibilities. Even contributors were not spared: even though they were not paid, they were still expected to do several rewrites if requested. Some embarrassing mistakes meant close attention was paid to proofreading: articles were often proofread three or four times. This fanatical attention to detail and quality and the dedication of staff and volunteers helped MT to appear to have more money behind it than it did.

There were two waves of volunteers, however, which also gives some indication of the way in which MT was reaching the public: the first wave was attracted by its political ideas during the early 1980s; the second wave was attracted in the mid- to late 1980s, but they were primarily interested in gaining media experience (Turner 1994). One of the dilemmas constantly facing MT was the lack of funds to keep trained and talented individuals (Jacques 1996). Nevertheless, the organisation of the production process and its volunteer labour contributed to MT's success in reaching out beyond the party, into the marketplace.

Finances

One important aspect of the left press is the recognition that in the capitalist marketplace it is the advertisers who determine which ideas will be successful (i.e. profitable): since socialist ideas have been unpopular with advertisers they have to be paid for by their readers and producers (advertisers, in effect, act as censors) (Curran 1986). Second, because the left recognises that the production and circulation of socialist ideas is an integral part of their work, there is a willingness to subsidise publications. However, a consequence of this approach makes a truism of the synergy between commercial and political decisions, particularly as long as CP agencies were involved in MT's production and distribution. The leadership often had to be won over on commercial decisions, while political decisions made about MT's production clearly had commercial consequences.

While some in the leadership expressed concern that party agencies should continue servicing MT, Jacques was more concerned to meet the necessary requirements for competing in the marketplace. A series of disputes arose over typesetting, printing and subscriptions between 1981 and 1986, which required a lot of negotiating before they were eventually won by MT. Both printing and subscriptions took years to negotiate; MT had to collect evidence to prove that it was losing revenue because party agencies were unable to provide the necessary technology or service to meet the demands of the marketplace.[8] For example, with national newsagent distribution, MT had to meet strict deadlines and provide a large monthly print run over expected sales to ensure that newsagents could be supplied with enough copies to meet demand. By 1986 all aspects of production and distribution had been made independent of the party, except for bookshop distribution.

Table 8.1   Finances 1979–1989[a]

	1979	1983	1985	1987	1989
Income					
Sales					
Newstrade		16.5	21.8	23.4	19.2
CB wholesale		22.9	12.0	6.0	5.0
Subscriptions		14.6	28.3	25.4	29.8
Misc. sales		1.0		1.0	
Total sales		55.0	62.1	55.8	54.0
Advertising		40.9	32.4	40.0	37.1
Miscellaneous		4.1	5.5	4.2	9.0
Total (%)		100.0	100.0	100.0	100.1
Total (£)	15 524.00	77 740.00	120 580.98	210 850.00	241 321.84
Expenditure					
Printing		48.0	31.2	26.0	22.9
Typesetting		11.0	10.3	6.8	4.8
Design		12.0	9.0	9.3	11.6
Promotion		5.3	4.0	7.6	8.2
Distribution		–	19.3	14.8	15.6
Wages		14.4	14.9	15.9	23.3
Office expenses		8.0	5.3	12.6	7.6
Miscellaneous		1.5	6.0	7.0	5.3
Total (%)		100.2	100.0	100.0	99.3
Total (£)	15 817.00	90 271.00	125 515.05	262 918.00	292 079.62
BALANCE (£)	(293.00)	(12 531.00)	(4 934.07)	(52 068.00)	(50 757.78)

[a]There is no breakdown for 1979, although the overwhelming income would have been from sales, with a small amount from advertising. The figures for 1985 are for October 1984 to September 1985 but do not actually include a number of costs which were only charged to MT later in 1985.

When the CP granted MT a bank account in 1984, it provided the necessary financial wherewithal for MT to operate autonomously. This meant MT could budget and plan ahead without having to constantly secure consent for business and technical expenditures. Nevertheless, the CP continued to provide subsidies to MT while it re-invested all its additional earnings from advertising, sales and subscriptions into production, publicity and distribution.

An examination of MT's finances in the 1980s demonstrates a number of important points (Table 8.1). First of all, it shows that it is possible, and indeed necessary, to produce high-quality publications in order to increase sales and recruit advertising: MT received substantial increases in revenue from advertising, newsagent sales and subscriptions during the second half of the 1980s. Second, however, these increases in revenue in turn necessitated expenditures to ensure the high turnover: distribution and publicity costs also increased substantially during the same period, as did design and printing costs (in absolute terms). However, MT experienced a series of problems[9] between 1986 and 1987 which led to substantial financial losses, despite increased revenues, and a reliance on substantially larger subsidies from the CP of around £50 000 per annum.

Social formation

Marxism Today went through a series of shifts in terms of both its contributors and its constituencies during the 1980s. During its first two decades, 1957–77, all aspects of its content, production and distribution pointed towards its role as an internal publication for party intellectuals, with only occasional contributions from non-party writers. However, during the 1970s there had been a broader engagement between non-aligned socialists and CP reformist intellectuals through the Communist University of London (CUL), which drew in 1 500-plus intellectuals at its peak (Andrews 1995). This grouping of party and non-party intellectuals influenced by various currents of Marxism provided a new constituency and new contributors for MT. However, the CUL went into decline and was replaced in 1982 by MT's first event, 'The Great Moving Left Show', which attracted tremendous interest and participation from outside the party, and its first favourable reviews in the national press.

Many of MT's new audience were part of the 1960s generation of working- and middle-class students, who had begun the 'long march through the institutions' after the failure of '68, and many of whom subsequently became lecturers, teachers and public-sector and white-collar workers. This younger generation had grown up with a certain amount of affluence and was influenced by popular culture ('sex and drugs and rock'n'roll') (Waite 1995), civil liberties, feminism, identity politics and the new social movements, and demonstrated a strong antipathy towards most kinds of authority, including the CP (many reformists were children of party members)

(Andrews 1995). MT, though, also retained a contingent of allies among an older generation of (non-party) New Leftists and anti-Stalinist Marxists, some of whom had remained in the party after 1956.

Two surveys carried out for MT demonstrated that its readership included a substantial, well-educated, ABC1 socio-economic grouping: 67% were graduates and 24% had a second degree; more than one-fifth (22%) were students; over half were employed full-time, and nearly one-third of the total were employed in the public sector. Although taken 4 years apart (1986 and 1990), the surveys revealed a readership that remained similar in terms of its socio-economic profile; the truly significant changes in readership had taken place between 1977 and 1986, which an examination of MT's contributors over three different years will reveal.

In 1975, as the CP still saw itself as a vanguard on the left, CP officials and intellectuals accounted for nearly four-fifths (78%) of all feature articles and other contributions, and all contributors were party members.[10] By 1983 the number of academics contributing features amounted to just over half, while trade unionists and social-movement activists contributed nearly one in eight feature contributions each (12%); overall, one in three feature writers (33%) were party members. However, of other (non-feature) contributions, academics, unionists and social activists contributed less than one in five items (17.8%). This was in keeping with the shift in alignment in the CP's new 1977 programme with its emphasis on establishing alliances with anti-Thatcherite forces. However, the most significant development by the late 1980s was the increase in media professionals.

Feature articles by media professionals had increased from none in 1975 to 30% by 1983 to 37.4% in 1988. By 1988 media professionals supplied more than half (53.3%) of all other items, while all contributions by unionists and social activists had dropped down to between 1 (features) and 4% (other), even less than in 1975. With increases in space (increased pagination and format sizes), MT needed to have copy that could be produced to tight deadlines, especially for topical issues. Journalists and other media professionals were well placed to contribute because of their skills, their access to technology (which helped them write to deadlines) and their contacts (needed to get interviews with public figures). However, MT also acted as a training ground for future journalists and media professionals (e.g. Suzanne Moore) and provided a space for other journalists to explore issues in greater depth than their usual outlets did. The use of media professionals also reflected changes in MT's format, from an internal party journal to a popular political magazine.

Parallel to these developments was the rapid decrease in contributors' explicit (stated or known) political affiliations. While 1975 can be taken as the benchmark year, when all contributors appeared to have been party members, by 1983 only one-third (33.3%) of feature and 10.7% of other contributors were CP members and 9% and 6.3%, respectively, were Labour Party members. By 1988 the number of feature and other contributors who were CP members had dropped to 23.1% and 9% respectively, while similar figures for LP members showed some decreases (to 8.8% and 2.4% respectively). Readership figures for 1986 and 1990 also demonstrate a decrease in overall political commitment from 17% CP and 39% Labour members in 1986 to 10% CP and 31% Labour in 1990 (*Marxism Today* Editorial Board 1977–91, Summertown Research Consultants 1990).

Significantly, the increase in contributions from journalists and media professionals mirrors the increase in press coverage. This relationship was a symbiotic one because as MT's public profile rose through events, promotion and media coverage it attracted interest from the media, and, in turn, journalists writing about MT in the national press sometimes also wrote articles for MT or participated in its events. Clearly, with the media professionals writing for it, MT had a better chance of getting media coverage than a publication without such contributors. Out of 16 journalists contributing in 1983 only six were affiliated to national newspapers; however, out of 49 journalists contributing in 1988, no less than 31 were affiliated to national newspapers (nine each from the *Guardian* and the *Financial Times*, seven from *The Independent*, four from the *Observer*). Clearly, the majority of journalists writing for MT were affiliated to newspapers that were closest to MT politically (e.g. centre-left).

Finally, it should also be noted that MT won over contributors by the close attention paid to articles by staff, attention rarely invested by mainstream media and which writers themselves seemed to appreciate: deputy editor, section editors or, in the case of features, usually Jacques himself. MT's close attention to detail, careful and rigorous proofreading and sub-editing work, and its seeking out the best possible commentators for different topics, helped to establish its credibility with the media, assisted by occasional 'news scoops', such as the Lech Walesa interview[11] published in October 1981. This reliability was important in establishing MT's credibility with the media (which could also draw upon its articles without worrying about their authenticity).

The medium

However, it was not only the changes in production and distribution, its editorial and organisational autonomy and financing that enabled MT to reach out beyond the party networks and even the left, but also the shift in its cultural form, from a 'journal' into a 'magazine'. This is more than just a case of semantics. Too often in the past, the left press in particular have marked themselves out as a distinctive genre by an unflattering disregard for production values, attractive layout and design, accessible formats, a close attention to detail, strong visuals and a clear writing style. Although there has been more attention to such details since MT's success in the 1980s, the exclusion of left periodicals from the national public sphere was at least in part due to their often forbidding look as densely printed, text-only 'journals'.

MT's first cultural form, 1957–77, was that of a 'journal': narrow audiences, no or limited advertising, in-depth articles covering areas of interest to a specialised audience, conventional design and format, few or no images, specialised language or jargon and an opaque or difficult writing style. Its overall defining quality was a 'seriousness' which was reinforced by the closely printed text set in two columns per page, 32 pages per issue, 384 pages per year (with few exceptions). The types of article published represented the different CP constituencies: party documents and speeches, with their formal, stilted prose; international communist speeches and documents, with similarly formal, stilted prose; a variety of articles by party intellectuals and ordinary members, some mirroring the official line, others trying to extend the boundaries of debate, the writing styles a mixture of the difficult and the accessible, the formal and the informal.

Jacques knew that he would have to change MT's look if it was to have any hope of reaching an audience outside the party. The process began shortly after he took over as editor; there were two major format changes plus a number of internal changes. Both the new formats, the second format, 1979–86, and the third (and largest) format, 1986–91, are more closely related to the cultural form of the 'magazine': addressing a general, educated audience; a range of advertising; topical subjects; contemporary design and an extensive use of images, graphics and cartoons; eschewing 'jargon' and promoting a writing style closer to periodical journalism. MT's shift in writing style meant a mimicking of some of journalism's conventions, even if it could not actually be defined as journalism (Taylor 1995).

The first changes to MT included the removal of articles promoting the official line, domestic and international communist documents and speeches. It was not just the type of article, however, but the subject matter that changed as well. Gradually, historical and theoretical articles were dropped in favour of those which dealt with more current developments in politics, society and culture. Although the writing style changed, as did the terminology, it did not necessarily mean that it was always more accessible or 'jargon-free'. Contributors who engaged in esoteric Marxist debates, such as that over the 'dialectics of nature', were attacked for appearing to mask more than they purported to explain, which was an affront to working-class members (e.g. Alce 1977). While the changes in the types of article were welcomed by both new and old readerships, letter-writers still complained about the inaccessibility of articles and the opacity or pomposity of the prose (e.g. Kingsford 1988).

Jacques's attempt to develop a new writing style by merging the scholar's 'deep thought' with the journalist's writing skills was a mixed success, though representative of MT's two key constituencies. MT also developed new modes for presenting ideas and different voices, such as the round-table discussion, which evolved as an attempt to include those who might not otherwise be able to contribute (like those workers without the confidence or the skills to write a 5000-word article), and it drew upon the British cultural-studies approach in developing its coverage of (popular) culture, which was almost unique.[12] Under the third format, personal and special columns were introduced, as was a more adventurous use of design and layout than in the second format.

Distribution

A key obstacle to alternative publications reaching a wider audience is distribution. There are no legal requirements for commercial distributors and newsagent chains to take on alternative publications; and under British libel laws distributors are as liable as publishers. Therefore, in order to be distributed and sold in newsagents, MT had to demonstrate that it was not likely to be libellous or scandalous. In addition, it also had to prove that it had the potential to sell well, which could be demonstrated by interviews with public figures, high production values, media coverage, etc. MT's initial one-year trial run in London with W.H. Smith's was successful enough for the company to agree to sell it through its national chain of newsagents (Jacques 1996). During the first month (October 1981) that it was sold through newsagents nationally its sales doubled, proving that there was a broader potential audience, despite its name and publisher.[13]

This move into national distribution meant that MT was no longer limited to party networks and independent radical bookshops. From October 1981 the CP began advertising for new members in MT, which proved more effective in recruitment than the party's daily newspaper (McKay 1982). However, just as these developments could not have happened without all the other changes taking place, MT also had to undertake supplementary activities, such as campaigns to promote newsagent sales, and to keep investing in production in order to maximise sales and compete in the marketplace. As different strategies were developed to increase sales via newsagents or subscriptions, by the mid-1980s party and bookshop sales had fallen below one-quarter, with subscriptions accounting for 30% and newsagents for 44% of all sales. By the late 1980s, though, subscriptions had outstripped newsagent sales in terms of income.[14]

National press coverage

The cornerstone of MT's access to the national public sphere was its publicity strategy to gain coverage in the news media. Each issue had anywhere from one to four or more press releases targeted at specific journalists and editors, followed up with telephone calls. Basically, there was a four-level hierarchy for stimulating media coverage. In descending order of importance, these were: ideas and analysis; interviews with public figures; contradictions between the title and the content or images; and promoting spin-offs. On a monthly sale of 12 000 this worked out to around one in 30 copies earmarked for publicity (Taylor 1995).

Nevertheless, despite the enormous publicity efforts, the results were mixed. For example, there were six press releases for the June 1989 MT: two promoted an interview with the Conservative secretary of state for health, Kenneth Clarke; two targeted the trade press; one focused on cultural coverage; and the sixth was the CP's press release for its new manifesto, bound on to MT as a 'special supplement'. Out of 17 items in the press, seven dealt with the manifesto (and did not discuss MT), six were responses in the trade press, and there were no national press references to the Clarke interview. However, MT's first interview with a Conservative minister, Edwina Currie, generated 11 articles in the national press alone, including tabloids.

The timing was also important, with the most energy and expense spent on the October edition and special issues. Starting with the October 1980 Tony Benn interview, almost every October issue was targeted at the Labour Party's annual conference. Feature articles were often reprinted in the *Guardian*, the one broadsheet which supported Labour throughout the 1980s, and where public debates and divisions over Labour's strategy and future were aired. The timing was meant to maximise the impact on Labour, and some of the ideas MT promoted found a willing audience in the national press.

Liberal broadsheets accounted for nearly four-fifths (77.9%) of the total national (broadsheet) press coverage between 1978 and 1991 (507 items) which concern MT in some way: the *Guardian* 45.3%; the FT[15] 10.7%; the *Observer* 9.9%; *The Independent* 9%. These liberal newspapers, spanning the centre and centre-left, were also the closest to MT ideologically, indicating that coverage is dictated by a paper's editorial line (Table 8.2).

More than two-fifths of all items (43.8%) were 'brief': anything from an event listing to a one- or two-paragraph news item. Though these items might be peripheral and of little consequence, they did contribute to promoting a particular public image, especially since many 'brief' references were quirky items (about a 'Marxist' periodical and merchandising, etc.). The remaining 285 articles had greater significance within the broadsheets. MT articles and excerpts reprinted in the broadsheets accounted for 43 items (8.5%), while MT articles acted as the 'primary source' (providing 40% or more of the content) for 62 newspaper articles (12.2%). Forty-eight articles were primarily focused on MT itself (9.5%), while another 84 items (16.6%) included MT as an 'important reference' within a story, most often about the CP's internal battles.

We can see patterns emerging in general subject matter covered by the press (Table 8.3). Nearly one in four items (23.3%) centred around the Labour Party and movement, one in five (20.5%) dealt with the CP and

Table 8.2 National press coverage by article type and/or use, 1978–1991[b]

Broadsheets	1978	1979	1980	1981	1982	1983	1984	1985	1986	1987	1988	1989	1990	1991	Total
Editorials	–	–	–	–	1	2	2	5	2	1	2	–	2	3	20
Reprints	–	–	1	1	3	1	3	8	4	4	6	2	5	5	43
MT source	1	–	–	1	11	8	15	6	5	6	7	–	–	2	62
On MT	–	–	–	1	4	5	4	2	3	6	9	4	1	9	48
Important reference	–	–	–	3	5	11	5	8	5	9	9	16	9	4	84
Brief reference	–	–	1	2	4	9	10	30	23	35	34	23	25	26	222
Letters	–	–	–	–	1	4	3	5	3	3	6	–	3	–	28
TOTAL	1	0	2	8	29	40	42	64	45	64	73	45	45	49	507

[b]Only those articles which mention or draw upon *Marxism Today* in some capacity are included.
Reprints = include whole or edited extracts.
MT source = articles either wholly or primarily based upon MT articles or interviews.
On MT = articles primarily about MT.
Important reference = articles with important references or substantial space (up to 40%) devoted to MT.
Brief reference = this includes all references to MT, no matter how short: listings, one paragraph items, etc.
Letters = only letters that mention MT or refer explicitly to reprinted items.

Table 8.3   National press coverage by subject, 1978–1991

Subject[c]	1978	1979	1980	1981	1982	1983	1984	1985	1986	1987	1988	1989	1990	1991	Total
CP or communism	–	–	–	–	4	10	7	14	4	7	17	20	19	2	104
Labour Party and movement	–	–	1	3	10	12	18	23	11	18	9	5	6	2	118
On MT[d]	–	–	–	2	4	3	–	5	6	13	9	10	3	16	71
Culture	–	–	–	–	2	2	1	1	1	8	3	–	3	4	25
General politics[e]	–	–	–	–	4	8	–	10	12	6	4	8	5	11	68
MT events	–	–	–	–	3	–	2	–	7	3	10	1	–	1	27
Interviews[f]	1	–	1	3	2	3	10	2	4	7	16	1	6	11	67
Miscellaneous	–	–	–	–	–	2	4	9	–	2	5	–	3	2	27
TOTAL	1	0	2	8	29	40	42	64	45	64	73	45	45	49	507

[c] The 'subject' is defined as the primary focus of the reference to MT within the article concerned.
[d] This refers to items which have focused upon MT itself.
[e] This refers to the area in which articles would discuss Thatcherism or intellectuals in British politics, etc.
[f] This is the one area in which the subject of the interview, the person, is of primary importance rather than a topic.

nearly one in five (19.3%) focused on MT and its events. Only 68 items (13.4%) made reference to other aspects of general politics, such as Thatcherism, government, single-issue movements, etc. Thus, 320 items out of 507 (63.1%) revolved around the left, Labour, the CP or MT itself. The primary interest of the press was MT's role on, relationship to and critique of the left and Labour, and not so much its other contributions on Thatcherism, the Conservative government, feminism, etc.[16]

The coverage of subjects varied throughout the decade. When press coverage first began to pick up in 1982–3 there was still a sense of unity in supporting the Labour left. However, as divisions arose over competing analyses of Labour's disastrous 1983 electoral defeat,[17] nearly three out of five items (59.3%) on the Labour Party and movement were published in 1984–7. This period was marked by an increasingly bitter, divisive debate over what went wrong and what should be done; MT criticised the left's shibboleths and was in turn attacked by many from across the left. However, during MT's last 4 years, only 22 items (18.6%) were published, indicating its declining importance for the press, and especially the *Guardian*, as Labour Party reforms had begun during this period. Equally important, however, was that MT contributors could be read in other publications and no longer exclusively in the CP's theoretical and discussion journal.

Conclusion

It is evident that *Marxism Today*'s success in reaching the national public sphere must be qualified. Although it utilised new distribution outlets, marketplace techniques and developments in production and technology to produce and circulate a high-quality periodical, MT was also dependent upon other organisations, the Communist Party and the national press, with their own agendas. These developments enabled MT, on the one hand, to increase its revenues enormously, feeding all the money back into production, publicity and distribution, which helped raise its profile and increase sales. However, on the other hand, MT never broke free of CP subsidies, the result of a combination of continuing to re-invest in production, publicity and distribution, occasional mistakes by MT, lack of proper administrative procedures and a periodic lack of good staff.

On the one hand, MT's association with the CP and its name held it back from expanding past its all-time high of 18 000 sales, and yet, on the other, the party provided the organisational capabilities that enabled MT to launch itself into the wider public sphere. For its efforts, the CP gained national prestige as MT's publisher, and it provided the CP with its best possible public face. The press coverage of MT is also without parallel among left and alternative media and enabled its access to the national public sphere. This must be qualified, however, because, despite the level of press coverage, it was selective. Clearly, MT's associations with the CP and labour were important in the media coverage of its criticisms of traditional left shibboleths, which would not have been as 'newsworthy' if they had come from virtually any other group; the liberal press were promoting MT's critiques as part of their own agenda of urging changes in the Labour Party. Therefore, access to the mainstream public sphere is dependent not only upon changes in production and distribution, cultural form, organisation, finances and autonomy, but also upon the degree of interest or sympathy manifested by the relevant news media.

Notes

1 This chapter draws upon original research carried out in the course of the author's Ph.D. thesis, in the Department of Media and Communications, Goldsmith's College, University of London. Original documents used in this chapter have been included in the References and further reading rather than being referenced throughout.
2 In 1957, 'Marxism' was still understood as the ideology of Soviet communism.
3 The PC was elected by the EC who, in turn, were elected by delegates sent to the biennial national party congresses. Although the EC was the leading party body, *de jure*, the PC was the *de facto* power. The PC was made up of full-time party officials and leaders.
4 These are the author's terms and are used solely to indicate two essentially broad, antagonistic wings within the CP, which were not even necessarily ideologically and organisationally cohesive, since they encompassed a number of different groupings and even contradictory beliefs (see Samuel 1985, 1987, Thompson 1992).
5 Though even these percentages are a little high, since a few hundred sales of each issue went overseas.
6 The editor only had the equivalent of one secretary's help for three days per week.
7 A round-table discussion on the CP was published in the November 1983 MT, just prior to the CP's national congress, to pre-empt complaints against MT.
8 This is not to say that MT did not experience problems with commercial enterprises.
9 These factors included Jacques's absence (due to illness), inexperienced staff, inadequate administrative procedures, relaunch costs, etc.
10 Before 1977 there was usually an indication when a contributor was not a party member.
11 Walesa was the leader of the free Polish trade union, Solidarity.
12 Another CP journal with a similar approach was *Comment* under Sarah Benton's editorship, 1978–80.
13 The name remained an obstacle to wider sales, although the subtitle was removed from the cover after September 1981.
14 This is because publishers earn more money per copy through subscriptions than through newsagents, because of the greater overheads involved in distribution for national newsagents.
15 The FT is harder to characterise because, although some FT journalists helped to promote monetarism in the 1960s and 1970s, the FT also came out in support of Labour during the 1992 general election (Tunstall 1996: 358).

16 Though arguably here as well, interest in some of these other issues may have been helped by divisions on the left (e.g. Live Aid).
17 Labour narrowly beat the Social Democratic Party, formed by a split from Labour, to second place with only 28% of the vote.

References and further reading

Alce, J. (1977) Letter to the editor, *Marxism Today* (Oct.).

Andrews, G. (1995) 'Young Turks and Old Guard: Intellectuals and the Communist Party Leadership in the 1970s', in G. Andrews *et al.* (eds), *Opening the Books: Essays on the Social and Cultural History of the British Communist Party*, London: Pluto Press, pp. 225–50.

Benn, T. (1980) 'Eric Hobsbawm Interviews Tony Benn,' *Marxism Today*, 24.10: 5–13.

Campaign for Press and Broadcasting Freedom (1996) ' "WH Smenzies" and Press Freedom', *Free Press*, 92: 5.

Chippindale, P. and Horrie, C. (1988) *Disaster! The Rise and Fall of the News on Sunday*, London: Sphere.

Cooper, L., Landry, C. and Berry, D. (1980) *The Other Secret Service: Press Distribution and Press Censorship*, London: Minority Press Group/Comedia.

Curran, J. (1986) 'The Impact of Advertising on the British Mass Media', in R. Collins *et al.* (eds), *Media, Culture and Society: A Critical Reader*, London: Sage, pp. 309–35.

Downing, J. (1984) *Radical Media*, Boston: South End Press.

Executive Committee, Communist Party of Great Britain (1967) 'Questions of Ideology and Culture', *Marxism Today*, 11.5: 134–8.

Hall, S. (1979) 'The Great Moving Right Show', *Marxism Today*, 23.1: 14–20.

Hall, S. and Jacques, M. (eds) (1989) *New Times: The Changing Face of Politics in the 1990s*, London: Lawrence and Wishart.

Hobsbawm, E. (1978) 'The Forward March of Labour Halted?', *Marxism Today*, 22.9: 279–86.

Jacques, M. (1996) Interview, 2 Sept.

Khiabany, G. (1997) 'Red Pepper: A New Model for the Alternative Press?' Unpubl. M.A. diss., University of Westminster.

Kingsford, P. (1988) 'Recondite Article', *Marxism Today*, 32.12: 11.

Landry, C., Morley, D., Southwood, R. and Wright, P. (1985) *What a Way to Run a Railroad*, London: Comedia.

Lane, T. (1982) 'The Unions: Caught on the Ebb Tide', *Marxism Today*, 26.9: 6–13.

Marxism Today (1983) 'The Long and Winding Road: Britain's Communists in 1983', *Marxism Today*, 27.11: 26–30.

Marxism Today Editorial Board (1977–91) Minutes, London: Martin Jacques Papers.

Marxism Today Press File (1978–91) Press clippings, London: Martin Jacques Papers.

McKay, I. (1982) 'Membership: Renewing the Force', *Comment*, 20.11: 7.

Rustin, M. (1989) 'The Trouble with "New Times" ', in S. Hall and M. Jacques (eds) (1989), *New Times: The Changing Face of Politics in the 1990s*, London: Lawrence and Wishart, pp. 303–20.

Samuel, R. (1985) 'The Lost World of British Communism, Part One', *New Left Review*, 154: 3–53.

Samuel, R. (1987) 'Class Politics: The Lost World of British Communism, Part Three', *New Left Review*, 165: 52–91.

Summertown Research Consultants (1990) *Marxism Today Readership Survey*, MTEB minutes, London: Martin Jacques Papers.

Taylor, J. (1995) Interview, 16 July.

Thompson, W. (1992) *The Good Old Cause: British Communism, 1920–1991*, London: Pluto Press.

Tunstall, J. (1996) *Newspaper Power*, Oxford: Oxford University Press.

Turner, J. (1994) Interview, 26 Sept.

Waite, M. (1995) 'Sex 'n' Drugs 'n' Rock 'n' Roll (and Communism) in the 1960s', in G. Andrews *et al.* (eds), *Opening the Books: Essays on the Social and Cultural History of the British Communist Party*, London: Pluto Press, pp. 210–24.

MEDIA AS CULTURAL PRODUCT

VI

9

Literary editors, social networks and cultural tradition

JAMES CURRAN

There is a score-settling tradition in British fiction. It features literary critics as brainless bouncers for the literary establishment, blurb-lifting sots, corrupted snobs, sterile scolds, cuckolded inadequates and heartless vigilantes. The vehemence of this tradition – to which Thomas Hardy, Rudyard Kipling, Henry James, George Gissing, Somerset Maugham, Graham Greene and Martin Amis have contributed (Curtis 1998) – is a reminder that book reviews matter at least to one constituency: the writers of books.

There is another tradition, based in literary studies, which is almost equally critical. 'Concerted and conscienceless misguidance' is F. R. Leavis's verdict on book reviewers in the commercial press (Leavis 1972: 221). 'An inert and timid coterie reluctant to take up the necessary adversary positions' is J. A. Sutherland's no less acerbic assessment (Sutherland 1978: 83). Similarly, D. J. Taylor (1989: 80) rounds on the 'coteries, deference, false standards' of the 'literary Establishment'. The central themes of these critics (their formal use of initials reflects their stern, unbending style) is that book reviewers are corrupted by friendship, write inadequate reviews, and fail to exercise literary leadership.

This chapter comes out of a different tradition, and reaches a different conclusion. It is not interested (save in passing) in whether book reviews are sufficiently critical, or whether they improve literary standards. What it seeks to understand is how literary editors do their job, and how their judgements reflect and influence the hierarchy of knowledge in society.[1]

Predestination and chaos

Interviews were conducted with 11 literary editors of national newspapers and weekly periodicals in 1986 and in 1999.[2] The term literary editor has stuck, partly because the alternative title of books editor is easily confused with editors in publishing companies. But, as one broadsheet literary editor pointed out, 'books editor would be better ... the whole point about being a literary editor is that you should have this huge range of antennae about all sorts of books'.

A stock response from almost all 22 literary editors who were interviewed was that books 'select', 'elect', 'choose', 'present' or 'speak for' themselves. Literary editors merely respond, it was claimed, to the external world. There are important authors, with established reputations and successful track records. There is also a pre-set agenda shaped by what readers are interested in, and what is being talked about. The job of the literary editor is really very straightforward, and calls for only limited intervention.

Beneath the surface of these assured responses, however, were sometimes indications of anxiety. Some books, it turned out, were easier to select than others. Novels by first-time authors were especially difficult to pick, and in general fiction was thought to pose more problems than non-fiction. Indeed, the more literary editors were pressed to explain their decision-making processes, the more they emphasised contingent considerations: what books were available within an irregular cycle of production; who was free to review; which title lent itself to illustration; what combination of reviews produced the right internal balance; how to avoid duplication with other parts of the paper; and so on. This second level of explanation emphasised the randomness, complexity and unpredictability of the books editor's life that defied simple generalisation. 'Half of it happens completely by accident ... whoever picks up the phone, what pops into your mind, or even if you are scrolling down the name and address list, whether X comes before Y', explains one literary editor. This is why the very idea that there is a general explanation of what books editors do 'amuses' her and needs to be 'be taken with a pinch of salt'. 'The trouble with sociology', pointedly commented another broadsheet literary editor as he ushered me to the lift, 'is that it pigeonholes and simplifies things that are fluid.'

Books editors thus gave two bafflingly different accounts of what they did, often in the same interview. One account invoked a theory of predestination in which books were not chosen but chose themselves. The other summoned up an image of improvisation and randomness, of actions governed by instinct and insight, without a clear pattern.

Good intentions

One way of seeking to shed light on this contradiction is to understand the objectives of literary editors. There was wide agreement about the purpose of book reviews even among literary editors who worked for very different types of publication. One key objective was thought to be alerting readers to 'books they ought to know about'. Time and again literary editors returned to this theme. Book sections should be a 'noticeboard of what is new and important'. They should 'keep people in touch with what is written and thought'. They 'should monitor the intellectual and cultural life that's going on'.

A variety of arguments, from different intellectual traditions, was advanced to justify this conception of book sections as a means of cultural and intellectual surveillance. It fulfilled the press's role as a journal of record. It stretched readers, in a Reithian way, by drawing their attention to important books in all areas of knowledge and literary endeavour. It extended the intellectual range of the press since 'under the guise of book reviews you can cover all sorts of things that would not necessarily pass muster if you had to go into a features conference'. However, the most often cited justification for this approach is that it was what readers wanted. In particular, it is widely believed that 'a lot of reviews are read as a substitute for reading a book' so that book pages provided a way for readers to keep abreast of important developments in different fields. Thus, the conception of book reviews as an intellectual monitor was widely shared, carefully considered and strongly defended by literary editors. It is absolutely central to how they approach their work.

Another key objective of book reviews is to engage, interest or entertain. One literary editor talked of constructing his book review section like a 'good dinner party' with the right mix of people and interests. Another invoked the image of 'intellectual cabaret' with 'a contrast between light and shade, seriousness and a bit of levity'. A third editor talked of 'floating along in a stream of signifiers', yet 'being exciting and playful and splashing around in it'. More pointedly, a tabloid literary editor explained, 'one is often looking for an angle to produce an entertaining review'. Her rival on another tabloid sought to generate reader interest through unlikely conjunctions such as highbrow A. S. Byatt praising Terry Pratchett.

A third objective is to offer a critical impression of a book, and evaluate its worth. However, this was often conceived as an aspect of the book review as a literary form that could be negotiated, rather than as an overriding objective. There is a subtle but important difference between the orientation of some in the literary-studies tradition who expect reviews to discriminate between good and bad, interpret meaning in a contextualised way, guide public understanding, and regulate literary standards (e.g. Sutherland 1978) and the attitude of some literary editors who see book reviews almost as feature articles – as a platform for someone to be interesting and intelligent, using books as a cue.

Indeed, there was often more resistance than appeared on the surface to a literary-studies approach. The requirement to be 'bright', to be a good guest at a dinner party, militates against textually supported, literary scholarship.

The conception of book sections as radar screens monitoring important new ideas and developments in the world of books is essentially a reporter's approach: it is about witnessing rather than regulating through praise and censure.

Actual practice

However, this broad measure of agreement among literary editors about the purpose of book reviews adds to, rather than dispels, confusion about how they work. For what they set out to do does not correspond to what they do in practice.

If one of their objectives is to identify books that are important, they manifestly fail in this. The radar screen they operate has serious and recurrent faults. Foremost among these is a failure to identify important works in the fields of science and technology. Indeed, science and technology accounted for no more than 2 per cent of book-review space in every national newspaper that was examined[3] (see Table 9.1). It was only a little higher in the weekly press (see Table 9.2).

Another area that receives relatively little attention is the social sciences (sociology, economics, psychology, anthropology, social administration and politics) and business studies. Most of the books in this category were about politics, and were written not by political scientists, but by politicians and journalists. If the latter are excluded, the attention given to social science is minimal.

Books judged to be important are concentrated in four areas: biography, literary fiction, history and general humanities (of which the leading category is literary criticism). In 1997, these four genres accounted for between 75 and 90 per cent of review space in sample broadsheet papers, and between 61 and 76 per cent in sample tabloid papers.[4]

In general, the book-review agenda of the broadsheet, mid-market tabloids and weekly press is relatively similar. Tabloids found more space for fiction (though still less than 20 per cent), and the weeklies found more space for politics. While changes occurred between 1984 and 1997, these were relatively modest.

The results of this analysis conflict with the claims of some literary editors, made in interviews, that they review 'masses' or 'loads' of science. But subjective impression, however informed, is not as reliable as systematic analysis based on careful measurement, using social-science procedures. It should also be noted that the pattern of book reviews identified in this analysis is consistent with that revealed by Noble and Noble (1974) in the only other major, statistical analysis of book reviews to have been undertaken in Britain.

Table 9.1 Distribution of book-review space (per cent) in national newspapers

Category	Observer 1984	Observer 1997	Sunday Times 1984	Sunday Times 1997	Sunday Express 1984	Express on Sunday 1997	Guardian 1984	Guardian 1997	Daily Telegraph 1984	Daily Telegraph 1997	Daily Mail 1984	Daily Mail 1997
Literary fiction	19	14	17	19	6	21	22	23	14	15	14	11
Popular fiction	4	4	2	4	4	14	3	4	4	6	11	14
SUB-TOTAL: ALL FICTION	23	18	19	23	10	35	25	27	18	21	25	25
Biographical	34	28	34	44	41	44	29	25	32	43	28	36
Historical	8	18	14	10	13	6	16	12	19	11	12	9
General humanities	16	15	9	15	1	5	13	18	6	11	4	5
Visual & performing arts	5	7	8	–	3	–	2	4	10	2	3	1
Politics, social science, business	8	8	9	7	6	4	7	7	9	8	10	10
Science, medicine & technology	1	2	1	2	*	–	–	2	2	1	1	–
Children's books	1	–	–	–	–	–	–	2	–	3	–	1
General interest	4	2	4	*	25	6	7	3	4	1	17	12
(Audio books)	(–)	(–)	(–)	(1)	(–)	(–)	(–)	(–)	(–)	(–)	(–)	(4)
(Paperbacks)	(–)	(6)	(–)	(7)	(–)	(13)	(–)	(9)	(–)	(6)	(–)	(5)

*Less than 1 per cent.
Sample: 180 issues.

Table 9.2   Distribution of book-review space (per cent) in selected weeklies

Category	Spectator 1984	Spectator 1997	New Statesman 1984	New Statesman 1997	Economist 1984	Economist 1997
Literary fiction	19	16	15	16	–	–
Popular fiction	2	3	3	–	1	10
SUB-TOTAL: ALL FICTION	21	19	18	16	1	10
Biographical	31	35	28	29	35	24
Historical	14	12	8	27	7	25
General humanities	14	14	18	3	4	15
Visual & performing arts	2	4	4	1	5	–
Politics, social science, business	11	10	19	14	34	21
Science, medicine & technology	–	–	2	7	4	3
Children's books	1	–	*	–	9	–
General interest	6	4	2	4	1	2

*Less than 1 per cent.
Sample: 90 issues.

Self-elective or selective

The books which 'choose' themselves in the eyes of books editors seem still less self-elective when they are considered in relation to book production and consumption.

The number of new books published in the United Kingdom doubled between 1978 and 1992 (Euromonitor 1993: Table 8.1), and rose still higher thereafter, with an estimated 88 032 new titles being published in 1996 (UNESCO 1997). Literary editors thus have a dauntingly wide choice.

The lack of attention given to science and social science books is not due to their scarcity. In 1996 11 198 new titles concerned with science or medicine were published in the United Kingdom, and a further 5275 titles covering the principal social sciences (UNESCO 1997: table 7.59). Their production is merely part of a vast flow of books that subdivides, so to speak, into a delta of smaller rivers traversing different subject areas. Books editors take up positions along certain riverbanks, fishing mainly from shoals of history, biography and fiction. These accounted for a mere 27 per cent of new stock in 1996 (UNESCO 1997, table 7.59). Some big fish are missed because great stretches of riverbank, vast areas of knowledge, are rarely visited.

If book reviews appear selective in the context of book production, this is even more true in relation to what people actually read. The public reads mainly paperbacks: yet, hardbacks account for over 90 per cent of all book reviews in national newspapers, with one exception (see Table 9.1).[5] In the most recent, publicly available survey (1992),[6] 66 per cent of book readers were currently reading fiction (Euromonitor 1993, table 9.5). Yet, over two-thirds of review space in 1997 was allocated to *non*-fiction.

The divergence between reviewing and reading becomes even more marked in relation to novels. Among those currently reading a book, only 5 per cent were reading a 'general novel' and 3 per cent were reading classics, contrasted with 58 per cent reading popular fiction (Euromonitor 1993: table 9.6). In other words, people were seven times more likely to be reading popular than literary fiction. However, popular fiction received less space than literary fiction in all but one newspaper in our analysis (see Table 9.1).

Another source of information about public preferences is market expenditure. According to not entirely reliable Euromonitor estimates, science, technical and medical books generated 61 per cent more expenditure than history and biography books in 1992, and were the biggest-selling category of non-fiction (Euromonitor 1993: table 8.3). This was similar to the pattern of previous years. Some science expenditure would have been on reference works, or would have been funded by institutions rather than consumers. Even so, the high level of spending on science books does not suggest that it is a subject about which the public is phobic. Book expenditure data also reveals that people distribute their spending across a wide range of fiction and non-fiction books, from food and travel to romance and crime. Preferences are highly fragmented, in contrast to the narrow focusing of review attention on a small range of books.

It may be objected that the readers of the broadsheet and middle-market press differ from the general public in being overwhelmingly middle-class. This was indeed an argument advanced by a number of literary editors. However, it is misleading on two counts.

First, book reading is strongly associated with higher levels of education and social class (Mann 1971, Publishers Association 1985). In other words, social background influences the reading not only of newspapers but also of books. Second, class influences book reading in complex ways that are different from those imagined by some literary editors. For example, historical fiction has a strong appeal among the higher social-economic groups; romance among the lower ones; while crime, thrillers, war and adventure books have a wide cross-class appeal (Publishers Association 1985: table 7.7). Readers of the prestige press, it seems, are not an island of elite culture differentiated from mass preferences.

Thus, the book-review selection in the national press is not so axiomatic that it requires no further explanation. It does not reflect what is published. It does not mirror what is important. And it does not correspond to what is popular. How, then, has it come to be like this?

Cultural values

The initial mystery surrounding books editors is easily dispelled. When they say that books select themselves, what they are actually saying is that they choose books within a framework of values they see no need to question. When some literary editors talk about the myriad, unpredictable things that determine their actions, they appear not to be fully aware of the routines they have adopted to control their environment, and of the interlocking chain of influence that leads them to choose books in a highly patterned, uniform and predictable way.

Literary editors' choice of book is influenced by their cultural values. These are not monolithic or unchanging. But what nearly all literary editors, in both 1986 and 1999, had in common was a perception of literature as a hierarchy. At the peak are works of outstanding literary merit reflected in their quality of writing, originality of vision, and depth of insight and observation. At the bottom are various forms of genre fiction whose literary value is undermined by their adherence to repetitive formula. Romantic fiction was usually identified as being especially impoverished, and crime fiction as exhibiting some redeeming features.

This hierarchical view results in different levels of attention being given to popular and literary fiction. Literary works are privileged because these are judged to be important, and to generate interesting reviews. Space for 'trashy' (a favourite adjective) books is rationed because these are thought to be of limited value and to produce dull reviews. It was widely assumed that this system of values is shared by readers of the prestige press. As one Sunday broadsheet literary editor explained, his paper's readers 'may read Jilly Cooper on the beach, perhaps. But they wouldn't want us to devote space to covering her'. It was in deference to his readers' wishes, he insisted, that he would not 'slum intellectually'.

This cultural traditionalism was undisturbed by the anguished rethinking which has taken place in university English literature departments in response to the rise of postmodernism, feminism and post-colonial theory. This has given rise to multicentred 'regimes' of value (Connor 1992, Frow 1995) different from the simple model of hierarchy adhered to by most literary editors. In addition, they were little influenced also by the positive reassessments of popular culture that have taken place in cultural studies departments in new universities in Britain and increasingly also in the United States (Modleski 1982, Radway 1984, Geraghty 1991, Landy 1997).

Part of the explanation for the intact nature of literary editors' traditional cultural values has to do with their age and education. Literary editors in 1999 were predominantly middle-aged, and educated at elite universities – as were their predecessors in 1986 (see Table 9.3). Most were also drawn to literary journalism through a love of literature. Significantly, nearly all those in 1999 who admitted taking pleasure in promoting particular books mentioned works of literary fiction or poetry, not non-fiction.

Table 9.3   University education of literary editors (per cent)

University	Oxbridge	Civic	New	Overseas	None/ not Av.	
1999	64	27	–	–	9	
1986	55	–	–	18	27	
Degree:	English	History	Other arts/hum.	Total arts/hum.	Social science	Sciences
1999	70	20	10	100	–	–
1986	37	37	19	94	6	–

Sample: 22 literary editors, 11 in 1999 and 1986. Non-graduates are excluded from degree distribution. English and philosophy degrees (2) have been tabulated as English, while Oxford PPE has been classified as half social science, half humanities.

Arts orientation

A number of literary editors said that they selected books that interested them on the assumption that they were like their readers. But, in fact, they were not at all typical of their readers. Not only had the majority gone to Oxford or Cambridge, they had tended to study just two subjects – English or history. Indeed, out of a sample of 18 university graduates, 17 had studied a humanities/arts subject (see Table 9.3). None had a science or straight social-science background.

The belief that readers were like themselves led some literary editors to take a hospitable view of some books that were relatively esoteric or difficult because these were in areas they had studied or were interested in. For example, a recondite reception study of Shakespeare in Asian countries was picked as the lead review by one literary editor of a broadsheet daily on the grounds that 'many people will find it interesting'. What he found compelling as someone who had worked on a literary studies Ph.D. may not have been viewed in the same light by his readers.

The same intellectual hospitality was not often extended to demanding or obscure books outside the arts/humanities family. Indeed, *all* books in the social sciences tended to be thought technical, specialist and, in 1999, to be of diminished authority. 'Social science is rather boring,' explained one Sunday broadsheet editor who deliberately shunned this general area. 'It's badly written ... full of jargon, full of statistics, rather uninteresting.' The problem, according to another Sunday broadsheet editor, is not only to find an interesting social-science book to review but to find anyone suitable to review it who does not 'write gobbledegook, such stodgy, jargony prose that you can't use it'. Social science (with the exception of economics) is also thought to lack the legitimacy needed to make it relevant to a general audience. 'Things have to be quite established in the culture before they appear in this paper,' explained a tabloid literary editor who avoided all books in the social-science category, however popular. But perhaps the most telling comment came from the literary editor of the *New Statesman*, a magazine that took over *New Society* in the 1980s. 'What do you mean by social science?', he asked. When the term was explained, he responded 'hasn't it been subsumed by cultural studies?'.[7]

Science was thought to have greater intellectual authority than the social sciences. There was also a sea-change of opinion among literary editors who were much more likely to say in 1999 than in 1986 that science books ought to be reviewed. Back in the 1980s, the familiar complaint had been, in the words of the late Terence Kilmartin (*Observer*), that science books were either 'technical and unintelligible' or 'popular and superficial'. The popular success of a number of critically acclaimed science books in the 1990s modified this prejudice. Yet, as our content analysis shows, a reluctance to review science books persisted. This was based partly on fear of *terra incognita*. Science was viewed as a vast area where it was difficult to distinguish good from bad, and know whom to trust. This cultural unease with science was expressed openly and candidly. For example, one literary editor confessed herself 'daunted by all these books that come in, genes and so forth'. 'Science', she continued,

> I find very difficult. . . . It is easier for us to handle science in a featurey way rather than by reviews, and I think that is probably a weakness on my part because I think that I am not sufficiently clued up in that area. I suspect that our readers may not be either, but then that is all the more reason why one should be informing them. I would find it quite difficult to know how to select reviewers in that area.

There was also a residual suspicion that public interest in science was in reality quite shallow. Consequently, science was best left to other parts of the paper (where to judge from available research (McQuail 1977, Curran and Seaton 1997) it is also neglected).

In short, literary editors are educated in the arts/humanities, within a highly specialised educational system, which disposes them against books outside this tradition. This finds extreme expression in the rule-of-thumb proscription adopted by a minority of literary editors: any book with graphs or tables is judged to be a 'technical' book of no interest to a general readership, and therefore unsuitable for review.

Occupational values

Book reviewing is also shaped by the occupational values of journalism. Only one out of 22 literary editors had not worked as a journalist before their appointment. Although they had mostly risen through what Tunstall

(1996) identifies as an elite track, and were rather untypical journalists (especially in 1986), they had all internalised journalistic norms. These stress immediacy, the over-riding importance of up-to-the-minute topicality in what Schlesinger (1978: 83) calls the 'stopwatch culture' of journalism. This largely explains the neglect of paperbacks. Hardbacks were associated with what was new, while paperbacks were identified with yesterday's news, an old story warmed up in new covers. Significantly, this prejudice is now weakening not out of recognition that most people read paperbacks but in response to the packaging of more new titles as first-edition paperbacks. A traditional news value lives on, even as it is being modified.

Another journalistic axiom is that 'people are more interesting than things'. This is the key to understanding why biographies are the most reviewed books in the press. They are favoured because they are about people, and 'tell a story'. They are also widely thought to generate interesting reviews that are easy to write and illustrate. They are the book-review equivalent of the human-interest story, an editorial category that has won steadily more space in the press because it appeals to a wide cross-section of the market (Curran et al. 1980).

However, literary editors are both literary people and journalists, and this duality gives rise to value conflicts. Many literary editors despise formula novels, yet publish reviews which follow journalistic formulae. They disdain market values in fiction, yet compete in the market place. Their first love is generally literature, yet they allocate more space to biography.

Role tensions are lessened through emphasising those things that literary and journalistic traditions have in common. One thing both traditions value is good writing, and this tends to be elevated into a fetish. Thus, it is thought logical that not only a review but also the book it assesses should be well written. 'You wouldn't expect us to review books that are badly written,' declared one literary editor, adding proudly that his paper 'celebrates good writing'. This excessive reverencing of style has the effect of excluding authors, like Jürgen Habermas, who write badly but have important things to say.

Literary editors are also drawn to books that succeed in both literary and journalistic terms. For example, A. N. Wilson's biography of Hilaire Belloc was given in 1984 the *lead* review position in three broadsheet papers, one tabloid paper and two leading magazines, in addition to being very extensively reviewed elsewhere. This book proved to be neither a bestseller nor a landmark study. But, as a well-written study of a literary figure by a journalist of note, it conformed precisely to what is considered a key book in the literary-journalistic community. Similarly, the three most-reviewed books in 1973, identified by Noble and Noble (1974), were all 'celebrity on celebrity' books with a literary-journalistic dimension.[8]

Pre-selection

The personal preferences and values of literary editors provide only one part of the explanation of the book-review agenda. The 'gatekeeper' strand of media research, initiated by David Manning White (1997 [1952]), is inclined to overstate the importance of the views and experiences of senior media workers because it tends to pay too little attention to wider cultural and institutional influences. The nature of these wider influences is highlighted by this case study.

Even before a book reaches a literary editor, it has been subjected to a filtering process that influences the attention it receives. In effect, the literary editor's selection is merely the culmination of a complex process of *pre-selection*.

The differential resources available to rival publishers constitute the first filter. Major publishers have, generally, larger budgets and greater prestige than smaller ones. Although some literary editors emphasised that they tried to help small publishers as a matter of principle, there was general agreement that a book from a major, prestige publisher tended to be approached with 'greater hope' than one from an obscure publishing house. This was because top publishers were perceived to offer the highest rewards and attract the best writers, and because some of them had track records which indicated good judgement.

Book covers are the second filter. These are widely thought to reveal much about a book. Why this should be the case remained obscure until one literary editor patiently went through two cupboards of books commenting on each cover. The conventional cues of blurb, endorsements and note about author were not what elicited most comment. It became immediately apparent that there are visual codes denoting a book as 'library fodder', run-of-the-mill, genre, specialist-academic or – the ultimate visual interpellation that invited further attention – a book on which money and time had been lavished to give it a distinctive, designed appearance. Book covers are 'read' by insiders in a way that is different from the rest of us. In this case, they were interpreted as revealing what publishers really thought about a book, as distinct from what the book's publicity proclaimed.

The third filter is the level of commitment made by a publisher to a book. Publishers respond to the unpredictability of the market by overproducing titles (Hirsch 1972). In this way, they avoid investing only in a few titles that may fail, and hedge their bets. But they also back their judgement by putting extra effort into those titles which they think will succeed. These internal organisational decisions have a way of being self-fulfilling.

The amount of resources committed to winning reviews varies enormously. On a ascending scale, this can be an unprominent announcement in a publisher's catalogue; the routine dispatch of a review copy; a cursory phone call to check that the book has arrived; a personalised note drawing attention to the book's virtues; the distribution of free copies not only to literary editors but also to reviewers known to the author or publisher; the dispatch of advance proof copies to selected literary editors; threnodies of praise for a book as one of the key titles of the season in personal meetings with literary editors (usually over lunch or at a party); a planned campaign of TV and radio appearances, press interviews, launch party, serialisation and paid advertising; or the fullscale mobilisation of the literary-journalistic community in a way that will be described in a moment.

Circuits of influence

Literary editors follow certain routines in order to control uncertainty, avoid mistakes and ensure a smooth flow of work. One of these routines is to maintain regular contact with leading publishers. They are the literary editors' equivalent of the 'news beat': their key source of information, gossip and data for planning ahead. As in conventional news beats, information is facilitated by professional intermediaries. Major publishing houses have publicity departments employing up to a dozen or more people, one of whose key tasks is to help and influence literary editors.

It is tempting to see literary editors as an extension of this publicity machine, as mere secondary agents who respond to prior processes of selection within the publishing industry. However, this view is both simplistic and misleading because it fails to take account of the unequal relationship between publicists and literary editors. At the end of the day, publicists make a case: literary editors decide whether to listen. Consequently, publicists have to adapt (to their private irritation, sometimes) to the preferences of literary editors in order to be effective. This results in promotion that generally reinforces rather than challenges these preferences.

For example, publishers print many titles without sending a single review copy to a national newspaper (as distinct from journals and magazines). Among these underpromoted books are large numbers of academic social-science books, which is one reason given by literary editors for why these books are so rarely reviewed. However, the reason why review copies are often not sent to national papers in the first place is because publishers have learnt from experience that it is usually a waste of time and money to do so. The pattern of promotion thus follows rather than dictates the book-review agenda.

The same logic applies to other aspects of promotion to the national press. Publicists from 11 publishers, with different lists and experiences, were asked in 1986 to list in order (1–4) from a prepared list of categories which types of book they thought were easiest to get reviewed in the national press. The choices were then weighted in terms of 4 for first choice, 3 for second, and so on, in a descending scale. What publicists thought closely resembled what actually got reviewed. They knew what worked, and prioritised their efforts accordingly.

Table 9.4   Publicists' assessment of review prospects

Biography	38
Literary novels	25
Literature and criticism	17
History	14
Politics and social science	8
Arts	7
Popular fiction	7
Science and technology	0

Sample: 11 publishers' public-relations executives. The points system was 4 for first choice; 3 for second choice; 2 for third choice; and 1 for fourth choice. The maximum possible score is 44, i.e. 4 for first choice × 11 executives.

If promotion follows rather than challenges, however, it can also canalise attention towards particular titles. That is to say, it can influence which books within favoured categories get reviewed. For example, it can affect which first novel is taken seriously, as is illustrated by the publication in 1984 of Iain Banks's first novel, *The Wasp Factory*. Its success began with a rumour spreading in Macmillan's offices that there had been a 'discovery', a brilliant, unsolicited first novel sent in by an unknown solicitor's clerk who worked in an office all day and wrote fiction by night. The story became a full-page feature article in the London *Evening Standard*, under the headline 'A Flying Leap from the Junk Pile' (30 Dec. 1993), six weeks ahead of publication. Copies of the *Standard* article were sent out; the trade was flooded with proof copies of the book; a major feature was inspired in *Publishing News*; and a trade advertising campaign was initiated. By this time, the mythic story of an unknown clerk working by night on a masterpiece had become part of the word-of-mouth buzz of the literary-journalistic community. A literary editor, who had decided not to review *The Wasp Factory* after a negative reaction from a regular reviewer, changed his mind when his editor told him excitedly what he had heard about it on the grapevine. This concerted word-of-mouth promotion resulted in the book being reviewed (though in a mixed way) in 10 national newspapers and eight national magazines; obtaining spots on BBC 2's *Bookmark*, TVS and prestige radio programmes (*Kaleidoscope* and Radio 4 *Midweek*); and generating over 600 standard column centimetres of additional feature articles in the press.[9] The book almost immediately sold out, and was reprinted.

In this case, the promotional muscle of a major publisher promoted literary innovation. But the close relationship between literary editors and major publishers also has a conservative aspect in that it tends to freeze out small publishers based overseas. For example, Naguib Mahfouz's key works were widely reviewed when they were published by Doubleday, a Transworld subsidary, in 1991–3. Yet, they received very little attention when they were originally published in English translation by the American University in Cairo Press.

The one partial exception to this picture of public relations as an agency of reinforcement and canalisation rather than of change relates to the promotion of science. A number of science books, including one on quantum mechanics (*In Search of Schrodinger's Cat* (1984)), sold well in the mid-1980s. In 1988 a major publisher, Transworld, put its promotional muscle behind Stephen Hawking's *A Brief History of Time*. Encouraged by a favourable trade response, it increased its initial print-run from 5000 to 7500 copies. This information was then fed to literary agents to persuade them that the book was of interest to a general audience. But, as with *The Wasp Factory*, it was primarily the book as a 'story' – in this case, a masterpiece by a crippled British genius, stricken by motor-neurone disease – that was, in Mark Barty-King's words, 'the trigger for review and feature attention'. The book gained extensive coverage in the national press, and subsequently became a bestseller. But while it became a stalking horse for other best-selling science books, and was important in terms of contributing to an increased psychological acceptance of science books among literary editors, it did not in fact make a great deal of difference to reviewing practice.

Transworld's assault on established attitudes was unusual. In general public-relations executives double-guess literary editors, and in the process entrench their prejudices. If literary editors prove unresponsive, publishers bypass them by placing increased reliance on other forms of promotion.

Networks

One key network influencing literary editors is book reviewers. These are a mixture of professional writers, journalists and academics, with particular areas of expertise. Their influence has grown over the years because book reviewing has become more casualised. Broadsheets no longer rely on full-time, professional star reviewers. The tabloids have also stopped using literary editors who do virtually all the reviewing themselves.

However, the rise of repertories of reviewers has tended to reinforce a pre-set agenda. Literary editors inherit reviewers, and prune or add to them over time. Reviewers are thus an extension both of editorial tradition and of the literary editor's own preferences. These informal teams have knowledge and competence relevant to the categories of book that are regularly reviewed.

This gives rise to a self-reproducing tradition. Book reviewers sometimes propose books they want to review. They can respond negatively or positively to suggestions from the literary editor. They generate a field force of influence in favour of certain kinds of books – biographies, history, literary novels and literary criticism – because these are the books that most of them specialise in reviewing. The composition of review teams thus skews which books get reviewed.

Another key network of influence is what Tunstall (1971) calls 'competitor-colleagues', that is journalists working in the same positions on rival papers. Literary editors often scan other literary pages to see how they compare with their own (often identifying particular publications as 'the real opposition'). The anxious nature of this tracking is well described by Andrew Curtis, the long-serving literary editor of the *Sunday Telegraph* and *Financial Times*. He projects an imaginary situation in which his paper had led with a review of a biography of an obscure Victorian literary figure called Beddoes. He is the only person to do so and he worries, thinking that 'he has achieved a scoop with it – but was it a scoop worth having?' Perhaps he will be criticised for failing to lead with another important book. Then, 'two or more weeks later, the lit ed notices to his delight that long reviews of the Beddoes biography are appearing in the other papers in the wake of his' (Curtis 1998: 21–2). This fantasy captures the central dynamic of this competitor-colleague relationship: to be both first and the same.

In the mid-1980s this herd-like behaviour was disturbed by one man, William Webb, literary editor of the *Guardian*. He was perceived to be something of a loner by other literary editors, and was criticised for reviewing 'obscure' and 'boring' books. However, he was also acknowledged to have a certain standing in the literary-journalist world. Webb's sin was to deviate not from the basic book-review agenda – in fact the balance of subjects reviewed on his pages was rather conventional – but to give unusual prominence to certain kinds of book within this agenda: in particular, fiction from central Europe and Latin America, radical social history and feminist work. But in 1999 there were no respected outsiders among national-press literary editors, no one who was attacked and resented for doing things differently. The group was supported in its conformism.

Another key network is the literary community. Its core is made up of writers, publishers, literary agents and literary journalists, who are bound together by social ties based on friendship, sexual partnership, work, educational background, club membership or neighbourhood. Thus, novelist Julian Barnes is godfather to poet Craig Raine's daughter. Craig Raine lives in the same street as novelist Ian McEwan, whose wife is literary editor of the *Financial Times*. The *Financial Times* hired Craig Raine as a reviewer . . . and so on. It would require a sociometric diagram of immense complexity to document the multiple interconnections which exist between prominent writers, reviewers and literary editors.

The literary world also has an unusual degree of cohesion and reciprocal influence because it is sustained, in a sense, by corporate sponsorship. Its members are brought together in book launch parties, lunches and dinner parties paid for by the publishing industry as part of its promotional activity. This is not to ignore the rivalries that exist within it, which can spill over into reviews. But, notwithstanding these rivalries, the literary community is united in its commitment to literary values, and strongly supports literary editors in defending and upholding these.

This literary-journalistic network is part of a para-community that is London-based and links together the different worlds of politics, letters, academe, media and performing arts. Its members do not necessarily know each other, but they tend to know *of* each other and to have friends or acquaintances in common. Its leading members regularly propose each other's books in round-ups of the year's best publications. This community of status supports, and is supported by, the book pages of the national press.

Cultural tradition

Literary editors are the carriers of a cultural tradition. Their literary values and book preferences are shaped by patterns of thought formed long ago.

Striking confirmation of this is provided by the Victorian press. The *Edinburgh Review* and *Blackwoods* of 1870 have little in common with the *New Statesman* and *Spectator* of 1997, yet all four publications reviewed essentially the same kinds of books. Similarly, over half the review space of the *Sunday Times* was given in 1870, as in 1997, to literary fiction, history and biography. The paper's review blindspots were also identical: the Victorian *Sunday Times* was no more interested in science and technology than its modern counterpart. While there are differences between the Victorian and contemporary book-review agendas,[10] the most noticeable thing is how small these are.

This agenda was shaped when there was a settled hierarchy of knowledge, underpinned by the elite educational and social system. In 1870 the humanities (classics, history, theology and philosophy) enjoyed an unchallenged ascendancy in ancient universities and were the staple of public-school teaching. In addition, a discriminating love of poetry and literary fiction was also accepted as being part of 'humane' culture as a consequence of its endorsement by the cultivated elite.

The press's quarantining of science books and disdain for genre fiction also has roots in the snobberies of this period. The natural and physical sciences came low in the hierarchy of prestige. They were developed and taught in socially inferior institutions: Scottish universities, northern higher-education establishments, dissenting academies, some grammar schools. Science was associated with irreligion, and identified with commerce and manufacture. In 1870 Cambridge University graduated only 20 scientists a year (Sanderson 1983: 45). Even lower in the scale of value came the fiction books enjoyed by the masses.

But what becomes harder to explain is why book-review conventions established so long ago should have proved so resistant to change. After all, the production of knowledge was transformed during the intervening period. The sciences made a breakthrough in Oxford and Cambridge from the 1870s onwards, and came to be accepted, though more slowly, in public schools. They also won a prestigious position in the university system as a whole, with the 1940s representing a key 'moment' when the sciences were deliberately given preferential treatment over all other disciplines (McKibbin 1998). The triumph of science was followed by the rise of the social sciences in the 1960s and 1970s, business studies in the 1980s, and combined studies in the 1990s. The world of ideas, within a greatly expanded university system, became unrecognisably different from what it had been in high Victorian Britain.

The power structure and cultural landscape of Britain was also transformed. A landed oligarchy gave way to a welfarist capitalist democracy (Reid 1992, Clarke 1997, Cannadine 1998). The culture of society became more commercialised, pluralistic, individualistic and democratic (LeMahieu 1988, Hewison 1995, Gelder and Thornton 1997). It was not just literary editors who stopped wearing frock coats: the whole of British society became less culturally straitjacketed.

The explanation for the immobility of the book-review agenda over the last century has to do with the social history of Britain. One accusatory account sees the contemporary intelligentsia as being shaped decisively by the gentrified values of the upper class in the 1850s and 1860s, and to have been frozen ever since in an anti-science, anti-productivist, literary mould with a sentimental attachment to a vanished rural idyll (Wiener 1985). A second account sees the Victorian intelligentsia as the reformers rather than cultural satellites of the aristocracy, emphasises the ways its successors adapted to the embrace of modern science, and celebrates its progressive, moralising influence on society (Perkin 1989). A third view points to the ideological contradictions within the liberal intelligentsia, and to the deep roots of some of its attitudes going back to the early modern period. Everything, it suggests, is more complicated and ambiguous than anyone has yet acknowledged (McKendrick 1986). Without getting caught up in detail in this controversy, it is clear that the literary-humanities values of contemporary literary editors took shape more than a century ago, and have been resistant to change partly due to the distinctive education and cultural formation of Britain's literary intelligentsia.

However, part of the explanation for why literary editors did not respond more fully to the transformation of British universities has to do with the shortcomings of the universities themselves. Academic specialisation led not only to the 'two cultures' of science and the arts, lamented by C. P. Snow in the 1950s, but to a fragmentation of academic cultures, each with their own self-referencing debates, technical vocabularies and demarcated areas of knowledge. Universities as communities of learning ceased to be comprehensible even to their own members (as victims of obscure inaugural lectures will testify), still less to a wider public. In part, this may have been an inevitable product of professionalisation, but it was also fostered by the erosion of the public role of universities. The reward system within universities encouraged introspection. It revolved around elite academic review of research in a form that paid no attention to whether it was read by the wider public or even by students. Consequently, academics came to write primarily for each other. The succession of big-selling science books in the 1990s, for example, originated not in the main from academic scientists (few of whom were willing to lift their sights above refereed journals) but from talented scientist-journalists like Simon Singh. By and large, academics chose voluntary internal exile by writing books, with tiny print runs, for narrow niche publics.

In other words, the selection of books for review begins not with the historical formation of the cultural values of literary editors, nor with the social networks of which they are part, nor even with pre-selection by publishers, but with the narrow exclusivity of university academics, the only state-supported group of writers in Britain.

Independence

Does it matter that the books agenda of the national press has largely stood still since Victorian times? Before attempting to answer this in the last section, we will follow two brief digressions, the first touching obliquely on the question of diversity and independence and the second identifying key changes that are taking place.

Although convergence between publications has been stressed, there is some diversity in the book-review pages of the national press, reflecting differences of audience, editorial tradition and personality. For example, the range of books selected in the *Economist* is more cosmopolitan than that of other mainstream weeklies principally because the majority of its readers live abroad.

Even if there is considerable overlap between the books that are reviewed, evaluations are by no means the same. In 1999, 14 national newspapers regularly published book reviews,[11] and these were supplemented by leading specialist literary journals, like the *London Review of Books* and *Literary Review*, as well as educational weeklies. This is in stark contrast to the more restricted book review oligopoly of the American press (Coser et al. 1982).

If book reviews are influenced by coterie, they are also influenced by the ideal of independence. This is reflected in the strong stand taken by literary editors in 1986 that book reviews were not – and should not be – shaped by the editorial line of their papers. This claim was cross-checked through an examination of press reviews of two books about the Falklands War, published in 1982 and 1983, that ran counter to the belligerent, pro-war position adopted by most national papers.[12] These two books received neutral or positive reviews in 12 out of the 13 notices that appeared in national newspapers, with in some cases reviewers making explicit their own anti-war or critical stance. These reviews plainly did not follow an editorial house line: they seemed, if anything, to reflect reservations about the Falklands War among the liberal intelligentsia.

Literary editors in 1999 again stressed their editorial independence, but this time in a more qualified form. More references were made to the looming presence of the editor, and the internalisation of controls was more freely acknowledged. For example, one tabloid literary editor talked about 'an instinctive restraint' that came 'from knowing the place you work in', adding that she 'wouldn't choose a radical feminist to review a radical feminist book'. Similarly, a weekly literary editor said that the 'culture' of her office meant that 'it would be very difficult ... to run a review that praised the elimination of the motorcar or socialism as the way of the future'.

One important reason why literary editors felt more constrained was that they were less well established. The majority of literary editors in 1986 had been long-serving, in some cases for over 20 years. By contrast, only two out of 11 literary editors interviewed in 1999 had held the same job for more than 6 years. The other reason why they felt exposed to more pressure was because the nature of their job was changing.

Key changes

The picture that has been offered so far has stressed continuity with the past. But the 1980s and 1990s should also be viewed as a period of transition, arising from the conjunction of changes in both book and newspaper publishing.

The introduction of new low-cost print technology in the mid-1980s led to an enormous expansion in the size of newspapers. The mean number of pages of national dailies rose by over two-thirds between 1985 and 1995 (Tunstall 1996: 32, table 3.1). Newspapers had to fill a yawning void, and looked around for new sources of cheap copy, particularly in the area of features.

During the 1980s and 1990s, publishers were taken over by international conglomerates. They were transformed from small-scale enterprises which, according to Lane (1980: 27), saw 'their real job as bringing books out, not as selling', into market-focused organisations. For the first time, a large investment was made in the promotion of books, and in the employment of people whose job was to secure free publicity for new titles.

Literary editors thus found themselves at the interface of two industries undergoing change: the one eager for new raw material, and the other newly geared up to supplying it.[13] Novels were increasingly constructed as 'stories' centring on the author, who was made available for interviews. Non-fiction books were more often filleted as newspaper copy in recognition that book authors are cheap sources of labour. The role of the literary editor thus began to be redefined, from being concerned only with commissioning and writing book reviews to becoming a broker who recognises or responds to ideas for converting books into features, serials, excerpts, interviews or even news reports. This evolutionary change has taken place unevenly in the national press, with some literary editors belonging to the old way of doing things and others symbolising the new. Typical of the latter was a daily literary editor who compared her office to a 'pork butchery'. 'There is no [non-fiction] book we cannot find a use for,' she boasted, 'even if it is a trotter to go into the magazine.'

The book-review pages also began to change in a way that our content analysis, which is confined to book reviews, does not document. In some newspapers, new sorts of article were introduced: interviews with authors, features about authors, heritage articles (i.e. 'the book I have loved'), news about publishing, information about book sales.

The sort of person who was appointed literary editor also changed. In 1986 the majority of literary editors were authors of published books; in 1999 only one respondent was. In the 1980s literary editors were overwhelmingly recruited from literary journalism; now they have more varied backgrounds often with a more extensive grounding in mainstream journalism. In the 1980s literary editors were often rather hostile to publicists; now they are more positive (with one, very influential literary editor claiming to have lunch with a publisher four or five days a week). The defiantly Reithian tone of some tabloid literary editors in 1986 (one compared his job to being a 'ballet teacher in East India Docks') has become subdued. There has been a shift, in short, from the literary editor as 'man' of letters to professional journalist.

A further aspect of this change is that literary editors are no longer overwhelmingly men. In 1986 only two out of 11 interviewees were women, compared with just over half in 1999.[14] However, it is not at all clear that this gender shift has made much of a difference. Women tended to attend fewer early evening literary functions than men because they assumed a larger domestic load at home. There were some indications that for this and other reasons female literary editors were less embedded in the literary world, and less influenced by its internal hierarchies. Some women (but only some) were more oriented than men towards women writers, and to issues that are of specific interest to women. However, the book pages are shaped by a long tradition of male gender values (Women in Publishing 1987) which persist despite the gender shift. For example, crime fiction with a strong male following still receives more attention than romantic fiction with a strong female following.

Influence of book reviews

Returning to the central thread of this essay, does it matter which books are reviewed? The conventional response to this question is to consider the influence of book reviews on consumer behaviour. The evidence suggests that reviews can influence book sales, with 24 per cent in one national survey saying that reading a review had influenced their last book purchase (Mintel 1984: 84). Reviews can also influence which books are stocked and borrowed in public libraries (Ward 1977), while anticipated review publicity can apparently affect initial bookshop orders (Women in Publishing 1987). This said, the importance of book reviews has probably diminished as a consequence of the rise of publishers' public relations and the growth of interviews, features and chat shows featuring authors. Books that are excluded from reviews and this kind of publicity are also promoted in other ways: through publishers' catalogues, mail order, specialist bookshops, inspection copies and advertising.

However, this conventional approach to assessing the influence of book reviews – as an 'effect' on consumer behaviour – does not adequately comprehend their wider cultural importance. Book reviews are a form of peer review in which writers judge other writers in a public process of symbolic grading. As Pierre Bourdieu (1993) points out, in the context of late nineteenth-century France, this can influence estimations not only of individual writers but also of rival literary traditions. These can affect in turn the production and public reception of these traditions.

Bourdieu's insight can be extended from literary faction to areas of knowledge. Book reviews in the national press allocate prestige not only between authors but also between the areas they work in. The act of regular critical appraisal affirms the value of the field in which the appraisal is being made. It is a form of public recognition signifying that the area of knowledge is important and relevant, one which an informed person should be expected to know something about. It also implies that certain competencies necessary for understanding that field (such as knowledge of specialist language, concepts, cultural references and relevant analytical tools) are attributes that a cultivated person should possess. The reverse is also true. Areas of knowledge that are relatively invisible in book pages are symbolically shunted to the margins as technical, difficult or unimportant. They do not belong to the 'need to know' area of public knowledge, while the skills needed to understand them are optional.

In making visible the humanities, but rendering relatively invisible the sciences and social sciences, the national book pages are engaging in a public process of valorisation. They are signifying that literature, history, biography and literary studies are at the centre of literate culture. Other subjects are by implication outside the core cultural curriculum of society. They are less relevant, important or of general interest. The cultural skills needed to understand these other subjects, such as an ability to read a statistical table, are not essential.

The attachment of social value to certain areas of knowledge imparts status to the holders of this knowledge. The celebration of literary and humanities culture in the books pages underpins the prestige of the largely humanities-educated elite who dominate public life in Britain. It also sustains a 'generalist' culture, with its belief that education for no particular occupation is a preparation for all occupations (at least, at the level of leadership). Conversely, the symbolic marginalisation of science detracts from the cultural status of trained scientists and technologists.

Which books are reviewed – in addition to how they are reviewed – may also have some influence on how books are written. The literary skills of academic history are constantly reinforced by the existence of a non-specialist audience for its work, supported by book reviews in the national press. The reverse, unfortunately, also applies. The knowledge that there is almost no general audience for academic social science, as well as no general public appraisal, reinforces the self-absorption and needless obscurity that is a growing feature of its writing.

However, the single most important consequence of the national press's selective book agenda is that it narrows access to knowledge. By marginalising social science, the book pages obscure its central insight: that the individual is constrained by structures in ways that run counter to the individual-centred, idealist view of the world advanced by much journalism (and also much biography). And, by downgrading science, literary editors are endorsing an inherited system of classification that elevates some books as 'culture' and sees others as merely technical or useful. In fact, science is as important in making sense of ourselves and of the world, and the relationship between the two, as the study of history or literature. It is in this sense no less central to 'cultural' understanding. By shrinking the intellectual horizons of the book pages, literary editors are thus doing no service to their readers.

In sum, what is reviewed in the press should not be reduced to the issue of how it affects the sales of particular titles. Nor should it be judged only in the terms set out by literary critics, cited at the beginning of this essay. What is reviewed has important consequences for how different areas of knowledge are perceived and accessed. That, ultimately, is why it is worth examining what influences literary editors.

Notes

1 My thanks go to Keith Negus and Herbert Pimlott for their invaluable contributions to this essay, and to Goldsmiths College for providing a £600 research grant. Keith Negus (then an undergraduate on research placement) undertook the content analysis for 1984, and undertook a number of interviews with publicists. Herbert Pimlott did the content analysis for 1997. Both also identified data on book production and consumption, and made important contributions to the ideas contained in this essay.

2 The 11 literary editors interviewed in 1996 were divided between broadsheets (4), tabloids (3) and weeklies (4). Those interviewed in 1999 were again divided between these three sectors: broadsheets (6), tabloids (3) and weeklies (2). Fewer weekly literary editors were interviewed the second time round because the

decline of the weeklies' influence had by then become fully apparent. All interviews were recorded. The overwhelming majority of comments that are quoted are taken from the more recent batch of interviews.

3 The content analysis was based on 270 issues of the nine titles, in 1984 and 1997 (the latest year for which copies are available in the Colingdale Newspaper Library), selected to be representative of the annual output of each publication. A code–recode test of 398 items revealed a 91.2 per cent agreement in their classification.

4 A study of lead or joint-lead reviews in 1984 produced results that resembled the overall distribution of space between categories of book, though it tended to emphasise still more the prominence given to biography.

5 The paperbacks tabulated in the content anlysis are those that are explicitly identified as such. Although some paperbacks would not have been detected through this method, their number is not large.

6 This is the most recent publicly available information deposited and classified in the British Library. More recent information is available on the Internet, but it proved too expensive to access – something that reinforces the central argument of Chapter 2.

7 The name of the publication is identified because it is relevant in terms of what was said, and also because this interview was conducted on the record.

8 They were a biography of Nye Bevan by the politician and former editor Michael Foot; a study of author parents, Harold Nicholson and Vita Sackville-West, by the author, journalist and former politician Nigel Nicolson; and a biography of Marilyn Monroe by the novelist and journalist Norman Mailer.

9 Our thanks to Marion Milne and Macmillan for making available office records.

10 In 1870 the range of books (from fables to stomach disorders) reviewed in the national press was more eclectic, reflecting a time when knowledge was less standardised by the university system. Classical learning received more attention, and genre novels even less, than now. The printed versions of plays and issues of periodicals were also sometimes reviewed as books, during a period when the book review had not fully stabilised as a literary form.

11 The *Sunday Mirror* dropped book reviews in 1998, but the *Daily Mirror* revived them in the same year.

12 The two books were David Tinker's *Message from the Falklands* (Penguin), and Robert Harris's *Gotcha!* (Faber). The fact that both were critical of official manipulation rather than overtly opposed to the war probably made them more acceptable. *Iron Britannia* (Anthony Barnett), an overtly anti-war book, would have provided a stronger test of independence but its publisher, Allison and Busby, had a very incomplete set of reviews.

13 A similar conjunction took place in the same period between television and publishing, in a process that awaits investigation.

14 This gender shift reflected that of the entire population of literary editors working for the national press. See Women in Publishing (1987) and Media Information (1998).

References

Bourdieu, P. (1993) *The Field of Cultural Production*, Cambridge: Polity.

Cannadine, D. (1998) *Class in Britain*, New Haven: Yale University Press.

Clarke, P. (1997) *Hope and Glory*, London: Penguin.

Connor, S. (1992) *Theory and Cultural Value*, Oxford: Blackwell.

Coser, L., Kadushin, C. and Powell, W. (1982) *Books*, New York: Basic Books.

Curran, J., Douglas, A. and Whannel, G. (1980) 'The Political Economy of the Human-Interest Story', in A. Smith (ed.), *Newspapers and Democracy*, Cambridge, MA: MIT Press.

Curran, J. and Seaton, J. (1997) *Power Without Responsibility*, 5th edn, London: Routledge.

Curtis, A. (1998) *Lit Ed*, Manchester: Carcanet.

Euromonitor (1993) *The Book Report*, London: Euromonitor Publications.

Frow, J. (1995) *Cultural Studies and Cultural Value*, Oxford: Oxford University Press.

Gelder, K. and Thornton, S. (1997) *The Subcultures Reader*, London: Routledge.

Geraghty, C. (1991) *Women and Soap Opera*, Cambridge: Polity.

Hewison, R. (1995) *Culture and Consensus*, London: Methuen.

Hirsch, P. (1972) 'Processing Fads and Fashions: An Organisational Analysis of Cultural Industry Systems', *American Journal of Sociology*, 77.4.

Landy, M. (1997) 'Melodrama and Femininity in World War Two British Cinema' in R. Murphy (ed.), *The British Cinema Book*, London: British Film Institute.

Lane, M. (1980) *Books and Publishers*, Toronto: D.C. Heath.

Leavis, F. R. (1972) *Nor Shall My Sword*, London: Chatto and Windus.

LeMahieu, D. L. (1988) *A Culture for Democracy*, Oxford: Clarendon Press.

McKendrick, N. (1986) ' "Gentlemen and Players" Revisited: The Gentlemanly Ideal, the Business Ideal and the Professional Ideal in English Literary Culture', in N. McKendrick and R. Outhwaite (eds), *Business Life and Public Policy*, Cambridge: Cambridge University Press.

McKibbin, R. (1998) *Classes and Cultures*, Oxford: Oxford University Press.

McQuail, D. (1977) *Analysis of Newspaper Content*, London: HMSO.

Mann, P. (1971) *Books: Buyers and Borrowers*, London: Deutsch.

Media Information (1998) *Editors Media Directories* (vol. 1), London: Media Information.

Mintel (1984) *Leisure Industry Report* (8), London: Mintel.

Modleski, T. (1982) *Loving With a Vengeance*, Hamden, CT: Archon Books.

Noble, D. H. and Noble, C. M. (1974) *A Survey of Book Reviews, October–December 1973*, London: Noble and Beck.

Perkin, H. (1989) *The Rise of Professional Society*, London: Routledge.

Publishers Association (1985) *The Book Trade Yearbook*, London: Publishers Assocation.

Radway, J. (1987) *Reading the Romance*, London: Verso.

Reid, A. (1992) *Social Classes and Social Relations in Britain, 1850–1914*, London: Macmillan.

Sanderson, M. (1983) *Education, Economic Change and Society in England 1780–1870*, London: Macmillan.

Schlesinger, P. (1978) *Putting 'Reality' Together*, London: Constable.

Sutherland, J. (1978) *Fiction and the Fiction Industry*, London: Athlone.

Taylor, D. J. (1989) *A Vain Conceit*, London: Bloomsbury.

Tunstall, J. (1971) *Journalists at Work*, London: Constable.

Tunstall, J. (1996) *Newspaper Power*, Oxford: Oxford University Press.

UNESCO (1997) *UNESCO Statistical Yearbook 1996*, Paris: UNESCO.

Ward, M. (1977) *Readers and Library Users*, London: Library Association.

White, D. M. (1997 [1952]) 'The "Gate Keeper": A Case Study in the Selection of News', in D. Berkowitz (ed.), *Social Meaning of News*, London: Sage.

Wiener, M. (1985) *English Culture and the Decline of the Industrial Spirit 1850–1980*, Harmondsworth: Penguin.

Women in Publishing (1987) *Reviewing the Reviews*, London: Journeyman Press.

10

Music divisions

The recording industry and the social mediation of cultural production

KEITH NEGUS

Researching cultural production involves thinking about the interconnections, and convergences or divergences, that come in between those practices conventionally labelled with the deceptively simple terms 'production' and 'consumption'. This is not only an issue for practitioners engaged in creating cultural items, whether film directors seeking to understand how to move audiences, novelists wondering about their readers or artists wishing to display and price a painting. It also poses dilemmas for those of us attempting to analyse media, arts and entertainment organisations with the aim of facilitating critical public engagement with, participation in and access to the worlds of cultural production. How we conceptualise and comprehend processes of mediation will have consequences for how we think about what producers are doing, their relationship to consumers, and any possible interventions or policies that may be advocated in order to make such practices more just or democratic.

In this chapter I will pursue these issues through a discussion of the recording industry and the production of popular music and focus on how music-industry personnel come in between performing artists and their listeners. In doing this I shall highlight how very specific patterns of intervention contribute to the formation of the music business and how this results in the institutionalisation of organisational routines which privilege certain musical styles over others. In turn, I will argue that the commercial priorities and aesthetic hierarchies that are established in music media organisations are directly shaped by broader social divisions and tensions (these are, effectively, brought 'into' and structurated 'within' music-producing organisations).

Two distinct senses of mediation are involved here. First, mediation as involving the intermediary activities of all the personnel who intervene as music is produced, distributed and circulated. This most obviously refers to workers employed by record companies, but it could also include journalists, retailers and the directors of music programmes on television and radio. As Raymond Williams (1976) has pointed out, this idea of intermediary action should not be understood as involving an arbitrating process of conciliatory activity. Although sometimes presented in such a light, the occupational intermediaries who work in the music industry are constantly engaged in disputes with each other, with their corporate bosses and with recording artists. Such conflicts can have a direct impact on how popular music is produced and presented to the public (Negus 1992).

At the same time as employing the concept of mediation to refer to occupational intermediaries, I am also using it in a broader way to signify the mediation of social relationships. By utilising the term in this way I am referring to how power and influence are exercised through such mediated relationships and how this has a direct impact on the creation and reception of entertainment products or works of art. This approach to mediation draws on a long tradition of Marxist analysis, with a particular issue concerning how human relationships and cultural forms are mediated by social class. While social class is clearly an important influence on the mediation of cultural forms in any class-divided society, there are further ways in which the social relations of race, gender, sexuality and ethnicity mediate the creation and reception of works of art and entertainment products. It is due to such factors that no music will ever simply 'reflect' a society or an individual performer's life or psyche, but instead be caught within, arise out of and refer to a series of unequal social relations and power struggles.

In this chapter I will be bringing together these two meanings of mediation to argue that when studying media organisations (in this case those in the recording industry) we need to consider how external processes and social divisions intersect with the industry, just as much as we conduct research focused on occupational activities within the organisations. To begin illustrating this argument, I shall provide a brief critique of the main organisation-centric approaches to the production of popular music. I will then move on to some broader perspectives which point to the connections between production and consumption (or organisation and audience) and which enable us to think about the wider relationships within which music is made.

Inside the music business: the musical mechanics

The work of staff within music-business organisations, and the activities of those engaged in commercial cultural production more generally, have often been explained through analogies with an 'assembly line' or 'production line'. The use of such mechanical metaphors can be traced back to Theodor Adorno's and Max Horkheimer's (1979) critique of the 'culture industry', a term they introduced in work first published during the 1940s, when arguing that cultural items were being produced in a way that had become analogous to how other industries were involved in manufacturing vast quantities of consumer goods. Employing what has subsequently become a familiar metaphor – the cultural 'assembly line' – they argued that all products were being produced solely for the purpose of economic gain and according to the same rationalised organisational procedures. The owners of the means of musical production had come to exert a decisive influence, and the commodification of culture had resulted in a mode of producing songs, along with Hollywood movies and novels, which resembled industrial manufacturing. This, they concluded, resulted in a standardised 'mass culture' which lacked individuality and originality. Following in this line of reasoning, critical observers began to explain commercial music production by evoking the image of bureaucratic 'song factories' engaged in the routine bolting together of standardised and interchangeable melodies, lyrics and rhythms.

The endurance of these mechanical metaphors can be detected in an influential 'filter-flow' model of music production proposed by Paul Hirsch (1972). His 'organisational set analysis of cultural industry systems' commences with the selection of 'raw materials', drawn from a 'universe' of potential recordings. These are admitted to a 'creative subsystem' where they are 'rank ordered and filtered' by producers and record-company policy-makers, regional promoters and the media, continually passing through a series of 'gatekeepers' until finally reaching the public. Hirsch presented a one-way transmission model of recording-industry personnel as bureaucratic administrators merely involved in selecting, classifying and rank ordering a vast quantity of completed items which flow through the music-business systems to the public.

More recently, the legacies of mechanistic models of the music industry have appeared in an argument about post-Fordism made by Scott Lash and John Urry (1994), who draw explicitly on the work of Hirsch. As part of a larger claim about major changes within capitalist economies, these writers have proposed that, at one time, the music business was heavily centralised and organised in 'Fordist' terms; utilising mass-production techniques similar to those developed by Henry Ford and selling standardised products to an undifferentiated mass market. According to Lash and Urry, the music business, like other sectors involved in cultural production, has undergone a profound change since the 1960s – from products being rationally 'assembled' to a more chaotic process of 'flexible disintegration'.

Such an argument may conveniently fit with a general theory about the universal emergence of a type of flexible 'post-Fordism', but it is profoundly misleading. It can be challenged in two main ways. First, it is historically inaccurate. The 'Fordist' label captures only the most superficial aspects of music production and ignores the historical specificity of how the recording industry has developed. Since its emergence at the end of the nineteenth century, the recorded music business has been organised according to small-scale productions and the selling to changing 'niche markets' alongside the creation of big hits and blockbusters. Most of the recordings issued throughout the twentieth century were never simply marketed to or purchased by a huge undifferentiated 'mass' audience. Instead, the industry has, since its formation, sold music to the fans of particular styles, through a variety of changing labels (whether using general categories such as 'topical', 'comic' or 'popular' or terms more indicative of changing music genre categories such as 'race', 'hillbilly' and 'ethnic' or blues, jazz, folk, polka, country, Latin, rock or techno). In addition, the recording industry has employed various legal and illegal, small-scale and team-based, marketing and promotional activities as a way of approaching consumers – practices which might well be labelled as 'flexible'.

The second shortcoming of Lash's and Urry's argument is that it misrepresents how the contemporary recording industry operates. As David Hesmondhalgh (1996a) has argued, recorded music production is still to a large degree dominated by a few major companies, and this dominance has tended to become more acute. The smaller units, labels and company divisions may appear to be operating in a decentralised 'post-Fordist' manner but these are by no means as autonomous or as 'flexible' as is sometimes believed. Instead, they are integrated through the economic imperatives of licensing deals, distribution agreements, stake holdings and outright acquisitions. In making this argument, Hesmondhalgh (1996a) has drawn from detailed research on the workings of small independent companies, suggesting that the music industry continues to be characterised by centralisation and consolidation rather than disintegration, decentralisation and flexibility. Hence, it is not only inaccurate to suggest that the music industry has become a less 'organised' entity which can be characterised as post-Fordist, it is also misleading to use this claim to imply that the music business was mechanical, factory-like and Fordist in the first place. Such grand theoretical models add little to our understanding of the dynamics of music production, and misleadingly divert attention towards the possibilities provided by small producers and away from the powerful influence that the major companies have continued to exert over the production and distribution of popular music.

Long before debates about 'post-Fordism', Richard Peterson (1976) challenged superficial parallels with manufacturing industries when calling for a 'production of culture perspective' which he also advocated in opposition to the idea that cultural artefacts are simply the work of individual artists ('raw materials' from whom are then filtered to the public). Stressing how culture is 'fabricated' by a range of occupational groups, Peterson published a series of detailed studies of the 'organisational structures' and 'production systems' within which country music has been created, culminating in his historical account of the 'institutionalization' of country music as a process involving a complex of people in an ironically knowing task of 'fabricating authenticity' (Peterson 1997).

Peterson's 'production of culture' perspective poses a challenge to those writers who approach creative work according to what he calls the 'rare genius of a few select people'. Instead he stresses 'the structural arrangements within which innovators work' (Peterson 1997: 10), arguing that we should pay attention to the specific conditions which have shaped how talent has been able to emerge and be recognised in the first place. In his own writings Peterson has shown how specific types of singers have become privileged as 'country' (white performers adopting specific rustic styles) and how a range of artists, managers, broadcasters, producers, musicians, songwriters and publishers have played a part in systematically selecting and shaping what is known as 'authentic' country music.

Peterson's 'production of culture' perspective analytically retains the complexities of the production process while moving us away from images of bureaucratic filtering systems, Fordist assembly lines or disorganised post-Fordist chaos. Yet, as an organisational sociologist, Peterson tends to focus solely on the dynamics of production within music media organisations. He has little to say about the broader social contexts within which music is received and appreciated and how this shapes occupational activities, nor the influential points of connection that link producers to audiences. However, a number of writers have provided useful insights into such relationships and pointers for pursuing these issues further.

Occupational intermediaries: connecting production and consumption

From researching the recording industry in France, Antoine Hennion (1983, 1989) arrived at similar conclusions to Peterson about the numerous people involved in the 'collective creation' of popular music, adding that music-industry personnel act as 'intermediaries', not only during the most obvious marketing and promotion activities, but also when 'introducing' the idea of an imagined audience into the recording studio. Stressing how this involves a large degree of human empathy and intuition rather than organisational formulae, assembly lines and corporate structures, Hennion argued that music-industry staff do not 'manipulate the public so much as feel its pulse' (1983: 191).

The work of mediators has also been pursued by Pierre Bourdieu (1986) who has adopted the concept of the 'cultural intermediary' to refer to workers providing 'symbolic goods and services' occupying a position *between* the producer and consumer, or artist and audience. Unlike Hennion, however, Bourdieu has stressed the importance of various social divisions which arise according to a 'habitus' of shared lifestyles, class backgrounds and ways of living (rather than the intuitive feeling of audience pulses) – admission to and advancement within cultural production is acquired by exerting influence within class-divided connections gained through shared life experiences formed among members of distinct social groups. Bourdieu (1993, 1996) has highlighted how artistic work is realised across a broad series of intersecting social 'fields' and not simply within an organisation. He has challenged simple political economy, with its stress on the consequences of corporate control of production, and emphasised the broader social, economic and political contexts through which aesthetic judgements are made, cultural hierarchies established and within which artists have to struggle for position. Such an idea can clearly be extended to consider the broader contexts within which musicians struggle to be recognised and rewarded and how this occurs *across* the social activities which are conventionally designated as 'production' and 'consumption'.

Despite the insights provided in his work, Bourdieu neglects how such struggles are part of the formal working world of media organisations and commercial corporations, and how members of organisations operate across and contribute to the formation of various 'fields' as part of their daily routine. In addition, while Bourdieu has perceptively analysed the impact of class divisions on cultural production and consumption, he has little to say about the influence of other social divisions of race, ethnicity, age, gender, sexuality and religious affiliation – all can become an integral part of music production, in different parts of the world and at specific moments in time.

In the next section I shall also be thinking about the connections between production and consumption and considering how a broader series of social divisions and ways of living intersect with the corporate organisation, informing and shaping cultural production. I will argue that production does not take place simply 'within' a corporate environment structured according to the requirements of capitalist production or organisational formulae, but in relation to broader culture formations, economic practices and social divisions. Cultural production is not confined to the formal occupational tasks within a corporate world, but stretched across a range of activities that blur such conventional distinctions as public/private, professional judgement/personal preference and work/leisure time. Many writers have provided insights into the 'production of culture', that is how *industry produces culture* as a product, but equally important is the 'culture of production' and how *culture produces industry* as a set of meaningful practices (Hall 1997) and as a 'whole way of life' (Williams 1961, 1965). The two dynamics are interwoven in the production of popular music.

The formation of the contemporary music industry in Britain: the dominance of the rock tradition

In order to provide some empirical body to the theoretical skeleton that I have just introduced, I shall illustrate these issues with reference to my own research on the music industry in Britain and the United States.[1] I began researching music production in Britain during 1988 and started by seeking to understand the processes through which artists are acquired, 'developed' and then marketed. I was concerned with how recording-industry personnel contribute to the construction of songs, styling of images and production of videos. In emphasising active 'collaboration' and direct intervention into the production of sounds and images, I was explicitly seeking to challenge models of music-industry workers as engaged in the routine task of filtering 'raw materials' and their portrayal as cogs in a corporate wheel.

In thinking about how artists were being acquired and marketed, I began to realise that a very particular set of criteria guided the judgements made by record-company staff, informing repertoire priorities and the level of economic investment accorded to different types of performers. These criteria were usually taken for granted by those applying them, and thought to be either 'obvious' or 'intuitive' by staff making the judgements. This was resulting in the hierarchical privileging of certain types of artists and music over others. Habitual and routine everyday beliefs about musical qualities and commercial potentials were not based on business decisions and objective aesthetic judgements in any simple sense, but instead were informed by broader social and cultural divisions. The 'intuitive' assessments that staff made about the most suitable artists to acquire were influenced by beliefs that had been shaped by a series of gendered and racialised class divisions and these were contributing to the structuration of the 'cultural worlds' of record-company departments.

In pursuing this issue, I discovered that most of the key decision-makers within the British music industry shared many features in common. Those executives who had been around for 20 to 25 years while establishing their reputations, and who were in senior management or running labels, were drawn from a very particular background. They had been recruited into the music industry during the 1960s and early 1970s, and were predominantly middle-class white males who had received a privately funded education at 'public schools', or attended state grammar schools and completed studies at university. Their formative experience had been shaped during the era when rock was gaining cultural value, becoming self-consciously intellectual and respectable, and when a simultaneous expansion of the universities and cultural production led to the recruitment into the recording industry of a group of mildly bohemian young people associated with the 'counter-culture'.[2] Many of these young executives had been booking bands, often as university entertainment officers, or they had played in bands. The 'genre culture' of British rock music had provided a particular series of orientations, assumptions and beliefs and these were carried into the organisations of music production and came to dominate agendas within the expanding recording industry. Despite often being presented as a fairly 'liberal' business, populated by personnel who are 'in touch' with the 'street', these agendas were in no way a 'reflection' of the diversity of music being played and listened to in Britain. Instead they represented, in condensed form, the preferences and judgements of a small, relatively elite-educated, middle-class white male constituency. One consequence was that, at a decisive phase in its expansion and growth, the British music industry was reorganised around a series of dichotomies in which rock artists were favoured over pop or soul performers; albums were favoured over singles; and 'organic' self-contained bands or 'solo artists' who 'express' themselves through writing their own songs were favoured over the more collaborative ways in which singers or groups of performers worked with arrangers, sessions musicians and songwriters in putting together a 'package'. Most obviously, conventional 'live' male guitar bands were treated as long-term propositions, while soul and rhythm and blues music came to be treated in a more ad hoc and casual manner.

As many feminist writers have observed, rock also instituted a particularly sexist approach to gender relations and a male-dominated mode of heterosexual expression (Meade 1972, Whitely 1992). This not only limited the range of expressive possibilities available to female performers, it also tended to marginalise women into specific sectors of the music industry. Apart from administrative and secretarial positions, the most notable area where women have established a presence over time has been in public-relations work. Women do not naturally gravitate to such work due to some inherent female characteristics; it is an aspect of a gendered division of labour that has been maintained through a very specific set of employment practices. In addition, most companies (with the notable exception of Island Records) tended to employ very few black staff, and then as an occasional accountant or more usually in the post room or as messengers. Hence, there were few women's voices contributing to key decisions about acquisition and artistic development, and not only conspicuously few black people in such positions but hardly any staff with knowledge and expertise in managing rhythm and blues and soul music. This was directly contributing to the deprioritising of the recordings produced by Britain's black musicians, with the Asian presence being even less visible at the time.[3] These dynamics were integral aspects of the 'culture of production' that constituted the context within which recordings were being made and mediated by the music industry.

In acquiring new artists staff in the British music industry were not simply responding, in any neutral or obvious way, to the 'talent available' or 'public demand'. Equally, the working practices that were employed to prioritise certain artists over others were not explicable in terms of formal occupational titles nor simply arguments about the type of pressures exerted by corporate capitalist control of production and distribution. These working practices had emerged and been shaped historically, as a result of broader social divisions within Britain and as a consequence of how the beliefs, practices and aesthetic preferences of those who constituted a 'rock-genre culture' had contributed to the formation of a particular type of music industry. This brought into the industry a whole series of orientations, prejudices and values and these were applied to administrative tasks and commercial decisions.

The findings from this research were published in 1992, and one of the issues that I raised when I was concluding the writing-up concerned whether the patterns that I had identified would be maintained or begin to break down during the years ahead. This is, I think, still something of an open question, and I certainly do not wish to attempt a final say on the issue here. My book was in many respects a critique of the agendas that had been institutionalised within the music industry, although I was certainly not the only person to have observed these cultural and economic priorities. It should also be noted that many members of the music industry, whether companies, individual executives or organisations, have subsequently sought to give greater representation to both women and black workers within the industry, while also attempting to invest equally in genres of music other than rock.

However, in certain respects things seem to have continued in much the same way. While the Spice Girls presented a fleeting, dubious and peculiarly British rendition of 'girl power' (and certainly superficial in its impact when compared to Madonna's or Janet Jackson's musical identities developed in different contexts in the United States), and although British artist Seal's idiosyncratic rhythm and blues has enjoyed considerable success in the United States (and been much under-appreciated in the UK), the British music business has been prominently promoting and gaining widespread coverage for very conventional all-male guitar rock bands, most notably Oasis and Blur. These bands have even been promoted with comparisons made to the Beatles and the Rolling Stones, establishing them as part of a very particular tradition. Although the local popularity of 'rave' and 'dance' music has prompted claims that repertoire agendas have profoundly changed, this has not necessarily been reflected in patterns of strategic long-term economic investment or when looking outside and considering the British artists prioritised for international marketing. In addition, much new dance music has come from a constituency of technology-fixated white boys with computers, not that different to the hordes of intense young men with electric guitars who continue to form into bands and stand in line waiting for recording contracts. Meanwhile, soul, rhythm and blues and the music of Britain's black and Asian populations continues to be treated in a more ad hoc and less strategic manner, finding outlets through affiliations and alliances with some of the more innovative and less easily labelled sounds that have circulated since the mid-1990s (such as the various collectivities associated with Bristol and the West Country, including artists such as Portishead, Massive Attack, Roni Size and Tricky). To end this section I shall quote from Ray Hayden, chairman of the British Rhythm and Blues Association, who explained in 1995 that he was gaining most of his investment for British black music from overseas sources because British companies were reluctant to commit themselves to it. He commented: 'it's taken

British companies to witness the overseas reception of British soul music (Des'ree, Omar) before they'll even grumble positively about it' (Springer 1995: 17).

The music business in the United States: fragmentation into genre divisions

If musicians in Britain have had to negotiate the way that the music business has been shaped by a series of interrelated social and aesthetic *hierarchies*, then their counterparts across the North Atlantic have had to deal with a recording industry which has increasingly confronted performers as a fragmented, multidivisional *polyarchy* of genre-specific boxes. Against the monological dominance of rock in Britain, the industry in the United States has often appeared to offer a plurality of possibilities. However, such potential cultural democracy is ultimately superficial, usually just as limiting and, as currently administered, socially divisive.

The fragmentation of social-cultural identities is a characteristic feature of life in the United States, with the commercial segmentation of markets for apparently neutral business reasons connecting uncomfortably with the social segregation of the country and breaking-up of cities into ghettos defined by class and ethnicity. The cultures of music production have been shaped by the way in which the US music business has been constituted within this broader context. The recording industry in the United States has come to deal with different genres according to discrete organisational units, promotional media and marketing routes. The major record companies divide their labels, genres and artists into strategic business units, enabling corporate surveillance of the performance, profile and financial contribution of each division – any 'underperforming' units can be cut from the 'portfolio' when necessary. Such a technique has been used within Britain (separating performers, and budgets, into classical, dance or pop divisions, for example) and some companies have considered introducing a pan-European version of such a system (co-ordinating production and marketing in one continental-wide rock or classical division, for example). However, this method has become well established in the United States, where contemporary record companies may use the jargon of 'portfolio management' which has developed since the 1970s, but where the basic way of dealing with different genres in discrete units has a long history. As Reebee Garofalo has pointed out in his history of US popular music: 'The marketing categories of the music industry have often classified performers as much by race as by musical style' (1997: 9), a practice that goes back to the 1920s, when performers and songs were allocated into three distinct categories: 'race' (African-American popular music); 'hillbilly' (white, working-class rural styles); and 'popular' (the type of music then produced by Tin

Pan Alley). Such practices have led to the division of black and white music, artists and audiences. Garofalo provides an example of how, for many years, this enduring division has informed the marketing and recording of music:

> When Syd Nathan, the founder of King Records, encouraged his r & b and country and western artists to record different versions of the same songs, he understood intuitively that pieces of music do not automatically have a genre, that they can be interpreted in many idioms. Still, in keeping with prevailing industry practices, he marketed his r & b releases only to black audiences and his country records only to white audiences. While Nathan was not limited in his choice of artists or material, he, like many others, accepted the notion that a separation of the races was 'the way things were'. These same prevailing industry practices led Leonard Chess, head of Chess Records, to inform Chuck Berry that his demo of *Ida Red* (*Maybellene*) had to be redone because it was too country sounding. In doing so, Chess was telling Berry in no uncertain terms that there was simply no way to market a black man as a country singer. Were it not for that reality, Chuck Berry might well have had a very different career trajectory.
>
> (Garofalo 1997: 11)

In his extended discussion, Garofalo notes instances when such practices were challenged and also refers to some of the confusions encountered in early song catalogues, where 'black' or 'white' artists were not so clearly classified or were simply labelled in the wrong way . Yet, these were usually exceptions, and the barriers referred to by Garofalo have endured and continue to operate just as strongly at the end of the twentieth century; a country singer is still expected to be white, and black musicians are dealt with by separate staff in an 'urban', 'r and b' or 'black music' division. Such divisions contribute to the separation of different groups of people and are far more than organisational arrangements that simply facilitate efficient marketing to a 'targeted' public.

While most major companies' black music divisions are located in New York City (with offices in Los Angeles), country music has been instituted as a company subdivision or label (a business unit within the 'corporate portfolio') located in Nashville and geographically separated from the day-to-day setting of agendas at corporate headquarters. For much of the genre's history, staff based at the head offices of the major companies had little interest in what went on in Nashville: the music was 'an exotic, regional music that outsiders – those record executives in New York and LA – could never really understand' (Gubernick 1993: 20). Such corporate neglect halted slightly during the 1960s and in the 1970s, and again during the country boom of the early to mid-1990s.

Yet, despite providing significant profits for the corporations, there are enduring divisions between those working with country artists and other parts of the record companies. The relationship between management in Nashville and corporate head office is not only informed by commercial concerns (is the country division meeting financial goals?) but influenced by the fact that Nashville is firmly part of 'the South' – with all the burden of accumulated meanings that small geographical signifier carries. As David Sanjek (1995) has observed, those involved in producing country music have had to deal with ignorance, antipathy and uncritically received stereotypes about their music and the place of the South within the United States: country production and intra-organisational working relationships are mediated by sentiments and beliefs formed as a result of the different cultural worlds which bifurcate along urban/rural and North/South divides, and residues of antagonisms and prejudices which can be traced back to the Civil War in the nineteenth century.

In a similar way, staff working US Latin music are located in regional offices in Miami and embroiled in a set of organisational relations which are not only symptomatic of institutional tensions between the English-language and Spanish-language cultures of the United States, but indicative of the relationships which uneasily connect the USA to Cuba, Puerto Rico and the Caribbean regions of Latin America on the East, and to the Latin populations of Texas, California and Mexico on the West. Such tensions endure as part of the cultural dynamics within the same corporations, influencing how staff interact and how artists are prioritised, produced and circulated.

There are complex working relationships involved here, not easily explained according to mechanical systems models of organisations or straightforward political-economic processes, and certainly not fully elaborated in my brief sketch above.[4] The working practices of staff are shaped by an unstable collision of commercial organisational structures; the activities of fan cultures; musician communities and historical legacies within broader social formations – all come together and inform the dynamics of cultural production.

This fragmented system does have one clear benefit. These separate units have provided a space for people who may not otherwise have gained employment in the industry; African-American staff, Latino/a personnel, and the 'hillbillies' from the South. In addition, such divisions have ensured that musicians are managed by personnel with knowledge, skills and understanding of their music. This could be a clear advantage over the situation that has developed in Britain, where soul bands have been dropped from rosters in the past simply because the rock-oriented A and R manager had neither the understanding nor the will to work with them.

However, these divisions lead to the separation of musical knowledge and result in a number of highly distinct, identifiable and institutionalised boundaries between listeners, musicians and workers within the same record companies. This is, in turn, reinforced by the equally divisive segmentation of listeners by radio broadcasters with the result that 'the audiences for hard rock, salsa and rhythm and blues are often mutually exclusive and divided neatly (and at times antagonistically) along racial and cultural lines' (Garofalo 1986: 81). A further consequence of these divisions is that creative practices and aesthetic discourses have come to be fragmented into genre-specific codes and conventions, boxed into social containers which either do not meet or meet under conditions of mutual incomprehension or contempt – 'I don't understand your music' or 'I don't like your music; it is boring/repetitive'. Such everyday statements are far more than musical judgements. As Simon Frith (1996) has argued, in his work on popular discrimination, such aesthetic judgements imply ethical agreements and disagreements, moral evaluations and assessments: the feelings that accompany aesthetic pleasure and displeasure are simultaneously emotional, sensual and social. Staying within or moving across musical genres is about more than music. Crossing genre boundaries is not only a musical act, it is also a social act, a way of making connections, of creating solidarities.

Much new music, including many of the most critically acclaimed sounds of the twentieth century, has been created when different cultural practices, peoples and musical traditions have met and got mixed up: when different genre cultures have interacted and combined. It is ironic that the music business has sought to capitalise on such mixtures, yet, in producing an organisation to profit from this, the industry has set up divisions within which music can be contained. As a consequence, the creation and crossing of bridges to other genre worlds is a process which has occurred and continues to happen despite, rather than because of, the ways in which the major record companies have sought to organise the production of contemporary popular music.

Conclusion

For many years now, studies of media organisations and cultural production have fallen one side or the other of a polarised divide that has separated arguments about the dire impact of corporate ownership and the constraints of production from arguments about the resistant, creative and transformative abilities of consumers and subcultures. On one side has been the pessimistic lament of political economy and the crushing juggernaut of modernity, on the other has been the liberating euphoria of an active audience and the endless possibilities of postmodernism. This has connected with a polarising of politics and policies between advocates of direct intervention into production and those adopting a more *laissez-faire* attitude towards consumer sovereignty as a corrective to capital.

Informed by the notion of mediation with which I started this chapter, my own argument is that to answer the policy questions we must dismantle this division. 'Cultural policies' cannot simply depend upon finding ways of dealing with 'the industry', occupational tasks or administrative concerns, nor the issues arising as a consequence of 'ownership' (corporate control, monopolies and oligopolies) in any simple sense: we also need to understand how industries are formed within a broader context or, to return to my earlier phrase, how culture produces industry. At the same time we need to recognise that 'consumers' cannot freely appropriate commodified music because the public do not 'get what they want', in terms either of products or of representation.

The possibility of gaining access to and participating in cultural production and becoming formally recognised as a cultural producer (whether in the domains of literature, painting, music, clothing design, theatre, film or investigative journalism) is clearly dependent upon presenting a 'marketable' product. But it is also informed by patterns of power and prejudice arising from how the formation of particular industries has been shaped by such factors as class, gender relations, sexual codes, ethnicity, racial labels, age, political allegiances, regional conflicts, family genealogy, religious affiliation and language. Depending where you are located in the world, some of these may appear to be more significant than others. In making this point, I do not wish to reduce the production of culture to a series of social variables or bodily distinguishing marks, but to emphasise how broader social divisions are inscribed *into* and become an integral part of business practices. The reason why one singer, and not another, may gain a recording contract is not only dependent upon the judgements of accountants and the expertise of producers with an ear to 'the market'. It is shaped by the cultures of production, the culture within the industry and the industry within culture.

Notes

1 For an extended analysis of the brief materials quoted here see Negus (1992 and 1999). I would like to acknowledge the financial support of the Economic and Social Research Council of Great Britain for the grant which enabled me to complete my Ph.D. study of musical production in Britain (1988–91) and for the award within the Media Economics and Media Culture Programme through which I completed research in the United States (1996).
2 For an elaboration of the culture of rock and its impact on the music industry see Frith (1983).
3 For discussion of the Asian presence and absence in the British music industry see Hesmondhalgh (1996b) and Sharma et al. (eds) (1996).
4 For further discussion of such divisions in the US music industry see Negus (1999).

References and further reading

Adorno, T. and Horkheimer, M. (1979) *Dialectic of Enlightenment*, London: Verso.
Bourdieu, P. (1986) *Distinction: A Social Critique of the Judgement of Taste*, London: Routledge.

Bourdieu, P. (1993) *The Field of Cultural Production*, Cambridge: Polity.

Bourdieu, P. (1996) *The Rules of Art*, Cambridge: Polity.

Frith, S. (1983) *Sound Effects, Youth, Leisure and the Politics of Rock'n'Roll*, London: Constable.

Frith, S. (1996) *Performing Rites: On the Value of Popular Music*, Oxford: Oxford University Press.

Garofalo, R. (1986) 'How Autonomous is Relative: Popular Music, the Social Formation and Cultural Struggle', *Popular Music*, 6.1: 77–92.

Garofalo, R. (1997) *Rockin' Out: Popular Music in the USA*, Needham Heights, MA: Allyn and Bacon.

Gubernick, L. (1993) *Get Hot or Go Home, Trisha Yearwood: The Making of a Nashville Star*, New York: St Martins Press.

Hall, S. (1997) 'The Work of Representation' in S. Hall (ed.), *Representation: Cultural Representations and Signifying Practices*, London: Sage, pp. 13–74.

Hennion, A. (1983) 'The Production of Success: An Anti-Musicology of The Pop Song', *Popular Music*, 3: 158–93.

Hennion, A. (1989) 'An Intermediary Between Production and Consumption: The Producer of Popular Music', *Science, Technology and Human Values*, 14.4: 400–24.

Hesmondhalgh, D. (1996a) 'Flexibility, Post-Fordism and the Music Industries', *Media, Culture and Society*, 18.3: 469–88.

Hesmondhalgh, D. (1996b) 'Independent Record Companies and Democratisation in the Popular Music Industry', Ph.D. thesis, Goldsmiths College, University of London.

Hirsch, P. (1972) 'Processing Fads and Fashions: An Organisational Set Analysis of Cultural Industry Systems', *American Journal of Sociology*, 77.4: 639–59.

Lash, S. and Urry, J. (1994) *Economies of Signs and Space*, London: Sage.

Meade, M. (1972) 'The Degradation of Women', in V. Denisoff and R. Peterson (eds), *The Sounds of Social Change*, Chicago: Rand McNally, pp. 173–7.

Negus, K. (1992) *Producing Pop: Culture and Conflict in the Popular Music Industry*, London: Edward Arnold.

Negus, K. (1999) *Music Genres and Corporate Cultures*, London: Routledge.

Peterson, R. (1976) 'The Production of Culture: A Prolegomenon', in R. Peterson (ed.), *The Production of Culture*, London: Sage, pp. 7–22.

Peterson, R. (1997) *Creating Country Music, Fabricating Authenticity*, Chicago: University of Chicago Press.

Sanjek, D. (1995) 'Blue Moon of Kentucky Rising Over the Mystery Train: The Complex Construction of Country Music', in C. Tichi (ed.), *Readin' Country Music: Steel Guitars, Opry Stars and Honky Tonk Bars*, *The South Atlantic Quarterly*, 94.1 (Winter): 29–55.

Sharma, S., Hutnyk, J. and Sharma, A. (eds) (1996) *Dis-Orienting Rhythms: The Politics of the New Asian Dance Music*, London: 2ed Books.

Springer, J. (1995) 'Hayden on The Edge', *Blues and Soul*, 694 (1–14 Aug.): 16–17.

Whitely, S. (1992) *The Space Between the Notes: Rock and the Counter-Culture*, London: Routledge.

Williams, R. (1961) *Culture and Society*, Harmondsworth: Penguin.

Williams, R. (1965) *The Long Revolution*, Harmondsworth: Penguin.

Williams, R. (1976) *Keywords*, Glasgow: Fontana.

11

Media, cultural identity and the state

The case of Hong Kong

ERIC KIT-WAI MA

In the postwar decades, both the Hong Kong colonial government and the nation state of mainland China, for different political reasons, refrained from imposing strong cultural imperatives in the colony. However, in the run-up to the sovereignty transfer in 1997 China was much more intrusive in the cultural affairs of Hong Kong. Comparing Hong Kong of the 1970s and 1990s, there is an obvious difference in the degree of state intervention in cultural politics which provides an opportunity to explore the role of media and the state in the formation and maintenance of cultural identity. By examining the specific case of Hong Kong, this chapter seeks to combine the insights of political economy and cultural studies in explaining the shifting relations between media, culture and politics in political change. The differences between political-economy and cultural-studies approaches are highly general and differentiating,[1] but they do represent prestige-bound preferences across the divide which have persisted for years, leaving what Murdock (1989, 1997) calls a 'missing link' at the heart of media studies. As he contends, critical political economy is at its strongest in explaining who gets to speak to whom and what forms these symbolic encounters take in the major spaces of public culture. He also contends that cultural studies, at its best, has much of value to say about how dominant and popular discourse and imagery are organised in complex and shifting patterns of meanings, and how these meanings are reproduced, negotiated and struggled over in the flow and flux of everyday life. Combining historical, textual and organisational analyses, this chapter will demonstrate the strengths of these two traditions in explaining the case of Hong Kong identity.

Minimal state intervention, strong media structuration

In the years after the communist take-over of China in 1949, waves of refugees from China poured into Hong Kong.[2] In the 1950s the colony had nearly 2 million newcomers, representing about two-thirds of the population. Subsequently, Hong Kong changed rapidly from an entrepôt to an international financial centre. The colonial government adopted a *laissez-faire* economic and non-interventionist social policy. Culturally, Chinese traditionalism was smoothly replaced by a secular indigenous culture. The colonial government did not intervene in the local culture and even discouraged the promotion of a Hong Kong identity among the younger generations. Britain sought to uphold Hong Kong as a commercial entrepôt in order to avoid antagonising the Chinese government, which also wanted to temporarily maintain a commercial and apolitical territory for economic and diplomatic reasons. Concerned primarily with sustaining economic and social order, the colonial administration therefore sought to stay away from identity politics. Schools and other government institutions did not provide any coherent historical narrative of national or political identification with which the younger generation could make sense of their world. Popular media subsequently filled this cultural space left by both Britain and China. Without any state-imposed shackles, popular media, in particular film and television culture, evolved to become a cradle of indigenous cultural identity. The simple term 'Hongkonger' gathered weight in films, television serials and Cantonese pop songs. Popular media, in particular television in the late 1960s and 1970s, absorbed western ingredients, transformed Chinese cultural particulars, articulated local experiences, and crystallised a distinct Hong Kong way of life.

Case 1: a television serial in the late 1970s

Within this period of minimal state intervention and strong media structuration, I choose a television serial as a case study of the reciprocal processes by which social power, instead of state power, was translated into and in turn reinforced by media representation. The case presented here illustrates the socio-cultural differentiation process in which a sharp symbolic division is developed between an established majority and a newer group of residents. The newcomers in this case were Chinese immigrants who came from mainland China in the 1970s. They were stigmatised as people lacking the superior human virtues, which the dominant group attributed to itself. The differentiating process not only stigmatised the newcomers, but was also essential in the 'discovery' of the collective identity of those immigrants who had settled in Hong Kong many years earlier. Once established, these people came to be called 'Hongkongers', leaving their Chinese identity in the shadow,[3] while the newcomers were given a collective name 'Ah Chian', a label carrying a derogatory sting. In Hong Kong, 'Ah Chian' has been the most popular name for the newcomers from mainland China for two decades. The name originated from a television melodrama in which a character, nicknamed Ah Chian, came to Hong Kong from China to rejoin his family.

The 80-episode melodramatic serial, *The Good, the Bad, and the Ugly* (henceforth abbreviated as GBU), was produced by TVB[4] in 1979. It was ranked the second favourite drama serial of the 1980s by local audiences.[5] When the serial was first released, a new membership category (Sacks 1992), 'Ah Chian', was quickly enacted. Ah Chian of the serial became the public face of the newcomers. What he did in the serial was seen as reflecting the activities of the newly enacted group. It is a case that reveals an insider/outsider configuration, in which a group possessing greater power, in terms of both material and symbolic resources, was asserting itself as superior to the others (Elias and Scotson 1994). The serial actually coined a group name, supplied the cultural imagery of the group, and set in motion a stigmatising process that has persisted for years.

The serial is a story of a 'typical' Hong Kong family of the 1970s. The parents are Chinese refugees who came to Hong Kong some decades ago. The elder son, Ching Wai,[6] a university graduate, and his younger sister, a factory worker, are brought up in Hong Kong. The opening episode quickly moves into a conflict situation when the Chings receive a letter from China telling them that their second son, Ching Chain, nicknamed Ah Chian, is on his way to Hong Kong to rejoin the family after 20 years of separation. This turns out not to be a happy reunion, but a threat to the family.

In the serial, Ah Chian is akin to a clown, a comic figure, or a Shakespearean fool (Cheng 1990). Most of the humour springs from his ignorance of social norms and his violation of the sense of good taste among the established Hongkongers. The awkwardness of Ah Chian's behaviour marks him as an outsider. Frequent in the stigmatisation of outsiders is the belief that they are ill-disciplined and lawless. Ah Chian dozes off at work, stays in bed till late afternoon, wants to get rich but is reluctant to make any effort. Ah Chian throws bottles out of the windows of a high-rise building, jumps the queue to apply for an identity card at the immigration office, and steals from the jewellery shop he is working in. Ah Chian is not case-specific. Stigmatisation of Ah Chian as a social group has many features in common with other kinds of insider/outsider configurations. Established groups usually have a code of conduct which demands a higher degree of self-restraint than newly arrived groups. They claim their superiority by being more 'civilised'; their social code prescribes a more firmly regulated behaviour, asks for a greater refinement of manners, and has more elaborate taboos. Outsiders are unusually 'uncivilised' in the sense that they have unrestrained desires, an unrefined manner and are often seen breaking norms long cherished by the established group. Ah Chian, like many other imagined outsiders, is uncivilised, undisciplined and lawless.

Prejudice against the new immigrants to Hong Kong were recorded in a series of research surveys carried out during 1979–82 and found evidence of widespread discrimination. In one of these surveys, more than half of the respondents felt that new immigrants competed with locals for jobs and public resources, and agreed with the impression that they were the usual offenders in petty crimes; some even thought that the newcomers were responsible for the increase in violent crimes in the early 1980s. These prejudices had real social consequences. In a study carried out in December 1980, it was found that 80 per cent of the menial jobs in restaurants were given to new immigrants. They were also taking dangerous short-term work on construction sites. Out of 165 work-related deaths from January 1979 to August 1980, 70 per cent involved new immigrants. Many work-related injuries occurred within the first six months of arrival. Not only were immigrants getting the most undesirable jobs, but they were also systematically being paid less than local workers were (Siu 1986). These data do not prove that GBU is directly responsible for social discrimination, but they suggest that it may have reinforced it. Textual and social domination reinforce each other. In the GBU case, the serial *does not create* the negative sentiments against mainlanders; as the survey data show, these sentiments were already felt by the general public at that time. The effect of the serial was more on the construction of identity categories, which objectified and consolidated the antagonism into relatively stable stereotypes.

As argued above, socio-historical contexts in the 1970s contributed to the formation of a relatively autonomous television culture. The colonial government did not impose any cultural imperative on commercial television and, besides, a large proportion of the population at that time shared the same social memories of settlement and rapid economic development. In addition, there was a surplus television economy, which allowed for a creative autonomy rarely found in the hostile television economy of the 1990s. Thus, for the local generation, the newly established television medium became a homogenising cultural force. As in other countries when television was in its infancy, the viewing public was enthusiastic about the new medium. It was not uncommon to have viewing figures shooting up to 70 or even 80 per cent on weekday prime time, which meant that a large proportion of the population participated in a daily ritual of television viewing. They were sharing meanings, adjusting differences, confirming common values and fostering an indigenous cultural identity with which the majority of the community could comfortably and proudly identify. Indeed, this identity-formation process is to be celebrated, especially by the transient refugee society of postwar Hong Kong.

If Hong Kong television in the 1970s was a ritual space of shared meaning, however, it was also a site of ideological domination. Television provides a cultural space for confirming cultural identities, but this is always a dual process, confirming and discriminating at the same time. It involves demarcation of symbolic borders between cultural groups. The building up of in-group pride, which is in itself a positive feature of a community, often goes hand in hand with the process of stigmatising outsider groups (Hagendoorn 1993, Elias and Scotson 1994, Jenkins 1994): it fosters cultural solidarity and encourages suppression of differences (Schudson 1994). In the case of GBU, we can see the ideological tendencies of television and identity formation in a very simple form. The textual domination was not the direct result of the intervention of the 'state ideological apparatus'; because the Hong Kong media in the 1970s was characterised as a minimally integrated media-political system (Kuan and Lau 1988), the colonial government did not meddle in media affairs in an obtrusive manner. The textual domination was also not the direct result of the distortion of the capitalistic media system. With a surplus television economy, there were relatively fewer production constraints connected to commercial considerations. Thus, in the specific circumstances of Hong Kong television in the 1970s, the ideological domination could be seen as the working of the internal logic of television ideologies and cultural identities.

Intrusive politics, polysemic media

In the 1970s the contextual factors so far discussed combined to give popular media a significant role in identity formation and reinforcement. However, these factors had gradually diminished after the signing of the 1984 Sino–British Declaration, which proclaimed the inevitable return of Hong Kong to China. By contrast to the surplus television economy of the 1970s, the television economy of the 1990s was much more competitive and hostile and the creative autonomy of television producers was greatly reduced. Since television production was more affected by political and commercial calculations, identity categories were articulated by television culture in a much more complicated way. The identity categories of mainlander and Hongkonger, as presented in television programming of the 1970s, were more stable and distinct; but in the 1990s they became unstable and contradictory. The stigmatised mainlanders, in an ironical turn in the 1990s, were potentially set to become the dominant group in Hong Kong. In the transition period, the colony was gradually reversing to Chinese rule. The former 'Ah Chians' were backed up by mainlanders with political and economic power far greater than the Hongkongers possessed. Fuelled by new-found pride in its economic vitality, China was promoting a brand of nationalism that claimed its superiority over a unique Chinese culture.[7] China repeatedly claimed that the people of Hong Kong were 'sacred and inalienable' members of the Chinese community. An ahistorical Chinese identity was created to foster patriotism and political commitment (see Chai 1994).

The Hong Kong identity emerged in the 1960s and 1970s from a cultural space with virtually no nationalistic imperative. Political movements in China were prevented from influencing the colony, while the colonial government vouchsafed its colonial subjects no political commitment. Neither had the Hong Kong identity in the colonial years a strong nationalistic component nor a political affiliation with sovereignty. However, the reversion of sovereignty has initiated a nationalisation process of the kind that changes the spaces of public culture so as to limit or expand the realm of what might constitute meaningful choice and identity positions (Chun 1996). Previously absent nationalistic discourse and icons have been introduced to the media, crafting new spaces of identity for Hongkongers as a result. The changing power hierarchy of the larger society was mapped onto mediated discourse in ways which were very different from those operating in the 1970s. In the next case study I attempt to capture the changing media representations of Hong Kong identity by examining in detail a television serial produced in the 1990s.

Case 2: a television serial in the early 1990s

Great Times[8] (GT below) is a serial in 40 episodes produced by TVB[9] in 1992, the story of which spans the period from the 1970s to the 1990s. The Chinese title, *Dashidai*, motivates the audience to look for the sign of the times. In the run-up to 1997, nationalist and democratic political discourses were prevalent in public debate. However, GT is extremely restrained in terms of political discourse: there is no hint in any of the 40 episodes that Hong Kong has any problem related to politics. Hong Kong, as constructed in GT, is an apolitical society all through the 1970s, the 1980s and the 1990s. In reality, the Hong Kong stock market was very much bothered by political debates, but, in the drama, the ups and downs of the stock market are only the push and pull between the villains and the heroes of the story.

The stock market is the central arena of the drama. The leading character, Fong, comes from a rich family. His father is bankrupted and then killed by the leading villain, Ting Hian. Fong becomes a street idler in his twenties, but he suddenly realises that he is talented in stock speculation and is destined to fulfil his potential in the stock market. Meanwhile, Ting's family, the villains, deliberately or accidentally kill all of Fong's three sisters and his stepmother. Despite these tragedies, Fong manages to work his way up to become a billionaire, just like the myth that has been retold many times in Hong Kong. Finally, Fong takes revenge on Ting's family by outsmarting them in the stock market.

The initial versions of the script had obvious political overtones: in one version, the story began with a stock-market crash in 1997. But in the serial as broadcast, the political discourse of Sino–Hong Kong antagonism is highly suppressed. Critics have long pointed out that commercial television tends to avoid controversial political issues, and GT shows a similar bias. On the surface, GT is apolitical. The majority of the audience took it that way, although a significant minority of them read it as a political allegory. GT's executive producer said he was surprised by the letters he received from viewers. Some of them commented on the 'meaning' of the characters. The most analytical was a letter published in a very popular magazine (*Next Magazine*, 4 Dec. 92, p. 18). The author noted that he took tremendous pleasure in reading the character of Ting Hian as an allusion to the Communist Party of China. So we have an 'apolitical' text that nevertheless triggers political readings.

Identity politics appear in the serial in a very complicated way. While the Fongs are seen as typical Hongkongers, the Tings are seen by some as mainlanders. In the story, Fong's father is educated in the West and his leisure life is associated with bars and western music. By contrast, Ting Hian is always found quoting traditional Chinese proverbs. All the names of Fong's family are common in Hong Kong, but the Tings have atypical names with negative connotations, all containing the Chinese character Hian, which means crabs, a symbol of transgression and fierceness. The character of Ting Hian alludes to the stereotyped image of the communists in mainland China: he is violent and corrupt, yet always claims to be honourable and blameless. He kills and prosecutes in the name of righteousness and for the purported well-being of his victims. He has patriarchal control over his sons; they comply even when Ting asks them to commit suicide.[10] Although some viewers read these characterisations apolitically, with public sentiment against the Chinese take-over widely shared by the people of Hong Kong at that time, political meanings were activated by a strong social desire among many members of the audience to read politics into the texts.

Articulations between socio-political contexts and televisual discourse, as indicated in the above analyses, vary from one period to another. Comparing GBU and GT across time, the identity category of the mainlander, as inscribed in televisual texts and circulated in social discourse, was relatively more stable in the 1970s than in the early 1990s, when the identity categories of mainlander and Hongkonger, as presented on Hong Kong television, became unstable and polysemic. The polysemic configurations reflected the contradictions within and between the Sino–British dual political powers and also the populist demands of the people. The complexity of the articulation asks for a more refined analysis of the discursive relations between the social and the televisual.

Institutional dispersion

I have spent quite some time exploring how television ideologies can be overdetermined, in multiple articulations, by 'contextual definers' on the wider social level. The general argument, simply put, is that television ideologies converge to a considerable extent with the dominant assumptions within society. Textual producers, regardless of which kinds of television organisations they belong to, are influenced by a world of widely circulated common-sense meanings embedded in the wider social, cultural and political contexts. This text/context articulation can be illustrated by the relatively stable representations of Hongkongers and mainlanders of the 1970s, which resonated with the socio-cultural differentiation of the two groups in the larger social context of the time. Also, the unstable, polysemic and sometimes contradictory identity categories in the 1990s were related to cleavages in the dominant social discourses in the run-up to 1997. Textual representations give symbolic forms to pre-existing power relations.

However, contextual articulation alone is inadequate to account for the discursive relationship between the media and society. Beyond the general level of signification, there is another level: the institutionalised encoding practices of media organisations. At the institutional level of signification, dominant contextual discourse is differentially articulated and/or dispersed into different forms and patterns of televisual ideologies. Though not always directly, the production side of television regulates, delimits or dramatises the kind of discourses that can be produced. Neglecting this institutional level of signification would result in a misconception of the media as *always* overdetermined by dominant contextual discourse to yield a convergent output, irrespective of the possible divergence between different media (Curran 1990).

In the Hong Kong case, the differentiation and dispersion effects of television organisations were less prominent in the 1970s because of specific circumstances: the 'minimally integrated media-political system' (Kuan and Lau 1988) and the surplus television economy of the 1970s produced a relatively autonomous organisational environment for media workers, who were, by and large, left alone. However, in the 1990s the media came into play in more influential ways. Television ideologies were increasingly articulated by the interplay between contextual and institutional influences.

One obvious ideological difference was between the television outputs of public and commercial television organisations. Of course, different television organisations in the 1970s also produced different kinds of televisual discourses, but the differences in the early 1990s were much more prominent. Because of the drastic socio-political changes in the 1990s, the quasi-public broadcaster RTHK[11] produced dramas, particularly in the early 1990s, with political overtones far more controversial than in any other Hong Kong television drama thus far, and this was in direct contrast to mainstream commercial television, which deliberately avoided political controversies in its entertainment programming. To examine how organisation factors come into play, I will contrast GT, the commercial drama discussed above, and *Below the Lion Rock* (henceforth BLR), produced by the public broadcaster RTHK.

Case 3: comparing public and commercial television dramas

Both GT and BLR were positioned by the executives of their respective television stations as the most important production of 1992. All TVB production staff interviewed said that GT was a prestigious assignment, while BLR was considered by staff to be the most ambitious production of RTHK's drama unit in recent years. The production teams of GT and BLR consisted of the best and most experienced staff available at each station. Out of the 20 RTHK and TVB staff interviewed in this study, all except three had worked, at the time of the interviews, in their respective television stations for more than 10 years, five of them more than 20 years. The two dramas can therefore be regarded as among the exemplary productions of their respective television systems. Both also generated a great deal of public discussion.

TEXTUAL COMPARISON

The public TV drama BLR is a series of eight single stories on the same theme: Hong Kong in the 1990s. In direct contrast with GT, BLR gives a general depiction of the exploitative nature of the capitalistic system of Hong Kong. For instance, one episode tells the story of a successful entrepreneur who participates in the first Legislative Council elections in 1991. Behind his good public image, his real motive for running for election is actually to further his commercial interests by obtaining a political position. Indeed, BLR differs from GT in that politics is made very explicit. For instance, one episode is a fable about the relationship between a country named Red Circle and a small city called Fragrant Harbour, mirroring the relations between China and Hong Kong. The story opens with a crackdown on democracy in Red Circle and then focuses on the dilemma of a television-station editor over how to handle an interview with Red Circle's senior leader. As a professional journalist, the editor wants to be critical and ask for factual details about of the crackdown. However, he is constrained by his boss, who insists that a critical interview will harm the station's commercial interests. The dilemma built around the character makes a strong statement against totalitarianism.

With regard to television ideologies, the non-commercial drama BLR exhibits an ideological pattern which is diversified and negotiatory in its stand towards the capitalistic economy of Hong Kong and the totalitarianism of communist China. It deals explicitly with political materials, constructing Hong Kong as a society caught in political controversies. It contests the myth of Hong Kong's economic success, exposes political and social conflicts and rethinks long-cherished cultural categories. By contrast, GT constructs Hong Kong as a capitalistic and apolitical society. Hong

Kong's capitalistic system is represented affirmatively as the territory's greatest asset. Political discourse is suppressed, but the narrative sublimi-nally presents a widely shared political ideology which sees China as a cor-rupt invading force that threatens the well-being of Hong Kong. The categorisation of Hongkonger/mainlander is hidden below the surface. It only comes out via implicit category-bound inferences which define main-landers as hostile outsiders and Hongkongers as victims. The Hongkongers can only fight back by virtue of their God-given economic vitality.

These discourses echo popular myths and mainstream ideologies which stress Hong Kong's economic success and see Hong Kong as an apolitical city. The emphasis on the economic myth and the avoidance of political dis-course are articulated into the television ideologies of GT in complicated, polysemic ways. A textual comparison shows that the ideological differ-ences between BLR and GT are paradigmatic (see Table 11.1).

These paradigmatic differences in television ideologies can be classified under the concepts of 'choric' and 'lyric' drama proposed by Newcomb and Alley (1983). The term choric is taken from Greek drama, in which the cho-rus expresses the ideas and emotions of the group, as opposed to the indi-viduals. Its focus is on the widely shared, the remembered and conventional responses. When an individual's voice becomes distinct, it stands out from the chorus as lyric. GT can be classified as a 'choric drama' which 'sings' in resonance with the mainstream capitalistic ideology, while the RTHK drama BLR can be called 'lyric drama', which stands out from and negoti-ates with the ideology of the establishment in a personal voice. In lyric drama we hear a distinct voice with less polysemic arrangements. On the other hand, choric drama has monolithic ideologies; it has limited ideologi-cal diversity and is pro-establishment in nature; it wants to please as many audiences as possible and does not want to offend dominant powers. However, beneath the harmonious resonance there are multiple layers of polysemic voices, since the chorus involves compromise and adjustment between a variety of interests.

Table 11.1

	GT	BLR
Economics	endorsing HK's capitalistic economy	negotiatory to HK's capitalistic economy
Politics	suppressed; critical towards take-over of China; expressed in oblique terms	explicit; diversified; critical yet negotiatory
	pro-establishment; limited diversity; mainstream	*negotiatory; diversified; alternative*

ORGANISATIONAL ANALYSIS

The textual analysis has shown that GT is choric while BLR is lyric. The next step is to see how this pattern can be related to the production contexts of the two dramas. The analysis is based on 32 hours of taped interviews with key production and creative staff of the two dramas. Statements used repetitively by the interviewees were singled out, and concepts thus formulated were categorised. From these categories, possible factors that influence the selection of drama content were then identified.

Organisational schemata[12]

'Since TVB is a commercial broadcaster, inevitably its dramas have to be popular, commercial, tamed and safe entertainment.' This line of reasoning appeared frequently among TVB staff. It infiltrated their perceptions of TVB's organisational orientation and their evaluative criteria and aesthetic norms for TV dramas. Most noteworthy is that whenever the interviewees complained about the lack of creative space at TVB, the complaints were usually followed by this reasoning as an excuse for the organisation: 'They [TVB management] should not be blamed, they have commercial considerations that we don't quite understand.'

Commercial considerations acted powerfully and unobtrusively at the idea-development stage. Initially there were four idea options:

1 An Alvin Toffler type of futuristic prediction to depict what Hong Kong would be like beyond 1997.
2 A drama centred around a major collapse of the stock market just before the take-over of Hong Kong by China in summer 1997.
3 A drama centred around an accident at Daya Bay Nuclear Plant[13] before or after 1997.
4 A drama beginning and ending with a miracle day in 1994 in which the Hang Seng stock-market index gained 4000 points.

Option 1 was social, 'serious' and analytical; options 2 and 3 were controversial and politically sensitive; option 4 was safe, optimistic and pleasing. Option 4 was adopted. The script supervisor gave the following explanations:

> If we talk about what Hong Kong would be like in 1997 or beyond, we are afraid that some people might be very unhappy. The audience might find the negative descriptions disturbing too. Besides, if it is concrete (realistic), people think it is too heavy. If it is vague (imaginative), it lacks the appeal.

The decision was autonomous; it was not made under any direct influence from management. All initial proposals for TVB drama are passed to the management meeting for approval. Before the meeting, the proposal will be tailored according to the perceived criteria of the management. No one wants a veto, because a veto means that two months of preparatory work are wasted. Besides, it harms the personal prestige of the creator. So favourable options are incorporated. Commercial logic screens out complicated and controversial content.

RTHK staff reasoned along different lines: all the RTHK interviewees thought that RTHK should provide non-commercial, alternative programming that commercial television would not provide. They all thought that RTHK was using public resources, so its programmes should have a social dimension and the content should serve the public interest. The making of BLR came out of their collective sense of responsibility as a public television drama producer to react to social issues at that critical point in Hong Kong's history.

It should be noted that RTHK is officially a government department. However, it enjoys the editorial independence claimed by most public broadcasters in other open societies. Editorial interference from the government is rare. The link between RTHK and the BBC, the political vacuum created by the decolonisation process and the non-interventionist policy of the Hong Kong government contributed to RTHK's dual role as government and public broadcaster. It is not unusual at all to find RTHK programmes that are severely critical of the Hong Kong colonial government as well as of the communist government in mainland China. BLR is one illustrative case among many others. The organisational schema of RTHK is closer to the non-commercialism of a public broadcaster than to a role as an instrumental mouthpiece of the government.

Feedback

Ratings. All TVB interviewees were serious about ratings. They were reportedly very upset by the poorish ratings in the first few weeks after GT's release. Good and bad ratings directly affect commercial producers' track records and prestige. They circulate openly among colleagues and attract media attention. Ratings pressure is translated from the psychological to the cognitive level: the need for mass appeal exerts a strong mainstreaming influence on content choice. At RTHK, meanwhile, audience feedback in the form of ratings is not so influential. All BLR producers either ignored the ratings or treated them as secondary. Some did not even know what their programme's ratings were. Freed from ratings pressure, BLR producers had a much wider range of ideological options. They did not have a mass audience in mind and did not develop content according to perceived audience taste. As a result, BLR's ideological content was not as restricted to the mainstream as that of GT.

Critical review. TV dramas also have another audience: media critics. TVB producers were generally more sceptical about media reviews, which they thought 'unfair', 'biased', 'subjective', 'written on purpose by some interested parties [TVB's rivals]', 'nonsense', 'out of context'. Many said they didn't bother to read them. However, most RTHK interviewees were very much affected by media reviews, especially in elite newspapers. When RTHK dramas met with critical acclaim in the elite papers, that type of drama, in terms of content and style, would be highly endorsed by the RTHK management and producers.

Feedback within the organisation.   Within the television organisation, evaluative feedback is rare. All TVB and RTHK interviewees said they seldom held evaluative discussions about their programmes with colleagues. Those in supervisory positions said they might talk about the programme with their subordinates, but when their subordinates were cross-checked they said that such discussions rarely happened. When asked about the criteria for good TV drama, answers were extremely diverse. Aesthetic norms ranged from concrete factors such as 'good characterisation' and 'strong conflicts' to vague notions such as 'look good', 'feel good'. The lack of shared norms in television drama is most obvious when compared with journalistic programmes. Journalists can easily come up with standards such as objectivity, balanced reporting, etc. But there are no such established norms in drama production, and in their absence creative measures of success tend to overlap with corporate factors such as those discussed above. TVB staff are inclined to value commercially attractive elements such as emotional impact and conflict, while their counterparts at RTHK are biased towards social significance – they lay more stress on sophistication and subtlety.

Resource allocation

Commercial television has a clear standard of cost-effectiveness. Resource allocation has a clear-cut profit margin. A TVB script supervisor claims that restrictive resource allocation limits creativity: 'Every time your story leads to some expensive scenes, you have to stop right there and think of something else.' Another TVB executive producer dramatised the situation with a metaphor:

> They give you one dollar to cook them a dish of fried rice. But you have had too much fried rice and you want some modest changes – you want ten more cents to add a little spice, and the answer is no.

On the other hand, non-commercial TV organisations provide cultural products whose utility is difficult to measure (McQuail 1991). As a result, the level of resource support for BLR was to a certain extent arbitrary. The episode with the highest ratings, 'Stormy Weather', had cost double the allocated production budget!

Television studies that describe a higher degree of individual autonomy tend to talk more of content innovation and diversity (Ettema 1982, Newcomb and Alley 1983, Feuer 1987). Those that describe a higher degree of creative constraint usually concern the production of media content

Table 11.2

	GT	BLR
Corporate objectives	commercialism; avoid controversy; maximise appeal	non-commercialism; social significance; complementary programming
Feedback	ratings; mass audience	critical review/ratings; elite audience
Aesthetics	ambiguous; commercial	ambiguous; non-commercial, elitist
Resource allocation	formalised; restrictive	flexible; ambiguous

which is mainstream and stereotypical (Tuchman (ed.) 1974, Gitlin 1983, Cantor and Cantor 1992). The findings of the present study support these patterns. BLR and GT are two cases which illustrate how the relatively more restrictive context of TVB produces choric TV drama while the less restrictive context of RTHK allows the production of lyric (or controversial) dramas. The ideological differences are not arbitrary but have contextual roots which are set out in Table 11.2.

The schema of commercialism, working together with a mass ratings system and popular aesthetics, creates an unobtrusive cognitive framework which predisposes producers of television dramas towards creative options that fall in with mainstream ideology. More restrictive administrative controls limit individual autonomy and thus the ideological diversity of television dramas. By contrast, the schema of non-commercialism, working together with critical feedback systems and elitist aesthetics, creates an unobtrusive cognitive framework which predisposes producers of television dramas towards a negotiatory ideology. Less restrictive administrative controls on resource allocations allow a greater degree of individual autonomy and thus a greater measure of ideological diversity.

Contextual articulation and institutional dispersion[14]

Our comparative analyses have shown that the media, cultural identities and the state are articulated by linkages which are effective only at specific conjunctures: they can be disarticulated and rearticulated in shifting and contingent power hierarchies. In the late 1970s minimal state intervention and a surplus television economy produced in Hong Kong a relatively autonomous organisational environment for media workers. When political and economic interventions were weak, socio-cultural powers took the dominant role in ideological articulations. Television producers drew on the prevalent public sentiments of the time and constructed identity categories in the interests of the established social powers. This symbolic order was structured predominantly by the hierarchy of society, in which the established group had social power over outsiders. Thus contextual definers, via the socio-cultural route, played a dominant role in the process of identity formation and confirmation.

However, in the 1990s political and economic intervention became more prominent. The dual political power centres of China and Britain were intrusive in media politics; the hostile television economy was much more constraining. The identity categories of mainlander and Hongkonger, as presented in the television of the 1990s, became unstable. Polysemic configurations reflected the contradictions within and between the dual political powers and the populist demands of the people. Out of the desire for reconciliation, commercial television suppressed the derogatory categorisation of mainlanders, resulting in polysemic patterns of televisual discourse in GT that would make little sense without an understanding of the wider contexts.

Beyond the general contextual level of signification, however, there is another level which is connected with the institutionalised encoding practices of media organisations. Different types of television organisations and production contexts have tendencies and predispositions to produce televisual texts with different ideological patterns. Differentiation between television organisations was less prominent in the 1970s, because the political economy was less intrusive and ideology was articulated mainly socio-culturally. However, in the 1990s, as television production was more affected by political and commercial calculations, power relations were increasingly relayed into television dramas through the interface of the television institutions.

Contextual influences of political economy are differentially absorbed by and dispersed and translated through different television organisations, which engage with socio-political contexts in different ways. Media producers, inhabiting different institutionalised habitats, relate differentially to the general ideological/cultural context. Organisational analysis can only tell us the institutional predispositions of media discourses; it cannot tell us why dominant cultural and ideological patterns pop up in those institutionally predisposed discourses (Grossberg 1995).

Within the general ideological/cultural context of the 1990s, the deep-seated two-set categorisation of mainlander and Hongkonger was strongly activated by social and political conflict. Sino–Hong Kong antagonism was so strong that it had mapped onto television discourses as the most dominant point of reference of the times. Even when commercial television, out of the desire for reconciliation, opted for 'amnesia' and suppressed the dominant membership categorisation of the 'dirty', 'delinquent' and 'dangerous' mainlanders, the ghostly representation of the mainlander still found its way into the polysemic discourse of GT. The sense of Hongkonger-under-threat in the wider social discourse also pushed the televisual discourse towards the reaffirmation and strengthening of the myth of Hong Kong's economic success, thereby contributing to, and reflecting the desire for, social stability in face of imminent social change. In contrast, the ideological articulations between the general ideological/cultural context and the televisual discourse of BLR worked in a very different direction. Out of the social mandate of public television, BLR amplified the Sino–Hong Kong conflicts as the signs of the times and questioned the viability of *laissez faire* and the category collection of Hongkonger/mainlander in the new socio-political milieu. Thus, despite institutional dispersions, both dramas drew from the general ideological/cultural context the dominant discursive agendas of the time. This dialectic interplay between contextual definers and organisational definers contributes to the divergence and convergence of the textual forms located in the textual analyses of the selected dramas in this study. In sum, the mediated processes of identity formation, maintenance and transformation should be conceptualised as involving contextual articulations and institutional dispersions related to and managed through the intentionality of the human agents in specific historical conjunctures.

Notes

1 Some contest this separation as too simplistic (see Carey 1995, Garnham 1995).
2 In the first six months of 1950 more than 700 000 refugees poured into Hong Kong from the mainland.
3 In a survey in 1985, about 60 per cent of locals chose 'Hongkongers' over 'Chinese' as their identity (Lau and Kuan 1988).
4 TVB is the most popular broadcast television station in Hong Kong. Its drama serials dominate prime time and attract the largest public audiences.
5 The survey was done in 1990 by TVB. GBU got 3823 votes and rated second in the top-10 list of favourite serials in the 1980s.
6 Ching is the surname, which goes first in Chinese naming.
7 In October 1994 a large-scale conference was organised in Peking to celebrate the 2545th birthday of Confucius. The celebration received unprecedented support from the communist government, which had denounced Confucianism for many years after seizing power.
8 The Chinese title *Dashidai* literally means 'great times'. The serial's title is translated into English by TVB as *The Greed of Man*. Here I use the English title *Great Times* because this translation better captures the connotations than the Chinese title.
9 The same television station that produced GBU in 1979.
10 The executive producer, K. F. Wei, said that the inspiration for this suicide-cum-homicide scene came from the open firing on protesting students in the crackdown of 4 June.
11 Radio Television Hong Kong (RTHK) produces television programmes that are released on borrowed airtime on the commercial television channels. RTHK is officially a government broadcaster and relies on government funding. However, the television section, particularly the drama unit, had been operating autonomously with minimal government interference. The programming is similar to that of other public television. Since the mid-1980s the government had

been working on a corporatisation project to turn RTHK into a public broad-caster. The project suffered from prolonged political procrastination and was eventually abandoned in the early 1990s.

12 'Organisational schema' is defined as a coherent set of premises that works as a reference frame for decision-making within the organisation.

13 The building of the plant caused a series of Sino–Hong Kong disputes. China insisted on the project despite strong opposition from Hong Kong. It has been a symbol of the political and psychological threat to Hong Kong ever since.

14 For a more elaborate discussion of contextual articulation, please see Ma, 1999.

References

Cantor, M. G. and Cantor, J. M. (1992) *Prime-Time Television: Content and Control*, 2nd edn, London: Sage.

Carey, J. W. (1995) 'Abolishing the Old Spirit World', *Critical Studies in Mass Communication*, 12: 62–71.

Chai, S. 'Patriotism and Civilisation', *Hong Kong Economic Journal*, 3 Oct. 1994 (in Chinese).

Cheng, Y. (1990) 'Uninvited Guests', in *The China Factor in Hong Kong Cinema*, Hong Kong: Urban Council.

Chun, A. (1996) 'Discourses of Identity in the Changing Spaces of Public Culture in Taiwan, Hong Kong and Singapore', *Theory, Culture and Society*, 13.1: 51–75.

Curran, J. (1990) 'Culturalists' Perspectives of News Organisations: A Reappraisal and a Case Study', in M. Ferguson (ed.), *Public Communication: The New Imperatives*, London: Sage.

Elias, N. and Scotson, J. L. (1994) *The Established and the Outsiders*, London: Sage.

Ettema, J. S. (1982) 'The Organizational Context of Creativity: A Case Study from Public Television', in J. S. Ettema and D. C. Whitney (eds), *Individuals in Mass Media Organizations: Creativity and Constraint*, London: Sage.

Feuer, J. (1987) 'The MTM Style', in Horace Newcomb (ed.), *Television: The Critical View*, 4th edn, Oxford: Oxford University Press.

Garnham, N. (1995) 'Political Economy and Cultural Studies: Reconciliation or Divorce?', *Critical Studies in Mass Communication*, 12: 62–71.

Gitlin, T. (1983) *Inside Prime Time*, New York: Pantheon.

Grossberg, L. (1995) 'Cultural Studies vs. Political Economy: Is Anybody Else Bored with this Debate?', *Critical Studies in Mass Communication*, 12: 72–81.

Hagendoorn, L. (1993) 'Ethnic Categorisation and Outgroup Exclusion: Cultural Values and Social Stereotypes', *Ethnic and Racial Studies*, 16.1: 26–51.

Jenkins, R. (1994) 'Rethinking Ethnicity: Identity, Categorisation and Power', *Ethnic and Racial Studies*, 17.2: 197–223.

Kuan, H. C. and Lau, S. K. (1988) *Mass Media and Politics in Hong Kong*, Hong Kong: Institute of Social Studies, Chinese University of Hong Kong.

Lau, S. K. and Kuan, H. C. (1988) *The Ethos of the Hong Kong Chinese*, Hong Kong: Chinese University of Hong Kong Press.

Ma, E. (1999) *Culture, Politics and Television in Hong Kong*, London: Routledge.

McQuail, D. (1991) 'Media Performance Assessment in the Public Interest: Principles and Methods', *Communication Year Book*, 14: 111–45.

Murdock, G. (1989) 'Cultural Studies: Missing Links', *Critical Studies in Mass Communication*, Dec.: 436–40.

Murdock, G. (1997) 'Base Notes: The Conditions of Cultural Practice', in M. Ferguson and P. Golding (eds), *Cultural Studies in Question*, London: Sage.

Newcomb, H. and Alley, R. S. (1983) *The Producer's Medium: Conversations with Creators of American TV*, Oxford: Oxford University Press.

Sacks, H. (1992) *Lectures on Conversation*, Oxford: Blackwell.

Schudson, M. (1994) 'Culture and the Integration of National Societies', in D. Crane (ed.), *The Sociology of Culture*, Oxford: Blackwell.

Siu, H. S. (1986) 'Immigrants and social ethos: Hong Kong in the 1980s', *Journal of the Hong Kong Branch of the Royal Asiatic Society*, 26: 1–16.

Tuchman, G. (ed.) (1974) *The TV Establishment*, Englewood Cliffs, NJ: Prentice Hall.

|12|

Media organisations and non-media people

NICK COULDRY

This chapter introduces a new approach to analysing the social impact of the media and, in particular, media organisations. This is to study the direct interactions between media organisations and non-media people as processes of sociological interest in their own right. There are many ways of doing this, but they have one thing in common: to shed light on the power relationships at work in routine processes of media production and thereby yield insights into the social sources of media power.

By 'the media' here I mean television, radio and the press – the 'common-sense' definition of 'the media' – without any emphasis on the possible differences between how those particular media operate. My concern is more how people deal with and think about 'the media' in general and less the detailed question of whether in fact they interact with particular media differently. For, as yet, even the most general issues about how non-media people interact with media institutions have rarely been explored empirically.

By 'media power', I mean media institutions' differential symbolic power, the concentration of symbolic power in media institutions. If we just take the British case as our starting-point, it is generally taken for granted that the media (in the broad sense just proposed) have a particular authority to speak on behalf of society as a whole. The media have the power to speak 'for us all' – indeed to define the social 'reality' that we all share[1] – a power which individuals, corporations, pressure groups, professional bodies and even perhaps the state do not have. This raises the larger question: how is this differential symbolic power of the media legitimated? I return to this question in my conclusion.

Initially, however, we must address a more basic question: why believe that studying the 'direct interactions' between media organisations and non-media people can help us in understanding those wider issues of power? 'Interactions' between the media and non-media people are, after all, generally *indirect*: they are 'mediated' by media texts and the routine processes of media consumption. Most approaches to media power have tended to reflect this unproblematically, either by foregrounding such 'indirect' inter-actions (studying the processes at work in media texts and their reception) or by shifting attention away from non-media people entirely and onto the institutional structures which produce media texts. Of course, both these approaches remain important, but to imagine that together they exhaust all the options is too limiting. It suggests that 'the media' are a social process with two quite separate poles – production and consumption – our only choice being as to which pole we study.

In fact, however, if we stand back and consider the vast mass of social processes to which we give the overall name 'the media', there are important areas which this 'bipolar' model excludes. First, there are the direct interactions between media people and non-media people that occur during media production itself: from organising an interview to recruiting a studio audience. Second, there are the attitudes of non-media people towards the media as an institutional power (and towards media people in particular), general attitudes which persist beyond particular acts of media consumption. Combining these two points, there is a vast area which the bipolar (production/consumption) model of the media leaves out: the whole field of media people's and non-media people's *dealings with each other*.

It is true that some work within media studies has touched on that field, often illuminatingly; for example, the work on the sociology of television journalism and production (Elliott 1972, Burns 1977, Hall et al. 1978, Schlesinger 1978, 1990, Gans 1980, Tunstall 1993). Paradoxically, much of this work has shown how *little* contact media people normally have with non-media people (for example, Schlesinger (1978: 107)). Recently, there has developed a body of work on the strategies of social or political activists to obtain media coverage (for example: van Zoonen 1992, 1996, Hansen (ed.) 1993, Gamson 1995, Gitlin 1980, Camauer forthcoming), and there is the tradition of work on the media's 'sources' (see Davis, Chapter 7 in this volume). Inevitably such work tends to focus on those who are 'experts' in this role, becoming in effect proto-media professionals themselves (Greenpeace, for example). Then, and from a very different direction, there is important work on media fans, including their dealings with media institutions (for example: Vermorel and Vermorel 1985, Jenkins 1992).

Even so, we still know little about important forms of interaction such as people's experiences of being interviewed in the press, or appearing on television.[2] What of non-media people's attempts to be represented and the difficulties they may encounter, let alone their reflections on the whole process of selection that precedes media representation? And what of the spaces and contexts where such interactions go on? This gap in our knowledge becomes all the more urgent with the growth of 'reality television' where non-media people routinely appear. The only work so far in this area relates to appearing on talk shows (Livingstone and Lunt 1994, Priest 1995, 1996). But, as those authors acknowledge, they have written against a background of general ignorance: 'It is not obvious why ordinary people go on television and little research has addressed this question' (Livingstone and Lunt 1994: 116); 'Virtually nothing is known about talk show participants' (Priest, 1995: 5). I aim to suggest various ways in which such gaps in our knowledge can be filled.

There is one other objection which needs to be addressed first: surely interactions between media institutions and non-media people are, *by definition*, infrequent, and, if so, offer little to study apart from some incidental areas of limited significance. But just because a social process is relatively rare does not mean that it is insignificant. Indeed the fact that non-media people rarely do have free access to media people may *itself* reveal much about the power disparity between those two groups! To take a broader analogy from the study of religion, the fact that many ritual experiences (such as pilgrimage, communion) are either rare or at least ritually controlled does not make them any less worth studying. On the contrary, such ritual interactions, when they occur, tell us much about how the social power of religious institutions is reproduced. Similarly, if people's general attitudes to the media are shaped by their normal *separation* from the process of media production, then their accounts of what happens when (rarely) they see that process close up may bring to the surface their background assumptions about the media: background expectations and judgements which normally remain unarticulated. There is a parallel here with how the sociologist Harold Garfinkel sought to analyse the 'background expectancies' which we make in everyday social interaction by studying what happens when those expectancies are breached (Garfinkel 1984 [1967]: ch. 1, Heritage 1984: ch. 4).

Meeting the media face to face

What can a detailed examination of people's talk and reflections on interacting directly with the media tell us about how the media's differential symbolic power is reproduced? The examples are drawn from interviews conducted for a larger study of this subject (Couldry forthcoming).

(A) 'I ended up outside again'

My first example will probably seem banal: a studio-audience member's account of the frustrations of waiting to enter a television studio. Yet even to discuss such an example is to challenge the neglect in media studies of studio spaces and other places of media production (cf. Scannell 1996: 141).[3]

I interviewed John, a 49-year-old clerical worker from Dorset, as part of a study of visitors to the external set of the soap *Coronation Street*, the main attraction at Granada Studios Tour, Manchester.[4] In the course of the interview, he told me about the time he had been in the audience for the BBC's live National Lottery draw. John's account of what happened in the television studio was suggestive: his initial feeling of being patronised when the audience were told the rules for when to laugh, and so on; his subsequent willingness to enjoy his role as part of the performance; the fact that from his vantage-point some parts of the live show were not clearly visible.[5]

More important for my argument, however, were John's experiences outside the studio, in particular the long wait to enter. Here is his description:

> Having enjoyed the studio thing [i.e. the programme], I did not enjoy the BBC itself, it was dreadful the way you were treated. You were told to get there, 6 o'clock I think it was, but the programme doesn't go live until 7.50, so you think, Oh well, I'm going to be in the studios, it'll be nice and warm. And you get there and you stand outside on the main road, at the BBC studios, it was freezing cold, it was November, and it started to rain. So after about half an hour, they then let you in and you go to a Portakabin and you're searched, frisked … and you go through a barrier like you do at an airport … and then you get out of there and you queue up again for about another 20 minutes and they take you round where it says BBC … and then you stand in another queue outside and then they take you in, and you think, Oh, I'm going into the studios, wonderful.
>
> And then they take you into this enormous room which is geared to very expensive … tea, coffee, BBC videos, BBC books … it's like an airport lounge, and you sit there for an hour, and you think, Oh, the studios must be just there, just off this room, no such luck. Then they start calling you in groups … and they put you there and there, and they say, right, we'll march you out … so you go through a set of double doors and the ushers open the doors, I was expecting to go into the studio and I ended up outside again …
>
> It was just a way of getting you into sections so they can do what they like with you … so I ended back where I was in the first queue, freezing cold it was … and you stand outside the studio where the lottery was for another … ten minutes … and THEN you get into the studio … I felt it was a bit like a cattle market.

John's frustrations, and the way his entry to the studios was carefully managed, are, perhaps, what one would expect from accounts of visiting any corporate space: the reinforcement of power through the control of territory has been studied by Michel Foucault (1979), Robert Sack (1986), and others. What is striking, however, is that *media institutions* have *not* generally been studied from this perspective: that is, for the way they seek to control the actions of those who do not work for them. This omission is all the more striking when dramatic examples of the spatial impact of media operations abound: consider, for example, the crowd of photographers on the driveway of someone in the media eye.

Not only have such spatial aspects of the media process generally been ignored, but with them their social and symbolic dimensions. One reason for John's frustration at the delays was, I suggest, his *desire* to enter the studio, the actual place where filming occurs: as someone outside 'the world of television', he invested his anticipated entry into the studio with a special (perhaps even a ritual) significance, which was undermined by the indignity of 'ending up outside again'. Much more could be said about how the scarcity value (for non-media people) of visiting the places of media production is now being commercially exploited (Davis 1996, Couldry 1998): visits to studios (Granada Studios Tour) or exhibitions (The BBC Experience), the marketing of places for their status as filming locations, and so on.

At this point, I simply want to focus on the broader empirical questions which John's account suggests:

1 How are social interactions between media organisations and non-media people managed in media spaces (such as studios)?
2 How are such interactions managed in other spaces (for example, when interviewing and filming on location)?
3 What do such interactions tell us about the power relations between media organisations and non-media people?
4 What questions do such power relations raise about the ability (or inability) of non-media people to intervene in and challenge the media process?

In case these questions seem curious, it is worth asking a more basic question: is it *necessary* for entry to the spaces where media (both press and broadcasting) are produced to be strictly controlled? Why should such spaces not be freely accessible 'public' spaces? This question is no more 'naive' than Bertolt Brecht's famous proposal in the early days of radio that 'radio should be converted from a distribution system to a communication system . . . making the listener not only hear but also speak' (Brecht 1979–80 [1932]: 25).[6] The reason that my question and Brecht's proposal seem 'naive' is simply that we have grown used to the idea that radio, television and before them the press are 'one-to-many' media, not 'many-to-many'. An inevitable consequence is that both the spaces where media inputs are made and the social interactions occurring there are strictly controlled. Scannell and Cardiff's history of British public broadcasting (1991) offers a glimpse into an alternative history. They relate (pp. 311–14) how the early regional radio stations, such as '2ZY' in Manchester, developed a more intimate relationship with their audience than the early BBC (until, that is, they were absorbed into the BBC). Not only did 2ZY's audience often contact the programmes but sometimes they even visited the studios themselves, treating them as if they were any other public space or public forum. Such openness now seems inconceivable, almost bizarre, until, that is, we realise that it is *the normal impossibility* for members of the public visiting studios to intervene directly in a publicly addressed production process that needs explaining!

(B) 'Awe, not respect'

John had seen aspects of the media production process, but they were limited: certainly, as an audience member, there was no question of him being represented on television beyond, perhaps, a brief shot. If he was on camera at all, it would have been as a spectator. What, then, is it like to be an active participant in events that are mediated, especially if those events are conflictual and therefore the resulting media coverage is likely to generate disputes? What do people's accounts of such a potentially disruptive experience tell us?

I interviewed a number of people who had protested against live animal exports in the east-coast English port of Brightlingsea in 1995. None of them had been close to the means of media production before. The shock of seeing the media process face to face – and realising the gap between media coverage (that of a previously trusted 'window onto the world') and their own direct experience of the protests – encouraged many to reflect on their earlier attitudes to the media. Such reflections took their most elaborate form in my interview with Rachel, a social-services worker in her early forties.

First, a word of introduction about the Brightlingsea protests, which received, at least in their early stages, intense local, national and international media coverage.[7] Of all the protest sites against live animal exports, Brightlingsea was the most disrupted by the trade. A seaside town of 8500 people on a little-known part of the East Anglian coast, it is reached by one main road that, when it approaches the small privatised port, is no wider than a suburban street, lined with houses and gardens on either side. As a result there was something particularly intense about events at Brightlingsea: the sight, sound, and smell of animals crammed onto lorries shocked those along the route, often leaving them in tears. Unlike at other ports, protesters were close enough to *touch* the animals as they passed, certainly to speak to the drivers. Events were played out on a small, almost 'personal' scale, the exact opposite, of course, of detached viewing of televised events in the comfort of your living-room. Tension was greatly increased by insensitive policing: there were many allegations of violent assaults on young and old people, verbal abuse and general intimidation. Policing soon became, for many, a protest issue in its own right. For almost everyone – as the media emphasised – this was their first experience of protesting. In fact, people came 'in touch' with a whole other world: of cruelty to animals, police intimidation, morally questionable business practices, behind-the-scenes government influence. In addition, the small town seemed to come together in a way which it had not done before: the camaraderie of 'wartime' was a frequent comparison made.

At the same time, emerging through all these other factors was a disruptive dimension which the media did not highlight. The events provided protesters with their first direct experience of the process of media reporting.

Indeed protesters suddenly found themselves 'subject[s] of media representations as distinct from ... consumer[s] of media images' (Benton and Redfearn (1996: 68)). Journalists, camera crews, press photographers, satellite transmission dishes – all the trappings of media production on location – were there. Protesters as non-media people were interacting directly with media institutions (or at least their representatives).

Rachel was middle-class, living with her husband and children in Brightlingsea. She wanted to be involved in the protests from the outset, but could not through illness. However, since her bedroom overlooked the route where protesters, lorries, police and media passed, she was still able to question media reports. She was shocked when early in the protests, local radio reports of a small, low-key police presence contradicted her own witnessing of 23 vans of police in semi-riot gear driving past her window:

> So I phoned the news desk and I said, 'I'm just enquiring how you know that there's 26 police in normal uniform?' And they said, 'From the police press officer'. And I said, 'Well, I think perhaps the information you're getting is drastically wrong' (...) And also by the time I got through to the newsroom there were officers walking (...) they certainly weren't in normal uniform (...) And they looked so sinister. And I was so incensed, because SGR was putting out '26 police officers are policing this huge crowd in NORMAL UNIFORM', it's like they were stressing it. And I wanted them to put me on the radio to say, 'This is just not true'.

This was one of many conflicts between her or her friends' accounts of the protests, and media reports. It was the most acute, because it revealed directly how the media report had been constructed: from a *police* press briefing. In other words, Rachel experienced for herself the role of 'primary definers' in news production which Hall et al (1978) analysed. Most important, Rachel realised that she was powerless to alter the report.

When around the same time Rachel saw pictures of friends in the national press, surrounded by police, apparently involved in conflict, she was concerned that people who didn't know them would misunderstand the photos and assume her friends were committing violence: 'I was privileged because I knew who they were. But nobody else would ... they [the media] could have put any sort of headline on those pictures and told a completely different story.'

Like many others at Brightlingsea, Rachel felt forcibly the impact of media stereotyping – *applied to herself*. Rachel was, perhaps more than others, aware before the 1995 events of media stereotyping of protesters: she also classed herself as already broadly sympathetic to strikes and protests. Others at Brightlingsea, however, experienced a more abrupt reversal: having before believed the stereotype of protesters as 'rentamob', with its visual associations of 'youths with earrings', 'punks', and so on, they resented those stereotypes being applied to them in media coverage. Rachel spoke for

them: 'this is US! ... This is no loony lefties or (...) Socialist Worker people, all the people you've ever been led to believe are the only people that
would "do that sort of thing" '. As a result, many protesters grasped *the
process of* stereotyping for the first time: 'we started to become mobs', 'you
look at that [pointing at the television] and you're a mob'. They experienced
directly the force of Raymond Williams's insight into massification: 'to
other people, we also are masses. Masses are other people' (1961: 289).

Like many also, Rachel lost her trust in the media, and her reflections
bring out vividly the normal background assumptions about the media (and
the media's social authority) which those disruptive events had dislodged:

> NC: What effect do you think it had on you, being so close to the media?
> (...)
> Rachel: I think it completely took away ... any awe that I may have had
> ... respect isn't the right word.
> NC: Awe rather than respect? (...)
> Rachel: Yeh, I suppose yeh, because things on the telly aren't always real,
> are they? It's all exciting, and it happens to other people, so the oppor-
> tunity to be right in the midst of it ... didn't have an effect that if you'd
> asked me two or three years ago, it might have done. I'd have said,
> 'Ooh, I'd have pushed myself, or I'd hide so that nobody could see me'
> (...) I don't think my reaction could have been predicted at all (...)
> You know, [I would have said] 'I'd have hidden and not had anything
> to do with it, out of coyness' or 'I'd have been really brave and I'd have
> said something, I'd have told them what I really thought'. But it was
> still with that sort of feeling, [a click sound, indicating surprise] 'Ooh!
> these big people have come from the television!' you know.
> NC: So what had changed? Why didn't you feel that this time, do you
> think?
> Rachel: Because they let me down, I think. Because I had enough short
> term experience of what they were doing ... to feel that ... they
> weren't getting it right. It still needed me to tell my friends what was
> going on (...) I think, resentment, that we were totally at their mercy,
> as to whether anything was said at all.

Her loss of trust is presented as part of a complex shift in attitudes. She felt
the media were 'not getting it right': it was down to her (with her special
knowledge) to tell the true story, revealing the lack of control which she
normally had over what the media do. Her old attitudes to the media had
changed. Previously she had felt more than respect for the media: she had
felt '*awe*', expressed in her sense of 'media people' as 'big people'. This
reveals something important about the social power which the media have:
'awe' after all is a strong word to use.

Rachel's own analysis of her likely previous reaction to the chance of
appearing on the media is rather sharp. There were two alternative ways the
media would previously have affected her: either she would have avoided

the media through nervousness; or she would have overcome that hesitation, 'pushing herself' and 'telling them what [she] *really* thought' (compensating, perhaps, for her anxiety with an intense involvement and self-revelation). Either way, as she sees, she would have been acknowledging the *boundary* which media participation involves: 'it was still with that sort of feeling, "Ooh, these big people have come from the television!" '. But now she had lost that awe and, she implied, respect as well. One phrase sums up the conflict between her old trust and her new doubts: 'things on the telly *aren't always* real'.

Rachel's interview shows how people's accounts of being close to the media's workings can reveal background assumptions about the media and the media's authority which normally, perhaps, would not be articulated at all.

(C) 'We're just ordinary people'

We can push this argument one stage further by looking at an interview with Louise, another animal-rights campaigner, who became active herself in relation to the media, using a camcorder to film maltreatment of animals at a local livestock market. A phrase of Louise's summed up her feeling of the shift this represented for herself and others: 'It's all changed. We're just ordinary people with no experience of the media or protests or anything.' Before, in other words, and perhaps still now, she had associated being an 'ordinary person' with having no experience of the media (compare Rachel's reference to television: 'it's all exciting and it happens to *other people*'). As an 'ordinary person', she assumed, she was automatically outside the 'media world' with no expectation of taking part in it. Gradually, however, she became more active in relation to the media. Her account of the transition from non-media person into media activist suggests how it took place *against the grain* of her previous assumptions about the 'media world'.

Louise was a self-employed university graduate in her twenties. She had gone with a friend in 1995 to a protest against live animal exports at one of the ports, protests which like those at Brightlingsea had received considerable media coverage:

> we'd never protested or anything before. We just saw the TV coverage of [the port] (. . .) and watched the coverage, just saw just so so many normal ordinary people, you know, we'd always thought of protesters as being not like us [short laugh] and we just saw (. . .) ordinary people (. . .) It was just like seeing the ordinary people and just thinking, we can do that.

Before, Louise had thought of protesters as 'weird', 'like the edge of society'. Seeing images of 'ordinary people' protesting flatly contradicted this. She felt able to act.

She avoided the cameras at the port through shyness and to avoid bad publicity for her business. However, what she saw (including police behaviour) was so shocking that she decided to buy a camcorder 'to capture it all on camera'. Someone else at the protests had visited a nearby livestock market to observe the conditions in which animals were kept. Suddenly, Louise realised that she too could go to her local market and film it:

> I used to avoid it [the local market] (...) but all of a sudden, through having seen everything at [the port], through having a camera and through having spoken to someone else about markets who was going there, we thought, Yeh, we can do that, you know, *we're ordinary people, but we can go and make a difference.* (added emphasis)

Note the phrasing: she is 'ordinary' *but* she 'can go and make a difference'. As the social psychologist Michael Billig has argued, it is partly in the 'small words' of people's talk – 'the unnoticed small words which seem beyond rhetorical challenge, and which are routinely and widely repeated' (1997: 225) – that power relations are subtly revealed (and at the same time reproduced). Being 'ordinary', Louise suggests, normally means *not* going and making a difference. But now the camcorder provided the purpose which made Louise's watching animal suffering at the market bearable: 'it's only because we know that, everything that happens, we're recording it all the time and that's what makes a difference'.

So far, she was using the camera purely to gather evidence to present to the market authorities. She did not regard herself as doing anything connected with 'the media'. This changed when a journalist she knew from the protests suggested that her work might interest the local press. This surprised her, although other protest organisations had already advised her on the importance of getting media coverage:

> [A leaflet] said (...) tell the media whenever you're having meetings with people or if you try and talk with the auctioneers. And I thought, I didn't know whether to believe it, I thought that was a bit strange, the media aren't going to want to know that [laughs] I'm having a meeting with [auctioneers] who are a company that are 100 years old (...) it just seemed a bit weird. And the whole idea of going to the media (...) I wouldn't dare, because that's going to be printed, what I say is going to be printed, what if say something wrong? It sounds very naive now.

The advice to use the media had made no sense before, I suggest, because she understood herself and the media to belong to mutually exclusive categories: 'we had no idea we were *even worthy* of coverage', she said elsewhere. She was also afraid: 'I wouldn't dare, because that's going to be printed, ... what if I say something wrong?' The media operated in a different world from her, the other side of a boundary policed by restrictions and fears.

Her story did reach the local press and she received regular coverage for a while. When, eventually, the publicity fell away, she did not automatically turn to doing her own publicity, since until then she had understood the publicity as something that had *happened* to her, rather than something she had done herself. When she did start generating her own publicity, it was because her way of understanding her relation to the media world had changed. This enabled her to reflect on her previous attitudes (just as Rachel had done):

> It's funny how things click (...) [A friend] was going on about, people who can't get publicity making their own publicity through leaflets, and that stuck in my mind (...) And I hadn't really thought about it, because I wouldn't have thought (...) *leafleting, that's not publicity, publicity to me meant newspapers* (...) we'd given out a couple of leaflets and things, but we hadn't really thought of the impact that was having (...) we *hadn't really thought of that in terms of publicity*. (added emphasis)

Previously she had discounted even the acts of publicity she was already performing. 'Publicity', she assumed, was something on a bigger scale, done by others. Before, it had been 'just ... us', 'a couple of leaflets and things'. Now, she saw her actions as 'worthy' of being in the 'media frame'.

Subsequently, she became active in generating storylines for the media to use and in telling activists elsewhere about her work. Reversing her earlier fear of saying the wrong thing, she found herself thinking: 'if I say the right thing here (...) I'm going to inspire these people'. Her previous silence in relation to the media world had been transformed into the possibility of action. We should not, of course, exaggerate the impact of her actions. She remained largely reliant on the coverage which the local press provided and her knowledge of how to attract that coverage. Her own self-publicity (through leaflets) could not hope to reach the same audience as a press story. But what is most important for my argument is Louise's changed understanding of her relationship to the media world once she came into contact with the process of media production (first as a witness of mediated protest events, and then as a camcorder user herself). Her account of that change reveals an earlier set of background assumptions about her *lack* of a place in the media world – assumptions which previously she had not challenged, and perhaps barely articulated.

Conclusion: the reproduction of media power

This chapter has offered an unorthodox empirical approach to media organisations, and I want in conclusion to consider briefly its wider implications.

First, we have seen how analysing interview accounts of people's dealings with the media is a way of bringing out people's normal, background assumptions about the media and their status. Each example (Rachel's and Louise's most explicitly) has raised the question of power – the massive concentration of symbolic resources and symbolic authority in media organisations – and with it the question of hierarchy. Just as Louise regarded herself as an 'ordinary person'[8] who therefore had nothing to do with the world of media production, so too Rachel had once felt 'awe' (not 'respect') before media people. We feel 'respect' for someone on a comparable level to us, but we feel 'awe' for someone or something on a completely different level from ourselves. It was a similarly absolute distinction (quite different from ordinary status rankings) that according to Durkheim distinguished the 'sacred' from the 'profane' in his analysis of the 'elementary forms of religious life' (1995 [1912]). We do not need to push the comparison between the media's authority and forms of religious authority very far[9] to see suggestive parallels between media power and Durkheim's theory of symbolic power. There is no space to develop them further here.

More specifically, foregrounding the detailed interactions between media organisations and non-media people seems a promising entry-point to analysing apparently radical programming developments such as BBC2's *Video Diaries* series. These gave participants some editorial involvement, although those who took part had already been selected by the producers.[10] Have such programmes shifted audiences' background assumptions about their place in the 'media world', assumptions such as Louise's? It was one of the *Video Diaries* producers (Jeremy Gibson, quoted in Keighron 1993) who remarked that very few 'video diarists' took the next step of making their own independent programme or video. Whereas Gibson expressed surprise at this, we should not, remembering how Louise's eventual progress to a limited form of media activism continually contradicted her assumptions of how little was possible for her as an 'ordinary person'. The *Video Diaries* (through scheduling and other means) remain framed as the exceptional interventions of 'ordinary people' into the institutional process of media production.

Third, underlying this chapter as a whole is a conception of power which I should at this point make explicit, although there is no space to defend it here in detail. Following Foucault, Giddens and a number of other recent social theorists,[11] I regard power not – or at least, not simply – as a 'thing' or 'asset' which the 'powerful' simply possess, but as the complex outcome of practices at *every level* of social interaction (Foucault 1979: 26–7). This is sometimes referred to as a 'dispersed' conception of power. Applying this to the media case, I understand the media's differential symbolic power as deriving not simply from the fact that there is a broadcasting or press distribution system and media institutions sit in control of it, but from the fact that everyone believes in the authority of media discourse and media people in countless local contexts, everyone believes others believe exactly the same, and everyone then proceeds to act and argue on that basis. In other words, media power rests not only on an institutional structure, but also on an intricate web of background assumptions about the media and non-media people's relationship to them. These assumptions do not persist in the abstract, but persist, quite simply, by being repeated and reworked in countless individual interactions.[12] We might call this the 'culture of belief' in the media. This 'culture' (as I have argued elsewhere: Couldry, forthcoming) is indispensable to the reproduction of media power *as legitimate*. It is an important social source of media power, which suggests we need a cultural dimension in political economy debates about the power of media organisations.

To analyse this culture of belief – and this is the methodological issue which this chapter has sought to highlight – we need to move away from an exclusively 'bipolar' conception of media studies: as either studying production (the structure of media organisations) or studying consumption (the structure of media texts and their reception). We need to examine the wide area of social interaction that lies between these two poles. The challenge for media analysis, then, is clear: to address the largely unexplored territory where media organisations and non-media people deal (or fail to deal) with each other.

Acknowledgements

This chapter (like Couldry, forthcoming and 1998) is based on research conducted under an ESRC Grant.

Notes

1 On 'symbolic power' as the 'power of constructing reality', see Bourdieu (1991: 163–70). See also Bourdieu's recent (1998) controversial analysis of television itself.
2 For an important early discussion of these issues, see Root (1986: ch. 5).
3 Again, the exceptions relate to talk shows: see especially Livingstone and Lunt (1994), Grindstaff (1997).
4 For this study see Couldry (forthcoming, Part Two) and Couldry (1998).
5 For a pioneering study of the differences between seeing an event live and seeing it on television, see Lang and Lang (1969). Cf. Corner (1995) for recent discussion.
6 Cf. Enzensberger (1972), Williams (1990 [1974]: 23–31).
7 See for more detail Benton and Redfearn (1996), Couldry (forthcoming: ch. 7).
8 A phrase Rachel also used of herself.
9 Compare however Curran (1982) for a fascinating historical comparison between the concentration of symbolic power in contemporary media organisations and the Medieval Catholic Church. See generally Couldry (forthcoming, chs 1 and 3).
10 The ratio of accepted to rejected was approximately one in 50 (Keighron, 1993: 25).

11 Foucault (1979, 1981), Giddens (1984): cf. Bourdieu (1977), Callon and Latour (1981).
12 For a general parallel, see especially Anthony Giddens's analysis of social structure in terms of continual processes of structuration (1984: 16–28).

References

Benton, T. and Redfearn, S. (1996) 'The Politics of Animal Rights: Where is the Left?', *New Left Review*, 215: 43–58.
Billig, M. (1997) 'From Codes to Utterances: Cultural Studies, Discourse and Psychology', in M. Ferguson and P. Golding (eds), *Cultural Studies in Question*, London: Sage, pp. 205–26.
Bourdieu, P. (1977) *Outline of a Theory of Practice*, Cambridge: Cambridge University Press.
Bourdieu, P. (1991) *Language and Symbolic Power*, Cambridge: Polity.
Bourdieu, P. (1998) *On Television and Journalism*, London: Pluto Press.
Brecht, B. (1979–80 [1932]) 'Radio as a Means of Communications: A Talk on the Function of Radio', *Screen*, 20.3–4: 24–8.
Burns, T. (1977) *The BBC: Public Institution and Private World*, London: Macmillan.
Callon, M. and Latour, B. (1981) 'Unscrewing the Big Leviathan: How Actors Macro-structure Reality and How Sociologists Help Them to Do So', in K. Knorr-Cetina and A. Cicourel (eds), *Advances in Social Theory and Methodology: Toward an Integration of Micro- and Macro-sociologies*, London: Routledge and Kegan Paul, pp. 277–303.
Camauer, L. (forthcoming) 'Women's Movements, Public Spheres and the Media', in L. van Zoonen and A. Sreberny-Mohammadi (eds), *Women's Politics and Communication*, Cresskill, NJ: The Hampton Press.
Corner, J. (1995) *Television Form and Public Address*, London: Edward Arnold.
Couldry, N. (1998) 'The View from Inside the Simulacrum: Visitors' Tales from the Set of Coronation Street', *Leisure Studies*, 17.2: 94–107.
Couldry, N. (forthcoming) *The Place of Media Power: Pilgrims and Witnesses of the Media Age*, Routledge: London.
Curran, J. (1982) 'Communications, Power and Social Order' in M. Gurevitch, T. Bennett, J. Curran and J. Woollacott (eds), *Culture, Society and the Media*, London: Routledge, pp. 202–35.
Davis, S. (1996) 'The Theme Park: Global Industry and Cultural Form', *Media, Culture and Society*, 18.3: 399–422.
Durkheim, E. (1995 [1912]) *The Elementary Forms of Religious Life*, New York: Free Press.
Elliott, P. (1972) *The Making of a Television Series: A Case Study in the Sociology of Culture*, London: Constable.
Enzensberger, H. M. (1972) 'Constituents of a Theory of the Media', in D. McQuail (ed.) *Sociology of Mass Communications*, Harmondsworth: Penguin, pp. 99–116.
Foucault, M. (1979) *Discipline and Punish: The Birth of the Prison*, Harmondsworth: Peregrine.
Gamson, W. (1995) 'Constructing Social Protest', in H. Johnston and B. Klandermans (eds), *Social Movements and Culture*, London: UCL Press, pp. 85–106.
Gans, H. (1980) *Deciding What's News: A Study of CBS Evening News, NBC Nightly News, Newsweek and Time*, 2nd edn, New York: Vintage.

Garfinkel, H. (1984 [1967]) *Studies in Ethnomethodology*, London: Routledge and Kegan Paul.

Giddens, A. (1984) *The Constitution of Society*, Cambridge: Polity.

Gitlin, T. (1980) *The Whole World is Watching: Mass Media in the Making and Unmaking of the New Left*, Berkeley: University of California Press.

Grindstaff, L. (1997) 'Producing Trash, Class and the Money Shot: A Behind-the-Scenes Account of Daytime TV Talk Shows', in J. Lull and S. Hinerman (eds), *Media Scandals: Morality and Desire in the Popular Culture Marketplace*, Cambridge: Polity, pp. 164–203.

Hall, S., Critcher, C., Jefferson, T., Clarke, J. and Roberts, B. (1978) *Policing the Crisis: Mugging, the State, and Law and Order*, London: Macmillan.

Hansen, A. (ed.) (1993) *The Mass Media and Environmental Issues*, Leicester: Leicester University Press.

Heritage, J. (1984) *Garfinkel and Ethnomethodology*, Cambridge: Polity.

Jenkins, H. (1992) *Textual Poachers*, London: Routledge.

Keighron, P. (1993) '*Video Diaries*: What's Up Doc?', *Sight and Sound*, 3.10: 24–5.

Lang, K. and Lang, G. (1969) 'The Unique Perspective of Television and its Effects: A Pilot Study', in W. Schramm (ed.), *Mass Communications*, 2nd edn, Urbana: University of Illinois Press, pp. 544–60.

Livingstone, S. and Lunt, P. (1994) *Talk on Television: Audience Participation and Public Debate*, London: Routledge.

Priest, P. (1995) *Public Intimacies: Talk Show Participants and Tell-All TV*, Cresskill, NJ: The Hampton Press.

Priest, P. (1996) ' "Gilt by Association": Talk Show Participants' Televisually Enhanced Status and Self-Esteem', in D. Grodin and T. Lindlof (eds), *Constructing the Self in a Mediated World*, London: Sage, pp. 68–83.

Root, J. (1986) *Open the Box*, London: Comedia.

Sack, R. (1986) *Human Territoriality: Its Theory and History*, Cambridge: Cambridge University Press.

Scannell, P. (1996) *Radio, Television and Modern Life*, Oxford: Blackwell.

Scannell, P. and Cardiff, D. (1991) *A Social History of British Broadcasting, Vol. 1: 1922–39 Serving the Nation*, Oxford: Blackwell.

Schlesinger, P. (1978) *Putting Reality Together: BBC News*, London: Methuen.

Schlesinger, P. (1990) 'Rethinking the Sociology of Journalism: Source Strategies and the Limits of Media-Centrism', in M. Ferguson (ed.), *Public Communication: The New Imperatives: Future Directions for Media Research*, London: Sage, pp. 61–83.

Tunstall, J. (1993) *Television Producers*, London: Routledge.

Williams, R. (1961) *Culture and Society: 1780–1950*, Harmondsworth: Penguin.

Williams, R. (1990 [1974]) *Television: Technology and Cultural Form*, 2nd edn, London: Routledge.

van Zoonen, L. (1992) 'The Women's Movement and the Media: Constructing a Public Identity', *European Journal of Communication*, 7.4: 453–76.

van Zoonen, L. (1996) 'A Dance of Death: New Social Movements and the Mass Media', in D. Paletz (ed.), *Political Communication in Action*, New Jersey: Hampton Press.

Vermorel, F. and Vermorel, J. (1985) *Starlust: The Secret Life of Fans*, London: W. H. Allen.

Index